T0212506

Lecture Notes in Computer Science 10075

Commenced Publication in 1973
Founding and Former Series Editors:
Gerhard Goos, Juris Hartmanis, and Jan van Leeuwen

Editorial Board

Atsuyuki Morishima · Andreas Rauber
Chern Li Liew (Eds.)

Digital Libraries: Knowledge, Information, and Data in an Open Access Society

18th International Conference on Asia-Pacific
Digital Libraries, ICADL 2016
Tsukuba, Japan, December 7–9, 2016
Proceedings

 Springer

Editors
Atsuyuki Morishima
University of Tsukuba
Tsukuba
Japan

Andreas Rauber
Vienna University of Technology
Vienna
Austria

Chern Li Liew
Victoria University of Wellington
Wellington
New Zealand

ISSN 0302-9743   ISSN 1611-3349   (electronic)
Lecture Notes in Computer Science
ISBN 978-3-319-49303-9   ISBN 978-3-319-49304-6   (eBook)
DOI 10.1007/978-3-319-49304-6

Library of Congress Control Number: 2016956498

LNCS Sublibrary: SL3 – Information Systems and Applications, incl. Internet/Web, and HCI

Printed on acid-free paper

This Springer imprint is published by Springer Nature
The registered company is Springer International Publishing AG
The registered company address is: Gewerbestrasse 11, 6330 Cham, Switzerland

Preface

This volume contains the papers presented at the 18th International Conference on Asia-Pacific Digital Libraries (ICADL 2016), held during December 7–9, 2016, in Tsukuba, Japan. Since starting in Hong Kong in 1998, ICADL has become a premier international conference for digital library research. The conference series explores digital libraries as a broad foundation for interaction with information and information management in the networked information society.

ICADL 2016 was jointly organized with the Asia-Pacific Forum of Information Schools (APIS) under the umbrella of the International Forum 2016. The theme of the International Forum 2016 was "Knowledge, Information and Data (KID) in Open Access Society." Open access is widely recognized as a key concept for the progress of the networked information society – open science, open government, open data, etc. This forum is aimed at promoting discussion around novel frameworks, technologies, and services related to the theme and at facilitating human networks for advancing KID research, education, and services. We believe digital libraries and information schools play important roles in the open access society, and we hope this conference provides the platform for exploring these further.

The ICADL series has traditionally been focused on advanced information technologies for the development of digital libraries. In its long history, ICADL 2016 was the first conference to explicitly solicit papers that investigate and discuss social and cultural issues related to the design and development of digital libraries, digital archives, and digital information services. We believe this multi-disciplinary approach is crucial to the development of a truly open access society.

ICADL 2016 presented three keynotes – by Prof. Ronald L. Larsen, Prof. Ee-peng Lim, and Prof. Katsumi Tanaka, and two thematic sessions – one on "The Future of Digital Library Research and iSchools" and another on "Natural Disasters and Information Technologies." Also unique to ICADL 2016 was the explicit solicitation of not only academic research papers but also practitioner papers. The integration of theory, research, and evidence-based policies and practice is critical to the discussion of research problems and future directions for digital library research. This encourages academics and researchers to more consciously embody our roles as the "critic and conscience" of society by actively engaging with practitioners and in demonstrating that theorization and constructive critiques are situated within meaningful practices. Practitioners, on the other hand, are exposed to new visions and perspectives for the future, driving the evolution of best practices in their environments.

Out of the 80 submissions from 16 countries received, we accepted 18 full papers, 17 work-in-progress papers, and seven practitioner papers. Collectively, these papers cover topics such as community informatics, digital heritage preservation, digital curation, models and guidelines, information retrieval/integration/extraction/recommendation, privacy, education and digital literacy, open access and data, and information access design. We would like to thank all members of the Program Committee for their effort in assisting us in the timely review of all the submissions. We are especially grateful to Prof. Shigeo Sugimoto of the University of Tsukuba, who is the general-co-chair of the International Forum, for his relentless enthusiasm and effort in connecting all the dots, and to the members of the Organizing Committee, who lent their support in making ICADL 2016 a success. We gratefully acknowledge the University of Tsukuba for hosting the forum and the support of our industrial sponsors. The forum was partially organized by JSPS Kakenhi (#16H01754, #25240012).

December 2016

Atsuyuki Morishima
Andreas Rauber
Chern Li Liew

Organization

Organizing Committee

Organizing Committee Co-chairs

Shigeo Sugimoto   University of Tsukuba, Japan
Atsuyuki Morishima   University of Tsukuba, Japan

ICADL Program Committee Co-chairs

Atsuyuki Morishima   University of Tsukuba, Japan
Andreas Rauber   Vienna University of Technology, Austria
Chern Li Liew   Victoria University Wellington, New Zealand

Publication Chair for ICADL

Akira Maeda   Ritsumeikan University, Japan

Publication Chair for APIS

Emi Ishita   Kyushu University, Japan

Doctoral Consortium Co-chairs

Christopher Khoo   Nanyang Technological University, Singapore
Taro Tezuka   University of Tsukuba, Japan

Publicity Co-chairs

Gobinda Chowdhury   Northumbria University, UK
Mitsuharu Nagamori   University of Tsukuba, Japan
Bhuva Narayan   University of Technology Sydney, Australia
Sueyeon Syn   The Catholic University of America, USA

Public Relations Chair

Hiroshi Itsumura   University of Tsukuba, Japan

Local Arrangements Chair

Tetsuo Sakaguchi   University of Tsukuba, Japan

Local Arrangements and Publicity

Tetsuya Mihara   University of Tsukuba, Japan

Treasurer

Masao Takaku   University of Tsukuba, Japan

ASIS&T Asia-Pacific Liaison

Songphan Choemprayong   Chulalongkorn University, Thailand

Advisory, PNC Liaison

Shoichiro Hara   Kyoto University, Japan

SIGIR Liaison

Edie Rasmussen   University of British Columbia, Canada

Program Committee

Palakorn Achananuparp   Singapore Management University, Singapore
Robert Allen   Yonsei University, South Korea
Toshiyuki Amagasa   University of Tsukuba, Japan
Kanwal Ameen   University of the Punjab, Pakistan
Lu An   Wuhan University, China
Naveed Anwar   Northumbria University, UK
Thomas Baker   Dublin Core Metadata Initiative
Christoph Becker   University of Toronto, Canada
Eric Boamah   The Open Polytechnic of New Zealand, New Zealand
Artur Caetano   University of Lisbon, Portugal
Shu-Jiun Chen   Academia Sinica, Taiwan
Gobinda Chowdhury   Northumbria University, UK
Euan Cochrane   Yale University Library, USA
Fabio Crestani   University of Lugano, Switzerland
Sally Jo Cunningham   Waikato University, New Zealand
Koji Eguchi   Kobe University, Japan
Miguel Escobar Varela   National University of Singapore, Singapore
Pavlos Fafalios   L3S Research Center, Germany
Schubert Foo   Nanyang Technological University, Singapore
Edward Fox   Virginia Polytechnic Institute and State University,
                                USA
Nuno Freire   INESC-ID, Portugal
Dion Goh   Nanyang Technological University, Singapore
Annika Hinze   University of Waikato, New Zealand
Jieh Hsiang   National Taiwan University, Taiwan
Jane Hunter   University of Queensland, Australia
Isto Huvila   Uppsala University, Sweden
Fidelia Ibekwe-Sanjuan   Aix-Marseille Université, France
Daisuke Ikeda   Kyushu University, Japan
Emi Ishita   Kyushu University, Japan

Kiduk Yang   Kyungpook National University, South Korea
Masatoshi Yoshikawa   Kyoto University, Japan
Marcia Zeng   Kent State University, USA
Maja Žumer   University of Ljubljana, Slovenia

Contents

Community and Digital Libraries

When Personal Data Becomes Open Data: An Exploration of Lifelogging,
User Privacy, and Implications for Privacy Literacy.................. 3
  Zablon Pingo and Bhuva Narayan

The Value of Public Libraries During a Major Flooding: How Digital
Resources Can Enhance Health and Disaster Preparedness in Local
Communities 10
  Feili Tu-Keefner

Current Situation and Countermeasures of the Legal Protection of Digital
Archives User's Privacy in China 16
  Jing Zhang and Jiaping Lin

Involving Source Communities in the Digitization and Preservation of
Indigenous Knowledge 21
  Eric Boamah and Chern Li Liew

Students and Their Videos: Implications for a Video Digital Library 37
  Sally Jo Cunningham, David M. Nichols, and Judy Bowen

Digital Library Design

Supporting Gender-Neutral Digital Library Creation: A Case Study Using
the GenderMag Toolkit 45
  Sally Jo Cunningham, Annika Hinze, and David M. Nichols

Developing Institutional Research Data Repository: A Case Study 51
  *Zhiwu Xie, Julie Speer, Yinlin Chen, Tingting Jiang, Collin Brittle,
  and Paul Mather*

Cultural Digital Map Prototype of Tourist Attractions in NirasSuphan
Written by SunthonPhu, Poet of Thailand 57
  *Watcharee Phetwong, Bhornchanit Leenaraj, Nanthiya Charin,
  Chadaphon Janchian, and Krisorn Sawangsire*

The Rise and Fall of the *Wonder Okinawa* Digital Archive: Comparing
Japanese and American Conceptualizations of Digital Archives........... 63
  Andrew Wertheimer and Noriko Asato

Toward Access to Multi-Perspective Archival Spoken Word Content   77
Douglas W. Oard, John H.L. Hansen, Abhijeet Sangawan, Bryan Toth,
Lakshmish Kaushik, and Chengzhu Yu

Information Access Design and User Experience

Rarity-Oriented Information Retrieval: Social Bookmarking vs.
Word Co-occurrence   85
Takayuki Yumoto, Takahiro Yamanaka, Manabu Nii,
and Naotake Kamiura

Proposing a Scientific Paper Retrieval and Recommender Framework   92
Aravind Sesagiri Raamkumar, Schubert Foo, and Natalie Pang

Investigating the Use of a Mobile Crowdsourcing Application for Public
Engagement in a Smart City   98
Chei Sian Lee, Vishwaraj Anand, Feng Han, Xiaoyu Kong,
and Dion Hoe-Lian Goh

User Testing of Prototype Systems in Two Different Environments:
Preliminary Results   104
Tanja Merčun, Athena Salaba, and Maja Žumer

Finding "Similar but Different" Documents Based on Coordinate
Relationship   110
Meng Zhao, Hiroaki Ohshima, and Katsumi Tanaka

Information Extraction and Analysis

Rule-Based Page Segmentation for Palm Leaf Manuscript on Color Image . . .   127
Papangkorn Inkeaw, Jakramate Bootkrajang, Phasit Charoenkwan,
Sanparith Marukatat, Shinn-Ying Ho, and Jeerayut Chaijaruwanich

Exploiting Synonymy and Hypernymy to Learn Efficient Meaning
Representations   137
Thomas Perianin, Hajime Senuma, and Akiko Aizawa

Entity Linking for Mathematical Expressions in Scientific Documents   144
Giovanni Yoko Kristianto, Goran Topić, and Akiko Aizawa

Improved Identification of Tweets that Mention Books: Selection of
Effective Features   150
Shuntaro Yada and Kyo Kageura

A Visualization of Relationships Among Papers Using Citation
and Co-citation Information   157
Yu Nakano, Toshiyuki Shimizu, and Masatoshi Yoshikawa

Education and Digital Literacy

A Lecture Slide Reconstruction System Based on Expertise Extraction for
e-Learning   167
   Yuanyuan Wang and Yukiko Kawai

Developing a Mobile Learning Application with LIS Discipline Ontology . . .   180
   Chao-Chen Chen, Wei-Chung Cheng, and Yi-Ting Yang

Heuristic Evaluation of an Information Literacy Game   188
   Yan Ru Guo and Dion Hoe-Lian Goh

Models and Guidelines

Guideline for Digital Curation for the Princess Maha Chakri Sirindhorn
Anthropology Centre's Digital Repository: Preliminary Outcome   203
   Sittisak Rungcharoensuksri

Describing Scholarly Information Resources with a Unified Temporal Map   212
   Robert B. Allen, Hanna Song, Bo Eun Lee, and Jiyoung Lee

Issues for the Direct Representation of History   218
   Robert B. Allen

Preserving Containers – Requirements and a Todo-List   225
   Klaus Rechert, Thomas Liebetraut, Dennis Wehrle, and Euan Cochrane

Development of Imaginary Beings Ontology   231
   Wirapong Chansanam and Kulthida Tuamsuk

Open Access and Data

MathDL: A Digital Library of Mathematics Questions   245
   Chu Keong Lee, Joan Jee Foon Wee, and Don Tze Wai Chai

Interleaving Clustering of Classes and Properties for Disambiguating
Linked Data   251
   Takahiro Komamizu, Toshiyuki Amagasa, and Hiroyuki Kitagawa

A Framework for Linking RDF Datasets for Thailand Open Government
Data Based on Semantic Type Detection   257
   *Pattama Krataithong, Marut Buranarach, Nattanont Hongwarittorrn,
   and Thepchai Supnithi*

An Attempt to Promote Open Data for Digital Humanities in Japanese
University Libraries   269
   Emi Ishita, Tetsuya Nakatoh, Kohei Hatano, and Michiaki Takayama

Redesigning the Open-Access Institutional Repository: A User Experience
Approach   275
    Edward Luca and Bhuva Narayan

Opinion, Sentiment and Location

Expanding Sentiment Lexicon with Multi-word Terms for Domain-Specific
Sentiment Analysis   285
    Sang-Sang Tan and Jin-Cheon Na

Twitter User Classification with Posting Locations   297
    Naoto Takeda and Yohei Seki

Temporal Analysis of Comparative Opinion Mining   311
    Kasturi Dewi Varathan, Anastasia Giachanou, and Fabio Crestani

Social Media

Social Q&A Question-and-Comments Interactions and Outcomes:
A Social Sequence Analysis   325
    Sei-Ching Joanna Sin, Chei Sian Lee, and Yin-Leng Theng

Why Do People View Photographs on Instagram?   339
    Chei Sian Lee and Sei-Ching Joanna Sin

Sharing Brings Happiness?: Effects of Sharing in Social Media Among
Adult Users   351
    Winston Jin Song Teo and Chei Sian Lee

Analyzing and Using Wikipedia

DOI Links on Wikipedia: Analyses of English, Japanese, and Chinese
Wikipedias   369
    Jiro Kikkawa, Masao Takaku, and Fuyuki Yoshikane

Cross-Modal Search on Social Networking Systems by Exploring
Wikipedia Concepts.   381
    Wei Wang, Xiaoyan Yang, and Shouxu Jiang

Suggesting Specific Segments as Link Targets in Wikipedia.   394
    Renzhi Wang and Mizuho Iwaihara

Author Index   407

Community and Digital Libraries

When Personal Data Becomes Open Data: An Exploration of Lifelogging, User Privacy, and Implications for Privacy Literacy

Zablon Pingo$^{(\boxtimes)}$ and Bhuva Narayan

School of Communication, University of Technology Sydney, Ultimo, Australia
{zablon.pingo,bhuva.narayan}@uts.edu.au

Abstract. This paper argues that there is a need for an awareness and education about privacy literacy in an age where lifelogging technologies are ubiquitous and open up private data to commercial and other uses, wherein commercial entities build up huge digital libraries of private data that they then mine with big data analytics. Often, data is represented as if they are the raw material of information and algorithms, and as neutral agents for processing these pieces of information, but in our digital society, this so-called neutral data can become open data that can be processed easily to reveal informational metadata on individuals' behaviors. Whilst much of this may be beyond individual control, and simply an unavoidable part of our information society, there are certain types of personal and private data that can be, and need to be, under individual control, and not open to integration or 'hashing' with public data. This requires a new type of data literacy on the part of users that we term as privacy literacy.

Keywords: Lifelogging · Privacy literacy · Personal data · User awareness · User education · Digital literacy

1 Introduction

People leave a digital trail of data or "electronic breadcrumbs" in their daily routines; through electronic fare cards, traffic and street cameras, internet surfing, paying for purchases with credit/cash cards, creating text messages or by making calls, and so on [1]. Additionally, with an increased awareness of personal health and individuals to keep fit and healthy, the use of lifelogging devices to track one's fitness, diet, sleep, exercise, and other activities is increasing also. These tracking applications or lifelogging devices also collect other incidental and behavioral data such as location, patterns, and related metadata and can be combined and re-combined to discover new data. This lifelogged information generated by individual consumers is often privatized by service providers and provided to third parties through their terms-and-conditions-of-use and end user license agreements (EULA). Users are required to read lengthy legalese in privacy policies before signing up to use devices and services, which hardly anyone

© Springer International Publishing AG 2016
A. Morishima et al. (Eds.): ICADL 2016, LNCS 10075, pp. 3–9, 2016.
DOI: 10.1007/978-3-319-49304-6_1

reads [2,3]. Increasingly, several retail-store loyalty programs have also adopted strategies that motivate users to link up their loyalty cards with fitness-device data and insurance companies' plans. This raises an important issue in regard to privacy, which surrounds data collection strategies, surveillance, and monitoring of people through technologies and related privacy risks, especially in light of corporate mergers, take-overs, and other synergies between commercial entities. This study will focus on understanding this disconnect between the intentions of service providers with respect to lifelogging devices and apps and the trust that individuals place in them in regard to their own personal information and privacy through a mixed methods study.

2 Literature Review

One of the difficulties in defining the realm of the private is that privacy is a notion that is strongly culturally relative, contingent on such factors as economics as well as technology available in a given cultural domain [4]. This literature review considers all perspectives of privacy around the domain of lifelogging data created by users for purposes of health and fitness.

2.1 The Concept of Privacy

Warren and Brandeis' argument for the right to be left alone was among the first works to define privacy, and its ideas are regarded by many as underpinning in privacy studies, it provides clear demarcation of the boundaries between the private realm and the public sphere [5]. Altman [6] further suggests that individuals should have control over sharing of their information and that, if another person or organization takes control of an individual's personal information without the individual's permission, that is an invasion of their privacy. With digital technologies deeply embedded into our social lives in the information age, the meaning of privacy is continually being debated and shaped by global technology corporations like Facebook, Google, Apple, Microsoft and so on [7]. Solove argues that it is almost impossible to discuss privacy in the abstract, removed from specific contexts, because it is an aspect of a wide variety of practices, each with a different value, and in a constant state of relational flux [8].

2.2 Privacy in the Digital Age

Increasingly, several service providers have merged their systems and converged, share their data, and leverage it for business and marketing purposes, this being the driving force and core for knowledge economies. Users are required to agree to terms and conditions as a form of negotiation for signing up to use the services or devices, but hardly anyone reads them [9]. Retail-store loyalty programs have also adopted strategies that motivate users to link up their loyalty cards with fitness data and insurance companies' plans. Although Facebook CEO Mark Zuckerberg argument that "people have really gotten comfortable not only sharing more information and different kinds, but more openly and with more people" [10], he does not address the use of the "derived" or "discovered" data from the digital technologies activities [SNs, lifelogs, search engines] which props up the privacy risks debate [11]. For instance, combination of personal data collected in different databases pose growing privacy risks and threats in two distinct ways: (i) using information other than its originally perceived approved purpose, and collected at one point in time ("spot information"), and (ii) combining the fruits of "spot information" to piece together information with other data to generate new information for profiling purposes [12]. Such re-use of data for purposes other than originally intended has become common commercial business practice in the current big data analytic era. Social Network Services provide the means for people to be seen online and to share experiences in real time, and for many, "the desire to be visible is stronger than the desire to protect private information" [13]. Currently the volume of data that people create themselves - communication from voice calls, emails, and text messages, to uploaded pictures and videos, is compelling. Moreover, as Agnellutti [14] argues, we are also at the "nascent stage" of the Internet of Things where our appliances and devices have started to be integrated to communicate with each other, sometimes without individual's awareness.

2.3   Lifelogging Metadata

We all use a variety of applications including online calendars, diaries, social networks, blogs, podcasts, and messaging apps etc. All these are offering a total recall of our lives through a total capture of personal relevant information [15], and along with the advances in wearable sensors, networking capabilities, and a massive increase in digital-storage they have also unlocked possibilities for misuse [23].

Personal data we share like photos has embedded metadata (including time, location, resolution, settings, time on device etc.), and all these pieced together can be used to construct our profiles. Schneier [16] distinguishes different sets of data in social networks, but these data classes equally apply to lifelogs data:

- Service data given to the service provider in order to use the application.
- Disclosed data is what one posts on one's own page including photos, video, comments, messages, shared to the "public" or "friends".
- Incidental data is what other people post about you that you don't have control for example somebody shares or re-posts your picture.
- Behavioral data is data the sites collects on users habits by recording what you do, who you do it with, etc. In short is a total engagements on the website.
- Derived/discovered data is data about an individual that is derived based on combination of data sets from one or more sources.

Often data is represented as if they are the raw material of information and algorithms, and as neutral agents for processing these pieces of information [17], but in our digital society, this so-called neutral data can become big data and open data that can be processed easily to reveal informational metadata on individuals' behaviors. Given the richness of this data and metadata it raises concerns on what secondary use it can be put to; Schneier [16] notes that the data is given in confidence, expecting the entities to safeguard the data. But ultimately at the receiving end, service providers can monetize all of it, generally by selling for targeted advertising or for other purposes based on the interests of third parties [18]. Lemov argues that, "Big data is people" [19], essentially a digital library of people. This is what makes the data different and significant, and they're being generated continuously [19].

To use digital technologies, the understanding of their terms and conditions before giving consent is imperative [20], but increasingly the products are offered in highly incentivized environments which might hasten and influence one's consent on use of the personal data without understanding the implications. The continued partnership of loyalty programs, insurance companies and fitness gadget raises serious privacy problems. For example, in Australia, one of the major retail supermarkets Coles encourages the users of health trackers such as Garmin, Fitbit, Jawbone and Polar to link their gadgets to their loyalty card programs for points towards insurance companies etc. The users are encouraged to establish this link with an incentive of 25000–50000 loyalty program points for 10000 steps per day for 10 points. Although this could motivate users to stay fit, it is not clear if users understand the consequences of such synergy on their own personal and private information. For instance, Social Intelligence Corporation notes that 55 % of the so-called millennial generation are ready to share their data (data stored on digital devices or online applications, SNs, etc.) in exchange for discounts, which turns into a great opportunity for businesses [21].

In the UK, the National Health Service (NHS) sparked a controversy on care.data where NHS had planned to give access to the database for commercial functions, ostensibly to sell the data to private enterprises such as insurance companies [22]. In the USA researchers have expressed a lack of sufficient protection to the data collected on the health wearable devices. Though most of the data is health-related, it is not covered sufficiently under the *Health Insurance Portability and Accountability Act* (HIPAA) on privacy [23], which covers primary health data collected by healthcare institutions, and even then, only allows for limited identification such as 5 digit zip code (the 4 digit extension is not allowed), dates of birth, death, admission, discharge, and all geographic subdivisions other than street address [24]. On the other hand, non-healthcare-related entities can utilize the health data from fitness trackers and apps such as geo-location, activities, behavioral data, sleep analysis, buying habits, biometric data, reproductive health data, fingerprints, voice, and face recognition data.

This discrepancy between legislation for registered health organizations and for health apps has resulted in the transport of health data to entities that operate outside the legal boundaries of confidentiality that we expect from medical professionals [25]. Some third parties can grab usernames, names and email addresses from the apps, others received data on exercise and diet habits, medical symptom searches, zip codes, geo-location and gender [26].

3   Implications for Research and Research Questions

In summary, privacy can be treated as a phenomenon that is constructed and negotiated in social processes, valued for the norms and practices that it makes possible [27], and hence we can understand it only through a social constructionist approach. For purposes of this study, we use Westin's [28] definition of privacy as "a claim of individuals, groups or institutions to determine for themselves when, how and to what extent information about them is communicated to others." Determining how people understand the risks and opportunities can help to better protect both parties' interests in the long run. Increasing user awareness and education on privacy implications and risks is important to help them make a rational and proactive decision when using lifelogging devices and applications for various purposes. Hence, in this study, we concentrate on the users of the fitness and lifelogging devices themselves, and seek to answer the following questions about user perceptions:

RQ: Do users understand the eventual use and implications of their personal data collected though lifelogging devices and apps, and the sharing of their fitness data with retail store loyalty programs and insurance companies?

4   Methodology and Research Design

In order to answer the research question, we are using a social constructivist approach though a qualitative interview method; this is because it is important to understand users' own perceptions in their own words using open questions while also giving them an opportunity to expand on their understanding and their behaviors. For this pilot study, we interviewed five participants who use lifelogging devices and had a detailed structured discussion about their use of these devices and apps and also their understanding of privacy issues. The findings presented in the next section are based on a pilot study with the five users.

5   Findings, Discussion and Conclusion

Initial findings from five Australian users of lifelogging technologies (the FitBit device and app) show that even amongst the most digitally capable users, there was a lack of understanding of the broader implications in regard to how their data is collected, stored, shared, connected, and used by their service providers and by third-party organizations. All participants were alarmed at the prospect of the private data from their exercising and their diets being shared with insurance companies and other entities. People indeed understand that they leave a digital trail of data or "electronic breadcrumbs" in their daily routine use of digital devices but are not aware of how it can be used by external companies. Whilst much of this may be beyond individual control, and simply an unavoidable part of our information society, there are certain other types of personal and private data that users say they need under individual control, such as their lifelogged information – this information, which is generated by individual consumers from their bodies, movements, and behaviors, is not expected to be privatized by service providers. Users demonstrated that they don't read terms and conditions when signing up for devices and apps, but did not see this as a loophole that can open up their private data; they perceived this as an invasion of their bodies through a digital proxy. Hence, in order to exercise individual control over their devices and the private data they generate, users require a new type of data literacy that we term as privacy literacy. The findings have implications for the design of lifelogging devices and apps in order to improve users' privacy awareness and also implications for policy and guidelines regarding the secondary use of data collected by them.

References

1. Pod Academy: Digital breadcrumbs: the data trail we leave behind us (2016)
2. Potter, W.J.: Media Literacy. Sage Publications, Santa Barbara (2015)
3. Solove, D.J.: Introduction: privacy self-management and the consent dilemma. Harvard Law Rev. **126**, 1880 (2012)
4. DeCew, J.: Privacy. The Stanford Encyclopedia of Philosophy (2002)
5. Warren, S., Brandeis, L.: The right to privacy. Harvard Law Rev. **4**(5), 193–220 (1890)
6. Altman, I.: The Environment and Social Behavior: Privacy, Personal Space, Territory, and Crowding. Brooks/Cole, Monterey (1975)
7. BBC News: EU court backs 'right to be forgotten' in Google case. BBC News, UK (2014)
8. Solove, D.J.: Conceptualizing privacy. Calif. Law Rev. **90**, 1087–1155 (2002)
9. Gindin, S.E.: Nobody reads your privacy policy or online contract: lessons learned and questions raised by the FTC's action against Sears. Northwest. J. Technol. Intell. Prop. **8**, 1 (2009)
10. Johnson, B.: Privacy No Longer a Social Norm, Says Facebook Founder. The Guardian, Las Vegas (2010)
11. King, N.J., Forder, J.: Data analytics and consumer profiling: finding appropriate privacy principles for discovered data. Comput. Law Secur. Rev. **32**(5), 669–796 (2016)
12. Etzioni, A.: A cyber age privacy doctrine. In: Privacy in a Cyber Age, pp. 1–18 (2015)
13. Jacobs, B.: Two of the grand changes through computer and network technology. In: Hansen, M., Hoepman, J.-H., Leenes, R., Whitehouse, D. (eds.) Privacy and Identity Management for Emerging Services and Technologies, pp. 1–11. Springer, Heidelberg (2013)
14. Agnellutti, C.: Big Data: An Exploration of Opportunities, Values, and Privacy Issues. Nova Science Publishers Inc., New York (2014)
15. Whittaker, S., Kalnikaitė, V., Petrelli, D., Sellen, A., Villar, N., Bergman, O., Clough, P., Brockmeier, J.: Socio-technical lifelogging: Deriving design principles for a future proof digital past. Hum. Comput. Interact. **27**, 37–62 (2012)
16. Schneier, B.: A taxonomy of social networking data. IEEE Secur. Priv. **8**, 88 (2010)
17. Lupton, D.: Digital Sociology. Routledge, London (2015)
18. Mortimer, R.: The camera never lies. Marketing week (2010)
19. Lemov, R.: Big data is people: why big data is actually small personal and very human. In: Aeon (2016)

20. Potter, W.J.: Media Literacy. Sage Publications, Thousand Oaks (2013)
21. Social Intelligence: social media reports (2016)
22. Keeley, A.: The society which used data on every NHS patient - and used it to guide insurance companies on premiums. Daily Mail (2014)
23. Doherty, J.K., Yu, C., Palfrey, Q.: Lack of comprehensive privacy legislation leaves consumers at risk. TechTarget, vol. 2016, online (2016)
24. HIPAA Personal Health Identifiers, vol. 2016. University of California, San Fransisco (2015)
25. Ifeoma, A.: Do You Know Where Your Health Data Is? Hufftingtonpost Impact (2015)
26. Kaye, K.: FTC: fitness apps can help you shred calories - and privacy (2014)
27. Möllers, N., Hälterlein, J.: Privacy issues in public discourse: the case of "smart" CCTV in Germany. Innovation: Eur. J. Soc. Sci. Res. **26**, 57–70 (2013)
28. Westin, A.F.: Privacy and Freedom. Athenaeum, New York (1967)

The Value of Public Libraries During a Major Flooding:

How Digital Resources Can Enhance Health and Disaster Preparedness in Local Communities

Feili Tu-Keefner[✉]

University of South Carolina, Columbia, SC, USA
feilitu@sc.edu

Abstract. In October 2015, several counties in South Carolina experienced catastrophic flooding that caused severe damage, including loss of residential homes and other calamities. Using a framework for risk communication preparedness and implementation about pandemic influenza for vulnerable populations recommended by public health experts, this case study investigates public libraries' value to their communities and their legitimacy as partners of public health agencies during and after a disaster. Public libraries' situation-specific information services in the target areas affected by flooding during and after the disaster were explored. The methodology was qualitative-based. Focus-group meetings with public library administrators and librarians, one-on-one interviews with community members, and an in-depth interview with a FEMA agent were conducted. Preliminary results reveal essential needs regarding health information and technology access during and after the disaster. Recommendations on the use of digital library resources and social media for disaster and health information dissemination are discussed.

Keywords: Public libraries · Digital library resources · Natural disasters · Disaster preparedness · Health information

1 Introduction

The general public today has become more demanding in searching for a variety of health information sources. Because public libraries are community outreach centers devoted to information services, especially to underserved populations [1], many adults rely on them for accessing technology and Internet resources [2, 3]. Kwon and Kim (2009) show that about 6 % of American adults consider public libraries their primary source for health information [2]. Public health professionals recognize that local public libraries have the potential to intervene effectively in delivering health information services to the public [2].

Public libraries, in addition to respected local and national government agencies such as health, fire, and police departments, are sources of credible information at difficult times [4]. During natural disasters and crises, people need to seek information to answer questions regarding the nature of the threat and how to respond to it. Studies indicate

© Springer International Publishing AG 2016
A. Morishima et al. (Eds.): ICADL 2016, LNCS 10075, pp. 10–15, 2016.
DOI: 10.1007/978-3-319-49304-6_2

that people are more satisfied with the information received about a particular threat when needed facts are provided [5]. Source credibility is the key to successful risk communication [6]. Public libraries have a long history of providing community outreach programs and services to their diverse user population, including aiding access to reliable consumer health information and electronic health resources and offering health-information literacy programs [5]. Public libraries are uniquely positioned to aid community members in developing specialized health information services [7]. A good example is the creation of the HealthLink infrastructure connecting with the library's programs on cancer awareness and screening for adults in the Queens Library System in New York City [7]. Ever-changing information technology has become embedded in every aspect of communication, and public libraries have begun using social media to communicate with their patrons. However, Zach reports that in 2011, within a month after the Mississippi River flooded, not many public libraries posted alerts about emergency situations on their websites [8].

2 Research Background and Theoretical Framework

In October 2015, several counties in South Carolina (SC) experienced catastrophic flooding that caused severe damage, including loss of residential homes and other calamities. This study investigates public libraries' value to their communities, especially to vulnerable populations, and their legitimacy as partners of public health agencies during and after a disaster. This includes various aspects of information, technology, and user support. The targeted public libraries are the Richland Library, the Orangeburg County Library, and the South Carolina State Library. The Richland Library is the major local public library system in the Columbia metropolitan area and Richland County. The Orangeburg County Library is the major local public library system in the Orangeburg County area. The South Carolina State Library is the primary administrator of federal and state support for the state's libraries.

A framework for effective health risk communication preparedness and implementation about pandemic influenza for vulnerable populations recommended by public health experts [9] is used to examine the role of public libraries during the catastrophic flooding (between October 4–10, 2015) in Richland and Orangeburg Counties. The focus of investigation is on the (1) process (including the use of multiple channels and technology for information distribution and services); (2) people (how libraries used community-first approaches for the provision of services and dissemination of trusted and credible information resources); (3) partners (how libraries collaborated with multilevel agencies to facilitate the building of community capacity and resources for emergency response and recovery.

3 Research Questions

Given the above background, the researchers asked the following questions:

During the catastrophic flooding (between October 4–10, 2015) in the target areas affected by flooding (i.e., Richland and Orangeburg Counties in South Carolina)

- What types of information services did the public libraries in the target areas provide to the community?
- What types of technology access (including computers, Internet, and social media) did the public libraries in the target areas provide to the community?

4 Research Design and Methodology

In order to gain a deep understanding of the phenomena related to this catastrophic flooding, the methodology for this case study was qualitative-based, using focus-group meetings and one-on-one interviews. The purposes were to collect comprehensive information regarding librarians' activities (for example, processes for information gathering, distribution, and services), libraries' partnerships with other agencies, and community members' information needs and technology access [10, 11].

4.1 Investigation of Public Libraries' Partnerships and Librarians' Operations

Focus-group meetings with public library administrators and librarians were used to examine how librarians responded during this time. The intention was to encourage library personnel to fully discuss and comment on personal experiences, and to compare their views with those of other participants [10]. Part of the discussions centered on the use of resources to provide information services as well as on users' information needs and technology access during and after the disaster. Purposive sampling was used to recruit as subjects library administrators and professional librarians from several locations specifically affected by flooding, i.e., the Richland Library Main Library and its three branches, as well as the Orangeburg County Public Library system. [12] A pool of potential subjects was identified based on their involvement in the library operations during and after the disaster, after which the researchers formally invited them to participate in this study.

4.2 Examination of Community Members' Information Needs and Technology Access

Community members who were affected by flooding in the target areas were the potential subjects for this component of the study The researchers are still recruiting subjects and conducting interviews with community members. Selective sampling has been used to identify subjects for one-on-one, semi-structured in-depth interviews. Altogether 20 subjects will be invited to participate in the study, with each receiving an incentive of $25. The subjects described in 4.1 served as the main sources in identifying this population. Several community member subjects dropped out during the interview process due to logistics and to personal reasons. A main reason is related to the trauma suffered by those who had gone through this catastrophic flooding.

4.3 Understanding of Public Libraries' Partnerships with Other Agencies

During the catastrophic flooding, public librarians in both Richland and Orangeburg Counties worked extensively with volunteers and responders to provide situation-specific and community-based information services. The U.S. Federal Emergency Management Agency (FEMA) [13] dispatched agents to help with response and recovery in South Carolina before, during, and after the flood. Many FEMA agents were stationed at the local public libraries to work with community members and help them file damage claims online. An in-depth interview with a FEMA agent was held to identify issues regarding the collaborations with public libraries and the technology ability needed for community members to file damage claims.

4.4 Protection of Participants and Confidentiality

Approval for the research protocol was sought from the University of South Carolina Institutional Review Board (IRB). Each person participating in the project was informed about the nature of the project and provided a cover letter as instructed by the IRB. Personal information on the subjects is kept confidential by the researchers. The researchers used email as the primary channel to contact the subjects, and the subjects' e-mail addresses are archived separately. Any files that contain personal information on the subjects will be destroyed after the completion of the project. The results of this research may be published, but no information that could identify subjects will be included. The results will be reported based on all participants collectively.

5   Results

Preliminary results are presented in this section. Altogether, twenty-five library administrators (13/25, 52 %) and librarians (12/25, 48 %) were invited to participate in this study. Three focus-group meetings with public library administrators and librarians were held. Eighteen out of twenty-five members (18/25, 72 %) attended the meetings. Eight of them are library administrators (8/18, 44.4 %), and the rest of them are librarians (10/18, 55.6 %). Three meetings were held at the University of South Carolina, and each meeting lasted around 60 min. The meetings were recorded digitally using Camtasia software. The transcripts of the meetings were prepared by a commercial transcription service. Two research assistants were onsite taking notes. Five one-on-one interviews were conducted; each session lasted around 60 min. A FEMA Regional Manager who served as the site manager in South Carolina was granted permission to meet with the researchers for 90 min. The same commercial transcription service was used to prepare the transcripts of interviews. The researchers decided to manually analyze all the transcripts individually and then compare the results. The topics selected for our analyses are related to the following: the processes librarians used for information gathering, distribution, and services; the community members' information needs; and the partnerships the libraries built with multi-level agencies to facilitate emergency response and recovery.

One of the research purposes is the investigation of public libraries' value to their communities and their legitimacy as partners of public health agencies during and after a disaster. The Richland Library administrators and librarians worked with the offices of South Carolina State Senator Joel Lourie [14] and U.S. Congressman James E. Clyburn [15] to help get FEMA to the local communities, and created disaster recovery centers for FEMA. In fact, 14 % of all FEMA applications were filed at the Richland Library's main and branch libraries. The Richland Library was a water distribution site; librarians took books, toys, and computers to shelters. This successful collaboration with public health agencies shows the value of public libraries in facilitating emergency response and recovery during this disaster.

This research also examines how librarians use technology (including social media) to provide situation-specific information and services. Preliminary results reveal that technology access was crucial to obtaining credible information and disseminating resources and services to the community. The Internet was predominantly used by librarians to gather and distribute resources to community members. Librarians used social media sites to answer patrons' questions with an average nine-minute response time. On the Richland Library's Facebook site, the library's posts were shared 1,386 times, an average of 98 shares for each post. From October 4–12, the library's Twitter account "gained 242 new followers.

However, the findings also show that a discrepancy exists between the reliable resources vital to consumers and the health information shared with them by the public libraries. Public librarians were not fully prepared to provide sufficient essential disaster and health information for adult users, especially through an online venue, before and after the natural disasters hit South Carolina. Information and technology literacy issues created barriers for many community members in accessing FEMA applications and filing claims online.

6 Conclusion and Recommendations

Even though public librarians are skilled at helping users find local information and resources [16], the results also show that the public libraries and librarians in our study were not well prepared in identifying, gathering, distributing, and promoting the use of disaster and health information. The researchers recommend that public libraries provide well-selected, reliable disaster and health digital resources for adult users, making them available permanently, and updating the information consistently. In addition, it is also critical to ensure that these resources can be easily located on the library websites. In recent years, social media have been increasingly popular as a venue for online infor- mation exchange. Social media network sites, such as Facebook and Twitter, can be used to increase the awareness of these library resources and to distribute real-time messages of interest by library personnel. By promoting the use of such resources and services, public librarians can help community members overcome issues related to information and technology literacies by simply clicking on links on the public libraries' websites anytime, anywhere. In addition, health sciences librarians can support the selection and dissemination of trustworthy health resources and train public librarians in the delivery of effective health information services.

References

1. Kreps, G.L.: Disseminating relevant health information to underserved audiences: implications of the digital divide pilot projects. J. Med. Libr. Assoc. **93**(Suppl. 5), S68–S73 (2005)
2. Kwon, N., Kim, K.: Who goes to a library for cancer information in the e-health era? a secondary data analysis of the health information national trends survey (HINTS). Libr. Inf. Sci. Res. **31**, 192–200 (2009)
3. Tu, F., Zimmerman, N.P., Jefferson, R.N.: It's not just a matter of ethics III: current status of the ethical provision of consumer health information services in public libraries in california and south carolina – a preliminary report. In: Mendina, T., Britz, J.J. (eds.) Information Ethics in the Electronic Age: Current Issues in Africa and the World, pp. 107–113. McFarland, Jefferson (2004)
4. Wray, R., Jupka, K.: What does the public want to know in the event of a terrorist attack using plague? Biosecur Bioterror **2**(3), 208–215 (2004)
5. Barr-Walker, J.: Health literacy and libraries: a literature review. Ref. Serv. Rev. **44**(2), 191–205 (2016)
6. Blendon, R.J., Benson, J.M., DesRoches, C.M., Weldon, K.J.: Using opinion surveys to track the public's response to a bioterrorist attack. J Health Commun. **8**, 83–92 (2003)
7. Michel, T.A., Sabino, E., Stevenson, A.J., Weiss, E., Carpenter, A., Rapkin, B.: Queens library healthlink: fighting health disparities through community engagement. Urban Libr. J. **17**(1) (2011). http://academicworks.cuny.edu/cgi/viewcontent.cgi?article=1109&context=ulj
8. Zach, L.: What do i do in an emergency? the role of public libraries in providing information during times of crisis. Sci. Technol. Libr. **30**, 404–413 (2011)
9. Vaugh, E., Tinker, T.: Effective health risk communication about pandemic influenza for vulnerable populations. Am. J. Public Health **99**(Suppl. 2), S324–S332 (2009)
10. Thomas, E., Magilvy, J.K.: Qualitative rigor or research validity in qualitative research. J. Spec. Pediatr. Nurs. **16**(2), 151–155 (2011)
11. Luo, L., Wildemuth, B.M.: Semistructured interview. In: Wildemuth, B.M. (ed.) Applications of Social Research Methods to Questions in Information and Library Science, pp 233–241. Libraries Unlimited, Wesptport (2009)
12. Wildemuth, B.M.: Sampling for Extensive Studies. In: Wildemuth, B.M. (ed.) Applications of Social Research Methods to Questions in Information and Library Science, pp 116–128. Libraries Unlimited, Wesptport (2009)
13. The U.S. Federal Emergency Management Agency, Department of Homeland Security. http://www.fema.gov/
14. Senator Joel Lourie. http://www.scstatehouse.gov/member.php?code=1124999865
15. Congressman Clyburn, J.E.: https://clyburn.house.gov/
16. Makizia, M., Hamilton, R., Littrell, D., Vargas, K., Olney, C.: Connecting public libraries with community emergency responders. Public Libr. **51**(3), 32–36 (2012)

Current Situation and Countermeasures of the Legal Protection of Digital Archives User's Privacy in China

Jing Zhang and Jiaping Lin[✉]

School of Information Management, Sun Yat-Sen University, Guangzhou, China
1024527910@qq.com

Abstract. In order to protect the digital archives users' privacy interests and wins more solid social foundation and wider living space for the development of the digital archives career, the article begins with the privacy and network privacy and lists the new connotation of digital archives users' privacy. It also analyzes the privacy right when digital archives collecting, transporting, storing and using the users' personal information. Then it describes the current situation of the legal protection of digital archives users' privacy in China. In regard to the protection of the digital archives users' privacy in China, the author thinks three steps should be taken. Firstly, privacy should be protected directly as an independent right of human dignity and unitary protective laws of privacy should be made. Secondly, protective regulations of digital archives users' privacy should be made. Thirdly, the contents of protecting users' privacy should be added to the *Archives Laws*.

Keywords: Digital archives users' privacy · Network privacy · Legal protection · Current situation · Countermeasure · China

1 Introduction

Digital Archives is a new proposition in the development of 21st century archives career, and it is also a new concept that has been widely used in the archival community in recent years. It initially appeared in the European countries,which the information level was in the leading position. The emergence and rise of digital archives has brought a serious problem that the users' privacy issues that are less obvious in traditional archives environment now becoming more and more prominent. Traditional archives users' privacy also presents new features in a networked environment. Neglect of this issue is bound to affect the construction and operation of digital archives. In the construction of digital archives, effectively protecting the user's privacy interests is not only the respect for others as an independent existence, but also reflects the user-centered spirit of digital archives services. It can establish a good social image in terms of privacy protection for digital archives and win more solid social foundation and wider living space for the development of the digital archives career, so we need to strengthen the research on digital archives privacy issues.

© Springer International Publishing AG 2016
A. Morishima et al. (Eds.): ICADL 2016, LNCS 10075, pp. 16–20, 2016.
DOI: 10.1007/978-3-319-49304-6_3

2   Basic Concepts and Theory

2.1   Digital Archives Users' Privacy

The network service environment of digital archives makes the user's privacy with the characteristics of the network privacy, and it places more emphasis on conformity, domination and disposal of the personal data. Also because of the virtual network environment it is more vulnerable to infringe. On the one hand,people enjoy the great convenience of digital archives network services, on the other hand, bear the risks and troubles that their personal privacy information will be collected unfairly and unlawfully disclosed. Digital archives should fully protect the security of user's information and the rights and interests of its related subjects, and avoid the violation of user's privacy when meet the archive information needs of the public. On the basis of traditional archives user's privacy, digital archives user's privacy right places more emphasis on: collection and possession of personal data; use and security of personal data; disclosure and publicity of personal data; rights and obligations of the data subject; tort relief and legal liability.

2.2   User's Privacy Issues in Digital Archives Information Service

In the traditional archives environment, since the collection of user's personal information is limited by technical means, there are not much privacy violations generally. However, digital archives has inherent characteristics of collecting, disseminating,using user's information in the network environment and this makes the construction and services of digital archives easy to produce users' privacy risks.

User's information collection.   Firstly, as long as the user login the website of digital archives website, its server "loggers" will automatically record the user's IP address, access time, and results. And it can accurately grasp the user's online behavior just to use the network tracking technology. Secondly, digital archives often require users to register as a member before accepting services. For example, registering as a member in Qingdao Digital Archives, it is required to complete the personal information including name, gender, age, identity, ID number, address, e-mail, education, occupation and unit names, etc. After paying a fee to upgrade to premium membership, the archives will provide users with personalized service,but it also needs to provide personal information. Digital archives using advanced technological means to collect personal information is not out of malice, but if collect personal information without the user's knowledge or willingness, it will infringe on the rights of concealing and dominating personal information in the privacy right.

User's Information Transportation and Storage.   As the security of network is unreliable and the current technology is incomplete, third party (such as hackers, etc.) use illegal means to intercept information in the process of users transporting personal information through the network or digital archives storing user's personal information. Digital archives collect personal information intentionally or unintentionally, but it must be done intentionally in terms of the protection of personal privacy information. Digital archives should provide the necessary technical and non-technical support to ensure the safety, completion and authenticity of the user's personal information and not to be stolen and leaked. And the users own information security awareness will affect the security of personal information when access to services of digital archives.

User's Information Use. Qingdao Digital Archives made it clear in its service terms that "respect user's privacy is a basic policy of this site. Therefore, as a supplementary of above mentioned second point about personal registration data analysis, the site will not open, edit or disclose the non-public contents that saved in this site without user's legal authority." Digital archives use the user's information mostly for the routine work or management functions, therefore it's difficult to control and prevent its infringement. For example, some users asked questions on the message board and if the problem is typical and representative, it will be placed inside the digital archives FAQ consulting database for other users to use and reference. If the archives didn't block or delete user's personal information in advance, the user's privacy will be vulnerable to a direct threat.

3   Related Legal Protection of Digital Archives User's Privacy

China has not yet to build a complete privacy protection system and privacy is not directly protected as an independent personal right of the civic. It takes an indirect, decentralized way to protect the privacy in the aspect of law. Provisions related to the privacy scattered Constitution of the People's Republic of China,Criminal Law of the People's Republic of China (hereinafter referred to as Criminal Law) Civil Law of the People's Republic of China, Criminal Procedure Law of the People's Republic of China, Civil Procedure Law of the People's Republic of China and the judicial interpretation made by the Supreme People's Court. In dealing with actual cases, it tends to incorporate privacy into reputation category. There weren't the provisions of privacy until the first Civil Code draft was introduced in new China. And the network privacy can also find the relevant legal provisions in some sectors and local regulations. The adaptation of the traditional archives user's privacy to the network environment produces the digital archives user's privacy. The laws and regulations of network privacy will directly or indirectly protect it in the very great degree before the industry legislation of the digital archives user's privacy come out.

Specific provisions of Criminal Law article two hundred and eighty-sixth stipulates that "violating the provisions of the State to delete, modify, add, interference computer systems and if causes serious consequences, it will be sentenced to five years imprisonment or criminal detention; if the consequences are particularly severe, sentenced to five years imprisonment." This is an earlier and more clearly defined provision in the criminal legal protection of network privacy. In the Criminal Law Amendment (VII), the addition of "crime of selling and illegally providing information of citizen" and "crime of illegally obtaining personal information of citizens" are considered to be the special protection of the network privacy of citizens in the field of Criminal Law. Tort Liability Law of People's Republic of China article thirty-sixth stipulates that "Network users and network services providers using the Internet to violate the civil rights of others shall assume the tort liability." And it is considered to be the norm of using law to regulate network infringement. On the one hand, the network services providers should ensure the security of user's information; on the other hand, Internet users have the right to require services providers to adopt the necessary measures to ensure the security of their personal information. Law on the Protection of Minors of People's Republic of China article thirty-ninth stipulates that "No organization or individual may conceal or destroy the letters, diaries, e-mail of minors." Wherein the email belongs to the category of network privacy. Law on the Protection of the Rights and Interests of Women of People's Republic of China article forty-second stipulates, "Privacy and other personality rights of women are protected by law. Forbidden to damage or belittle the personality of women by the mass media or otherwise." And the mass media includes the way of communication under the network environment.

In addition to the above-mentioned several major laws, there is also the special protection for the network privacy. December 7th, 1997, the State Council promulgated Interim Provisions Implementation Measures of Computer Information Network International Networking Management and article eighteenth stipulates that "forbidden to enter the computer system to tamper other's information without authorization and permission; forbidden to distribute malicious information on the web and send a message on behalf of impersonation to violate other's privacy." December 30th, 1997, the Ministry of Public Security under the State Council promulgated Safety Protection Measures for the Administration of International Networking of Computer Information Network and article seventh stipulates, "User's freedom and privacy of communication are protected by law. No unit or individual may violate the law to use the Internet to violate the user's freedom and privacy of communication." October 8th, 2000, the Ministry of Information Industry promulgated Internet Electronic Bulletin Service Management Stipulation and article twelfth stipulates, "Electronic bulletin services providers shall keep the Internet user's personal information secret. Forbidden to divulge the Internet user's personal information to others without the consent of the users, except as otherwise provided by law." December, 2000, the Standing Committee of the National People's Congress promulgated The Standing Committee of the National People's Congress on Maintaining Internet Security and article fourth stipulates that "Using the Internet to insult others or fabricate facts to slander others and illegally intercept, tamper or delete other's e-mail or other's data to violate citizens' freedom and privacy of correspondence, if constitutes a crime, will be held criminally responsible by the criminal law." Computer Information System Safety Protection Regulations in Guangdong Province applied officially in 2003, and one of the important purposes is to safeguard the legitimate rights and interests of Internet users. It stipulates that that stealing other's account, sending a message on behalf of impersonation, violating the privacy of citizens, disclosing others e-mail address to third parties without permission, sending spam to others are illegal behaviors, which will be punished.

4 Conclusions

Digital archives users' privacy is gradually revealed and established in network service environment. The research on the digital archives users' privacy in China has a late start and the research on the theoretical basis of digital archives user's privacy protection is not systemic enough, also the research on the legal basis of digital archives user's privacy protection is exile. It is obviously that theoretical research in this aspect does not keep pace with the practical development. Using the current protection laws and regulations of network can directly or indirectly protects the digital archives user's privacy to a certain degree and the Personal Information Protection Law has been on the legislative agenda, but digital archives user's privacy has its own particularity. Therefore, development of specialized protection regulations of digital archives user's privacy is the fundamental way out, and it is imminent. For the legislation protection of digital archives user's privacy, the author thinks three steps should be taken. Firstly, privacy should be protected directly as an independent right of human dignity and unitary protective laws of privacy right should be made. Secondly, protective regulations of digital archives users' privacy right should be made. Thirdly, the contents of protecting users' privacy right should be added to the Archives Laws.

References

1. Wang, L.: New Theory of Personal Right, p. 15. Jilin People's Press, Jilin (1994)
2. Yin, L.: Experts on performance of the online contract and the protection of online privacy. Procuratorial Daily **5**, 22–26 (1999)
3. Li, J.: Research on Legislation of Network Privacy Protection. Ocean University of China, Qingdao (2009)
4. Zhao, Q.: Innovation of digital archives user's privacy, pp. 35–37. Lantai World (2012)
5. Li, Y.: Research on long-term mechanism of digital archives user's privacy protection. Lantai World **24**, 15–16 (2008)
6. "Qingdao Archival Information Network" Service Terms 02 November 2015. http://digital.qdda.gov.cn/front/frontlogin/information.jsp
7. Ren, Y., Cui, X.: Analysis of network privacy legislation protection. J. Law **4**, 24–26 (2007)
8. Jin, P.: Research on Network Privacy Protection. Hebei Normal University, Shijiazhuang (2013)
9. Zhang, Z.: Research on Chinese E-commerce Enterprise Restructuring and Its Legal Issues, p. 329. Wuhan University Press, Wuhan (2002)
10. Wang, H.: Research on Library User's Privacy Protection Legislation. Heilongjiang university, Harbin (2009)
11. Li, J.: Research on Legislation of Network Privacy Protection. Ocean University of China, Qingdao (2009)
12. Lei, J.: Protection of Citizens Privacy in the Internet Age. University of International Business and Economics, Beijing (2002)
13. Shen, Y.: Status and role of archives law of People's Republic of China. Law Review **4**, 58–59 (1991)

Involving Source Communities in the Digitization and Preservation of Indigenous Knowledge

Eric Boamah[1] and Chern Li Liew[2(✉)]

[1] School of Social Science, Open Polytechnic New Zealand, Lower Hutt, New Zealand
Eric.Boamah@openpolytechnic.ac.nz
[2] School of Information Management, Victoria University of Wellington,
Wellington, New Zealand
ChernLi.Liew@vuw.ac.nz

Abstract. The digital era has transformed the ways people share information and preserve knowledge for the future. Increasingly, Web 2.0 technologies have been used for participatory practices aimed at constructing cultural heritage knowledge. Memory institutions, including libraries and museums have become keen on opportunities to engage with potential partners and collaborators. For such participatory construction of cultural knowledge to be successful however, some underlying contradictions between traditional documentary practices that privilege 'expert knowledge' and the distributed social Web practices that emphasize the allowance for multiple (at times contradictory) perspectives need to be resolved. This interpretive qualitative study examines the values and challenges of collaborating with communities who are the originators, owners and/or guardians of the traditional beliefs, expressions and other cultural artifacts that bear the indigenous knowledge of a cultural group, as well as people who are recognized by indigenous communities to hold the knowledge. Data was collected through 27 semi-structured interviews in Ghana.

Keywords: Cultural heritage · Digitization · Digital preservation · Indigenous knowledge · Participatory cultural heritage · Source communities

1 Introduction

In this paper, we discuss the importance and challenges associated with involving source communities in the digitization and preservation of Indigenous Knowledge (IK). IK encompasses all forms of traditional information and wisdom that have accumulated over centuries of generational cultural activities within a specific society [1]. The digital era has transformed the ways people share information and preserve knowledge for the future. Increasingly, Web 2.0 technologies have been used for participatory practices aimed at constructing cultural heritage knowledge. Memory institutions, including libraries and museums have become keen on opportunities to engage with potential partners and collaborators. For such participatory construction of cultural knowledge to be successful however, some underlying contradictions between traditional documentary practices that privilege the authoritative ('expert') and the distributed social Web

© Springer International Publishing AG 2016
A. Morishima et al. (Eds.): ICADL 2016, LNCS 10075, pp. 21–36, 2016.
DOI: 10.1007/978-3-319-49304-6_4

practices that emphasize the allowance for multiple (at times contradictory) perspectives [2] need to be resolved. Digitization and digital preservation of IK can be challenging when disconnection occurs between the 'expert' practice and the perspectives of the originating source communities (and the custodians of IK) that has been developed through centuries of practices [3].

This paper builds on the main author's doctoral study which explored various contextual factors influencing the management and preservation of digital cultural heritage resources in Ghana [4] and the second author's research on participatory construction of cultural heritage [5, 6]. The study gives insight into the values of involving source communities. In this study, "source communities" refer to the people who are the originators, owners and/or guardians of the traditional beliefs, expressions, and other cultural artefacts that bear the IK of a cultural group, as well as people who are recognized by indigenous communities to hold the knowledge of the area. The term "involving" means to collaborate with and include the people in the community in every stage of the process digitization their cultural knowledge.

Following a literature review of relevant aspects of IK management and preservation, we discuss relevant findings from Boamah [7] relating to the discussion of involving and collaborating with source communities in the preservation of IK in Ghana. The paper concludes with a discussion of the benefits and challenges associated with involving source communities in the digitization and preservation of IK.

2   Literature Review

Researchers explain that IK is the various forms of principles, truths and ideas that a cultural group acquires as it interacts with its natural environment [8–10]. IK is seen as a cultural reference point for the native people in Ghana. Given the many different indigenous groups in Ghana, it is not surprising that some social, cultural and political issues have been found to prevent source community groups from allowing their IK to be digitized and captured into the national digital preservation management program [7]. In the rush to digitize and to support interoperability and universal access to IK, many memory institutions have applied traditional, often Anglo-American standards that do not account for the often multiple meanings and ontological perspectives associated with traditional cultural knowledge and objects.

Issues affecting the digitization of IK are varied and could be peculiar to each specific cultural group or society where the IK is found. Whaanga *et al.* [3] reported on the ethics, processes and procedures associated with the digitization of the manuscripts, works and collected treasures of key cultural personalities in New Zealand, with emphasis on the late Dr. Pei Te Hurinui Jones. They described how these materials were transformed into a digital library, including the decision-making processes and the various roles and responsibilities of the researchers, family members and local institutions in the process. The researchers found that the digital era has transformed how people interact with the knowledge systems around them. This transformation helps with the collaboration that is required between researchers and the source communities to facilitate the digitization of IK.

A group of Australian researchers explored the various issues that arise through working with indigenous communities in the development of pragmatic and effective data management strategies for higher education researchers [11]. Their analysis suggests that respect for the owners of the IK is critical for enabling engagement with sources communities.

It has been identified especially in the last twenty years that many memory institutions have heeded the calls by indigenous activists to integrate indigenous models and knowledge into mainstream practices [12]. Christen used a case study to examine a collaborative archival project aimed at digitally repatriating and reciprocally curating cultural heritage materials of the Plateau tribes in the Pacific Northwest. She observed that the digital terrain poses both possibilities and problems for indigenous peoples as they seek to manage, revive, circulate and create new cultural heritage within overlapping colonial/postcolonial histories and oftentimes-binary public debates about access in a digital age. She further emphasized that digital technologies allow for items to be repatriated quickly, circulated widely and annotated endlessly. These same technologies however, pose challenges to some indigenous communities who wish to add their expert voices to public collections and to maintain some traditional cultural protocols for the viewing, circulation and reproduction of some materials [12].

Some indigenous communities refuse the digitization of their IK due to fear that they can easily be stolen, misinterpreted or misused when they are made accessible online. Through effective source community involvement, such issues could be addressed and resolved. An example is the Australian Institute of Aboriginal and Torres Strait Islander Studies (AIATSIS) Digitization Program [13]. This project enabled source communities to establish their own local archives and create educational projects with appeal and relevance to the younger members of the communities. The main aim was to preserve important cultural heritage materials to encourage young indigenous Australians to engage in the educational system. It also sought to facilitate and promote the development of the value of materials with focus on the experiences of indigenous people. Examples of community engagement efforts included the creation of new employment opportunities for members through indigenous traineeships in the professions of collection development, preservation, photocopying, audio engineering, film and video etc. [13].

More recently, Filson and Afful-Arthur [14] survey how knowledge on indigenous medicines are preserved in Ghanaian university libraries. Their study reveals that there is scant indigenous medical knowledge for the libraries to curate because most of the practitioners have not considered documenting their knowledge. They hesitate putting their knowledge out in the public domain for fear of losing their intellectual property right. One of the goals of this study was to seek the perspectives of thirty traditional medicine practitioners and to encourage them to document their traditional knowledge. Digitization and digital preservation activities are in their very initial stages in Ghana [7, 15, 16]. Filson and Afful-Arthur's [14] call for alternative healthcare practitioners, such as herbalist, traditional birth attendants, spiritualists, traditional psychiatrist and bonesetters to start to document their knowledge can provide a base for involving key members of source communities as partners and collaborators in IK digitization and preservation.

The importance of involving source communities in IK digitization in Ghana has also been stressed by Plockey [17]. Ghanaian cultures are largely oral in nature, taking the forms of traditional songs, appellations, folklore and storytelling about cultural superheroes and gods (traditionally called 'Ananse' stories). In recent times, advancements in digital technologies are enabling the capturing of some of these Ananse stories into digital forms to showcase them to the rest of the world. For instance, Leti Arts [18] released an interactive digital comic and a mobile app that presents Ananse Superhero games for Windows Phones. In Ghana, traditional games such as 'Oware', 'Dame', 'Abatuo', 'Aso' and 'Ampe' are also a very important aspect of Ghanaian IK. When information about these games is digitized, they form part of IK preservation in Ghana. An example is the development of Kobla Nyomi's Oware 3D mobile application [19].

In a society where everything with a Western connotation is perceived to be an adulteration of the purity of the culture, the adaptation of these computer software programs - which are also seen as signifiers of the Western culture [20] leads to the discussion of which aspects of the Ghanaian IK can be digitized. In modern times, it is very uncommon to see people play these games as it used to be a couple of decades ago. The younger generations are increasingly turning to computer games, gradually losing interests in the physical traditional games. Moving these traditional games into the digital sphere helps Ghanaians preserves aspects of this tradition. The developer of these apps, Kobla Nyomi also emphasizes that if anyone is going to be responsible for digitizing the traditional aspects of the culture into a game like this in their possible best form, it is the people from the source communities rather than so-called information management 'experts' working in memory institutions [21].

The fact that these digitization initiatives and innovations are being done by people from the source communities themselves is pointing to the possibilities for transforming the practices of curation and documentation of aspects of IK to accommodate multiple voices and perspectives. Ghanaian cultural protocols are seen in the various forms of ceremonies and occasions such as festivals, naming ceremonies and marriage ceremonies in which aspects of the traditions such as rituals, myths, folklore and proverbs are performed in ways where specific procedures that follow laid down conventions, rules and practices. These protocols are not only meant to teach the people culturally-acceptable ways of living, but they also impart indigenous ecological knowledge for people to be aware of their environment and protect it [22].

Despite the people's commitment and adherence to cultural protocols, these aspects of the Ghanaian cultural knowledge are either not properly managed or often missing from materials being curated in the various cultural institutions [7]. Most institutions have been found to not deal well with oral traditions [17]. Another important aspect of Ghanaian IK is traditional law relating to cultural patrimony and kinship. When these are effectively documented, they can form a basis for future IK digitization project. A way of documenting these aspects of IK is through studies such as Korang-Okrah and Haight's (2015) ethnographic exploration of Ghanaian (Akan) women's experiences of widowhood and property rights violation in the Ashanti and Brong-Ahafo regions of Ghana. These researchers have found that the way some local customary laws are applied can sometimes constrain the implementation of national progressive law.

Research and activities that take the researcher to the specific context of the people performing traditional activities can help with effective digitization and preservation of IK utilizing grassroots evidence. Again, Korang-Okrah's [24] exploration of the experiences of Ghanaian (Akan) widows and their property rights violation is a good example. She visited specific villages in the Ashanti and Brong-Ahafo regions where these traditional activities are strongly performed with the objective of uncovering the subjective experience. She used digital devices to record the stories and the experiences shared by the twenty widows interviewed – narration of the events that took place during the performance of their widowhood rites. This approach of recording the IK from the people on the ground in the source communities can best be described as a grassroots approach of documenting cultural knowledge and it is a useful basis for future IK digitization.

The review of current literature also reveals issues that inhibit involvement of source communities in the curation, digitization and preservation of IK. The main institutions found to be in charge in the management and preservation of aspects of the documentary cultural heritage resources in Ghana are the Public Records and Archives Administration Department (PRAAD), which serves as the National Archives of Ghana. Meanwhile, the Ghana Library Board (GLB) provides public library services in the country. But these institutions face several challenges in their management of IK in Ghana [4]. These include a general lack of interest in documentary heritage information resources and their management, lack of funding, lack of skilled personnel, inadequate facilities for training and poor infrastructures (e.g. inconsistent power supply). Plockey [25] also explored the various issues and prospects affecting to the role of Ghanaian public libraries in the digitization of indigenous knowledge and similarly, found that lack of human resource, finance, infrastructure, reliable Internet connectivity and copyright issues, among other concerns, pose challenges in the digitization of indigenous knowledge in Ghana, and thus suggested a need for training, research into IK digitization management and the development of a policy framework. In a subsequent study, Plockey [17] identified that academic libraries in Ghana fail to "recognize indigenous knowledge as a distinct system of knowledge that requires handling and management regimes for its materials that are different from those applied by the Western system of knowledge management" (p. 40). This attitude is believed to inhibit the effective management of heritage resources and the involvement of source communities in IK curation, digitization and preservation.

3   Research Design

An interpretative qualitative research approach was employed. A semi-structured interview technique using the snowball sampling technique was employed. Interviewees included information and cultural heritage experts, representing key personalities and representing the people of the source communities of IK in Ghana. Key personalities used in this study also include scholars, funders of information management and cultural heritage initiatives, school teachers who handled subjects for which ICT and cultural heritage resources in digital forms support the curriculum, and government officials involved in policy and decision making in Ghana. Participants were drawn from various cultural institutions, ministries, departments, agencies and district offices, traditional areas, chiefs' palaces, institutions involved with ICT education and those that dealt with digital information management.

In total, 27 interviews were conducted with key stakeholders from 23 institutions in Ghana. Each interview lasted between 45 min and 1 h and they were audio-recorded. Each interview was transcribed and to facilitate coding, the interviewees were grouped into five categories based on their institutions. Table 1 shows the institutional categories of interviewees and their codes.

Table 1. Institutional categories of interviewees and their codes

Interviewees	Code	Number
University Lecturers	UL	4
People from Cultural Institutions (Libraries, Archives, Museums, Chiefs' Palaces)	CI	8
ICT Teachers/Managers	IT	4
People from Ministries and Agencies/District Assemblies	MD	7
NGOs/Private Institutions	PI	4
Total Number of Interviewees		**27**

The Department of Information Studies (DIS), University of Ghana, is the main institution that educates information professionals in Ghana. From DIS, four lecturers with expertise in IK management were interviewed and labelled 'UL'. Specific interviewees from DIS were UL1, UL2, UL3 and UL4. There were eight participants from the different cultural institutions. These cultural institutions included chief palaces, palace museums, courtyards of clan heads and shrines of traditional priests. The participants from cultural institutions were labelled CI1 through to CI8. Participants from various institutions where ICT education and/or its management take place were also labelled as 'IT'. They included ICT teachers, practitioners and managers. There were four IT interviewees: IT1, through to IT4. The study also included participants from public institutions such as the ministries, departments, agencies and district assemblies. Altogether this group was labelled 'MD', resulting in MD1 through to MD7. The label 'PI' was used for participants from private institutions and Non-Governmental Organisations. There were four PI interviewees: PI1, through to PI4.

The interview transcripts were carefully read several times and different colour codes where used to mark and highlight key concepts that initially emerged. Different color codes were used to represent the major themes under which the main ideas were grouped. A table was created to organise the main ideas and to help identify the patterns and relationships between the emerging themes. Four main clusters of factors were identified as influencing the management and preservation of digital cultural heritage resources in Ghana. In the next section, findings from the interview data relevant to the understanding of the lack of involvement of source communities in IK digitization, and the values/benefits and challenges of involving source communities are presented and discussed.

4   Findings and Discussion

There is evidence in Ghana pointing to the involvement of originating communities in the capturing and documentation of IK to prepare them for digitization projects. Since the culture is oral, there is not much written documentation on the various aspects. The interview data revealed that most of the traditional indigenous performances are dying out because modern lifestyles are keeping people from performing them regularly. But upon recognizing the danger associated with the loss of some of these IK, there have been attempts in recent times to document them through digital photography and video recordings. An interviewee who is responsible for the management of a regional museum explained how they recaptured some of the aspects of the culture that were almost lost:

> Last year we had the privilege of the 10th anniversary of Otumfuo [title of Asante kings] where through his own request we brought onto the Apatakesie [the biggest auditorium] stage about, 15 of these almost dying traditional musical forms. We went searching for them and performed to the delight of His Majesty and His entourage. It was a rewarding experience but until then most of the groups were almost dead. (MD4)

The people who performed these musical forms were the indigenous people from the various villages. Using digital photography and video recording to document aspects of the culture is very relevant in the Ghanaian society as documentation through written text is a very limited. The lack of written documentation of the culture is due to high levels of illiteracy. Several interviewees reveal that people are not much concerned about the creation of a national memory through digitization. They are more concerned about where the documented aspects of the culture will come from. Some interviewees expressed this concern in the following way:

> We are an oral culture. We need to document our culture. The little that has even been done it is foreigners or let me say outsiders who do not understand the culture who have documented our culture. Basic knowledge about our culture and other things will be missing to generations to come because they have not been documented for them to read. (UL4)

> We should document, because the oral tradition our elders used are failing us. Things are changing, from text we move to microforms and now the latest form of storing information [digitization]. So I think we should move with the time. (CI5)

When it comes to digitization of IK, the literacy level of the people in the source community may not be a hindrance. But the process of involving the source communities may be difficult. The interview data shows that majority of the people in Ghanaian IK sources communities are illiterate and that is affecting their awareness of the values of digitizing IK. A curator from one of the national cultural institutions said:

> The Ghanaian by nature does not like reading. There is this saying that 'if you want to hide anything from the Ghanaian, just put it on paper', so when it comes to defense you just say I put it in writing you did not read it. (CI5)

It is for this reason that one of the academic interviewees believes that Ghanaians are not serious when it comes to management and digitization of IK:

> We don't take cultural heritage management and preservation as an area of priority. People don't want to write about our culture they are interested in other areas. Although we are an oral society we need to write to enhance knowledge transfer. But we allow foreigners to write on our culture.

The major factor is lack of interest. They don't have the interest and desire to write about the culture. (UL4)

Another interviewee indicates that a reason why people from the different cultural groups do not document aspects of their cultural heritage may be as a result of the fear of permanent loss of cultural information. A manager in charge of a regional traditional museum said for instance:

We need to protect our creative and intellectual materials. We need to be always conscious so that we don't get people stealing them from us. I think the idea of digitizing is laudable but I am sceptical because we do not have adequate protective measures for them when we put them online. What I know is that those people out there are good at stealing and if we don't take care they will steal everything from us and come back later to sell to us at very expensive prices (MD4).

A curator in charge of a palace museum of a major indigenous group described the issues:

People have their own cultural objects of historical significance hidden under their bedrooms, because they fear that once they give them out who is going to take care of those objects, who is going to preserve them?. Their forefathers of so many years ago gave those items which are mainly designed from pure gold. You see, everything is gold. Look, this key contains gold [holding up a key]. You see? But modern people, the moment you give this item to them they will go and sell it. But if people can be assured of a place, a secured central point to keep the item, they will donate. So in the future his grandson will visit the place and say oh my grandfather donated this or that and he will feel proud and the next time he will also do something to help. (CI2)

The points in interviewees' comments above illustrates what the literature describes about how some people in the source communities refuse to offer their IK for digitization projects because of fear of permanent loss [13, 14]. This fear can make IK digitization innovations in Ghana challenging. It could prevent people in the source communities from fully getting involved and bringing their heritage resources for the development of a national digital cultural heritage repository. A closer look at the interview data shows that apart from this fear, certain historical tribal conflicts have resulted in enmities among the various indigenous groups in Ghana. Interviewees traced the reason for these animosities to the precolonial era when British soldiers supported and used some smaller and weaker traditional groups to defeat major tribes who now feel a lack of trust and a loss of supremacy and control. As a result, every group appears to be keeping their IK to themselves. The same palace museum curator explained the issue of animosities this way:

Some people have been trampled upon in the past. It is not easy to heal those wounds. Asante [tribe] was more or less Ghana until the British came. After independence, the expectation was that some of Asante's heritages were going to be recognised by the constitution as national. But it was not accepted by the other tribes. So it shouldn't be now that somebody comes to tell us to give out the Golden Stool for national keeps, or make Akwasidae [a festival] a national celebration. Everywhere you go people speak Akan more than any Ghanaian language. But people don't want to accept it as a national language because they feel bitter. So we will also keep our [culture]. There are a lot of observances that we do that do not come to public especially in the celebration of our festivals people only see the celebration aspects but the behind the scene aspects no one knows, because it is for the Ashantis alone. (CI2)

These issues seriously affect the involvement of originating communities as key stakeholders in collaborative IK digitization programme and lead to lack of desire for a collective IK curation, digitization and preservation in Ghana.

Nevertheless, several comments from interviewees lend support to the importance placed on involving source communities in IK digitization and preservation. For instance, the manager in charge of regional tradition museum explained that the actual concern of some of the people is not just the about whether the creation of a national heritage institution will be feasible or not but how people from the various indigenous communities can be brought together to contribute their documented heritage so everybody can identify themselves with it and find value and benefits in the digitized IK:

> Some of us are not even concern about whether there is a national institution or not. If we should have, what should be there? That is the most important because if we should have such an institution and when you go there it is only foreign materials you will see there then we must not have it. What we are doing is to encourage our people to put these knowledge and information into books so that when we eventually have that national institution it will be filled with books and materials documented by our people about us, making us understand who we are, what our people have gone through, where we are now and where we are going. (MD4)

Several interviewees indicated that at the end of the day, the objective of IK digitization and preservation will be to ensure that there is a national memory that is available to everybody and can be tapped into at any point by anybody who needs it. Because of this, it is important to have a formidable institution that will need to review what is happening somewhere and come out with priorities to involve all Ghanaian traditional communities and cultures.

> Ghana should have a national institution where you can go and have access to cultures of different aspects of our people with our different tribes, the Asante culture, Dagombas, all the cultures and history at one point. So that it becomes a national thing. But for now everybody has their own separate culture. (CI2)

These views are consistent with discussions in the literature that stress the importance of involving source communities in IK digitization [17]. Plockey indicated that digitizing African and for that matter, Ghanaian IK will help to avoid cultural gaps between generations. The establishment of a national digital memory, as a result of IK digitization and preservation can also lead to sustainable development in the country.

The interview data shows interesting possibilities exist for transforming the practices of curation and documentation of cultural object and knowledge to accommodate multiple voices and perspectives. Evidence from the literature shows that Ghanaian cultural institutions lack adequate efforts in managing both physical and digital forms of heritage resources and IK [7, 14, 15, 25] and was identified in Plockey's [17] that academic libraries in Ghana do not deal with the management of oral traditions at all (p. 40). The interview data for this study supports that argument and shows that some university libraries have become conscious of the importance of incorporating the management of IK in their institutional repositories. An academic librarian in charge of an institutional repository in a Ghanaian university said:

> We created this digital repository in 2009, and it is the only University in Ghana with an institutional repository which is live online. Currently our institutional repository has been mandated to be the national institutional repository. We keep digital forms of thesis of post graduate

students, reports of graduate students, conference papers, research papers by lecturers and faculty. We also have some of our collection representing our heritage, for example, the *Adinkra* traditional signs and symbols like 'Gye Nyame', 'Asempa', all of them are represented in our database. (CI3)

This practice shows that there is a possibility for libraries and other cultural institutions in Ghana to transform their documentation and curatorial services to include other perspectives in their digitization and preservation of IK.

The interview data reveals the importance of cultural protocols and contextual experience and knowledge around cultural norms, objective and knowledge. But since the culture is mostly oral and people from the sources communities lack the interest to write about their culture, most of these protocols are missing from the traditional documentation records for the development of a memory institution for the country. Discussions in the literature show how cultural protocols are used to instill culturally accepted values and ways of living, and also to help the members of the source communities to be aware of their environment and protect them [22]. An interviewee from Kintampo traditional area explained the chiefs and traditional leaders have instituted taboos to 'protect' the IK in their areas:

There is an ancient dug out *oware* [traditional game] in the rocks inside the Kunsu forest. Pots used by slaves, the shackles use to chain them are still tacked into the trees; they are all still there. People's activities in the forest can easily result in the loss of these important heritage resources. So the chief and elders in Kunsu have rendered the forest evil and it is taboo for anyone to enter the forest for any activity. The people also listen; so the forest and the heritage in it are being protected. (PI1)

Most of the Ghanaian cultural protocols are kept in secrete and made known to only those seen to be fit to perform them. Because of this secrecy, it becomes very difficult for some aspects to be documented and made known to other people outside the culture. Interviewees assert that such procedures lead to issues that make the digitization, management and digital preservation of IK in Ghana very difficult to deal with. A cultural heritage academic expert described this situation in the following words:

We can face issues. First the legal, and secondly the privacy; But even there, most of our cultural things are not owned by any one particular tribe. The only privacy issue I may think of is that most of our cultural things are shrouded in secrecy and we need to draw a line between what to digitize and what not to digitize. (UL4)

Drawing a line between what needs to be digitized and what not to be digitized requires collaboration and understanding between peoples in the source communities and digital preservation experts and the involvement of all stakeholders. But with the sort of fear, animosities, lack of interest and other attitudes that affects the information culture in Ghana, it seems a lot of grounds work needs to be done before a fine line can be drawn between what aspects of the Ghanaian IK needs to be digitized and what should not. Some interviewees expressed concern that aspects of IK are missing because of the beliefs of of the custodians:

The leaders, chiefs, queen mothers and custodians of the culture, don't see the essence of preservation in modern times. Just consider how the traditional home operates, when children ask questions they are shouted at to keep quite because we think children are not supposed to ask elders too many questions. So it is not unusual to find kids being insulted by elders for even coming close to ask a question. Chiefs and queen-mothers don't interact with the youth. Children see them as a cult. They are not approachable. So if we do not find a way of documenting these cultures, all these heritage resources at their disposal will not be available to the youth in the future because there is a barrier. (PI1)

The point in PI1's comments is that since Ghana is an oral culture which is largely preserved through oral means, the custodians should involve children more so that they can learn most of the IK and keep it for the future. New digital technologies provide many avenues for learning. The television, computers and Internet, video games etc. are all competing for the children's attention. So if the elders keep telling the children not to come close to them, the children will lose interest in the IK and it will eventually disappear.

Nevertheless, other interviewees indicated that some of the custodians have seen the potential brought about by new digital technologies. An IT manager in charge of a Community Information Centre for instance, explained:

The chief and the [traditional] priest of this town are the custodians of the culture of this area. They both have their children in this center to learn about ICT. When I miss a class with their children, they get angry with me for not giving their children more time to teach them the computer, showing that even the custodians are striving to learn something about the computer. They have realized how the world is changing to digital. When these custodians die they leave the culture to their children. So they want the children to learn about the technology so that they can use it to manage and preserve the culture. (IT4)

There is evidence in the interview data that a grassroots approach to IK digitization in Ghana will be welcomed. Even though some interviewees indicated that there was fear and animosities among the people in the source communities, all interviewees believe IK digitization is important in Ghana. A manager of a private environmental sustainability institution said that:

Digital preservation is very necessary because the way things are going if we do not preserve heritage materials digitally, then it is not preservation at all. Photos on papers easily fade out, when water pours on them they spoil, the quality and everything get spoil. We can get the paintings of foreign artists on the internet. However, paintings of certain great but unknown African artist cannot be found because efforts were not made to preserve them either physically or move a step further to preserve them digitally. There is national pride in heritage resources this is what should motivate us to well manage and preserve our cultural heritage. The best way to keep them for future generation is to digitize them and collectively protect them. (PI1)

A rural radio journalist said that:

People are using digital technologies in the form of digital recorders, digital cameras and even mobile phones in the rural areas, but we take it as if that place is rural so we don't go there. I am advising you, go to the grassroots. It is there that the hardships that people go through in terms of ICT use can be found. If you go to Accra, they are already advanced you will not get any necessary information. (PI3)

Several interviewees also suggested that for a national digital repository to be feasible, it is important to start the documentation from the rural areas. For instance, a small cultural heritage office can be set up in every town or village with a computer or any recording device, where people can go and tell stories for it to recorded or those who have any cultural document can deposit them there. Then from the offices in the towns, they can be moved to the district heritage office before being transferred to the regional heritage office. After which liaisons can be made with relevant libraries, museums or archives to collate the documented heritage for a national-level collection.

The interview data also revealed a number of issues perceived to be barriers that hinder the involvement of source communities in IK curation, digitization and preservation in Ghana. For instance, a curator in a national cultural institution pointed out that there is lack of awareness of the importance of IK digitization:

> Most people are not aware of the importance of history and these heritage resources and why we need to preserve them. They need to know that for one to build the future they must know the past. How will they know, it is through studies such as you are doing, and practicing it to bring out the importance and the need for cultural preservation. (CI1)

Lack of interest in information management and IK digitization is apparently not only amongst decision makers at the institutional level. The interview data reveals that it occurs at the national level too. An academic and expert in heritage information management commented that many people, especially members at the base and middle levels of the social system lack awareness of the need to preserve IK while those at the top levels where awareness was present but decision makers were interested in other priorities. A manager in charge of an institutional repository at a university library expressed similar concern about commitment by leaders of the relevant cultural heritage management institutions:

> If the institutions are committed, we wouldn't have these problems with scanners. The leaders buy heavy, heavy cars; we buy $80,000 cars and all that. How much is a scanner? The institutional commitment is not there. It is not because we don't have the money, the money is there but they are used for other things. (CI3)

The lack of genuine interest and political interference has also been quoted as interfering factors. Interviewees explained that when someone has expert knowledge but is not part of the ruling government, their views are not considered. Positions of trust are only given to people who are found to be 'sympathizers' of the government, irrespective of whether those people are qualified or not. Accordingly, some institutions are afraid to embark on any serious digitization initiatives that involve huge costs because they do not want to be unduly investigated by government. Several interviewees believe that it is a strategy employed to frustrate institutions that are perceived to show signs of not being obedient to the government. An interviewee described a situation where a digitization initiative was stopped because of political interference:

> The Social Security and National Insurance Trust [SSNIT] is one institution that initiated a nice digitization project, but when the NPP came into power, they subjected SSNIT in an investigation on how their machines were acquired and how they finance the project. Because of this SSNIT was never able to continue with the digitizing. (UL1)

Some of these political interferences in information management projects have contributed to the overall poor perception of the field by people in the sources communities. A manager from a national cultural institution lamented:

> The Ghanaian perception of the value for records is very poor. If somebody in an institution or department is troublesome or not doing well in his area that person is thrown into the records office as a punishment and where are the record offices? They are usually under staircases where junks, old tyres, old furniture and obsolete things are kept. (CI5)

The lack of a regulatory body for the sector in Ghana is a big hindrance to progress towards effective information management. In countries like New Zealand where progress in cultural information management and IK digitization have been achieved, the role of the national library, national archive and the national museum as well as professional associations are very important. But Ghana does not have a national library. Instead, agencies such as the Ghana Library Board (GLB) who oversees the public library services and the Public Records and Archives Administration Department (PRAAD) who plays the role of a national archive and the Ghana Museums and Monument Board (GMMB) are not perceived to be effective. An interviewee who is a cultural heritage academic said:

> We lack a regulatory or controlling body. National Library is needed as a controlling body for the success of all these. It is needed to coordinate other institutions due to inherent issues and to avoid rivalry. But we don't have it. (UL1)

The lack of equipment was also believed to be a hindering factor. An interviewee from a leading national cultural heritage institution revealed this:

As we sit here now, we have not been able to put our finding aids onto computers. Being a government institution we look up to the government for funding, but it seems they are not interested. The other time I was compelled to confront our director and the accountant on whether they do not present our case when they go for budget hearing, but they said they do their best. But no funding is coming. The only two computers we have were donated by the MAMOTH Ghana when they came to digitize parts of our collection. (CI5)

This interviewee continued:

> The benefits of digitization would be immense to us. But we have not started. This is a government institution but the government is not doing everything for us. We have to look elsewhere for funding. They say it is capital intensive. These decision makers don't put value on records. (CI5)

For a leading national cultural heritage institution to have just two computers is problematic in itself. But for those two computers to be donated by a private organization shows how serious cultural institutions have been ignored by government. Even more serious is that sometimes when some of these private organizations donate to government institutions, there is a motive behind and at times some of the motives can compromise the use of public records or information. For instance, in addition to the quote above, CI5 revealed that when in return to MAMOTH's donated computers, they were allowed to digitize all the slave trade archives and keep for their own private use. As to what MAMOTH Ghana took these public records for, no one could tell.

Apart from these issues of lack of support from government and key decision makers, there was also mention of the lack of unity among the Ghanaian ethnic groups which was believed to hinder the progress towards the development of a collective memory. A cultural heritage expert for instance, stressed that there is no unity in Ghana. Every tribe looks at its culture individually and everybody makes sure that the government does not take over the management of their IK. So this interviewee believes that there are aspects of cultures that they will never release you see (CI1).

5   Conclusions and Going Forward

The conceptual argument for the need to include multiple interpretations and perspectives around the curation, presentation and preservation of cultural objects and indigenous knowledge has become more fervent in recent years with the emergence of participatory Web technologies that offer potentials for institutions to facilitate engagement and collaborative practices with communities from which the indigenous knowledge and cultural objects originate. As evidenced by the interview data, there is much enthusiasm and believe that involving source communities and public stakeholders in collaborative development of collective memory is a desired goal. However, there remain a number of historical, institutional, political and practical barriers. Participatory social Web technologies are offering interesting possibilities for facilitating collaborative development and preservation of collective memory. However, memory institutions need to consider them a development which necessitates investments in strategies and resources and must be willing to reconsider how they think about IK and cultural objects, how cultural objects and knowledge are described, and must be willing to reach out to build respectful and sustainable relationships with members of source communities and public stakeholders of indigenous and cultural knowledge.

A number of barriers are faced by Ghanaian cultural institutions in IK digitization and preservation. The interview data revealed that most institutions placed low priorities for digitization and preservation of IK, with limited funds dedicated to supporting IK digitization initiatives. Similarly, political leaders and key decision makers also lack interest in the information management field in general and subsequently, have little appreciation for IK digitization. The introduction of an independent regulatory body in Ghana is therefore perceived to be necessary not only to monitor IK digitization activities, but also to serve as the mouthpiece for memory institutions.

Involving source communities in IK digitization requires collaboration. It is therefore necessary to build understanding and trust among the stakeholders. Historical tribal wars and oppression from colonial rule has created disunity and animosity among the people. This kind of animosities and lack of unity among the various Ghanaian indigenous groups is a considerable barrier hindering effective heritage resources management. Lack of trust and enmity is preventing some members of source communities to agree to have their heritage resources curated and managed by one central national agency. At the moment, there is not a single cultural identity that is common to all Ghanaians. Every ethnic group is managing their IK separately. There is currently little evidence of the various groups' willingness to work together towards the creation of a unified, collective national memory comprising of all the different traditions, cultural objects and knowledge.

Nevertheless, the interview data reveals evidence of a number of positive practices at the grassroots that can be harnessed and developed to foster progress towards the establishment of a national digital memory for Ghana. Digital literacy is on the rise and people are increasingly using mobile technologies to capture traditional practices and activities. A collective cultural heritage memory programme for Ghana can therefore begin from gradually collecting documented heritage starting from the villages, to the districts before being transferred for management and preservation under a central agency. A study to investigate means to effectively and trustworthily collate and curate documented heritage in various forms from the grassroots-level to build towards a national collective memory that embraces all representative IK with collaboration and trust from sources communities is the next necessary step going forward.

References

1. Lodhi, S., Mikulecky, P.: Management of indigenous knowledge for developing countries (2010). http://www.wseas.us/e-library/conferences/2010/Tenerife/COMATIA/COMATIA-13.pdf
2. Srinivasan, R.S., Boast, R., Furner, J., Becvar, K.M.: Digital museums and diverse cultural knowledges: moving past the traditional catalog. Inf. Soc. **25**(4), 265–278 (2009)
3. Whaanga, H., Bainbridge, D., Anderson, M., Scrivener, K.I., Cader, P., Roa, T., Keegan, T.K.: He Matapihi Mā Mua, Mō Muri: the ethics, processes and procedures associated with the digitization of indigenous knowledge - the Pei Jones Collection. Cataloging Classif. Q. **53**(5–6), 520–547 (2015)
4. Boamah, E.: Ghanaian library and information science professionals' conception of digital libraries: a phenomenographic study. (Master of Arts), Tallinn University (2009). https://oda.hio.no/jspui/bitstream/10642/872/2/Boamah_Eric.pdf
5. Liew, C.L., Cheetham, F.: Participatory culture in memory institutions: of diversity, ethics and trust? D-Lib Mag. **22**(7/8) (2016)
6. Liew, C.L.: Collaborative construction of digital cultural heritage: a synthesis of research on online sociability determinants. D-Lib Mag. **21**(11/12), 5 (2015)
7. Boamah, E.: Towards effective management and preservation of digital cultural heritage resources: an exploration of contextual factors in Ghana. (Doctoral Disseertation), Victoria University of Wellington (2014). http://hdl.handle.net/10063/3270
8. Ayiku, R.: Symbolic meanings in the Ghanaian arts: a step towards developing cultural legacy. Marilyn Zurmumenhlen Working Papers in Art Education **14**(1), 2–11 (1997)
9. Kargbo, J.A.: Oral traditions and libraries. Lib. Rev. **57**(6), 442–448 (2008)
10. Moahi, K.H.: Promoting African indigenous knowledge in the knowledge economy: exploring the role of higher education and libraries. New Inf. Perspect. **64**(5), 540–554 (2012)
11. Gardiner, G., McDonald, J., Byrne, A., Thorpe, K.: Respect, trust and engagement: creating an Australian indigenous data archive. Collect. Build. **30**(4), 148–154 (2011)
12. Christen, K.: Opening archives: respectful repatriation. Am. Archivist **74**(1), 185–210 (2011)
13. Taylor, L.: Digitisation of indigenous cultural resources. Aust. Aboriginal Stud. **2007**(1), 1–2 (2007)
14. Filson, C.K., Afful-Arthur, P.: Knowledge management in indigenous medicine. Library Philosophy and Practice (e-journal) Paper 1388 (2016). http://digitalcommons.unl.edu/cgi/viewcontent.cgi?article=3809&context=libphilprac
15. Dadzie, P.S., van der Walk, T.: Digitising University Libraries in Ghana: How technology is facilitating access to digital content and services. Mousaion, **33**(3) (2015)
16. Koranteng, K.A.: Framework for digital preservation of electronic government in Ghana. (Doctor of Philosophy and Literature), University of South Africa, Pretoria (2015). http://hdl.handle.net/10500/20118
17. Plockey, F.D.-D.: Indigenous knowledge production, digital media and academic libraries in Ghana. J. Pan Afr. Stud. **8**(4), 32–44 (2015)
18. Leti Arts. Press Release: Leti releases Ananse Superhero Game for Windows Phone (2013). http://letiarts.com/now-available-ananse-origin-game/

19. Nyomi, K.: Making of Oware 3D. Exclusive behind the scenes footage of the making of Oware 3D (Part 3) (2013). https://www.youtube.com/watch?v=PG8n_biZo3I

20. Opoku-Agyeman, K.: Lost/gained in translation: Oware 3D, Ananse: the origin and questions of hegemony. J. Gaming Virtual Worlds **7**(2), 155–168 (2015). doi:10.1386/jgvw.7.2.155_1

21. Ashesi University. (n.d.). Bridging a divide: Kobla Nyomi '11 discusses his Oware 3D games, and why he us building it. http://www.ashesi.edu.gh/academics/45-bulletin/features/1486-bridging-a-divide-kobla-nyomi-11-discusses-his-oware-3d-game-and-why-he-is-building-it.html

22. Awuah-Nyamekye, S.: Indigenous ways of creating environmental awareness: a case study from Berekum Traditional Area, Ghana. J. Study Religion Nat. Cult. **8**(1), 46–63 (2014)

23. Korang-Okrah, R., Haight, W.: Ghanaian (Akan) women's experience of widowhood and property rights violations: an ethnographic inquiry. Qual. Soc. Work **14**(2), 224–241 (2015)

24. Korang-Okrah, R.: Risk and resilience: Ghanaian (Akan) widows and property rights (Doctor of Philosophy), University of Illinois at Urbana-Champaign (2011). https://www.ideals.illinois.edu/bitstream/handle/2142/29439/KORANG-OKRAH_ROSE.pdf?sequence=1

25. Plockey, F.D.-D.: The role of Ghana Public Libraries in the digitization of indigenous knowledge: issues and prospects. J. Pan African Stud. **6**(10), 20–36 (2014)

Students and Their Videos: Implications for a Video Digital Library

Sally Jo Cunningham[✉], David M. Nichols, and Judy Bowen

Department of Computer Science, University of Waikato,
Private Bag 3105, Hamilton, New Zealand
{sallyjo,d.nichols,jbowen}@waikato.ac.nz

Abstract. Personal information collections have expanded to include video files but users often organize their content with the same tools they use for other simpler media types. We analyze the 'native' video management behavior expressed in 35 self-interviews and diary studies produced by New Zealand students, to create a 'rich picture' of personal video collection size, formats, organization and intended usage. We consider how conventional digital libraries can better support usage of personal video material.

1   Introduction

Personal information collections have expanded to include a diverse set of multimedia digital objects; in particular users now regularly create and download video files. Video content typically consumes more storage space and bandwidth than other document types although users structure their content with the same organisational tools they use for smaller and simpler items.

In this paper we expand on previous work [2]: briefly reviewing research on video management (Sect. 2), then describing study methods (Sect. 3) and the emergent themes around collection size, contents and usage (Sect. 4). In Sect. 5, we consider how this nuanced understanding of behavior can inform personal video management systems.

2   Related Work

Users now regularly view video (via sites such as YouTube [7]), down-load video files and create their own video content (especially via mobile phones [10]). 46 % of a sample of Finnish students had downloaded at least one video to their personal storage and some users had downloaded over a hundred files [6]. Some users have adopted cloud storage services for their video content [9]. Cushing [3] notes the importance of control over media on online services: remote files are still regarded as theirs by users even if they do not have a local copy. Irrespective of the location or media type of their content, the organisational tools available to users are familiar: filenames, folders and some dedicated applications (e.g. iTunes) [1].

© Springer International Publishing AG 2016
A. Morishima et al. (Eds.): ICADL 2016, LNCS 10075, pp. 37–42, 2016.
DOI: 10.1007/978-3-319-49304-6_5

Work on personal digital information management does not usually focus on video content (e.g., [3, 8, 9])—often considering videos when they are primarily used for other purposes such as listening to music (e.g. [6]). The contribution of this paper is to focus specifically on video-centric behaviour using naturalistic methods to explore how users experience video storage, organisation and sharing.

3 Methodology

The data analyzed in this present study was collected in the context of a third-year tertiary university course offered in New Zealand in 2013. As the initial step in user requirements analysis for a video management system, the students first examined their own video collection creation behavior through a written self-interview/autoethnography, and then through a diary study focusing on video document behavior. These are here analyzed for 35 students: 21 (60 %) male and 14 (40 %) female, with 32 (91 %) aged 20 to 24 and 3 (9 %) aged 30 to 60. All 35 were New Zealand citizens and permanent residents and are hereafter referred to as P1, P2, ..., P35. Their self-interviews and diary study summaries totalled 175 pages. These were analyzed using grounded theory methods [5]; analysis proceeded through iterative reading, code development, and coding as the categories emerged inductively.

4 Results

We explore four aspects of the students' reported video collection behaviors: the size and formats of their videos, motivations for adding a video to their collection, and techniques for tracking their personal video consumption.

4.1 Collection Sizes and Formats

The students typically estimated the size of their collections in number of videos and/or in memory usage. Collections ranged from the miniscule (three students had fewer than 20 videos in their collection) to the enormous (1.85 Terabytes on the student's personal media server, with an additional 2332 videos bookmarked, favorited, or otherwise linked to in online sources). On the other hand, collection size can also be subjective; one collection of approximately 150 Movies, TV episodes, and short clips) was described as "very large" by its owner, while student another believed his 700 gigabyte collection to be "rather small for this day and age" [P20].

To store or track these videos, the students used a wide variety of storage devices and techniques (Table 1). An initial, striking finding is that the students' personal collections are highly diverse and not limited to video files stored on physical devices under the students' control (Physical storage, Table 1) or stored by the student 'in the cloud' (e.g., Virtual storage, Table 1); students also 'saved' videos virtually (Virtual storage, Table 1) by, for example, posting them to Facebook. Students also considered videos that they had viewed through large online collections such as YouTube (through channel subscriptions) as being in some sense 'their' videos, in that the students could access the videos for re-viewing. We note the obvious difficulties with maintaining a record of previously viewed videos, trusting that the video will not be removed from the collection, and maintaining a subscription for continued access.

Table 1. Number of students utilizing each collection storage method or technique.

Physical storage		Virtual storage		Personal record	
Laptop/desktop	28	Facebook, social media	14	Bookmarks, favorites, 'likes'	23
External drive	18	YouTube subscription	6	Open browser tabs	2
Mobile	7	Cloud	5	Word document	1
USB memory stick	7	Personal YouTube channel	3	Email message with links	1
CD-ROM/DVD	4	iTunes	2	Links posted on blog	1
SD card	2	Netflix	1	Pinterest	1
Video camera	1			Memory	9
Gaming console	1				

Students often relied on their memory to be able to re-find videos, rather than storing the file or a link. This option is generally taken for videos that they have no great attachment to. Contextual cues may make it easier to recall a video's location (e.g., associating a video with the friend who posted it on Facebook). Students are generally confident that they can easily re-find videos—though it is not clear how well founded that confidence is.

No student in the study stored his/her collection using only a single mechanism from Table 1; instead, their collections were scattered across an average of five. This can make it difficult to access a particular video in the collection: "It can get frustrating having to log in and use the different conventions on all of these apps" [P4].

4.2 Motivations for Adding a Video to a Collection

This section explores the two most commonly reported motives for adding videos:

To Watch Later (28 students). The primary reason for saving a video is, of course, 'to watch later'. This motivation can be teased apart to mean: to watch in the future, as watching now is inconvenient; to watch the video again, as it has been watched once and enjoyed, and the student anticipates that they will want to re-watch it in the future; to watch at a more appropriate time, given that the video appears interesting but the student does not presently have the time free to watch it in its entirety; to have something to watch when the internet can't be accessed or access is prohibitively expensive; to look more deeply into previously enjoyed videos; to 'use' the video, in the sense of gaining information from it; and to support the *possibility* of watching or re-watching the video, at some indeterminate future time. Given that collections can run to tens of thousands of hours of video footage, It seems unlikely that every video in a large collection will be watched ("...most people I know including myself just store videos because we can" [P28]).

For Sharing (26 students). Sharing is also a multi-faceted activity. Sometimes it is driven by practical issues, such as trying to minimize data usage in a home Internet connection. Sharing can also be an expression of closeness; the sharer knows enough about the others' tastes to be able to predict that they will enjoy it ("Most of my YouTube likes have been from friends sharing the videos to me or on their pages on Facebook" [P33]), or the video is shared to express something about the sharer ("these are videos that I enjoy and are a reflection of my personality" [P29]). The fact that two friends have viewed the same video can provide an opportunity to bring them closer: "once I share a video with people I can talk to them about it later" [P4].

4.3 "Keeping Track"

Another common task in managing a personal video collection is maintaining a record of one's interactions with it. Students reported a variety of interactions that they attempted to track, with varying degrees of success: marking their viewing progress through a sequence of videos (e.g., episodes in a season of a TV series.); marking the place to begin watching again in a video whose viewing has been interrupted; keeping a list of of videos that have been added to the collection but that have not yet been viewed; differentiating between watched and unwatched videos in a video stream; tracking which videos have already been downloaded/added to the collection; marking one's viewing position in a partially watched video, to be able to pick up viewing again at that spot; and selecting brief clips of interest embedded in longer videos.

These tasks are not well-supported in the file systems used to store video files, so the students with collections on their own devices (hard drives, external drives, etc.) either had to rely on memory to track their viewing, or had to develop their own tracking system. Given that metadata for downloaded videos is not saved with the file and that filenames often vary between download sites, it can be difficult even to know which videos are already in the collection. A major difficulty lies in the absence of a detailed viewing/usage history supported directly by the file system (beyond the date of modification, which is often too crude a measure). Simple work-arounds could only handle one or two of the tracking tasks above (e.g., "I also mark files with a (M) at the end of the file name to mark my place in a series of videos." [P18]). More complex schemes rely on the student's diligence in recording the relevant aspects of their viewing history—and these management techniques are often not rigorously applied.

Tracking video consumption in online video collections (e.g., YouTube) is also surprisingly fraught. If videos that the user intends to collect are stored in a list—for example, a YouTube playlist—then as the list grows one can 'lose' videos as they move off-screen. Though YouTube does maintain a history list, it is easily clogged with videos that the user does not intend to track ("I will click on videos then decide not to watch them, the annoyance of this for me is that these videos will automatically be added to my history playlist…" [P22]). Vimeo's 'watch later' function is useful, but is only available within that system. The solution to tracking short segments of interest embedded within longer videos is to extract the interesting clips and save them as new videos. In the process, however, all context and metadata from the source video are stripped and must be manually re-entered.

5 Discussion

Many of the participants' problems with managing video content stems from the large file sizes which leads to users distributing their content over local, removable, online and cloud storage. This in turn creates new problems for finding and retrieving videos, with many of the study participants stating that they rely largely on their memory for re-locating items they have saved or in someway bookmarked or referenced A common response is to simply store links to online content; which can lead to issues of persistence where the bookmarks are subject to link rot. The various forms of storage fragmentation (device, platform, local v. remote, content v. link) create challenges for users as their existing tools do not cross these boundaries.

The *Memsy* prototype [4] provides a cross-device and cross-service approach to addressing some of the fragmentation issues reported by our participants. Although Memsy supports cloud services such as Dropbox it does not appear to support the integration of links to online collections (such as YouTube) which were used to cope with storage limitations. The preservation of time markers (to support viewing across sessions) is not supported by native operating system file management (or by a system such as Memsy). Online video platforms such as YouTube and Twitch do support 'keeping track' of previous viewing (via cookies) but other systems need to add additional functionality to meet this user need. A broader conclusion might be that file management systems that have evolved for non-temporal documents (images, text files, ...) need specific augmentation to support temporal media.

Other aspects that emerge from our study that increase the challenges of managing videos include the fact that the concept of 'ownership' is often blurred, with many participants feeling they have ownership of videos that they have accessed, but also being aware of the impermanence of some online files (again leading to link rot) which in turn drives behaviours around downloading and sharing which become ways of preserving and 'owning'.

The videos themselves are multi-dimensional as they exist in different formats and can be categorised across multiple genres which lead to different usage patterns. Not only do we suspect that a light-weight and flexible management solution is required to support all of these aspects, but also that any solution needs to enable users to incorporate concepts of memory and sharing without the need to enter detailed metadata. Users appear wedded to light-weight mechanisms such as instant bookmarking, sharing etc. irrespective of the fact that they do not necessarily serve them well.

6 Conclusions

The key factors that emerge from our study are need for video management solutions that incorporate aspects of: indexing—supporting users in keeping track of what content they have, where it is located and how to access it; bookmarking—supporting users in finding sub-content at specific points in videos or keeping track of how far through a video has been viewed; and sharing—enabling users to share video, and keep track of what is shared. While some of these video functionalities can be supported in a straight-forward manner in the context of single-owner content providers (for example streaming services) it is more difficult to design tools for the real world, ad-hoc collections and behaviours described by the study participants.

References

1. Copeland, A.J.: Analysis of public library users' digital preservation practices. J. Am. Soc. Inf. Sci. Tech. **62**(7), 1288–1300 (2011)
2. Cunningham, S.J., Nichols, D.M., Bowen, J.: Personal video collection management behavior. In: Proceedings of JCDL 2016, pp. 219–220. ACM (2016)
3. Cushing, A.L.: "It's stuff that speaks to me": Exploring the characteristics of digital possessions. J. Am. Soc. Inf. Sci. Tech. **64**(8), 1723–1734 (2013)
4. Geel, M., Norrie, M.C.: Memsy: keeping track of personal digital resources across devices and services. In: Kapidakis, S., Mazurek, C., Werla, M. (eds.) TPDL 2015. LNCS, vol. 9316, pp. 71–83. Springer, Heidelberg (2015). doi:10.1007/978-3-319-24592-8_6
5. Glaser, B., Strauss, A.: The Discovery of Grounded Theory: Strategies for Qualitative Research, Chicago. (1967)
6. Liikkanen, L.A., Åman, P.: Shuffling Services: current trends in interacting with digital music. Interact. Comput. (2015). doi:10.1093/iwc/iwv004
7. Liikkanen, L.A., Salovaara, A.: Music on YouTube: user engagement with traditional, user-appropriated and derivative videos. Comput. Hum. Behav. **50**, 108–124 (2015)
8. Marshall, C.C.: Rethinking personal digital archiving, part 1: four challenges from the field. D-Lib Mag. **14**(3/4) (2008) doi:10.1045/march2008-marshall-pt1
9. Odom, W., Zimmerman, J., Forlizzi, J.: Teenagers and their virtual possessions: design opportunities and issues. In: Proceedings of SIGCHI 2011, pp. 1491–1500. ACM (2011)
10. Puikkonen, A., Häkkilä, J., Ballagas, R, Mäntyjärvi, J.: Practices in creating videos with mobile phones. In: Proceedings of MobileHCI 2009, Article 3, 10 pages. ACM (2009) doi: 10.1145/1613858.1613862

Digital Library Design

Supporting Gender-Neutral Digital Library Creation: A Case Study Using the GenderMag Toolkit

Sally Jo Cunningham[✉], Annika Hinze, and David M. Nichols

Department of Computer Science, University of Waikato,
Private Bag 3105, Hamilton, New Zealand
{sallyjo,hinze,d.nichols}@waikato.ac.nz

Abstract. Software is assumed by its creators and maintainers to be gender-neutral: that is, that it is equally well suited for use by any user, regardless of gender. We investigate this assumption in the digital libraries context through analysis of a significant digital library construction and maintenance tool—the Greenstone Digital Librarian Interface (GLI)—using the GenderMag toolkit. GenderMag provides personas whose approaches to software use fall across the spectrum of gender-stereotypic actions and motivations. The personas are used as the basis for cognitive walkthroughs of the system under investigation, to uncover potential gender biases in system functionality and interface design. We uncover significant such biases in GLI.

1 Introduction

Digital library collections have many configuration options reflecting the diverse design decisions (appearance, structure, search features … etc.) made in sharing digital content. DL software systems have attempted to simplify these indexing, design and deployment options by providing dedicated interfaces to support online publishing. For example, the Greenstone digital library system [8] has a Greenstone Librarian Interface (GLI) [7] that abstracts underlying text indexing packages into a graphical interface.

Usability for digital libraries is often focussed on whether the published collection supports the needs of users seeking information. Evaluations of the creation interfaces are less common; one example study used questionnaires of students who had used GLI as part of their course [6]. There are a variety of usability techniques that can be applied to software; in this paper we focus on a recent variant of a well-established inspection method: the cognitive walkthrough.

Burnett et al. developed the GenderMag (Gender-Inclusiveness Magnifier) cognitive walkthrough method [1–3] to explore gender differences in software use and user experience. This topic is particularly relevant for DL users as a survey of the characteristics of the library and information science workforce (graduates of LIS programmes in North Carolina) reported they were "predominantly female" [4]. Further, a review of teaching practices in tertiary digital libraries courses found that the courses were sited largely in library and information science programmes (which generally have a large proportion of female students) and that Greenstone and GLI were frequently mandated or

© Springer International Publishing AG 2016
A. Morishima et al. (Eds.): ICADL 2016, LNCS 10075, pp. 45–50, 2016.
DOI: 10.1007/978-3-319-49304-6_6

recommended for projects [5]. In this paper we outline the GenderMag approach and report on an initial evaluation of the GLI DL tool.

2   Background

GenderMag encapsulates the extensive body of research into gender differences in software use and problem-solving via the following five facets [1]:

- *Motivation:* whether the persona tends to use software in order to accomplish a task (typically a female characteristic) or whether the persona is primarily motivated by an enjoyment of technology use (typically male)
- *Self-efficacy*: a persona's level of confidence in their ability to use the software for a given task (typically female users have lower self-efficacy than males)
- *Risk aversion*: a persona's comfort with dealing with uncertainty and the possibility of error when using software (females tend to be more risk-averse)
- *Tinkering*: the degree to which a persona enjoys exploring the settings and functions of novel software (where males are more likely to engage in tinkering behavior than females)
- *Skills/knowledge*: while none of the personas have backgrounds in computer programming or formal IT experience, the male personas engage more strongly with technology in their leisure time (for example, updating and tailoring their mobiles and apps)

These facets are incorporated into a set of four personas derived from an extensive review of literature highlighting "statistically significant gender differences in the ways people tend to go about things" [2]: Abby, representing the statistically 'female' behaviors; Patricia and Patrick, whose behaviors are closer to female and male behaviors respectively; and Tim, representing the statistically 'male' behaviors. These personas are described in the conventional manner: each includes a photo, a brief backstory (hobbies, employment, age, etc.), and a discussion of the persona's facet-based behavior in an IT context (Abby's risk aversion, for example, is described as "She tries to perform tasks "the safe" (i.e., familiar) way, even if the less familiar features might promise a more direct solution"). The four personas share identical backstories in terms of a university degree in accounting, current employment as accountants, and knowing "how to think in terms of numbers".

To identify gender-related usability issues with an application, one or more of the personas are used as the basis for a streamlined cognitive walkthrough (described in the context of an analysis of GLI in Sect. 3). The choice of persona—Abby, Patricia, Patrick, or Tim—provides the perspective of a user at that point on the spectrum of stereotypically gendered user behaviors. The GenderMag methodology has been evaluated in multiple case field studies in major technology organizations [1] and was found to be of practical utility to real-world software developers in identifying software interface and interaction gender-inclusiveness issues.

3   Methodology

We explored potential gender inclusiveness issues with the Greenstone Librarian Interface by performing a GenderMag-based cognitive walkthrough using the materials in the GenderMag Toolkit [2]. The tasks and their associated actions of the walkthrough were drawn from the GLI tutorial as representing a fundamental set of activities for a GLI user, together with the developer-recommended actions to accomplish those activities. Specifically, we chose the scenario involving the creation of a new Greenstone collection from a set of documents, with four sub-goals (the fifth was added by the present researchers):

- Sub-goal 1: Start a new collection (give the collection a name and description)
- Sub-goal 2: Add documents to a collection (where the documents are pre-existing HTML documents on the user's local drive)
- Sub-goal 3: Build the collection ('build' is Greenstone terminology for creating the index and interface to the collection)
- Sub-goal 4: View the extracted collection (from within GLI, examine the interface to the new collection)
- Sub-goal 5: Confirm that the collection construction was successful (exit GLI, then locate and open the new collection)

As we were primarily interested in teasing inclusiveness issues likely to have their strongest impact on female GLI users, we took the 'Abby' persona as our point of view in the walkthrough. Key characteristics of the Abby persona are: low self-confidence in performing computing tasks, risk aversion, and preferring step-by-step tutorials to tinkering with software [2]. The three authors comprised the walkthrough team, with one serving as facilitator, a second as recorder and all three serving as evaluators (as standard in the GenderMag methodology). We performed a GenderMag cognitive walkthrough by stepping through the sub-goals from the standpoint of Abby, noting each point at which she would likely diverge from the 'ideal' path of actions listed in the tutorial.

For each sub-goal, we considered the following two questions: *Will Abby have formed this sub-goal as a step to her overall goal?*; and *Why (considering Abby's Motivation and Strategies)?* For each action in a sub-goal, we considered the analysis questions in Table 1.

We briefly describe the tutorial tasks through a series of screenshots: Step 1: The process of creating a new collection is started by selecting "New..." in the File menu

Table 1. GenderMag analysis questions for our scenario

Will Abby know what to do at this step?	If Abby did the right thing, will she know that she did the right thing and is making progress towards her goal?
Why? (considering Abby's Knowledge/Skills, Motivations/Strategies, Self-efficacy and Tinkering	Why? (considering Abby's Self-efficacy and Attitudes Toward Risk)

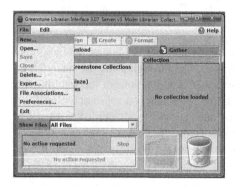

Fig. 1. Starting a new collection

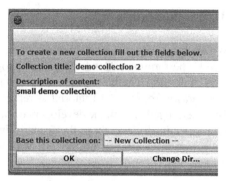

Fig. 2. Naming & description

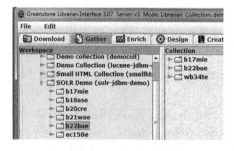

Fig. 3. Gather documents

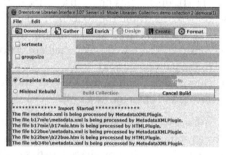

Fig. 4. Building a collection

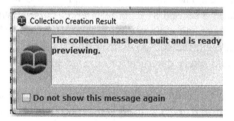

Fig. 5. Collection result

(see Fig. 1). The second step (un-named pop-up window, see Fig. 2) captures the collection title and description. The third step is to gather documents into the collection (via the "Gather tab", see Fig. 3) by drag and drop. Fourth, the collection is built (see Fig. 4). At completion, the librarian is informed of the built collection (see pop-up in Fig. 5).

4   Results

We present an overview of the significant gender-focused problems identified by our cognitive walkthrough. Note that a GenderMag analysis will identify both issues surrounding gender inclusivity (that is, problems associated with persona facet values) as well as general usability problems. In the discussion below, we focus on the former.

Three closely related issues became apparent as we stepped through the scenario: confusion over whether the computer or the person is the actor, a focus on artefacts over process, and a lack of feedback as to the effects of a user's actions.

Actor confusion: While it is Abby's goal to build a DL collection, as soon as she turns to the software, most tasks are presented *not* from her point of view but instead with a focus on the actions of computer. For example, the activity of "building" the collection is a task that the software performs (see Figs. 4 and 5). Some of the screen designs are ambiguous at best, such as the gathering of documents into the collection (see Fig. 3), in which the interface merely shows the objects rather than referring to the process (see discussion below). Similarly, while the on-screen instructions Step 2 (Fig. 2) refers to creating the new collection, from the interaction it becomes apparent that this, in fact, refers to the software process that will commence *after* Abby entered some information. This ongoing ambiguity over who is in control of the interaction—Abby or the software—is likely to be particularly stressful for a low self-efficacy user like Abby. Further, none of the on-screen instructions or labels seem to directly consider Abby, as a digital librarian, to be managing and leading the process but rather assign her to the role of assisting the software. As a consequence, users like Abby may feel marginalized— counter productive for an application designed with information professionals as one of the target user groups.

Artefact vs process: Most of the tasks that need to be carried out are not presented as processes but rather with a focus on the artefact or object. This lack of process or workflow support is particularly problematic for Abby, who heavily favors software that guides her work with a wizard, step-by-step prompts, or other explicit representation of the expected series of actions. For example, the creation process has to be started by selecting "File" and "New…"; while these standard labels would be reassuring to Abby (as she prefers to use features that she is 'already familiar and comfortable with' [2]), these labels are not particularly helpful in this instance (Abby wishes to create a new collection, not a new file). The interface for the gathering process (in which the documents for the new collection are identified; see Fig. 3) does not refer to or guide the activity. It merely shows a workspace (left) and files in the collection (right), which is initially empty for a new collection. The librarian's activity shown in Fig. 2 is not named (no window title). Overall, this reinforces the impression that the librarian is not the actor and their process of creating the collection is not the focus of the software, but rather the emphasis lies on the artefacts.

Lack of feedback: Abby has low self-confidence/self-efficacy in learning new applications and tends to blame herself rather than the software when software does not work as expected. When problems occur, she tends to avoid using those features in favor of work-arounds—or perhaps avoid using the software at all. The GLI interface gives very little feedback to users as they progress through the digital library creation process; we noted at most sub-goals that there was no dialog box or other message to inform Abby that the correct actions had been taken, and that the final dialog box indicating that a collection has been successfully created (Fig. 5) includes the option "Do not show this message again" (the ticking of which would eliminate any future indication of successful collection creation/re-creation). Further, there was no indication given at the end of the process of how to locate the new collection once Abby exited GLI. This constant state of uncertainty over the effects of her actions would be a powerful disincentive to future use of GLI for Abby.

5   Conclusions

Our analysis of the GLI interface uncovered three significant usability issues. These issues affect all potential users but would be particularly problematic for Abby, the GenderMag persona who exhibits the strongest statistically 'female' software use characteristics. Given the strongly female skew of the library and information science profession [4]—a major target user group for Greenstone and GLI—these issues could be a significant barrier to Greenstone uptake.

Additionally, we found the GenderMag methodology to provide a powerful tool for exploring the affective aspects of these usability issues on potential (female) users. By basing the cognitive walkthrough on a persona, the potential emotional impact of interface/interaction issues is magnified and made explicit—allowing the researchers to better differentiate between minor and major problems with the GLI software.

References

1. Burnett, M., Peters, A., Hill, C., Elarief, N.: Finding gender-inclusiveness software issues with GenderMag: a field investigation. In: Proceedings of CHI 2016, pp. 2586–2598. ACM (2016)
2. Burnett, M., Stumpf, S., Beckwith, L., Peters, A.: The GenderMag Kit: how to use the GenderMag method to find inclusiveness issues through a gender lens. In: EUSES Consortium (2015). http://eusesconsortium.org/gender
3. Burnett, M., Stumpf, S., Macbeth, J., Makri, S., Beckwith, L., Kwan, I., Peters, A., Jernigan, J.: GenderMag: a method for evaluating software's gender inclusiveness. Interacting with Computers (to appear). doi:10.1093/iwc/iwv046
4. Morgan, J.C., Farrar, B., Owens, I.: Documenting diversity among working LIS graduates. Libr. Trends **58**(2), 192–214 (2009)
5. Pomerantz, J., Abbas, J., Mostafa, J.: Teaching digital library concepts using digital library applications. Int. J. Digit. Libr. **10**(1), 1–13 (2009)
6. Tramullas, J., Sánchez-Casabón, A.-I., Garrido-Picazo, P.: An Evaluation based on the Digital Library user: an experience with greenstone software. Procedia Soc. Behav. Sci. **73**, 167–174 (2013)
7. Witten, I.H.: Creating and customizing digital library collections with the Greenstone Librarian Interface. In: Proceedings of International Symposium on Digital Libraries and Knowledge Communities in Networked Information Society (DLKC 2004), University of Tsukuba, Tokyo, pp. 97–104 (2004)
8. Witten, I.H., Bainbridge, D., Nichols, D.M.: How to Build a Digital Library, 2nd edn. Morgan Kaufmann, San Francisco (2010)

Developing Institutional Research Data Repository: A Case Study

Zhiwu Xie[(✉)], Julie Speer, Yinlin Chen, Tingting Jiang, Collin Brittle, and Paul Mather

University Libraries, Virginia Polytechnic Institute and State University, Blacksburg, USA
{zhiwuxie,jspeer,ylchen,virjtt03,rotated8,pmather}@vt.edu

Abstract. We introduce VTechData, a Sufia/Fedora based institutional repository specifically implemented to meet the needs of research data management at Virginia Tech. Despite the rapid maturity of Hydra and Fedora code bases, the gaps between the released packages and a launched production-level service are still many and far from trivial. In this practitioner paper we describe the strategy and efforts through which these gaps were filled and lessons learned in the process of creating our first Hydra/Sufia-based repository.

Keywords: Research data management · Institutional repository · Digital library

1 Introduction

In 2011, Virginia Tech Libraries began offering research data management services to university researchers in the form of data consulting services: assisting researchers in creating data management plans to comply with funding agency requirements and understanding and applying data management best practices. Four years later, we applied our knowledge gained through consulting and campus research environmental assessment efforts, to begin designing and developing an institutional research data repository for long-term preservation and access.

Research data have specific characteristics and requirements that call for different treatments and strategies for preservation and dissemination. This paper shares our experience building a data repository based on Fedora 4 [1] and Sufia [2], a specialized Hydra [3] implementation for self and proxy deposit.

2 Why A Separate Repository for Data?

Like many other institutions, Virginia Tech Libraries has operated an institutional repository (IR) called VTechWorks [1] for many years. Based on popular open-source IR software DSpace [4], VTechWorks is currently used to provide open access to a large number of textual documents including faculty publications, news, internal reports, and electronic thesis and dissertations (ETDs), etc. It also holds some non-textual collections, one of which has more than 7000 images and some audio/video content. Before

© Springer International Publishing AG 2016
A. Morishima et al. (Eds.): ICADL 2016, LNCS 10075, pp. 51–56, 2016.
DOI: 10.1007/978-3-319-49304-6_7

the launch of VTechData [6], data sets, in some cases fairly large ones, are also deposit in and published from VTechWorks. For example, in 2014 a 140 GB compilation of satellite remote sensing data set in ESRI[1] proprietary formats were split into multi-volume tar files and ingested into VTechWorks. It therefore begs the question: why do we need a separate repository for research data? Why can't we simply use VTechWorks for data publishing?

The first and foremost reason concerns data workflow. While DSpace workflow has worked well for sharing traditional publications, research data are in a constant state of flux and their sharing does not necessarily coincide with the publication. Over the years we have received many inquiries from researchers regarding using VTechWorks as temporary file storage or sharing uploaded files only with the chosen users and groups. We had to repeatedly explain that the IR is meant for publishing content in relative stable states, and once published, should not be changed or retracted without compelling justifications. The dilemma is that for data, the "stable stages" are relatively ambiguous as well as ephemeral. Often researchers are reluctant to publish preliminary results, or have passed the window to do so because they have modified the data for the next research ideas. Being able to take snapshots on work-in-progress copy of data, like the similar functions in version controlling software code, would certainly help to alleviate the issue. But the DSpace workflow supports neither sharing in-progress submissions nor snapshot, and its lack of fine-grained permission and sharing options certainly has not made it any more attractive. In contrast, cloud-based file storage and sharing services such as Google Drive, Dropbox, and Amazon S3 have become wildly popular among researchers exactly because they fulfilled these needs.

The workflow dilemma described above only reveals the tip of a larger problem with DSpace, that it is inherently difficult to customize for more diverse digital library needs. Virginia Tech used to develop specialized software for each of these needs, e.g., ETD-db [7] for ETDs, ImageBase [8] for some image collections with deep hierarchical structures, CONTENTdm [9] for image exhibitions, and custom built websites for newspaper articles and electronic journals etc. When it became more and more difficult to maintain all these systems, their content was under consideration to be migrated to VTechWorks, but usually had to undergo significant functionality reduction. For example, the folio structure in ImageBase, the compound objects in CONTENTdm, and the highly customized workflow in ETD-db were all to be lost. At the same time, many academic and administrative units on campus were not satisfied with VTechWorks' centralized management model. They want to have their own workflows and user interfaces, even if they all agree that the library should still take on the responsibility to manage and curate the deposit. DSpace appeared to have reached its limit.

The third significant problem we face is the rapid growth of content. We had to move VTechWorks to larger servers multiple times, yet the trajectory indicated that we might soon need an even larger server. Built for a single server operation, DSpace was not meant to scale horizontally.

From 2012, Virginia Tech Libraries started to seriously consider moving the IR to a Fedora/Hydra based system, since this technology stack attempted to separate various

---

[1] http://www.esri.com/.

digital library concerns and functions into different components and would allow many different deposit workflows and web interfaces (e.g., Hydra heads) to be built on top of a centralized Fedora based repository layer. Soon the Fedora Futures community initiative was established that promised a fully updated Fedora version with much better performance and the possibility to scale on computer clusters. This strategic change on technology direction coincided with a rapid growth of data management needs at Virginia Tech, spurred by the many funding agency data management mandates. During data consultancy we were frequently asked when faculty could publish data with us. While we kept pointing them to VTechWorks, we know that sooner or later we would need a more suitable repository for data.

We therefore were faced with two choices: (1) immediately start building a Hydra head on top of Fedora 3, migrate content from both VTechWorks and many other legacy systems to it, then migrate again after Fedora 4 releases; (2) wait till Fedora 4 is released, then build Hydra heads and migrate content. We opted for option 2, since by then it became clearer that Fedora 4 would not be backward compatible with Fedora 3. Instead it would be a fully rewrite on newer software framework, which makes content migration from Fedora 3 to 4 far from trivial. We then also had the option to either start Fedora 4/ Hydra with a new data repository or with content migration from VTechWorks. We opted to do the former, not only because the need for a data repository was more urgent by then, but also because content migration was known to be time consuming, therefore could have blocked data repository development for an extended period of time.

In retrospect, we believe we have made the right choice, considering we are able to provide a much-enhanced data management service in a relatively short period of time. The downside of this decision, however, is that we will have to maintain both DSpace and Fedora/Hydra for some time, potentially diverting development resources. We solved this problem by deciding not to develop new features for DSpace based VTech-Works, instead shifted its technology development to maintenance mode, and focused most resources on Fedora 4/Sufia based VTechData development.

3   VTechData Features

VTechData was built on Fedora 4 and Sufia, a specialized Hydra implementation for self and proxy deposit. Sufia has built in workflows that allow flexible sharing features immediately after file uploads, e.g., sharing only with designated users, groups, or with anyone with a time-limited link. This Google drive like feature allows researchers to upload work-in-progress data and use VTechData as a temporary storage and data workbench instead of the end product repository. This section, however, only describes the features we developed in addition to those already exist in the released Sufia package. These features arise from the in-depth discussions with the stakeholder group including the data service team, repository managers, and end users.

3.1   Refined Workflow

Recognizing the users' needs to use VTechData as a workbench, we redefine the action "publish" as being signified only by a valid DOI. In other words, a data curator will not even start to inspect the data and metadata until the depositor requests a DOI from Virginia Tech Libraries or associates an existing DOI with the deposit. We consider the ad-hoc sharing before the publication no different from those occurred at Google Drive or Dropbox, and do not prevent users from making changes and even deleting uploaded files. The DOI request, however, triggers the quality control and curation actions from data managers and once approved, a snapshot action will be taken and then the DOI will be assigned to the snapshot copy, which the depositor will no longer be able to change. The overall data workflow therefore consists of 4 distinct stages: Upload, when files are uploaded to VTechData; Describe, when metadata about the uploaded files are recorded; Organize, when described files are organized into data sets; and finally Publish.

The built-in Sufia workflow may be considered a superset of ours but we found it lack a clear overall picture about where a user stands. For example, at the Organize stage, multiple links on the page will suddenly bring the users back to Upload or Describe stage, which can be rather confusing. Even an experienced user can easily get lost. A user testing later conducted at University of Alberta library [10] indeed confirmed such experience. In an attempt to avoid rewriting the Sufia workflow which would create difficulties maintaining the future upgrade paths, we opted to add a visible dashboard banner on every page after login to indicate which stage the users are, as shown in Fig. 1.

Fig. 1.   Dashboard showing the 4 stages

3.2   Integration with External Systems

An institution repository naturally needs to be integrated with the university's enterprise systems. The stakeholder meetings indicated that we did not wish to open up the repository to external users unless an active Virginia Tech user was willing to act as the depositor. With this assumption in mind we disabled the Sufia database based authentication and replaced it with Virginia Tech's own single sign-on system. We then imported all faculty members' names to the system as a softer form of name control.

Consistent with other IR user experience research, VTechWorks user feedback also indicates users frustration with long forms to fill in at various stages of the workflow. To alleviate these pains, we embedded DataCite search, CrossRef search, and the university's people search to various form fields, so that many metadata may be gathered from external systems. We also integrated VTechData with ORCID, making it possible to load the user's full publication list to improve metadata quality and disseminate new data publication information.

3.3 DevOps

Considerable VTechData work has been dedicated to developing more efficient development and operations (DevOps) procedures. Through the participation of other community development projects, our team became familiar with deploying development, testing, and staging environments in the cloud with Puppet [11]. However the DevOps choices are inherently dependent on our IT department who will eventually take over the service operations. We therefore evolved from Puppet to bash scripts, then to Vagrant [12] and now towards Ansible [13]. After much effort, now spinning up a new development environment for a new developer will only take minutes. This also makes it possible for us to conduct hands-on, project-based interviews with applicants for developer and student employee positions.

4 Discussion and Future Work

In this paper we briefly summarize our path towards the launch of a new institutional data repository. We describe the rationales behind many of our strategic and tactical decisions, and highlight where the efforts were made.

The Virginia Tech scenario is far from unique. Many research libraries have been operating legacy IRs for many years. These IRs are still mostly functional and fulfilling their original design goals. But technologies, library services, and expectations have changed significantly over time, making these IRs more and more burdensome in terms of both maintenance and achieving new service goals. Moving towards newer technologies and broader services will eventually become inevitable. We therefore hope the Virginia Tech experience described here will contribute to a better orchestrated pathway for technology and service migration.

After the launch of VTechData, we will expand the Fedora/Sufia based effort to other specialized digitization projects and geospatial data archiving, and at the same time plan the migration of VTechWorks content. The mid-range, e.g., 5-year goal is to archive most if not all library held digital assets in a single expansive Fedora repository platform, but disseminate and curate them through various specialized front-end built in Hydra and/or similar technologies.

References

1. Fedora repository. http://fedorarepository.org/
2. Sufia. http://sufia.io/
3. Hydra project. https://projecthydra.org/
4. VTechWorks. http://vtechworks.lib.vt.edu
5. DSpace. http://www.dspace.org
6. VTechData. http://data.lib.vt.edu
7. ETD-db. http://theses.lib.vt.edu/theses
8. ImageBase. http://imagebase.lib.vt.edu
9. CONTENTdm. http://www.oclc.org/en-US/contentdm.html
10. Betz, S., Hall, R.: Self-archiving with ease in an institutional repository: microinteractions and the user experience. Inf. Technol. Libr. **34**(3), 43–58 (2015)
11. Puppet. http://www.puppet.com
12. Vagrant. https://www.vagrantup.com
13. Ansible. http://www.ansible.com

Cultural Digital Map Prototype of Tourist Attractions in NirasSuphan Written by SunthonPhu, Poet of Thailand

Watcharee Phetwong[1(✉)], Bhornchanit Leenaraj[2], Nanthiya Charin[1],
Chadaphon Janchian[1], and Krisorn Sawangsire[1]

[1] Faculty of Business Administration and Information Technology,
Rajamangala University of Technology Suvarnabhumi, Suphanburi, Thailand
phetwong.watcharee@gmail.com, krisorn.s@rmutsb.ac.th
[2] Library and Information Science Department, Faculty of Humanities,
Chiang Mai University, Chiang Mai, Thailand
aong_lee@hotmail.com

Abstract. NirasSuphan is poem written by SunthonPhu explaining the trip from ThepThida Temple, Bangkok to PahLuk, Danchang District in Suphanburi province. It was written in 2374 B.E. and recites the trip to find a leklai, a metal charm believed to melt when exposed to fire, which was believed to be a kind of elixir. The literature is significant to Suphanburi province since it describes how people lived in the past. The objective of this research was to design a digital map prototype of tourist attractions based on a sample of communities mentioned in the NirasSuphan and develop an accompanying web site to describe the communities along this route. One research study found that Thai tourists did not acknowledge having received guidance or having any existing awareness of cultural heritage. Developing a digital map for cultural tourist attractions could be a means of raising awareness of Thai cultural heritage.

Keywords: NirasSuphan · SunthonPhu · Cultural digital map · Thai heritage

1 Introduction

Tourism is a mechanism to increase national economies. It is an industry that adds value by enabling services related to tourist attractions to emerge and also by generating various streams of income for local communities near these attractions. We have seen tourism develop in different communities in which they sell community uniqueness based on national tourism research. This research applied information technology and communication systems to support the development of systematic digital maps of tourist attractions that showcase Thai cultural identity [2]. Suphanburi is a province with a long history and the NirasSuphan, written by SunthornPhu, is a poem showing this history. It narrates the story of SunthornPhu's journey along the Mahanak canal from ThepTida temple in Bangkok to Suphanburi. NirasSuphan narrated SunthornPhu's route and it has become a historic poem of Suphanburi. In the research by Pisutthakul, Thai tourists did not acknowledge having received guidance or having any existing awareness of cultural heritage [1]. We then assume that in the past, tourists travelling to Suphanburi were also

© Springer International Publishing AG 2016
A. Morishima et al. (Eds.): ICADL 2016, LNCS 10075, pp. 57–62, 2016.
DOI: 10.1007/978-3-319-49304-6_8

unaware of tourist attractions mentioned in the NirasSupan. In this research, we traced the journey that SunthonPhu travelled while incorporating tourist attractions mentioned in the poem NirasSuphan. Then we conceived a design that would apply information technology into the development of a digital map of this journey with accompanying website. The end product is significantly different from any other tourist map.

This research had 2 objectives.

1. To analyze the text of the NirasSuphan written by SunthonPhu and gather data about a sampling of communities mentioned in this poem.
2. To design a prototype for a digital map of tourist attractions along the route of the sample communities mentioned in the NirasSuphan and develop an accompanying web site to house the data collected on the present day communities.

2   Research Methodology

The scope of this research was limited to one district mentioned in the NirasSuphan in order to obtain a small sample of communities. This district was also significant because, according to the poem, it was the geographic location where SunthonPhu stopped and searched for a particular mineral. Gathering basic data about the current location and surroundings of the communities within the Samchuck district included walking in the physical village, using GPS, recording the longitude and latitude and describing some physical surroundings such as forests, canals or markets.

There were 3 steps in the research process based on the objectives including:

(2.1) Analysis of the NirasSuphan and gathering data about a sampling of communities by:

(1) Studying sections of the NirasSuphan referring to the Samchuk district.
(2) Extracting NiraSuphan data about communities within the Samchuk district.
(3) Drafting a map of the Samchuk district section as described in the NirasSuphan.
(4) Contrasting the draft map to Google Maps.
(5) Map observation in the community to collect data about the community
(6) Map adjustment based on suggestions by community leaders.

(2.2) Design of a prototype for a digital map of tourist attractions along the route of the sample communities mentioned in the NirasSuphan and develop an accompanying web site by:

(1) Illustrating different elements for the digital map and website.
(2) Designing the digital map and website.
(3) Developing a prototype of the digital map.
(4) Developing the accompanying website to illustrate the present day data collected.

3   Research Finding

3.1   A Review of the Poem to Confirm the Locations that Were Mentioned Within the Samchuk District, Provided Evidence of 16 Communities

Physical visits to the region within which the original communities were located revealed that the small communities and forests changed to urban communities and in fact only 11 of the original 16 villages were still in existence. The villages which were found and those that no longer exist are shown in Table 1.

Table 1. Community Data

Village	Current	Village	Current
1.Wanghin	found	9. Tueng	found
2.Yanyao	Found	10.Wadbarntueng	Found
3.Wonkonhard	Not found	11.Taotong Taonak	Not found
4.Wangchalarm	Not found	12.Kratua	found
5.Bangkwag	Found	13.Pongdaeng	found
6.Samchuk	Found	14.Klongkrasiaw	found
7.Sumpeng	Found	15.Bangwak	Not found
8.Chadhorm	Not found	16.Yangsongphinong	Found

Informal interviews with local officials in each community allowed the location of the original villages to be approximated and GPS to be used to obtain latitude and longitude coordinates for each community. This geographic data about each present-day community was added to short descriptions about the physical surroundings such as forests, canals or markets. This data was to be later used in the accompanying website.

3.2   The Analysis and Design of a Digital Map for Tourist Attractions in NirasSuphan Resulted in Two Companion Templates

Together, these templates list the key elements needed for a comprehensive illustration of both the geographical location and the cultural significance of each tourist attraction. The elements for the digital map are shown in Fig. 1 while the elements of the accompanying website can be seen in Fig. 2.

It should be noted that in Fig. 2, the element entitled "Niras excerpts about the community" would link to sections of the poem pertaining to each community mapped along the route. Similarly the "Historical animation" element refers to links that would imagine, in an animated fashion, how the original communities might have appeared in the time of the NirasSuphan.

The next phase of the design process for both the map and the website resulted in the following illustrations of how the elements would appear visually as shown in Figs. 3 and 4.

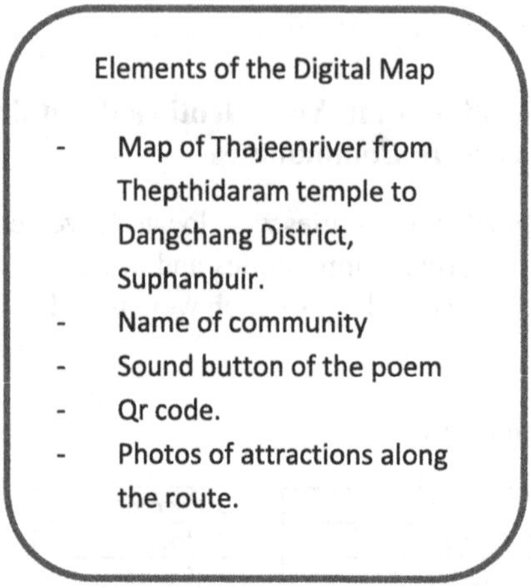

Elements of the Digital Map
- Map of Thajeenriver from Thepthidaram temple to Dangchang District, Suphanbuir.
- Name of community
- Sound button of the poem
- Qr code.
- Photos of attractions along the route.

Fig. 1. The Digital Map elements

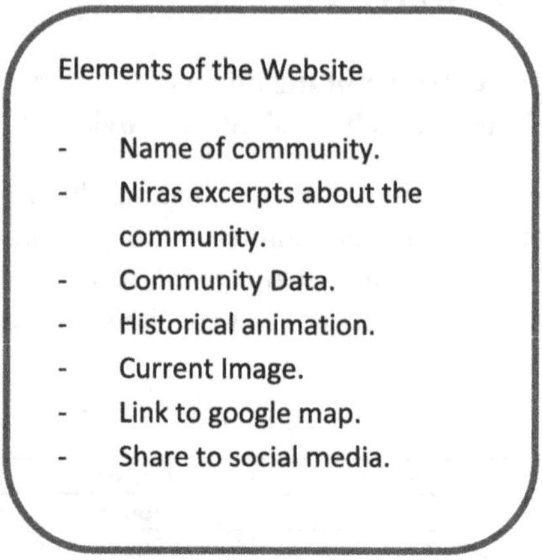

Elements of the Website
- Name of community.
- Niras excerpts about the community.
- Community Data.
- Historical animation.
- Current Image.
- Link to google map.
- Share to social media.

Fig. 2. The Website elements

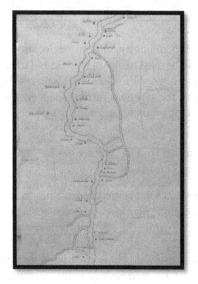

Fig. 3. The design of digital Map

List of Communi ty.
Detail of the communites
. - Name of community.
- Niras excerpts about the community.
- Community Data.
- Historical animation.
- Current Image.
- Link to google map.
- Share to social media.
Map

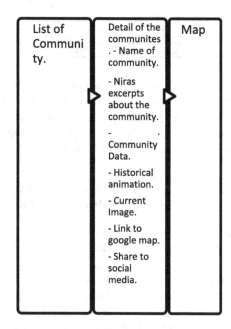

Fig. 4. Website design

3.3 The Design of a Digital Map Prototype for Tourist Attractions

The design of a digital map prototype for tourist attractions. In NirasSuphan revealed that this digital map could provide community data along the route in the poem and tourists could use the map by communicating through the QR Code which would link with different parts of the accompanying website. The website would display the 16 communities from the past through animated representations and offer present day information for the 11 villages that exist today. Samchuk District information would also be available. In addition, users could press the sound button to listen to readings from the NirasSuphan. These design ideas can be seen in Figs. 5 and 6.

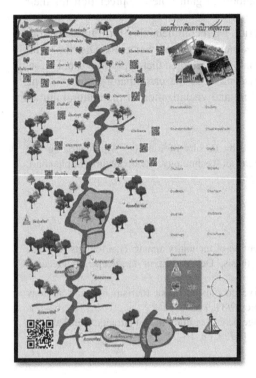

Fig. 5. Digital map prototype for tourist attraction in NirasSuphan written by SunthonPhu

Fig. 6. Website showing data about the community.

4 Conclusion

This is a model for Thai literature conservation and a tool to promote learning and retaining Thai culture for readers to better understand and appreciate the literature. The map can provide data to the community while tourists can utilize the map through QR code communication and link to the accompanying website which displays community data, animation, photos and sound clips of the NirasSuphan poem.

Presentation of the map allowed users to participate by communicating via QR Code or by pressing the sound button to listen to the NirasSuphan poem excerpts. The map was therefore different from cultural tourism maps designed by ManeewanChartvanich [3] and Nantanach Pisutthakul [1]. Previous maps only presented tourism routes and photos while this digital map allows a user to participate in the experience and responds to the user request. This participatory aspect addresses the results in the study by

Nantanach Pisutthakul [1]. Which found that memories about travel routes were best derived from participation. Such a digital map and accompanying website for cultural tourist attractions could be a means of raising awareness of Thai cultural heritage. Finally, it can encourage people in Suphanburi to gain a new appreciation for their ancestors.

Since our scope was limited to one district, we recommend that for future development of this research idea, it should be expanded beyond Samchuk District to all communities referred to in the NirasSuphan. It is anticipated that applying virtual information technology to the design would also increase the participatory aspect of the digital map and could improve understanding and visualization of the cultural attractions.

Acknowledgement. This research is supported by Faculty of Business Administration and Information Technology, Rajamangala University of Technology Suvarnabhumi, Suphanburi, Thailand.

References

1. Nantanach Pisutthakul 2554 B.E. The perception of mentality among Thai tourists at Tapae Road, Chiangmai. Doctor of architecture thesis, Department of landscape architecture, SilpakornUniversit
2. National research committee. Administrative conclusion about tourism research strategy (2555–2559 B.E.). www.kmutt.ac.th/rippc/nrct59/33s9.pdf
3. ManeewanChartvanich 2556 B.E. The management of cultural tourist attractions in TaladPlu community, Thonburi district, Cult. Trend J., 13920, pp. 16–32

The Rise and Fall of the *Wonder Okinawa* Digital Archive: Comparing Japanese and American Conceptualizations of Digital Archives

Andrew Wertheimer[✉] and Noriko Asato

Library and Information Science Program, University of Hawaii, Honolulu, USA
{wertheim,asaton}@hawaii.edu

Abstract. This paper examines the development of what once was Japan's largest local digital archive, *Wonder Okinawa*, created in 2003. It collected a diverse view of Okinawa's cultural properties as a treasure house for future generations. It was created under the banner of establishing an Okinawan "brand" to promote tourism, and to nurture human resources, so that Okinawa could foster a hub of IT industries. In the early 2000s, the national government envisioned digital archives as part of its scheme to become a highly networked society, as the means to address social problems, such as the low birthrate, graying population, and shrinking workforce. The digital archive project spearheaded the government's effort. However, the $13.5 millon project was dismantled less than a decade after its spectacular debut. The paper analyzes the causes of the failure and explores some key differences between the conceptual model of digital archives in Japan and North America.

Keywords: Digital archives · Regional digital archives · E-Japan strategy · Intellectual property · Cultural preservation · Funding digital archives · Regional identity

1 Introduction

In the digital era the terms "archives" and especially "digital archives" have become increasingly ubiquitous, although they are used with a variety of meanings. This situation has brought more people and funding to archives and archival studies, but also has created palpable tensions over definitions and ownership in the same way that "digital libraries" has challenged and offered new opportunities to our colleagues in librarianship. As this article demonstrates, this state of affairs is not limited to North America but also was the norm in Japan.

The present study explores one of Japan's earliest self-defined "digital archives" – *Wonder Okinawa*. This research paper examines the successes and failures of this pioneering online collection. At its peak, *Wonder Okinawa* was Japan's largest regional digital archive. It consisted of a total of 10,000 web pages, and around 10 h of high-definition digital video. It was one of the largest video digital archives seen on a global scale. Around 500 people (authors, creators, and performers) participated in generating

© Springer International Publishing AG 2016
A. Morishima et al. (Eds.): ICADL 2016, LNCS 10075, pp. 63–76, 2016.
DOI: 10.1007/978-3-319-49304-6_9

the content, 80 % of whom were people from Okinawa Prefecture. The total cost was 1.5 billion yen (roughly 13.5 millon USD at the time). Perhaps most amazingly, this digital archive is no more [1].

This article explores the history of *Wonder Okinawa* with an emphasis on (a) how it related to national IT policies, (b) the development of local economy and preservation of local tradition and culture, and to the (c) specific socio-political conditions in Okinawa. Our intent is to focus on the following questions: (1) How did those involved with *Wonder Okinawa* define "digital archive"?; (2) Was it doomed to fail because of its mandate?; (3) What were some unique contributions or elements of *Wonder Okinawa*?; and (4) How does this the creation of *Wonder Okinawa* relate to the archival profession and government policy in Japan today?

2   Methodology

This paper conducts a case study on a digital library project in Okinawa. It examines the digital project with the perspectives of archival studies and archival theory developed and practiced in North America. The approach will allow us to critically examine and compare the conceptual models of digital archives between North America and Japan. Our research source includes various bureaus of national government reports to examine their involvement to the Okinawa digital archive project, and also their policies towards general digital archives. The study also used correspondences, major local newspapers and independent smaller media outlets. These primary sources offer insight for the process of the digital project and help examine how it developed into a large scale government fiasco.

3   Okinawa, Social and Historical Context

Since the digital archive we are examining deals with Okinawa, it is important to have some brief understanding of this unique place before proceeding to examine a digital archive portraying it. At its most basic level, Okinawa is the southern-most prefecture of Japan. It is made up of 60 islands, with five main ones, including the Okinawa main island, where roughly 92 % of the prefecture's 1.3 million population live. Historians and Okinawans, however, would stress that Okinawa has a long history as the Ryukyu (Liuqiu or Liu-ch'iu) Kingdom with its own culture, belief system, dances, foods, and arts. It was formally made part of Japan in 1870s, although Ryukyu paid tribute to both Japan's Satsuma Domain and China.

Okinawa's modern history was troubled. It was the site of some of the most bloody battles of World War II, which meant the deaths of 12,500 Americans, around of a million Japanese and Okinawans [2]. After the war's end, Okinawa remained an American Territory until 1972 – twenty years after the end of America's occupation of Japan. Even after this point, US military bases remained a major controversial presence. During the quarter century of American rule, US authorities established a university, information centers (which were predecessors of public libraries) and championed awareness of a distinct Okinawan identity. American forces took most of their records to Washington, DC., and it was not until 1995 that the Okinawa Prefecture established its own Archives [3].

For a variety of reasons, four decades after reversion to Japan, Okinawa is the poorest of Japan's prefectures. The unemployment rate in 2010, for example was 7.5 %, almost double the national average of 4.0 % [4]. Okinawans claim the military bases occupy precious land and that Okinawa did not benefit from Japan's major postwar economic boom. Moreover, the economic impact of the bases declined as the value of the dollar declined compared with the Yen. Thus, Okinawa's economy shifted from being dependent on military spending to one based on tourism.

The national government has invested a great deal of funds on projects in Okinawa over the years. On one hand, these are supposedly to create jobs and build infrasturcture in the Prefecture. On the other hand, the government also is making these investments as a way of apoligizing to Okinawans for enduring the burden of the bases and having so many foreign soldiers.

4   National Strategy of Digital Archives

Wonder Okinawa emerged partly as a response to Tokyo's twin problem of Okinawa's straggling economy and its tensions with prefectural officials and Okinawa's public protest against American bases. The project was designed to be a key part of the national government's efforts to ignite Japan's cutting-edge digital economy, just as Korea and Taiwan were also doing in the early 1990s. It is important to remember that Japan at that time was facing a devastating crisis. The bubble economy of the 1980s had just burst, and Japanese found themselves facing serious social and economic problems. Beyond the bubble, Japan became aware that there was a real cost to the declining birthrate and the mass-migration from rural communities to the metropolitan cores of Tokyo-Yokohama and Greater Osaka. While a low birthrate could hamper any economy, that combined with limited foreign immigration meant trouble in sustaining a workforce. Basically, as the few young people fled to Tokyo and the other urban cores, rural communites struggled to provide basic infrastructure (rail and road connections without tax support) and basic social and medical services. Factories closed and farms were no longer as profitable, so many worried about empty communities – ghost towns without a future. People in rural Japan worried about who would maintain their communities, local infrastructure, and unique regional cultures. Concerned voters pressured their elected Diet (Parliament) Members for answers. Japan's ruling party, the Liberal Democratic Party or LDP, decided that the answer to high urban property costs and the evaporation of rural Japan's infrastructure was to promote employment of the next generation and encourage the preservation of local culture(s), as an ugent part of the government's agenda [5].

Thus, it should be understood that government officials determined that development of digital archives should be not only be part of traditional intellectual or cultural policy, but was seen as playing a key part of building a social infrastructure and even a strategy to solve some of the nation's most pressing problems. It also was seen as a strategy to nurture local IT industries to entice young people to remingrate or remain in the coutryside, in order to revitalize regional economies. Tokyo hoped to help advance the national goal of becoming a leader in an advanced IT world.

In January 2001, the Japanese government introduced *e-Japan Strategy:* a scheme to establish an evironment, in which education, culture, and art are all accessible for people living in an advanced and highly networked society. In March, its specific plans, the *e-Japan Priority Policy Program* was issued. The policy set goals for national transformation within five years. Its vision was through the Internet, people would be able to use online information about works of art and cultural assets without any geographical constraints. Museums and libraries were encouraged to digitize their cultural properties and arts and offer databases via Internet [6]. The *e-Japan Priority Plan-2002* envisioned Okinawa as Japan's "Headquarters of International Information and Communication" towards Asia and the world. It aimed to develop a global Internet infrastucture, create and aggregate content applications, and develop a vibrant IT industrial base in Okinawa. Three national government offices, the Cabinet Office (the national government's executive branch), the Ministry of Internal Affairs and Commmunications, and the Ministry of Economy, Trade and Industry were all involved with the project [7].

Okinawa and the Northern Territories, designated as special areas, receive unique government administrative treatment under the jurisdiction of the Cabinet Office. Okinawa was declared an "Information and Communication Speical Area," allowing the Okinawa digital archives project to be subsidized by a special government fund [8]. The Ministry of Economy, Trade and Industry approached the project with their agenda of promoting the tourism industry, training professionals involved with producing content, and promoting the inheritance of Okinawa's unique culture by "building a digital archive of the highest level" [9]. Among the government ministries and agencies, the Ministry of Internal Affairs and Communications was one of the most engaged with digital archives projects. It participated in the Japan Digital Archives Association (JDAA), which was a NPO (non profit organization) established in 1996 with the Ministry of Economy, Trade, and Industry (then the Ministry of International Trade and Industry), and the Agency for Cultural Affairs, along with private corporations. JDAA defined its digital archive vision as being able:

> to record tangible and intangible cultural properties in digital format, and [to] create and preserve a database of the information. It also involves browsing, viewing, and transmitting information by using an information network [10].

JDAA advocated for digital archives and advanced research on technology and intellectual property issues involved with digitization. As local communities became interested in digitizing their traditional arts and crafts, the Ministry of Internal Affairs and Communications began various research projects and conducted the "Local Culture Digitization Project," and also established the *Regional Cultural Asset Portal* (2006) to disseminate these digital projects [11]. In cooperation with the Agency for Cultural Affairs, the Ministry also later established the national digital archive portal, *Cultural Heritage Online* (2008) holding digitized images of cultural treasures from more than 950 museums and archives in Japan [12]. By 2006, 424 local governments received national government subsidies for digitization projects [13] while according to a 2009 National Diet Library survey, among over 2,000 responding agencies, 23 % had digital libraries and another 11 % were preparing to create them [14].

5 Digital Archives Project: *Wonder Okinawa*

5.1 Overview

The force behind *Wonder Okinawa* itself was the Okinawa Digital Archive Project. Established in Okinawa Prefecture in 2002, the Project's goal was to create a digital archive with two main streams "content production" and "content dissemination." Content production involved surveying a variety of Okinawa's cultural assets, nature and unique culture, and also gathering information that can be used for tourism and entertainment. Content dissemination was to work with the digitized images, videos, sounds, and texts so they could be best viewed not only via the Internet but also enjoyed even on large ultra high defintion screens, so as to demonstrate the potential of newly developed HDTV.

The underlying purpose of the Okinawa Digital Archive Project was to use the digital archives to promote tourism, international cultural exchange, and local culture and its development. For Okinawa's local communities, there was interest in preserving its unique cultural properties, and traditions, and passing them down to the next generation [15]. There was much hope for the process of making the digital archives and the product itself contribute to economic and cultural prosperity (Fig. 1).

The content was divided into six themes, "History", "Nature", "Arts and Crafts", "Entertainment", "Folklore", and "Others." Each theme had several topics. For example, "History" included "Shuri Castle" and "Ryukyu Kingdom," and other two topics, while "Arts and Crafts" contained "Okinawan Pottery", "Ryukyu Glass", "Okinawa's Dyed and Woven Textile", "Lion-Dog", "Ryukyu Lacquer Ware," and "Okinawan Art." Within the 26 main topics, there were additional pages exploring more specific content. For example, under "Okinawan Pottery" there are pages explaining or demonstrating various techniques, history, works, feature, using photos and videos. All of the text is written in both Japanese and English [15]. More than 10,000 pages and ten hours of high definition videos made *Wonder Okinawa* the largest local digital archives project to date [16] (Fig. 2).

5.2 Process

The Okinawa Digital Archive Project began with one billion yen from a digital archive project fund, along with another half billion yen from Okinawa Prefecture; thus making a total budget of about $13.5 millon. Beyond this, the Cabinet Office for IT industry infrastructure and promotion allocated an additonal $6 million to fund related infrastructure projects [17]. Of the total budget, one-third was used to produce content for a large screen demonstration version that would be used to promote Okinawa tourism in big cities outside Okinawa. Another third was spent on IT equipment and programing, and the final third went to produce the actual digital content [18] (Fig. 3).

Fig. 1. Artistic images welcoming the user to *Wonder Okinawa*

Fig. 2. Site map

Fig. 3. High-definition digital images of festivals and rituals

In April 2002, the Okinawa Prefectural Government established the Digital Archive Promotion Committee, which oversaw the project, chaired by a University of Tokyo professor [19]. The next month, the Okinawa Digital Archive Association (ODAA) was formed to collaborate technological research, share information, and promote digital archives. Over fifty groups, including IT related companies, content production offices, and video companies joined the Association [20]. The ODAA proposed the following as the project's objectives: (1) to nurture content production professionals, (2) build a state of the art database system which can administer and maintain the digital archives, and (3) utilize local IT businesses which can run, maintain, and improve the system [21]. Prefectural government officially announced the project initiative and invited proposals, especially from local companies [22].

On July 12, 2002, 32 proposals were accepted. Those included "Shuri Castle", "Gusuku Sites and Related Properties of the Kingdom of Ryukyu," which would be produced by a consortium led by the Ryukyu Broadcasting Corporation (RBC TV), and "Karate and Martial Arts with Weaponry" proposed by the *Ryukyu Shimpo* (the leading local newspaper) and others [23]. The newspaper reported the recording of Karate and martial arts started in Yomitan Village. Six karate instructors, designated as "human treasures" in Okinawa, demonstrated their highly trained skills in front of three video cameras [24]. In November 2002, the government reported that among 86 participating companies, 60 were local, and the number of people engaged in production was over 420. It exaplained that all of the 32 propsed themes had passed a midterm check by the project promotion committee. Here, the name of the digital archives was announced for the first time as *Wonder Okinawa* [25].

5.3   Internal Disturbance

Contrary to the government's proud announcement, the October 19, 2002 *Okinawa Times* revealed that three groups had withdrawn from the project due to the government's breach of the contract [26], while one fourth of the participating companies had discontinued their work [27]. The reason they withhold their contract was that the production commission was reduced by 20 % on one hand, while format and other technical requirements were changed from the terms specified in the original contract. Copyright was another sore point, as the government wanted to claim copyright on all recorded content – even including the still and video images that were not used in the archive. This situation became quite a scandal, since a national professional organization, the Japan Association of Cultural Film Producers, Inc. (or JACFP, presently Japan Association of Audiovisual Producers Inc.) sent a letter to the Okinawa government to protest the mistreatment of those companies [28]. However, the government later corrected the contract and the project moved forward again [28].

Although a key emphasis of the archive project was to bring the national government's special fund to incubate local IT development and businesses, it became apparent that a large part of the funds went to large companies located outside the Prefecture in order to produce high definition content, purchase computers, and hardware. The remaining one-third of the total budget was divided by more than 30 local consortia to create content for the archive.

Another controversy surrounding *Wonder Okinawa* was that the government attempted to start charging a fee to new participating organizations, although the initial stage was free of charge. Various areas of professionals' suggestions were often ignored. Critics also pointed out that the digital project was unpopular among people in the tourism industry. They criticized that the project specifications were formed by a university professor who had no idea about tourism, and that IT companies which had no ideas about tourism or Okinawa produced the content. Although there were companies and individuals who had been collecting actual ethnographic videos with detailed records for over several decades, they were either completely ignored or withdrew themselves from the project because of its absurdity [29].

Despite the many controversies, the *Ryukyu Shimpo* morning edition reported that *Wonder Okinawa* officially made its online debut on June 10, 2003 [30]. In December, *Wonder Okinawa* was received the largest national digital archives award at the Fifth Digital Frontier Kyoto. By the time, it recorded 3.5 million site visits. The 2003 Asia Digital Award coffered the Digital Design Award to Wonder Okinawa's system application "Ryukyu ALIVE (Galaxy)" [31]. The project team also was recognized with a special award in the Production Team category at the Digital Content Association's Grand Prix [32].

6 Development of Law for Intellectual Property of Contents

When the JACFP sent a letter to the Okinawa Government to mediate the situation, there was no legistation to regulate intellectual property rights of digital content produced with government subsidies. It automatically belonged to the goverment itself as custom of business practice. Indeed the Okinawa Goverment explained in its reply to JACFP that individual production costs were determined based on the consideration that copyright of the content would belong to the government [33]. In other words, the intellectual property rights to the content would have been specified when the producers signed the contract.

The legislative measures for government commissioned projects or research carried out by businesses had been in existence since 1999. At a conference to enhance Japan's industrial competitiveness organized by the Prime Minister, numerous recommendations to improve the status quo were proposed by the private sector, which led the establishment of the Industrial Revitalization Special Measures or Japan's "Bayh-Dole Act," modeled after the U.S. measure. It allows private businesses to maintain patents on government-consigned work [34]. However, it was prior to the advancement of IT businesses in Japan, and digital contents were not yet in its purview.

The aforementioned government IT policies recognized digital archives to be a key "knowledge infrastructure" that guide the creation of new content, intellectual property strategy in Japan and also increase its competitiveness internationally. Parallel to these IT strategies, the recent "Cool Japan" strategy promotes cultural content, games, manga, animé, food, and anything that foreigners may find attractive to expand the international marketplace for "Brand Japan." With this background, the Promotion of the Creation, Protection and Utilization of Content Act (Law No. 81 of 2004) was passed on

September 11, 2004 pursuant to the basic principles of the Intellectual Property Law (Law No. 122 of 2002) [35]. Article 25 of the Act provides intellectual property rights of the content as goverment consignment, the purpose of which is to promote the effective use of contents. It states that it is possible for the goverment not to take over from the contractors its intellectual property rights, if any of the following situation is applicable.

(1) The contractor promised to report the information on intellectual property rights relating to content.
(2) The contractor promised to allow the government to use the content at no cost if the government recognized and explained the legitimate reason for public interest clearly.
(3) The contractor promised to allow a third party to use the content if the government recognized that it has not been used for some time without obvious reasons and gave a legitimate reason for the content to be used effectively [35].

Since 2004, the act was revised several times but had not been enacted until April 1, 2016 [35]. Production of *Wonder Okinawa*, the funding of which was largely subsidized by both the national and prefectural governments, must have contributed to the insights to the provisions of the Act.

7 Analysis

In order to analyze Wonder Okinawa, we are going to use two lenses. In the first, we will consider it from our perspective as North American LIS educators with our definitions and theories of digital archives. We will then try to approach it from a less ethnocentric approach as a reflection of Japanese economic development policy.

7.1 Criticism from a North American LIS Perspective

Before critically analyzing this historic case, it is important for the authors to clarify that we are analyzing the situation on the basis of our standpoint as educators in North America following American archival practices. We recognized that Schellenberg launched American archival practice based on a practical approach that basically fit the challenge of applying library management approaches to coping with federal government records during the Roosevelt years, a period of the increasing output in terms of quantity and breadth. While we professionally embrace this philosophy, there is no basic consensus on any international definition or concept for digital archives.

In North America, digital archives are largely carried out by librarians and archivists, and adopting the ethics, policies, and approaches that governed our curating of print collections. These concerns led practitioners in North America to often spend considerable time first focusing on collaborating in order to create basic standards, controlled vocabularies (metadata), and mission statements, and collection policies that emphasize potential to develop networks, and also an emphasis on sustainability, so that one can add to pilot digital projects. From this North American perspective, we might say that

Wonder Okinawa was a very fancy website or web portal rather than a digital archive in the North American sense. A key difference is that digital archives in North America usually focus on digitization and providing sustainable access to the digital content, although born digital materials do not require the first step. Creating content itself, however, is not in their normal work parameters. In contrast, Wonder Okinawa consumed much of its funds on creating professional content, and there is no evidence to indicate that organizational systems or standards, such as metadata and format, were used in order to provide feasible and sustainable access. The government's requirement that the videos be in high definition made the site visually stunning, but also made it a very costly operation in terms of bandwidth, which predicted its inability to sustain itself. By operating in HD, the site also made it very difficult for citizens to participate in the project without making great expenditures. Perhaps our most critical point is that no librarians or archivists seemed to be part of the Wonder Okinawa team. A librarian or archivist would probably have asked these questions in terms of helping to focus the project on organization, access and sustainability. These arguments might not lead to as visually stunning sites, but Wonder Okinawa might still be operating today as a site if it had been operated with the existing prefectural library or archives and their staff, with their professional concerns.

7.2 Analysis from a Japanese Perspective

It would be shortsighted and ethnocentric of us to end our study by labeling Wonder Okinawa a failure simply on the basis of its demise. It is important to recognize that Japan has different definition and set of objectives for digital archives. We are working on a larger study that explores these differences in more detail.

We should admit that Wonder Okinawa was only part of a much larger investment by the national government in Okinawa. The point was not to advance the science of digital archives, but rather was part of the Ministry of Economy, Trade and Industry's developmental concept, based on the Michael Porter's Cluster Theory. Basically, the national government invested in Okinawa in hope of rejuvenating this depressed economy, trying to stimulate employment by fostering clusters of industries that would take advantage of Okinawa's resources and image. It is no surprise that the videos featured in Wonder Okinawa reflected these national emphasis on health and culture, that could translate into health tourism, sustainable heritage tourism and other avenues. Of course, the national government also hoped to develop an IT infrastructure. This explains why the government based much of the project in the private sector rather than simply giving the funding to either the prefectural archives or libraries. It is beyond the scope of this research to see if Wonder Okinawa led to the economic revitalization of the Prefecture.

With the understanding of the difference in mission and objectives assigned to the digital project, we still should not overlook critical problems derived from the governments' lack of knowledge of dealing with subsidized projects involved intellectual properties, especially digitalized images and information. Digital images have inherent intellectual property rights, which should be recognized separately from the production process. As we examined in Sect. 4.3, all digital images were expected to be submitted as part of their commissioned work. In addition, the content of the original contract was not honored and arbitrarily changed format and project participation fees. Again, a project manager who had a background in information knowledge and management would not have let the project begin without standards and policies were in place.

7.3 Comparative Analysis

As described in Sect. 7.1, the foundations of digital archives in North America were derived from the traditional archive and library theories and practices. For example, the Open Archival Information System (OAIS) Functional Model, a part of the OAIS Reference Model, which is an ISO (International Organization for Standards) Standards (ISO14721) describes six main functional entities; Ingest, Archival Storage, Data Management, Administration, Preservation Planning, and Access. Any organization or system whose mission is to preserve content and provide access over long term are responsible to meet those minimum functions [36, 37]. Each stage is governed by and managed with policies, standards, and guidelines. In this model, there is no component addressing or implying the "utility" of archived material or data. In other words, the North American paradigm of digital archives is less focused on how the collected information would be used. The underlying assumption of this is the understanding that utility of information is the user's prerogative.

Contrary to the North American theoretical model, the utility of digitalized materials are a quintessential part of a digital archive theoretical model. Guided by the national government's IT strategies that intended to address nation's various social and economic problems, digital archives projects in Japan had various missions, such as preservation of local culture, promoting livelihood and economic revitalization of the community, well-being of senior citizens, and women's participation in the workplace. Digital archives are perceived merely one of the means to achieve these national goals. Therefore, the national government subsidies were provided mostly to local governments, instead of to cultural heritage institutions such as archives, museums, or libraries, with the exception of some national museums and archives. Those digital projects launched without archivists or librarians who would strive to achieve the best professional quality in laying out plans, policies, and standards, tended to fall apart so quickly. Wonder Okinawa's digitized cultural property and treasures were now disassembled and parts of them became DVDs, which are available at the Japanese National Diet Library. For the Okinawa project, a policy guiding a digital archive's closure was not in the place either.

These theoretically polar opposite models compel the need to conduct more research on digital archives in different countries. Generally archival and library science researchers in North America assume that the theory and practice of archives, and other areas of information practice, are more or less similar throughout the world. The study demonstrated that this is indeed a myth and that there is a need for further research.

8   Conclusion

Wonder Okinawa entered the world with much hope and excitement, almost echoing the way that one entered the website in a visual orchestra of animation and sound that excited the user as they approached a site that truly was a wonder. It was not only visually stunning, but raised the bar in terms of HD video content that was professionally created working with local cultural practitioners. Although not visible on the site, many educators created teaching materials based on the content. The fact that hopes were so raised by the content and presentation of Wonder Okinawa made its demise an even hasher blow. The success and failure of Wonder Okinawa was an important learning experience for the national government as well as other communities that also experienced the same type of digital archive investments. Further research will show what lessons these governments learned from this experience.

In conclusion, our experience of studying Wonder Okinawa suggests a need for even more interdisciplinary and comparative research on digital archives, which recognizes the many definitions, concepts, goals, and situational settings for digital archives. Such a perspective could help us to understand the unique strengths and challenges of individual digital archives, as well as the complex legal, political, and economic context in which digital archives are created and used. They will help us to see the importance of issues, such as intellectual property legislation, technological infrastructure, and the potential of digital archives. Such research is important for LIS scholars, future digital archivists, and for policymakers in order to promote digital archives that can truly serve society.

References

1. The operation of Wonder Okinawa began in 2003 and was dismantled in 2011
2. Okinawa Prefecture. Encyclopedia of Japan. Accessed 22 Mar 2016
3. Tominaga, K.: A Decisive Absence: A Dissenter's View on the Archival Strategy in Japan. Japan-U.S. Archives Seminar (2007). http://www.archivists.org/publications/proceedings/accesstoarchives/05_Tominaga_KAZUYA.pdf. Accessed 5 Aug 2015
4. Statistics Japan, Annual Rate of Unemployment (2010). http://stats-japan.com/t/kiji/11187. Accessed 9 Aug 2015
5. Kanto ICT Promotion NPO Liaison Council. デジタルアーカイブまちづくり事例集 [Case Studies on Digital Archives for Building Communities] (2009). http://www.soumu.go.jp/soutsu/kanto/ai/npo/hokokusho/h210603.pdf. Accessed 5 June 2015
6. IT Strategic Headquarters. e-Japan Priority Policy Program Outlines (2001). https://www.kantei.go.jp/jp/singi/it2/dai3/jyuten/0329sum8.html. Accessed 1 July 2015
7. IT Strategic Headquarters. e-Japan Priority Plan-2002 (2002). https://www.kantei.go.jp/jp/singi/it2/kettei/020618-2-1.html. Accessed 1 July 2015
8. Cabinet Office, Government of Japan. 沖縄振興特別措置法に基づく沖縄の特区・地域制度について [Special district, area policy of Okinawa based on the Okinawa promotion special measures law]. http://www8.cao.go.jp/okinawa/seisaku/okishinhou/2014kaisei/toc.html. Accessed 1 July 2015

9. Media and Content Industry Division, Commerce and Information Policy Bureau, Ministry of Economy, Trade and Industry. デジタルアーカイブと地域産業振興について [Digital archives and promotion of local industry] (2002). http://www.meti.go.jp/policy/media_contents/downloadfiles/0406archives.pdf. Accessed 5 June 2015

10. Kageyama, K.: デジタルアーカイブ羅針盤 [Digital archive compass] (2010). http://www.infocom.co.jp/das/column/column1/column1.html. Accessed 19 July 2015

11. NPO Regional Culture Digital Archives. "当法人設立の趣旨 [Purpose of the organization]. http://www.digital-museum.gr.jp/outline/talk.html. Accessed 10 June 2015

12. Kasaba, H.: "デジタルアーカイブの歴史的考察 [A historical study of digital archives]." 映像情報メディア学会誌 J. Inst. Image Inf. Televis. Eng. 11, 1547 (2007)

13. Kawakami, K., Okabe, Y., Suzuki, S.: Web 上の地域映像アーカイブの調査と検証:デジタルアーカイブズの持続性に着目して = A Study in Communal Image Archive on Web: Focused on Sustainability of Digital Archives, 情報知識学会誌 [J. Inf. Knowl.] **21**(2), 249 (2011). Accessed 25 Mar 2016

14. Kasaba, H.: デジタルアーカイブ整備の近年の動向 [Present Sate of Development of Digital Archives]. Current Awareness Portal. http://current.ndl.go.jp/node/17888 Accessed 28 Feb 2015

15. Wonder 沖縄 [Wonder Okinawa]. Wonder 沖縄とは [What is Wonder Okinawa]. via Web Archiving Project (WARP). http://warp.ndl.go.jp/info:ndljp/pid/261751/www.wonder-okinawa.jp/jp/wonder.html. Accessed 25 May 2015

16. Denshi Shoko ni Okinawa o Marugoto [Contain the entire Okinawa in an digital archive], *Ryukyu Shimpo* (morning edition). The Ryukyu Shimpo Newspaper database (2003)

17. 電子図書館、IT 振興設備が事業復活 [Digital library, promotion of IT business resumed]. Ryukyu Shimpo (2001). http://ryukyushimpo.jp/news/storyid-110358-storytopic-86.html. Accessed 7 June 2015

18. Toguchi, A.: Okinawa Degitaru Akaibu ga Huhyo [Okinawa digital archives is unpopular]. The Okinawa: Tourism News, 625, December 2002. http://www.sokuhou.co.jp/backno/625.html. Accessed 28 Feb 2015

19. 22 日に構想案決定 [The plan was made on the 22nd]. Ryukyu Shimpo (morning edition). The Ryukyu Shimpo Newspaper database (2002)

20. 伝統を電子化し継承 [Inherit Tradition via Digitization]. Ryukyu Shimpo (morning edition). The Ryukyu Shimpo Newspaper database (May 18, 2002)

21. 地元業者の活用を [Use local businesses]. Ryukyu Shimpo (morning edition). The Ryukyu Shimpo Newspaper database (2002)

22. 観光振興や IT 支援 [Tourism promotion and IT support] Ryukyu Shimpo (morning edition). The Ryukyu Shimpo Newspaper database (2002)

23. "デジタルアーカイブ [Digital archive] Ryukyu Shimpo (morning edition). The Ryukyu Shimpo Newspaper database (2002)

24. 空手・古武術の撮影開始 [Karate, martial arts video shooting started]. Ryukyu Shimpo (morning edition). The Ryukyu Shimpo Newspaper database (2002)

25. DVD 配布など利活用案を承認 [DVD and other usage plans approved]. Ryukyu Shimpo (morning edition). The Ryukyu Shimpo Newspaper database (2002)

26. 三企業体参加辞退 [Three corporations withdrawn from participation]. Okinawa Times (morning edition). The Okinawa Times Newspaper database (2002)

27. Japan Association of Audiovisual Producers. 沖縄デジタルアーカイブの契約条件について [About the contract of the Okinawa digital archives]. http://www.eibunren.or.jp/wordpress/?page_id=858. Accessed 25 May 2015

28. Toguchi. Okinawa Degitaru Akaibu

29. Keijiban, K.: 観光情報プラットホームの問題点 (1)-(3) [Problems with Tourism Information Platform (1)-(3)]" originally from 観光とけいざい [Tourism and economics] 661, excerpts from reporters round-table talk (2004). http://ie.u-ryukyu.ac.jp/~tnal/kanko/index.php?%B4%D1%B8%A6%B7%C7%BC%A8%C8%C4%2F12. Accessed 28 Feb 2015

30. "電子書庫に沖縄を丸ごと [The entire Okinawa in the digital archives]," *Ryukyu Shimpo* (morning edition). The Ryukyu Shimpo Newspaper database (2003)

31. "デジタルアーカイブアウォードを受賞 [Received the digital archive award]," *Ryukyu Shimpo* (morning edition). The Ryukyu Shimpo Newspaper database (2003)

32. "沖縄チームに特別賞 [Special award to the Okinawa team]," *Ryukyu Shimpo* (morning edition). The Ryukyu Shimpo Newspaper database (2003)

33. Letter "Okinawa Digital Archive Project Contract Terms (Response)" Aug. 29, 2002, from Dept. of Commerce and Labor, Yoritaka Hanashiro to Association of Audio Visual Producers, Chiyuki Umehara and Tadashi Okubo. http://www.eibunren.or.jp/wordpress/pdf/okinawa02.pdf. Accessed 20 Feb 2016

34. Ministry of Economy, Trade and Industry. Japanese Bayh-Dole Act. http://www.meti.go.jp/policy/innovation_policy/bayh-dole.pdf. Accessed 24 Mar 2016

35. コンテンツの創造、保護及び活用の促進に関する法律 [Promotion of the Creation, Protection and Utilization of Content Act]," Law No. 81 of 2004. http://law.e-gov.go.jp/htmldata/H16/H16HO081.html. Accessed 24 Mar 2016

36. Corrado, E.M., Moulaison, H.L.: Digital Preservation for Libraries, Archives, & Museums. Rowman & Littlefield, Lanham (2014)

37. Ghaznavi, M., Bishoff, L.: Standards for Digital Archives. Presentation Handout. Society of American Archivists Webinar (2014)

Toward Access to Multi-Perspective Archival Spoken Word Content

Douglas W. Oard[1]([✉]), John H.L. Hansen[2], Abhijeet Sangawan[2], Bryan Toth[1], Lakshmish Kaushik[2], and Chengzhu Yu[2]

[1] University of Maryland, College Park, College Park, MD, USA
oard@umd.edu
[2] University of Texas at Dallas, Richardson, TX, USA

Abstract. During the mid-twentieth century Apollo missions to the Moon, dozens of intercommunication and telecommunication voice channels were recorded for historical purposes in the Mission Control Center. These recordings are now being digitized. This paper describes initial experiments with integration of multi-channel audio into a mission reconstruction system, and it describes work in progress on the development of more advanced user experience designs.

1 Introduction

In the four years between December of 1968 and December of 1972, nine Apollo missions flew to Earth's moon; six of those missions landed, two orbited, and one flew by [4]. While it's true that astronauts flew those missions in outer space, the vast majority of the people who participated in each mission never left the ground. Three astronauts flew on each Apollo mission, but each mission also demanded the expertise and engagement of more than one hundred flight controllers and other support personnel. As the movie *Apollo 13* illustrated, those flight controllers managed the enormous complexity of each mission, and much of their coordination was conducted using voice intercom circuits [2]. Dozens of those intercom circuits were recorded, continuously for the many days it took to conduct each mission, but most of those recordings have never been heard. We are now working to change that by digitizing nearly the full set of Mission Control Center recordings from an Apollo mission, and by integrating some of those recordings into an interactive system for mission reconstruction.

2 Mission Control

In the Apollo era, the Mission Control Center (MCC) in Houston, Texas consisted of a Mission Operations Control Room (MOCR) where the flight controllers worked, and several Staff Support Rooms (SSR) where technical specialists worked [3]. Three types of intercom circuits, known colloquially as "loops," were used. The most important of these, monitored by nearly everyone, was the

© Springer International Publishing AG 2016
A. Morishima et al. (Eds.): ICADL 2016, LNCS 10075, pp. 77–82, 2016.
DOI: 10.1007/978-3-319-49304-6_10

Flight Director loop. The Flight Director had the ultimate authority for all decisions made during a mission, and the flight controllers in the MOCR used the Flight Director loop to speak with the Flight Director. The most numerous set of loops were those used by each flight controller in the MOCR to speak with the technical experts in the SSR who supported their function. For example, during launch the Booster flight controller in the MOCR used the "Booster loop" to speak with SSR experts on (rocket) Engines and on Propellant (i.e., rocket fuel). The third type of loop was a "meet me" loop that flight controllers and SSR experts who were not normally on the same loop could use to have side conversations about specific issues.

Four 30-track tape recorders were used to record much of this audio, both to support subsequent engineering analysis and for historical purposes [7]. Two recorders ran simultaneously, with the other two being started just before the tape on the first two ended. Each of the two recorders was set up to record different channels, so a total of 56 channels could be recorded simultaneously (56 rather than 60 because one channel on each recorder was set to record a code indicating the time and a second was used for voice annotations of the tape itself). Some of these channels were set to record specific loops, but many channels were configured instead to record the headset audio of specific flight controllers. Flight controllers typically listened to many channels (including at least the Flight Director loop, the radio communication with the astronauts, and their own loop with their SSR experts), with some channels set to be loud (demanding their attention) and others softer (to provide awareness of other things going on at the same time). In addition to loops and headset audio, the radio communication with the astronauts was also typically recorded on one channel, and explanations of mission activity for the television audience that was provided by a Public Affairs Officer (PAO) was typically recorded on another.

3   Digitization

The tapes are stored by the United States National Archives and Records Administration, but they are difficult to replay because the 30-track reel-to-reel recording format is no longer in used. One SoundScriber player for these tapes does exist, but before our project it was able to play only one track at a time. But these old tapes are rather fragile (as is the SoundScriber tape player!) and it is simply not possible to play every tape 28 times to get every channel. We therefore constructed a new 3-track tape head to prove it was possible to capture multiple tracks at the same time without encountering cross-channel interference. Once we verified this was possible, we then set out to build a 30-channel digitization pipeline that now makes it possible to play each tape just once.

To verify the audio quality and to gain experience with the digitization process, in September and December 2014 we first conducted a pilot study of our digitization and processing pipeline using our newly built 3-track tape head. We selected portions of six tapes for six high-interest periods during the Apollo 11 mission (launch from Earth, lunar landing, start of the moonwalk, two other periods while on the Moon, and lunar liftoff) and digitized three tracks at a time. We digitized a total of 52 twenty-minute segments that together span 29 different headset-audio channels and 6 different intercom loop channels.

The National Aeronautics and Space Administration (NASA) must review all materials for public release to comply with U.S. law, so we have worked with NASA to develop a scalable review process. Listening to dozens of channels for many days of audio would be infeasible, so we used two technologies to accelerate the review process. First, we developed a Speech Activity Detection (SAD) system that is able to accommodate long periods of silences (which are common on many channels) and that can handle headset audio channels that include radio communication with the astronauts (as many do) [8]. We then manually transcribed the entire recorded radio communication between MCC and the astronauts for the eight-day Apollo 11 mission to the precise timing standards required for training a Large-Vocabulary Continuous Speech Recognition (LVCSR) system, and we used that transcribed data to train such a system [6].

Another challenge that we encountered was the pervasive use of acronyms to facilitate efficient communication during the Apollo program. This required that we supplement the term list used by our LVCSR system. To accomplish this, we searched all available NASA and Apollo related sites for (usually scanned) documents from which acronyms could be extracted. Pronunciations were then developed for each acronym, another challenging task because some acronyms were by convention spoken as a word (e.g., "fido" for FDO) while others were by convention spelled out (e.g., "c s m" for CSM). Next, we adapted acoustic models developed in our earlier work to match the statistical characteristics of the Apollo radio transmissions on which we trained the LVCSR system.

We then ran the resulting LVCSR system on each of the 52 twenty-minute digitized audio files from headset audio and intercom files and we provided the resulting automatically generated transcripts to NASA along with the audio files. NASA used the transcripts to identify portions of the audio that might require detailed review, and then they conducted a detailed review of those portions using the digitized audio. The net effect was a more efficient review process than would have been possible with the audio alone. NASA completed the review of the 52 twenty-minute segments in August, 2015, and those initial digitization results are now available for our use in multi-channel audio experimentation.

In the meantime, we designed and installed a new 30-track tape head on the one existing SoundScriber player. We initially tested that installation, and our new 30-channel digitization pipeline, using analog calibration test tapes that had been created to test the original 30-channel SoundScriber recorders (which no longer exist) back in the 1960's. We have to date digitized the entirety of the first lunar landing mission (Apollo 11), and portions of the Apollo 13 mission (which is of historical interest because of an explosion in space that prevented a lunar landing on that mission), obtaining more than 19,000 h of digitized audio over a three-month period in late 2015. We have run our SAD and LVCSR systems on that audio, and it is now being reviewed for release by NASA.

4   Mission Reconstruction

We originally developed the Apollo Archive Explorer (AEX) to serve as a platform for experimenting with time-synchronized replay of the multimedia records of an Apollo mission [5].[1] AEX performs time-synchronized replay of four types of media: audio, transcripts, video, and photographs. Additional synchronized content includes an animated map (showing where on the Moon the astronauts are during moonwalks), flight plans (showing what the astronauts had been planning to do at that time), and post-flight interviews (which are topic-linked rather than time synchronized). Three transcripts are available, one for the radio communication and one each for the (intermittently operated) tape recorders aboard the two Apollo spacecraft—the Command Module (CM) and the Lunar Module (LM). AEX is a Java application.

The original design goal of AEX was to provide a multi-perspective immersive experience that would give users a richer experience than any single source could provide in isolation. In the initial AEX design, one audio channel was available at a time. Initially this was radio communication with the astronauts (with PAO commentary), although we also have experimented with instead presenting audio recorded aboard the CM (which is available for parts of several missions). An ability to integrate audio from additional sources offers the potential for constructing different immersive experiences (e.g., from the perspective of an individual flight controller), but it also offers the potential to construct perspectives that no participant at the time could actually have experienced. For example, we might hear the astronauts talking among themselves in one ear, while we hear discussions on Earth about the same topic in the other.

While there's no practical way that users could hope to listen to dozens of channels at once, it is possible to play more than one channel. As a first step, we can use stereo replay to play different channels in each ear. As a second step, we can (as the flight controllers did) allow the user to make some channels loud and other channels softer. This capability is now implemented in the current AEX release. Presenting a mission reconstruction in which users could potentially access dozens of audio channels poses several new challenges, however.

One challenge revealed by our initial multi-channel audio implementation is that as the number of channels grows it becomes more difficult to clearly indicate to the user what they should expect to find on each channel. Another challenge is that when different channels (in different ears) contain some of the same audio, small timing differences in the replay can create a unpleasant "echo" effect. For demonstrations we can preselect channels that have no shared content, but for unrestricted mission replay we will need some way for users to see what's on each channel before making selections and to manage their selections in ways that minimize content overlap. Our initial design for this (using the spatial layout of the MCC as a visualization for the available headset audio channels) is useful as a starting point, but we will also need good ways of showing what's being

---

[1] AEX can be obtained from http://www.umiacs.umd.edu/~oard/aex.

listened to on each of the available headset channel and we will need some other way of indicating the availability of separately recorded loops.

Our initial work with multi-channel audio has focused on mission events such as launch from Earth and the lunar landing during which there is a lot of activity, and selecting almost any channel during such times will result in some audio content. But as we integrate multi-channel audio from less busy mission periods (e.g., the crew sleep periods, which lasted several hours), we will surely find that many channels the user might choose will have long periods of silence. We therefore also need some form of visualization to indicate to the user which channels will have activity in the near future. This is easily done using speech activity detection, although we do not yet have that capability implemented.

Indicating who is talking, and when they are talking, may suffice for less active mission phases, but during particularly intense periods (e.g., the lunar landing) users may need assistance in navigating among the available cacophony. One way in which me might seek to facilitate that navigation would be to visually indicate to users which of the available channels have activity that is related to what they are listening to now. Apollo flight controllers were skilled in selecting which channels to listen to, but casual users of AEX will likely require more support from the system to perform that task well.

A challenge that we had not anticipated is the need to help users think differently about channels that record loops (which the users can then combine as they wish) and those that contain headset audio (for which the selections might change as the flight controller being recorded selected and deselected specific loops for their headset). We may be able to use automated speaker identification to recognize which channels are available in a headset, and in the longer term we may be able to perform channel separation to isolate the content of specific loops that had been mixed on a single recorded channel. We might also use content-based alignment techniques to perform precise time alignment to at least suppress the annoying "echo" phenomenon that now arises when the same content is played from different channels. As we work through these alternatives, we will need to give thought to how best to indicate to the user the capabilities and limitations of each selection that they might make.

5 Conclusion

One major result of our project will be the creation of a newly digitized collection containing tens of thousands of hours of recorded audio that will potentially be of interest to people as diverse as historians, speech processing researchers, scholars who study decision making under stress, and educators. Another anticipated contribution will be the use of portions of that collection in the Apollo Archive Explorer. Although reconstruction of the Apollo missions is an interesting challenge in its own right, it is not hard to imagine other applications of similar techniques. The Apollo program was not unique in creating a centralized coordination activity that supported time-critical decision making—similar things happen every day in control centers for the electric grid, cell phone networks, stock markets, the Internet, newsrooms, police forces, and many other kinds of physical and social infrastructure. If we are able to go beyond creating immersive experiences and support productive analysis of multi-channel audio, then recording that audio might become more common.

Another potential application of similar techniques is to the product of what is colloquially referred to as "lifelogging," where people seek to capture information about events in their life, sometimes from multiple perspectives [1]. We presently think of lifelogging as an egocentric activity, but of course the lifelog of a family, or of a work group, would raise many of the same issues that we see in the archival Apollo materials. Indeed, we can think of the remarkable records available from the Apollo program as a sort of prehistoric lifelogging. Learning to reconstruct events from multiple perspectives may thus help to shape how we think about lifelogging in the future.

Many people know a little about what happened during Apollo, and some people know a lot. But no human alive at the time or since has ever heard every word that was recorded in the Mission Control Center. It therefore seems reasonable to expect that capabilities of the type we are developing in AEX will ultimately make it possible for historians to gain new perspectives, for engineers designing systems for a return to the Moon to analyze the Apollo experience in new ways, and for schoolchildren around the world to imagine themselves in that room at that moment.

Acknowledgments. This material is based upon work supported by NSF Grants 1218159 and 1219130. Opinions, findings and conclusions or recommendations are those of the authors and do not necessarily reflect the views of NSF.

References

1. Gurrin, C., Smeaton, A.F., Doherty, A.R.: LifeLogging: personal big data. Found. Trends Inf. Retrieval **8**(1), 1–107 (2014)
2. Kranz, G.: Failure is not an Option: Mission Control from Mercury to Apollo and Beyond. Simon and Schuster, New York (2009)
3. NASA: MCC Operational Configuration: Mission J1 (Apollo 15), NASA (1971). http://klabs.org/history/history_docs/jsc_t/mcc_operational_configuration_as15.pdf
4. NASA: Apollo Program Summary Report, NASA Johnson Space Center (1975). http://history.nasa.gov/alsj/APSR-JSC-09423.pdf
5. Oard, D.W., Malionek, J.: The Apollo archive explorer. In: Joint Conference on Digital Libraries, pp. 453–454 (2013)
6. Oard, D.W., Sangwan, A., Hansen, J.H.: Reconstruction of Apollo mission control center activity. In: SIGIR Workshop on Exploration, Navigation and Retrieval of Information in Cultural Heritage, pp. 1–4 (2013)
7. Swanson, G.: We have liftoff!: the story behind the Mercury, Gemini and Apollo air to ground transmissions. Spaceflight **43**(2), 74–80 (2001)
8. Ziaei, A., Kaushik, L., Sangwan, A., Hansen, J.H., Oard, D.W.: Speech activity detection for NASA Apollo space missions. In: Interspeech, pp. 1544–1548 (2014)

Information Access Design and User Experience

Rarity-Oriented Information Retrieval: Social Bookmarking vs. Word Co-occurrence

Takayuki Yumoto[✉], Takahiro Yamanaka, Manabu Nii, and Naotake Kamiura

Graduate School of Engineering, University of Hyogo, 2167 Shosha,
Himeji, Hyogo 671-2201, Japan
yumoto@eng.u-hyogo.ac.jp

Abstract. We propose rarity-oriented retrieval methods for serendipity using two approaches. We define rare information as relevant and
atypical information. We propose two approaches. In the first approach,
we use social bookmark data. We introduce tag estimation to our previous work. The second approach is based on word co-occurrence in a
dataset. In both approaches, we use conditional probabilities to express
relevancy and atypicality. In experiments, we compared our methods
with the relevance-oriented method, the diversity-oriented method, and
another rarity-oriented method. Our methods using word co-occurrence
obtained better nDCG scores than the other methods.

1 Introduction

The progress of information retrieval (IR) and recommendation allows users to
obtain the information they want to know. In research areas, relevancy to a
given query or user preference is thought to be most important. However, other
metrics such as serendipity are getting increasing attention [4]. Many approaches
such as diversification [1] have been designed for better seredipity. Among these
approaches, a concept of rarity was designed by us, and we utilized it for information recommendation [6].

Rarity is a combination of relevancy and atypicality. The rarity, relevancy and
atypicality have been defined as probabilities using social bookmark data. Social
bookmarking (SBM) is a Web service to manage and share bookmarks for Web
pages. When users bookmark pages, they can use tags. Tags are used in various
ways [3] and they are often used as a topic category such as "programming"
or "food". Therefore, we focused on such tags. We used words in tagged Web
pages and calculated the probability that the page belongs to a category when
it contains a certain word and the probability that the page belonging to a
category contains a certain word for obtaining relevancy scores and atypicality
scores. However, this approach is only applicable when we have large scale social
bookmark data and users' interest can be expressed as tags in it.

We propose two methods to overcome these limitations, both of which we
apply to rarity-oriented IR. In the first method, we use SBM data again. We
propose a method to estimate tags corresponding to queries. Then, we introduce

© Springer International Publishing AG 2016
A. Morishima et al. (Eds.): ICADL 2016, LNCS 10075, pp. 85–91, 2016.
DOI: 10.1007/978-3-319-49304-6_11

the tag estimation method to our previous work for applying our method to more varied queries. In the second method, we focus on word co-occurrence in a dataset instead of SBM data. We express relevancy and atypicality using probabilities derived from word co-occurrences. As evaluations, our rarity-oriented methods were compared with the conventional relevancy-oriented method, the diversifying method, and our previous method.

2   Rarity-Oriented IR Derived from Social Bookmarking

To solve the problems of the method based on the rarity score, we introduce a tag estimation method and relevancy-based filtering into our SBM-derived approach. First, we estimate a category tag corresponding to a given query. Then, we calculate the relevancy score and atypicality score using the category tag. We use the relevancy score and the atypicality score defined by previous work [6]. However, we do not calculate any rarity scores. Alternatively, we filter pages using their relevancy scores and rank them according to their atypicality scores.

2.1   Tag Estimation by Query

We focus on tags used as categories, and we only use tags consisting of one noun. From a SBM database, we obtain frequent N tags attached to pages that contains query q. Then, we rank them according to the naive Bayes approach defined in Eq. (1).

$$P(c|q) = \frac{P(c)P(q|c)}{P(q)} \propto P(q|c) = \prod_{q_i \in q} P(q_i|c) \qquad (1)$$

$P(c|q)$ is the probability that tag c is obtained when query q is given. Here, we regard $P(q)$ as a constant and $P(c)$ as the same for all tags. $P(q_i|c)$ is defined as $P(q_i|c) = |BM_c \cap BM_{q_i}|/|BM_c|$. BM_c is a set of SBMs where tag c is used and BM_{q_i} is a set of SBMs to pages containing word q_i. If $|BM_c \cap BM_{q_i}|$ is too small, we regard c as not being related to q and we eliminate c from the candidates. Here, we use c such that $|BM_c \cap BM_{q_i}| \geq 10$.

2.2   Page Filtering by Category Relevancy

We use $P(c|d)$ defined in [6] as the relevancy of d to c. Although the relevancy is used to calculate the rarity score in [6], we use it for page filtering in this method. We regard the pages that have relevance scores less than a predefined threshold as being irrelevant. $P(c|d)$ is the probability that page d belongs to category c when d is given. When all keywords in d are not related to c, we regard d as not belonging to c. Therefore, we define $P(\bar{c}|d)$, the probability that d does not belong to c when d is given, as being $P(\bar{c}|d) = \prod_{w_i \in d} P(\bar{c}|w_i)$. $P(\bar{c}|w_i)$ is the probability that word w_i is not related to category c when w_i is given. Then, we can calculate $P(c|d)$ as Eq. (2).

$$P(c|d) = 1 - P(\bar{c}|d) = 1 - \prod_{w_i \in d} P(\bar{c}|w_i) = 1 - \prod_{w_i \in d} \{1 - P(c|w_i)\} \qquad (2)$$

$P(c|w_i)$ means the probability that word w_i is not related to category c when w_i is given, and it is defined as $P(c|w_i) = |BM_c \cap BM_{w_i}|/|BM_{w_i}|$.

To extract keywords from pages, we use TF-RIDF, a product of a term frequency (TF) and residual IDF(RIDF) [2]. RIDF is defined by subtracting expected IDF using a Poisson distribution from the actual IDF. In both of TF-IDF and TF-RIDF, the values increase when the word frequently appears in a page, and the values decrease when many pages contain the word. In IDF, the number of the words used in each page is not considered. However, the RIDF score increases when the word appears in fewer pages and when it frequently appears in those pages. We calculate the TF-RIDF score of the words in each page, and we extract the top 10 words with the largest TF-RIDF score as being the keywords of the page.

2.3   Atypicality in Category

We use $P(\bar{d}|c)$ defined in [6] as the atypicality of d in c. $P(\bar{d}|c)$ is the probability that page d is associated with category c when c is given. When any keywords in d are not associated with c, we regard d as being atypical in c. Therefore, we define $P(\bar{d}|c)$ in Eq. (3).

$$P(\bar{d}|c) = \prod_{w_i \in d} P(\bar{w}_i|c) = \prod_{w_i \in d} \{1 - P(w_i|c)\} \qquad (3)$$

$P(\bar{w}_i|c)$ is the probability that w_i is not associated with c when c is given, and $P(w_i|c)$ is the probability that w_i is associated with c when c is given. These probabilities obviously satisfy $P(\bar{w}_i|c) = 1 - P(w_i|c)$. Then, $P(\bar{d}|c)$ is calculated using $P(w_i|c)$. We define $P(w_i|c)$ as $|BM_c \cap BM_{w_i}|/|BM_c|$.

3   Rarity-Oriented IR Derived from Word Co-occurrence

In the SBM-derived method proposed in the previous section, we need a high enough number of tagged pages. Furthermore, appropriate tags may not correspond to given queries. We propose another method for rarity-oriented IR to avoid these problems. In this method, we use the co-occurrence of words and a query instead of tagged pages. We conduct page filtering from the aspect of relevancy and rank pages according to their atypicality scores derived from word co-occurrence.

3.1 Page Filtering by Query Relevance

We select relevant pages in two steps, filtering based on pseudo-relevance feedback and filtering based on query word usage in pages. In the first step, we use relevancy defined using word co-occurrence Because queries consist of one or a few words in many cases, we conduct a query expansion to select relevant pages correctly. We utilize a pseudo-relevance feedback approach. First, we obtain seed pages of filtering. We use $P(q|d)$, which is the probability where given page d is related to query q. $P(q|d)$ is defined as $P(q|d) = \prod_{q_i \in q} tf(q_i, d)/|d|$, where $tf(q_i, d)$ is the frequency of noun q_i in page d and where $|d|$ is the length of page d. Because we only use nouns to express pages, $|d|$ is the same as the number of nouns in page d. $P(q|d)$ is the relevancy score defined using word co-occurrence.

We obtain three pages with the highest $P(q|d)$ and construct their feature vectors. We use summation of these vectors as an expanded query vector $\vec{q}$. In page vectors and query vectors, we use TF-IDF weighting. We use 100 nouns that have highest df values as stopwords. If the cosine similarity of the page with the query vector is higher than a predefined threshold, we regard it as a relevant page.

In the second step, we consider how query words are used in pages. We focus on keywords extracted by TF-RIDF mentioned in Sect. 2.2. When all query words are keywords, the page is regarded as being relevant to the query. We call this step keyword filtering.

3.2 Atypicality Derived from Word Co-occurrence

We express atypicality as the probability $P(\bar{d}|q)$ that page d can not be obtained when query q is given. Here, we regard the page as atypical when any keywords are not associated with the query. Then, we can define $P(\bar{d}|q)$ as

$$P(\bar{d}|q) = \prod_{w_i \in d} P(\bar{w}_i|q) = \prod_{w_i \in d} \{1 - P(w_i|q)\} \tag{4}$$

$P(w_i|q)$ is defined as $P(w_i|q) = df(q \wedge w_i)/df(q)$. $df(q \wedge w_i)$ is the number of pages that contain q and w_i in a dataset and $df(q)$ is the number of pages that contain q in a dataset.

4   Experiments

We obtained SBM data from Hatena bookmark[1], which is a popular SBM service in Japan. Hatena bookmark provides lists of hot entries on ten categories, including Web pages recently bookmarked by many users. We periodically collected lists of hot entries and social bookmarks to them via RSS feeds and APIs from April 14th to October 27th in 2011 and from April 28th to July 4th in 2014. We extracted the lists of users from the social bookmarks and obtained

---

[1] http://b.hatena.ne.jp/.

the lists of their social bookmarks, and we downloaded the Web pages in the obtained bookmarks. We obtained $4,019,427$ bookmarks with $121,270$ unique tags and $158,993$ pages. For extracting nouns from the pages, we used a Japanese morphological analyzer Mecab[2]. The pages contained $1,108,914$ unique nouns. This dataset was used for calculating the probabilities in the proposed methods and the baseline methods. Note that we could have used datasets other than SBMs to calculate the probabilities defined in Sect. 3 if they were large datasets containing various categories.

In our experiments, we used ten queries (stress, smartphone, diet, pollen allergy, caries, breakfast, headache, catarrh, interview exam, and medicine). One of the authors prepared ten typical pages and ten atypical pages for each query. The original queries and pages were in Japanese. Then, four evaluators who were not the authors rated each page 0 (irrelevant page), 1 (relevant and typical page), or 2 (relevant and atypical page). The κ of their ratings was 0.59, indicating moderate agreement.

4.1 Experiments for Relevancy

To evaluate the relevancy, we focused on two classifiers using the relevancy derived from SBM and the relevancy derived from co-occurrence. We regarded the pages rated as 1 or 2 to be relevant pages and the pages rated as 0 to be irrelevant pages. We use precision, recall, and F-measure for the evaluation. The precision is defined as $|R_{1,2} \cap R_{rel}|/|R_{rel}|$ and the recall is defined as $|R_{1,2} \cap R_{rel}|/|R_{1,2}|$, where $R_{1,2}$ is a set of pages rated as 1 or 2 and where R_{rel} is a set of pages classified as relevant by each method. The F-measure is a harmonic mean of the precision and the recall. We used the thresholds maximizing the mean of the F-measures. It was 0.02 in the relevancy derived from SBM, and it was 0.11 in the relevancy derived from co-occurrence. We calculate these measures for each rater and use their mean for the evaluation. The mean of the F-measures using SBM was 0.79, the one using co-occurrence without the keyword filtering was 0.87 and the one using co-occurrence with the keyword filtering was 0.89. In most queries, the relevancy derived from co-occurrence was better than the relevancy derived from SBM. This is because some estimated tags did not belong to the categories of the queries but hypernym categories in the SBM-based approach.

4.2 Experiments for Rarity

We evaluated our rarity-oriented ranking using nDCG [5]. As the baselines, we used the relevance, which is the cosine similarity of the page with the query vector, the maximal marginal ranking (MMR) [1], and the rarity score proposed in [6]. We show the mean and standard deviation of nDCG for each method in Table 1. The co-occur approaches were better than other methods, and the co-occurrence with the keyword filtering was best. However, unimportant words

---

[2] http://taku910.github.io/mecab/.

Table 1. nDCG by each method (mean ± SD)

Method	$nDCG_3$	$nDCG_5$	$nDCG_{10}$
SBM	0.50 ± 0.18	0.58 ± 0.16	0.64 ± 0.14
Co-occur(w/o keyword filtering)	0.79 ± 0.14	0.77 ± 0.15	0.81 ± 0.11
Co-occur(with keyword filtering)	<u>0.81</u> ± 0.13	<u>0.80</u> ± 0.11	<u>0.82</u> ± 0.08
Rarity score	0.49 ± 0.22	0.49 ± 0.23	0.58 ± 0.21
Relevance	0.67 ± 0.12	0.73 ± 0.09	0.80 ± 0.05
MMR	0.68 ± 0.08	0.73 ± 0.06	0.70 ± 0.07

were sometimes extracted as keywords in some pages, and they decreased the nDCGs. Although the nDCGs using the SBM-derived method were better than the ones using the rarity score, they were worse than the ones using the MMR and the method using the relevance. This was caused by the problem in relevancy using SBM discussed in Sect. 4.1.

5 Conclusions

We proposed rarity-oriented retrieval methods using SBM and word co-occurrence for serendipity. In both methods, relevancy and atypicality are expressed as probabilities. In the method using SBM, we introduced tag estimation to the previous work [6]. The method using word co-occurrence does not need SBM data. In this method, we rank the pages according to atypicality derived from word co-occurrence. In the experiments, we compared our methods with the relevance-oriented method, the diversity-oriented method, and the method of previous work. Our methods using word co-occurrence obtained better nDCG scores than other methods. The method using SBM did not work well because correspondent tags to given queries in the dataset did not always exist. We will focus on the co-occurrence approach and improve the method for a keyword selection as future work.

References

1. Carbonell, J.G., Goldstein, J.: The use of MMR, diversity-based reranking for reordering documents and producing summaries. In: Research and Development in Information Retrieval, pp. 335–336 (1998)
2. Church, K., Gale, W.: Inverse document frequency (idf): a measure of deviations from poisson. In: Armstrong, S., Church, K., Isabelle, P., Manzi, S., Tzoukermann, E., Yarowsky, D. (eds.) Proceedings of the 3rd Workshop on Very Large Corpora, pp. 283–295. Springer, Heidelberg (1995)
3. Golder, S.A., Huberman, B.A.: Usage patterns of collaborative tagging systems. J. Inf. Sci. **32**(2), 198–208 (2006)
4. Herlocker, J.L., Konstan, J.A., Terveen, L.G., Riedl, J.T.: Evaluating collaborative filtering recommender systems. ACM Trans. Inf. Syst. **22**(1), 5–53 (2004)

5. Järvelin, K., Kekäläinen, J.: Cumulated gain-based evaluation of ir techniques. ACM Trans. Inf. Syst. **20**(4), 422–446 (2002)

6. Yumoto, T., Tada, R., Nii, M., Sato, K.: Finding rare web pages by relevancy and atypicality in a category. In: Proceedings of IIAI International Conference on Advanced Applied Informatics, pp. 284–288 (2013)

Proposing a Scientific Paper Retrieval and Recommender Framework

Aravind Sesagiri Raamkumar[(✉)], Schubert Foo, and Natalie Pang

Wee Kim Wee School of Communication and Information,
Nanyang Technological University, Singapore, Singapore
{aravind002,sfoo,nlspang}@ntu.edu.sg

Abstract. In this paper, we propose a framework that combines aspects of user role modeling and user-interface features with retrieval and recommender systems components. The framework is based on emergent themes identified from participants feedback in a user evaluation study conducted with a prototype assistive system. 119 researchers participated in the study for evaluating the prototype system that provides recommendations for two literature review and one manuscript writing tasks.

Keywords: Scientific paper recommender systems · Scientific paper retrieval systems · Literature review · Manuscript writing · User roles · Personalization

1 Introduction

Special purpose information retrieval (IR) and recommender systems (RS) implementations have been devised for providing relevant research papers to different LR search and manuscript writing (MW) tasks [1, 2]. Two issues are observed in such implementations: First, the applications are piecemeal approaches thereby forcing the researcher to depend on multiple systems to complete important LR search tasks. Second, there are a wide variety of algorithms and data items used in these studies, making it a difficult proposition for a contextual integration of services. With the aim of addressing these issues, we selected two key LR search tasks and one MW task for developing a system called Rec4LRW [3]. The recommendation techniques of the tasks are based on a set of features that capture the important characteristics of the research paper and the constituent bibliographic references and citations. Along with the traditional metadata fields displayed with the recommended papers, new informational display features were introduced in the system to help the user in making faster and efficient decisions on the relevance and usefulness of retrieved/recommended papers. Using a quantitative and qualitative approach, an evaluation study was carried out with the system. A total of 119 university student and staff participants who had experience in writing research papers participated in the study.

In this paper, we first present the emergent themes derived from the feedback comments of the participants. Secondly, these themes are further utilized for conceptualizing a specialized framework called scientific paper retrieval and recommender

© Springer International Publishing AG 2016
A. Morishima et al. (Eds.): ICADL 2016, LNCS 10075, pp. 92–97, 2016.
DOI: 10.1007/978-3-319-49304-6_12

Framework (SPRRF). This framework is meant to guide our future studies with the Rec4LRW system and also to help researchers and developers in better designing systems meant for recommending papers. SPRRF integrates elements from user modeling, IR/RS, search user interfaces (SUI) and exploratory search; therefore most of the contextual entities related to a task are reinforced to complement each other.

2   Prototype System and User Evaluation Study

The three tasks offered by the Rec4LRW system are (i) building a reading list of research papers, (ii) finding similar papers based on a set of papers, and (iii) shortlisting papers from the final reading list for inclusion in manuscript based on article type preference of the user. In the task screens of the system, new informational display features are included for helping researchers in understanding the uniqueness of the recommended papers. For all the three tasks, information cue labels depicting the paper-type of the recommended paper are displayed. The four labels used are *popular, high reach, survey/ review and recent.* An extract from the ACM Digital Library (ACM DL) for the period 1951 to 2011, is used as the corpus of the system. The sample set for the evaluation study was formed by extracting papers with full text and metadata availability in the extract. The final corpus contained a total of 103,739 articles.

A user evaluation study was conducted to determine the usefulness and efficiency levels of the three recommendation tasks and the overall system. An online pre-screening survey was conducted to screen the potential participants. A user guide[1] with the necessary instructions was provided to the participants at the start of the study. The evaluation questionnaire in each task was accommodated at the bottom of the screen. The participants had to answer the survey questions and subjective feedback questions as a part of the evaluation. Participants' subjective feedback responses were coded by the corresponding author using an inductive coding style. The aim of the coding exercise was identifying the central themes from the comments of the 119 participants.

3   Emergent Themes from Participants Feedback Data

3.1   Distinct User Groups and Information Cues

Information Systems (IS) across different domains provide content based on the specific role of the user. The role can determine both the display features and the content to be displayed to the user. In industrial and corporate IS, these roles are utilized to enforce security settings simulating the hierarchy of employees. In academic digital libraries, these roles have not been considered extensively even though attempts have been made to classify users based on varying experience levels [1]. This type of classification can be challenged in relation to the task. Conversely, research papers can be classified on content-oriented aspects such as quality of research, extent of contribution, article-type and parent discipline. From the participants' feedback, the existence of two user groups

---

[1] Rec4LRW user guide http://goo.gl/dxUCuk.

was inherently visible. One group required control features in the UI for sorting the recommendations and viewing the articles through topical facets. These participants also gave preferences on the algorithm for retrieving papers as researchers tend to follow distinctive paths to arrive at the required papers. The other group of users was largely satisfied with both the recommendations quality and the ranked display of papers. They were not interested in manipulating the display for achieving alternative rankings. Secondly, they trusted the background algorithms used for the recommendations.

The utility of information cues in positively impacting users' perceptions has been underlined in earlier studies [4]. Rec4LRW's unique informational display features such as the information cue labels enabled the participants to better understand the recommended papers. Apart from the four cue labels from the current design of the Rec4LRW system, more labels indicating the interdisciplinary and article-type aspects of the recommended papers can be introduced. Cue labels appear to be a most promising feature for inclusion of such systems as most participants found them to be most useful.

3.2   Two Types of Serendipity and Algorithms

Serendipitous discovery of research papers is a challenging problem as it is complex to model the interestingness of particular unread papers to researcher's current interests. This problem has been handled before in earlier studies [5]. The approaches from such studies are to be classified under the *forced serendipity* category as the resultant recommendations are based on corresponding models. The alternate way of serendipitously encountering research papers is based on purely un-modelled scenarios. For instance, the 'View Papers in the Parent Cluster' feature in the Rec4LRW system helped participants in noticing papers which they have not read earlier. In addition, it can be stated that *natural serendipity* can be facilitated by incorporating more transparency in the recommendation process.

The recommendation and retrieval algorithms proposed in earlier studies have been predominantly static and fixed. The obvious advantage of fixed algorithms is the validity and reproducibility. Nonetheless, factors such as relevance feedback-based changes and choice of algorithms are to be considered for future systems. These two factors contribute to the fluidity level in algorithms. In the case of the first factor, user's actions and choices dictate future recommendations. For the second factor, users expect a list of appropriate algorithms to be presented to them. Some participants in the study suggested heuristics to identify papers for Task 1 and 2. Providing a list of algorithms is expensive in terms of computational capability as these algorithms need to be optimized for superior performance. Nevertheless, user satisfaction will probably improve with algorithmic independence.

3.3   Inclusion of Control Features and Bibliometric Data

In digital libraries, the importance of control features in UI cannot be overstated as these systems serve as an entry point to the large corpuses of papers. Even though, algorithms help in ranking the top most relevant papers for a user's search requirement, not all users would want to select the papers from the ranked list. During the user evaluation study, it was noticed that many users felt handicapped by the absence of control features such as sorting and advanced search features in the Rec4LRW system. Informational display features in RS mostly do not represent an extensive set of bibliometric data. In traditional digital libraries, the inclusion of this data has become commonplace as users rely on these metrics for relevance judgment. However, in the case of previous RS, only simple metrics such as the citation count and reference count were included. In the user study, participants explicitly stated the need to include metrics such as impact factor and h-index along with the other metadata. The main challenge for including these metrics in the user interface is the computing overhead for calculating these values for all the papers in the corpus. Further exacerbating this issue, most of the prototype systems use different datasets, thereby re-use of metrics data is not a viable option.

3.4 Diversification of Corpus and Task Interconnectivity

The evaluation of algorithms in most of the prior studies has been restricted to datasets from certain disciplines such as computer science and related disciplines. Even though there is large level of uniformity in hard and soft sciences on the approaches followed for scientific information seeking, not much is known about the differences in relevance heuristics for LR tasks. Therefore, future studies should include papers from "far-apart" disciplines for the evaluation. In systems where multiple search tasks are supported, task interconnectivity mechanism is an essential component. With this component, certain redundant user actions can be avoided. In the user study, a good number of participants appreciated the utility of seed basket and reading list towards management of the paper across the three tasks.

4 The Framework

There are three high-level components in the *Scientific Paper Retrieval and Recommender Framework (SPRRF)* as shown in Fig. 1.

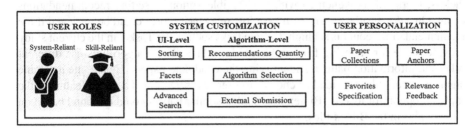

Fig. 1. Scientific paper retrieval and recommender framework (SPRRF)

4.1 User Roles

Our proposed classification of user-role is based on the levels of system customization and user personalization preferred by the user. The two proposed roles are (i) skill-reliant and (ii) system-reliant users. Skill-reliant user role caters to users who prefer to customize the UI and system-level features to a high extent. These users prefer to have sorting, advanced search and filtering options to sieve through the recommended results. They prefer to have control over algorithm logic and the required quantity of output papers. On the other hand, System-reliant role caters to users who prefer to trust the system in its default settings i.e. fixed algorithm logic, low levels of customization and non-personalized options. Research students mostly fall under this category since they preferred the system to a higher extent [3]. The characteristics of these user roles are influenced by the other two components in SPRRF. Assignment of the role to a new user to the system can be made with a simple selection from the user during the first visit. Accordingly, a user could change the role setting during future visits.

4.2 System Customization

Under this component, there are two sub-components. They are UI and algorithm customizations. The *UI Customization* sub-component involves control features. Although, there are different types of control features, three main features are considered adequate. These are (i) sort options, (ii) topical facets and (iii) advanced search options. Sort options provide alternative schemes such as sorting by publication date, citation count and textual similarity. Topical facets are hyperlinks provided in the navigation pane of the results page. The author-specified keywords from research papers are ideal candidates for topical facets. Advanced search options include more text boxes for executing field-specific search queries which can be combined using Boolean operators. These UI customization features in specialized RS will help in simulating a familiar experience for users who have been using traditional digital libraries. The second level of system customization - *Algorithmic Customization*, is related to the retrieval/recommender algorithm. There are three customization features. These are (i) setting the recommendations count, (ii) selecting the algorithm and (iii) submission of external papers through Bibtex files. In all the previous studies and the current study, the recommendations count has been fixed by the researchers based on different rationale. Nevertheless, users will be benefited with this flexible option of setting recommendations count. On a down side, papers with very low relevance scores could be retrieved if the recommendations count is set high. Certain tasks such as the Task 1 in the current study provide scope for choosing from different algorithms. These algorithms use different rules and information paths for identifying the candidate papers. Hence, the available algorithms could be provided as choices to users for selection. The third feature is the 'upload' option for loading Bibtex files so that similar papers could be found based on the citations in the Bibtex files.

4.3 User Personalization

The extent of user personalization applicable for scientific paper recommendations is limited in comparison with other domains such as e-commerce, films and music. Through the SPRRF, a different perspective of personalization is presented with four features. These are (i) paper collections, (ii) favorites specification, (iii) paper anchors and (iv) relevance feedback. The seed basket and reading list which are already available in the Rec4LRW system are apt paper collection features for enforcing explicit personalization at task level. Anchoring or pinning certain papers in the seed basket or reading list, is the second feature meant for exerting strong influence on recommendations. This helps in acquiring highly personalized results. Alternatively, different weights could be set to the seed papers so that recommendations could be formulated accordingly. User specification of favorites among authors, conferences and journals is the third personalization feature for manipulating recommendations. This feature is set at the user profile level, thereby making these favorites global for all the recommendation tasks carried out by the user. Relevance feedback based re-orientation of recommendations is the fourth feature of user personalization that can really benefit researchers in training the system to their individual tastes.

5   Conclusion

In this paper, we have proposed a specialized framework meant to cater for future studies in scholarly search tasks. A detailed version of the framework with proofs for the emergent themes has been made available as a technical report [6].

References

1. McNee, S.M., Kapoor, N., Konstan, J.A.: Don't look stupid: avoiding pitfalls when recommending research papers. In: Proceedings of the 2006 20th Anniversary Conference on Computer Supported Cooperative Work, pp. 171–180 (2006)
2. Küçüktunç, O., Saule, E., Kaya, K., Çatalyürek, Ü.V: TheAdvisor: a webservice for academic recommendation. In: Proceedings of the 13th ACM/IEEE-CS Joint Conference on Digital Libraries, pp. 433–434 (2013)
3. Sesagiri Raamkumar, A., Foo, S., Pang, N.: Making literature review and manuscript writing tasks easier for novice researchers through Rec4LRW system. In: Proceedings of the 16th ACM/IEEE-CS on Joint Conference on Digital Libraries - JCDL 2016, pp. 229–230. ACM Press, New York, USA (2016)
4. Tang, M.-C.: A study of academic library users' decision-making process: a Lens model approach. J. Doc. **65**, 938–957 (2009)
5. Sugiyama, K., Kan, M.-Y.: Serendipitous recommendation for scholarly papers. In: Proceedings of the 11th Annual International ACM/IEEE Joint Conference on Digital Libraries, pp. 307–310 (2011)
6. Sesagiri Raamkumar, A., Foo, S., Pang, N.: A framework for scientific paper retrieval and recommender systems (2016). http://arxiv.org/abs/1609.01415

Investigating the Use of a Mobile Crowdsourcing Application for Public Engagement in a Smart City

Chei Sian Lee[✉], Vishwaraj Anand, Feng Han, Xiaoyu Kong,
and Dion Hoe-Lian Goh

Wee Kim Wee School of Communication and Information,
Nanyang Technological University, Singapore, Singapore
{leecs,vishwara001,hanf0005,kong0112,ashlgoh}@ntu.edu.sg

Abstract. It has been reported that crowdsourcing applications are valuable to support smart city initiatives. However, there still remains a gap in using such applications to empower and engage city residents This study introduces a mobile crowdsourcing platform prototype known as My Smart Mobile City app (i.e. MSMC) that aims to help cities manage public engagement with their residents. The aim of apps like MSMC is to help cities to collect useful local information by empowering and motivating residents to contribute content related to the city's public spaces. Hence, motivations driving the use of MSMC will be explored. Preliminary results and implications of our work are discussed.

Keywords: Crowdsourcing · Motivation · Smart city · Public engagement · Android app

1 Introduction

Powered by the extensive and increasing access to the Internet, the use of crowdsourcing has grown tremendously over the last decade. Crowdsourcing is the act of gathering a large group of people to address a particular task through an open call for proposals via the Internet [1]. Indeed, crowdsourcing has become a major way of populating information-rich online environments such as digital libraries (e.g. annotating locations) as it harnesses diverse groups of online users to address specific problems [2] through the process enable information to be shared efficiently. In the context of smart city initiatives, crowdsourcing is able to efficiently democratize information among public [3] especially in the areas of public engagement [4].

This study explores the use of a mobile crowdsourcing application to engage city residents in the use and management of public spaces. Smart city projects are progressively prevalent because more than half of the world's population now lives in urban areas. Indeed, research on smart cities has become increasingly important but the focus in past research has been on Western cities [4] and studies on Asian cities are still limited.

There are two objectives in the present study. First, we develop a mobile crowdsourcing application prototype, My Smart Mobile City app (MSMC), that enables city residents to contribute and access content (e.g. comments, suggestions, announcements,

© Springer International Publishing AG 2016
A. Morishima et al. (Eds.): ICADL 2016, LNCS 10075, pp. 98–103, 2016.
DOI: 10.1007/978-3-319-49304-6_13

questions) about public spaces. Concomitantly, the content shared via the app will function like a digital library in a smart city that meets the information needs of other residents (e.g. details about events and facilities in the neighborhood) and also enable other stakeholders (e.g. government agencies, business) to better understand the needs of the residents. The second objective is to examine the factors motivating the use of such an app and to conduct an evaluation of MSMC to understand users' needs that affect the usage and sustainability of the app.

2   Related Work

2.1   Crowdsourcing in a Smart City

Crowdsourcing refers to the use of an online platform to collect innovative ideas, answers or solutions from a diverse group of individuals [5]. OpenStreetMap (www.onestreetmap.org) is a successful example of a crowdsourcing platform, where people with basic geographic skills and an affinity for digital mapping collaboratively contribute to the free wiki map of the world [6]. Traditionally, information to meet information needs in cities is typically provided by governments and other organizations. However, in smart cities, individuals are believed to be in the position to play an integral role [7]. Indeed, increasingly the untapped knowledge of city residents is utilized to support smart city initiatives via crowdsourcing. For instance, Brabham [4] investigated the use of crowdsourcing to improve public engagement in transit planning. Benouaret et al. [8] discussed methods for citizen participation and tasks distribution on crowdsourcing platforms. Collectively, these studies show that by employing crowdsourcing, local information can be collected in a structured manner effectively and efficiently.

2.2   Understanding Motivating Factors

Four motivational factors appear to govern most current crowdsourcing platforms and they are money, love, fun and glory [9, 10]. *Money* the common incentive mechanism and is effective in cases when the task is tedious and unpleasant [11]. Even though different norms for remuneration rates exist in different market or industry, generally higher monetary payment can encourage better quality [11]. However, it is also suggested that if people *love* the task because of interest, idealism or novelty, they will still be motivated to participate in crowdsourcing and contribute the time and effort for free [11]. Recent research has also indicated that the layering of games into crowdsourcing apps could modify usage behavior because of the *fun* element [10]. Finally, *glory* such as respect and recognition from one's peers can be an influential motivator [11]. In most practices, a crowdsourcing platform is built based on a combination of different motivation structures. In sum, both intrinsic (i.e. love, fun, glory) and extrinsic (i.e. money) motivating factors are important in crowdsourcing.

3   Introducing My Smart Mobile City App (MSMC)

My Smart Mobile City (MSMC) is a mobile crowdsourcing application prototype.

3.1   Foundation and Functional Requirements for MSMC

There are six components in smart city research [12]: smart economy, smart governance, smart people, smart living, smart mobility and smart environment. These six components form the foundation in our development of MSMC for public engagement in a smart city and the focus here is smart governance and people. Further, [7] elaborated that the main elements in crowdsourcing are clearly defined crowd, a task with a clear goal, clearly identified crowdsourcer, clearly defined compensation to be received by the crowdsourcer, and an online assigned process.

3.2   Application Developed

The current implementation of MSMC is developed using Java for Android Systems. In essence, the app collects location-based content contributed by users which represent the suggestions and feedbacks from users and connects the content with relevant stakeholders (e.g. government agencies or businesses) who are responsible or will be interested in the content of that location (refer to Fig. 1).

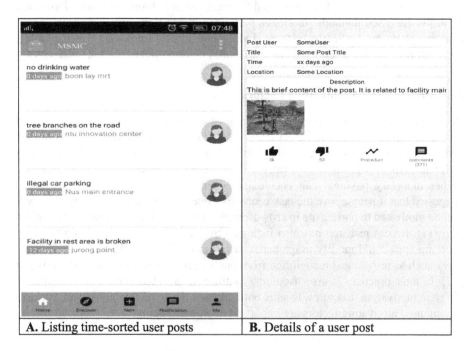

| A. Listing time-sorted user posts | B. Details of a user post |

Fig. 1.   MSMC's screenshots

Figure 1 shows two screenshots of MSMC. One shows a listing of the recent contributions and the other shows the textual and visual content posted by a user.

4 Methodology

This is an on-going project. The results reported in this paper was from an initial phase conducted in a large university in Singapore. Participants were undergraduate and graduate students who responded to the advertisements posted on campus.

4.1 Procedure

Prior to the study, participants attended a 10-minute briefing session. The usage of the app was demonstrated, followed by a short practice session. Four scenarios were identified and the participants were asked to create, browse and rate content based on these scenarios. The participants were also asked to observe the different features available on the app. After using the app, the participants were requested to answer an online survey to assess their perception and usability of the app, as well as motivations for usage and suggestions on features to be included. The participants were offered a compensation of 5 Singapore Dollars for their participation. Participation was voluntary.

4.2 Participants

A total of 80 participants, of which 53 were male, were recruited. Their ages ranged from 18 to 33 years with 36 participants were of the age group 18–24 and average age of the participants is 24.4 years old. Forty-four participants were university graduates with at least a bachelor degree and above. All the participants used their mobile phones extensively with 85 % indicated that they would share photos videos at least once a day and 65 % of the respondents indicated that they take photographs or videos using their mobile phones at least once a day.

5 Preliminary Results and Discussion

Our preliminary results demonstrate that the crowdsourcing concepts embodied in the application appeal to participants in our study and is a viable solution to encourage pubic engagement in a smart city. Overall, 77.5 % of the participants commented that the application was intuitive to use. Around 87.5 % of the participants were of the opinion that the app would help in better public engagement to aid in the governance of public spaces in Singapore.

In terms of motivations, our results reveal two main motivation drivers. The first group of factors are mostly content-related such as to seek information, to seek advice, to share information and to access up-to-date information. Our preliminary results show that these content-related factors are the primary drivers affecting usage intention of MSMC. It should be noted that the participants in our study further suggested that visual content and content related to the vicinity user were also valuable and should be incorporated in MSMC. Here are the quotations reflecting these suggestions, "*need to find nearby information*", "*need to be informed of congested public places*", and "*picture of the repaired facility*". Collectively, this study suggest that a highly interactive, mobile and informative app will be valuable for every day information seeking for residents in a smart city.

The second group of factors consists of social-related factors such as to show concern for others, to keep in touch with others, to interact with others and to be part of the community. Interestingly, the intrinsic motivations (e.g. love) appeal to the participants more than the extrinsic motivations such as financial awards. But when asked about long term sustainability issues, the participants in our study placed more emphasis on extrinsic motivations. However, the extrinsic motivations we found were not in the form of money as suggested by [9]. Specifically, 76.3 % of the participants said that the incentive mechanism of exchanging rewards with accumulated credit was attractive to them. Furthermore, several participants proposed to incorporate more ecommerce-related features such as "*online food delivery services*" and "*Internet banking*". Overall, our study indicates that a combination of both intrinsic and extrinsic motivations are important to motivate and sustain usage MSMC.

Besides connecting with one's social networks, several participants also articulated the necessity of establishing linkages with government agencies especially during crisis situations. Specially, one participant noted that "*online chat with government*" and one male participant further suggested that "*Emergency communication directly with govt[government agencies] should be incorporated*". This is supported by a female participant who also suggested that "*emergency features*" would be useful. Given the recent wave of terrorist attacks and crisis happening in different parts of the world, it is not surprising that participants in our study have highlighted such features. More specifically, these responses indicate that residents envision themselves to play important roles in ensuring the security and safety of the community and city.

6   Conclusion

In conclusion, our findings indicate that crowdsourcing apps are effective to engage city residents with regards to public space management and maintenance in a smart city. The majority of our participants who expressed a liking for MSMC supported the idea of using mobile crowdsourcing to contribute information or to seek for information related to public spaces in Singapore. In terms of motivations, we found that content-related and social-related motivating factors are primary drivers of apps like MSMC.

Our findings provide an important foundation for future research in the use crowdsourcing in smart city initiatives. Future work should conduct longitudinal study to ascertain the perceived usefulness and long term sustainability of apps like MSMC. In addition, fun and games can be incorporated in the app to motivate crowd workers to participate [13]. Caution must be taken when interpreting our results. Specifically, our participants were located in Singapore at the point of data collection, and thus replicating the study with a diverse group of population (in another city in Asia) would be beneficial to validate the present findings. Nonetheless, despite these shortcomings, the present study contributes to a better understanding of the use of a mobile crowdsourcing app in a smart city context from an Asian perspective.

Acknowledgement. This work was supported by NTU MOE/Tier 1 grant RG149/15.

References

1. Schneider, D., deSouza, J., Lucas, E.M.: Towards a typology of social news apps from a Crowd Computing perspective. In: 2014 IEEE International Conference on Systems, Man, and Cybernetics (SMC), pp. 1134–1140 (2014)
2. Doan, A., Ramakrishnan, R., Halevy, A.Y.: Crowdsourcing systems on the world-wide web. Commun. ACM **54**, 86–96 (2011)
3. Sherky, C.: Here comes everybody: The power of organizing without organizations, p. 106. Penguin, New York (2008)
4. Brabham, D.C.: Motivations for participation in a crowdsourcing application to improve public engagement in transit planning. J. Appl. Commun. Res. **40**, 307–328 (2012)
5. Surowiecki, J.: The Wisdom of Crowds: Why the Many are Smarter than the Few and How Collective Wisdom Shapes Business, Economies, Societies, and Nations. Doubleday, New York (2004)
6. Haklay, M.: How good is volunteered geographical information? A comparative study of OpenStreetMap and Ordnance Survey datasets. Environ. Plann. **37**, 682–703 (2010)
7. Estellés-Arolas, E., González-Ladrón-De-Guevara, F.: Towards an integrated crowdsourcing definition. J. Inf. Sci. **38**, 189–200 (2012)
8. Benouaret, K., Valliyur-Ramalingam, R., Charoy, F.: CrowdSC: building smart with large scale citizen participation. IEEE Internet Comput. **17**, 57 (2013)
9. Malone, T.W., Laubacher, R., Dellarocas, C.: Harnessing crowds: mapping the genome of collective intelligence, MIT Sloan Res. **51**, 21–31 (2009)
10. Goh, D.H., Pe-Than, E.P.P., Lee, C.S.: Games for crowdsourcing mobile content: an analysis of contribution patterns. In: JCDL Joint Conference of Digital Libraries, pp. 249–250. ACM, New York (2016)
11. Morris, R.R., McDuff, D.: Crowdsourcing techniques for affective computing. In: Calvo, R.A., D'Mello, S.K., Gratch, J., Kappas, A. (eds.) The Oxford Handbook of Affective Computing, pp. 384–394. Oxford University Press, New York (2015)
12. Griffinger, K., Gertner, C., Kramar, H., Kalasek, R., Pichler-milanovic, N., & Meijers, E., Smart cities: ranking of European medium-sized cities. Vienna University of Technology (2007). http://www.smartcities.eeu/download/smart_cities_fianl_report.pdf. Accessed 17 Jan 2016
13. Goh, D.H., Lee, C.S.: Perceptions, quality and motivational needs in image tagging human computation games. J. Inf. Sci. **37**, 515–531 (2011)

User Testing of Prototype Systems in Two Different Environments: Preliminary Results

Tanja Merčun[1]([✉]), Athena Salaba[2], and Maja Žumer[1]

[1] University of Ljubljana, Ljubljana, Slovenia
{tanja.mercun,maja.zumer}@ff.uni-lj.si
[2] Kent State University, Kent, OH, USA
asalaba@kent.edu

Abstract. The paper presents a preliminary report on two studies testing the same prototype system user interfaces in Slovenia and the USA. A comparison of results highlights some of the differences in performance and preferences between the two studies and leads to a discussion of possible implications for testing in different cultural environments on one hand and on the other hand, the question of universally accepted user interfaces.

Keywords: User interfaces · Evaluation · Bibliographic information systems · Information visualization

1 Introduction

In the competitive digital environment, user testing of digital libraries and bibliographic information systems is becoming increasingly important for developing systems that will not only provide access to valuable collections, but will also offer positive user experience that will attract users to return and explore the collections. However, empirical studies of quality and user's perception of usability show that the notion of usability may not be the same across cultures [2] and cross-cultural user testing can prove difficult as certain methods that are appropriate in some cultures do not work in other cultures [3]. But as the information society continues to become more global and digital libraries make information available across borders and cultures, there is more need than ever to develop user interfaces that not only accommodate individual differences, but also cultural diversity as pointed out early on by Marchionini [4]. Examining the usability of digital libraries in multicultural and cross-cultural environments and conducting evaluation in a wider variety of contexts is therefore necessary for building digital libraries that offer cross-cultural usability [1].

With the changes in the world of bibliographic data and problems connected to current bibliographic systems, the community is faced with new challenges when it comes to designing user interfaces for presenting and exploring the rich library collections. Building on new models, we have developed a prototype system based on the concept of bibliographic work families, using information visualization as a new approach for navigation and overview of bibliographic data. Implementing four different

© Springer International Publishing AG 2016
A. Morishima et al. (Eds.): ICADL 2016, LNCS 10075, pp. 104–109, 2016.
DOI: 10.1007/978-3-319-49304-6_14

hierarchical visualization techniques and a Baseline system, the prototype designs were first evaluated in a user study in Slovenia with the goal of identifying the design that provided best performance and user experience. However, because it was tested in a specific cultural environment that is influenced by a specific set of existing bibliographic systems, we questioned whether the same results would be obtained if the test was repeated in a different cultural environment. Therefore, part of the study was repeated with participants in the United States (US) to check whether the results could be more globally applicable. This paper presents a preliminary comparison of the results from the two studies and discusses some of the potential differences that will need to be explored further.

2   Study Background

Among the five prototype designs included in the study, one represented a typical bibliographic information system with faceted navigation and edition-based displays (Baseline), while the other four embodied the bibliographic work family concept and used an information visualization feature for overview and navigation (Fig. 1). Each of the four visualized displays (Sunburst, Indented tree, Circlepack, Radial tree) implemented a different hierarchical visualization technique (Fig. 2) while the other features were the same in all four.

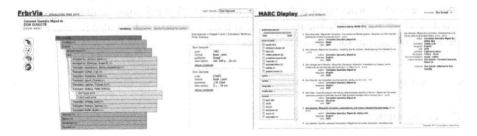

Fig. 1.   The visual prototype system (left) and the Baseline system (right).

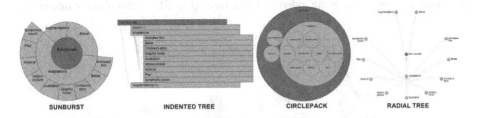

Fig. 2.   Four hierarchical visualizations used in the visualized prototype system.

The first study was completed in January 2012 in Slovenia, while the second study was conducted in April 2016 and took place in the United States. In both studies, students from different areas of study were recruited at each university and the sessions were recorded and analyzed using Morae software and the same set of measures. While some of the tasks between the two studies were different, the setup of the tests was the same and the Don Quixote work family example used in the first study was repeated in full also in the second study as it was seen as neutral and international enough for both environments. The analysis in this paper therefore takes into account only sessions testing the Don Quixote work set, which results in a sample of 90 tests from the Slovenian experiment and 94 tests from the United States experiment (Table 1). The representation of participants by gender, study area, and experience with bibliographic information systems was comparable in the two studies.

Table 1. The number of tests within each prototype design.

	Baseline	Radial	Circlepack	Indented	Sunburst	Total
SLO	18	18	18	18	18	90
USA	24	17	18	16	19	94

Each participant interacted with a randomly assigned set of prototype designs and completed 10 tasks in each of the systems. Tasks ranged from simple look-up tasks ("What year did Cervantes write a play titled Pedro de Udermalas?) to more exploratory tasks ("Browse through different editions of Don Quixote in English language and describe what you notice."). Each participant was asked to assign a difficulty score for each task, to select any number of positive or negative reaction cards that described the experience with a particular prototype design and to rank the designs from least to most favorite one. In addition to the user-reported measures, researchers also recorded task times and completion success scores for each task.

3   Results

3.1   Performance

In both studies, participants using the Baseline system needed considerably more time to complete the tasks and were also less successful than with any of the four visualized prototype designs. Comparing individual interfaces (Fig. 3), we can observe that in the

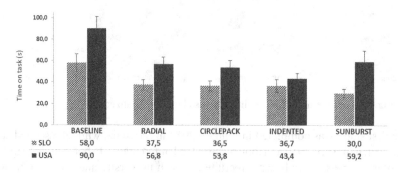

Fig. 3. Comparison by average (mean) time on task with 95 % confidence intervals.

US study, participants generally needed more time to complete the tasks in all prototype systems. The most important shift between the first and the second study was, however, that in the US study, participants using the Indented tree had the best time on task score and that using the Sunburst prototype was notably slower than using the Indented tree, a difference that did not appear in the first study.

Both studies also show that participants were least successful in completing tasks when using the Baseline prototype. There are, though, some noticeable differences between the two studies in the number of unsuccessfully completed tasks in the visualizations (Fig. 4). Slovenian participants had the highest number of unsuccessful tasks using the Radial prototype and the lowest when using Sunburst, while the US participants were more unsuccessful using the Indented Tree and had the lowest number of unsuccessful tasks when using Circlepack.

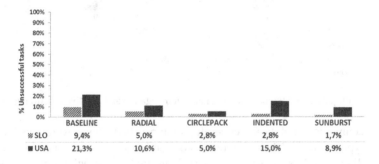

Fig. 4. Comparison by the percentage of unsuccessfully completed tasks.

3.2 Perception

Participants were asked to rate how easy or difficult it was to complete each task they performed, using a scale of 1–5, where 1 was very easy and 5 very difficult. As illustrated in Fig. 5, participants in the Slovenian study on average rated the tasks performed using the Baseline as more difficult and the tasks performed in Sunburst as easier than their counterparts in the US study.

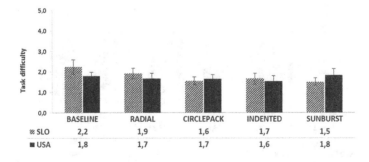

Fig. 5. Comparison by mean task difficulty with 95 % confidence intervals.

When all tasks using a particular prototype were completed, participants were asked to use reaction cards to express their perception of the prototype. Comparing the results of the two studies (Fig. 6), we see that in the US study, all visualized prototypes received a higher percentage of negative reactions while the Baseline received a lower percentage of negative cards. However, in both studies, the Indented Tree and Circlepack received the highest percentage of positive reaction cards. The Radial prototype received the highest number of negative reaction cards among US participants, while Baseline received the highest number of negative reaction cards among Slovenian participants.

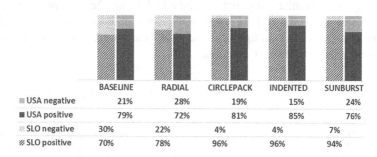

	BASELINE	RADIAL	CIRCLEPACK	INDENTED	SUNBURST
USA negative	21%	28%	19%	15%	24%
USA positive	79%	72%	81%	85%	76%
SLO negative	30%	22%	4%	4%	7%
SLO positive	70%	78%	96%	96%	94%

Fig. 6. Comparison by the percentage of selected negative and positive reaction cards.

At the completion of all tasks across all prototypes, participants were asked to rank each prototype by order of their preference, considering all aspects of their interactions with them. Figure 7 offers a summary of the rankings for the Don Quixote example based on the top two ranked prototypes by each participant. In both studies, Sunburst and Indented tree prototypes received the highest number of #1 and #2 rankings and Baseline the lowest number of top two rankings. Interestingly, it was the Sunburst prototype that received the highest number of #1 rankings by US participants, which is in contrast to some of the results from previously presented measures such as the time needed to complete the tasks or the relatively high percentage of negative reaction cards in the US study.

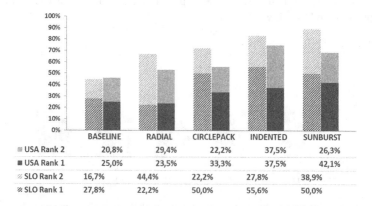

	BASELINE	RADIAL	CIRCLEPACK	INDENTED	SUNBURST
USA Rank 2	20,8%	29,4%	22,2%	37,5%	26,3%
USA Rank 1	25,0%	23,5%	33,3%	37,5%	42,1%
SLO Rank 2	16,7%	44,4%	22,2%	27,8%	38,9%
SLO Rank 1	27,8%	22,2%	50,0%	55,6%	50,0%

Fig. 7. Comparison by rank frequency (Rank 1 – most favorite, Rank 2–2nd favorite)

4   Discussion and Conclusion

Both studies confirm that overall, the Baseline prototype performed least favorably among all prototypes, in terms of performance (time-on-task and percentage of unsuccessful tasks) and perceptions (difficulty of task completion, ranking). When it comes to the use of reaction cards to describe the Baseline prototype, the US participants used more favorable terms (higher percentage of positive reaction cards) than their Slovenian counterparts. This could in part be explained by the fact that US participants often described the Baseline system as familiar and positively commented on the availability of faceted navigation. Such a feature is not very common in current Slovenian catalogues and therefore, Slovenian users were not influenced by the familiarity of facets.

The studies show a significant difference in the time it took to complete the same tasks by the two different groups of participants. There are two factors that may be contributing to this difference: (a) US participants were more willing to think-aloud and were prompted more often to remember to express their thoughts and opinions while performing the tasks, possibly contributing to the time it took to complete the tasks; and (b) although it was assumed that the majority of participants would be familiar or at least aware of Cervantes' Don Quixote work, the findings show that the majority of the US participants had never heard of this work. Further analysis on whether familiarity with the work has an effect on time-on-task is needed.

Despite the differences in performance and perceptions between the two studies, overall, Sunburst and Indented Tree are ranked as best systems in both studies, suggesting that it is possible to design a visualization prototype that appeals to users in different cultural environments. The study, however, also shows that when testing a user interface in different cultural environments, it is sometimes difficult to compare and interpret the data as there are many more factors influencing participants' interactions and perceptions than just the user interface itself.

Acknowledgements. Prototypes developed in cooperation with dr. Trond Aalberg (NTNU, Norway).

References

1. Borgman, C., Rasmussen, E.: Usability of digital libraries in a multicultural environment. In: Theng, Y.-L., Foo, S. (eds.) Design and Usability of Digital Libraries: Case Studies in the Asia-Pacific, pp. 270–284. Information Science Publishing, London (2004)
2. Clemmensen, T.: Towards a theory of cultural usability: a comparison of ADA and CM-U theory. In: Kurosu, Masaaki (ed.) HCD 2009. LNCS, vol. 5619, pp. 416–425. Springer, Heidelberg (2009). doi:10.1007/978-3-642-02806-9_48
3. Evers, V.: Cross-cultural applicability of user evaluation methods: a case study amongst Japanese, North-American, English and Dutch Users. In: CHI 2002 Extended Abstracts on Human Factors in Computing Systems, pp. 740–741. ACM Press, New York (2002)
4. Marchionini, G.: Interfaces for end-user information seeking. J. Am. Soc. Inf. Sci. **43**, 156–163 (1992)

Finding "Similar but Different" Documents Based on Coordinate Relationship

Meng Zhao[✉], Hiroaki Ohshima, and Katsumi Tanaka

Graduate School of Informatics, Kyoto University,
Yoshida Honmachi, Kyoto 606–8501, Japan
{zhao,ohshima,tanaka}@dl.kuis.kyoto-u.ac.jp

Abstract. Traditional search technologies are based on similarity relationship such that they return content similar documents in accordance with a given one. However, such similarity-based search does not always result in good results, e.g., similar documents will bring little additional information so that it is difficult to increase information gain. In this paper, we propose a method to find *similar but different* documents of a user-given one by distinguishing **coordinate relationship** from similarity relationship between documents. Simply, a *similar but different* document denotes the document with the same topic as that of the given document, but describing different events or concepts. For example, given as the input a news article stating the occurrence of *the Oregon school shooting*, articles stating the occurrence of other school shooting events, such as *the Virginia Tech shooting*, are detected and returned to users. Experiments conducted on the New York Times Annotated Corpus verify the effectiveness of our method and illustrate the importance of incorporating coordinate relationship to find similar but different documents.

Keywords: Coordinate relationship · Similar but different · Web mining

1 Introduction

Content-based information retrieval (CBIR), which allows people to retrieve documents based on the understanding of their contents and of their components, has attracted a lot of research interest in recent years. Traditional technologies are based on similarity relationship [2,4,7,10]. Therefore, with the help of CBIR technologies, people can get content similar documents in accordance with a given one. However, such similarity-based search does not always result in good results. One of the conceivable reasons is that similar documents will bring little additional information so that it is difficult to increase information gain.

For example, given as the input a news article stating the occurrence of *the Oregon school shooting*, such as Article 1 in our example, articles stating the occurrence of the same school shooting by other news agents, such as Article 2, are considered as better output by traditional CBIR technologies. In the most

© Springer International Publishing AG 2016
A. Morishima et al. (Eds.): ICADL 2016, LNCS 10075, pp. 110–123, 2016.
DOI: 10.1007/978-3-319-49304-6_15

extreme case, these news articles contain the same information, e.g., occurrence time, place. Therefore, people will not obtain more information when they read them. It seems that these similar articles are less likely to make people satisfied. We think the follow-ups of the inputted news article or articles stating the occurrence of other school shooting events are better choices for further understanding the whole topic. Especially, we target at the latter ones and name it **similar but different** documents. Simply, a similar but different document denotes the document with the same topic as that of the given document, but describing different events or concepts. For the before-mentioned news article that states the occurrence of *the Oregon school shooting*, articles stating the occurrence of other school shooting events, such as Article 3 about *the Virginia Tech shooting*, are regarded as its similar but different ones.

Article 1

*The Oregon shooting **occurred** on October 1, 2015 at the UCC campus near Roseburg, Oregon, United States. Christopher Harper-Mercer, a 26-year-old enrolled at the school, fatally **shot** an assistant professor and eight students in a classroom. Seven to nine others were **injured**. After being wounded by two police officers, the gunman **committed suicide** by shooting himself in the head.*

Article 2

Ten people were killed when a gunman opened fire at Oregon's Umpqua Community College on Thursday, forcing the nation to face yet another mass shooting. Seven other people were injured, and the shooter is dead. Earlier estimates had put the number of people hurt much higher. Multiple law enforcement officials familiar with the investigation identified the gunman as 26-year-old Christopher Harper-Mercer.

Article 3

*The Virginia Tech shooting **occurred** on April 16, 2007, on the campus of Virginia Polytechnic Institute and State University in Blacksburg, Virginia, United States. Seung-Hui Cho, a senior at Virginia Tech, **shot and killed** 32 people and **wounded** 17 others in two separate attacks, approximately two hours apart, before **committing suicide**.*

In this paper, we propose a method to retrieve similar but different documents of a user-given one by distinguishing **coordinate relationship** from similarity relationship between documents. Experiments conducted on the New York Times Annotated Corpus verify the effectiveness of our method and illustrate the importance of incorporating coordinate relationship.

The remainder of the paper is organized as follows. We explain the so-called coordinate relationship in Sect. 2 and formalize the problem in Sect. 3. In Sect. 4, we describe the details of our proposed method. In Sect. 5, we show experimental results which were conducted on the New York Times Annotated Corpus. We devote Sect. 6 to a discussion of the previous work. Finally, we conclude the paper in Sect. 7.

2   Coordinate Relationship Between Documents

In this section, we address the key concept "coordinate relationship" and discuss it at the document level.

Coordinate relationships exist at different levels, such as term, sentence and document levels. Here, we use the symbol "$\parallel$" to express the coordinate relationship between elements. Previous studies [13,15,18] concentrate on coordinate relationship at the term level and define it between terms as below:

$$t \parallel t' \Leftarrow \exists C(t \text{ belongs to } C \wedge t' \text{ belongs to } C)$$

where C denotes a concept. In other words, two terms are coordinate to each other if they share any common hypernym. For example, because both "Umpqua Community College" and "Virginia Polytechnic Institute and State University" belong to the *school* category, they are coordinate terms. Here, "school" is their common hypernym.

When considering coordinate relationship at the document level, we assume that a document, especially a news article, is a combination of subjects and actions, which are presented by nouns (to be specific, proper nouns) and verbs, respectively. Based on this assumption, it is intuitive to consider two kinds of "similar but different" documents: (1) documents with similar subjects but different actions; (2) documents with similar actions but different subjects. Note that documents should be under the same topic in both of the two situations. We know that with the development of a news event, its subjects change a little. In contrast, its actions change a lot. Therefore, in the former situation, a document is a follow-up[1] (or a followed-up) of another document. On the other hand, we know that similar news events have similar developments. We assume that actions can locate the development phase of an event. Therefore, in the latter situation, similar but different documents denote documents stating different events but in the same development phase.

Given Article 1, which describes the occurrence of *the Oregon school shooting*, its similar but different documents can be the follow-ups of this article, e.g., the launch of a campus-wide search for explosives, more executive action on the subject of gun control, corresponding to the first situation in the above discussion. Its similar but different documents can be also the articles stating the occurrence of other school shooting events, such as Article 3 about *the Virginia Tech shooting*, corresponding to the second situation in the above discussion. In this paper, we target at the latter one.

By carefully observing Article 1 and Article 3, we find that (1) the subjects are coordinate to each other in some way. For example, the occurrence time of the Oregon shooting, *October 1, 2015*, is coordinate to the occurrence time of the Virginia Tech shooting, *April 16, 2007*. The occurrence location of the Oregon shooting, *UCC campus*, is coordinate to that of the Virginia Tech shooting, *campus of Virginia Polytechnic Institute and State University*. (2) The actions

---

[1] Follow-up is an article giving further information on a previously reported news event.

in both these articles are similar (see terms or phrases in bold). For example, at the beginning of both these articles, it states the occurrence of the event, using exactly the same term "occurred". When it comes to the injuries and deaths of each shootings, Article 1 used the term "injured", while Article 3 used the term "wounded". Even though these two terms have different surface forms, they have the same semantic meaning.

Based on the finding, we assume that two documents are coordinate to each other if they have coordinate subjects and similar actions. Therefore, we give the definition of coordinate relationship between documents in this paper as follows:

$$d \parallel d' \Leftarrow \exists C(d \text{ belongs to } C \wedge d' \text{ belongs to } C \wedge$$
$$Subject(d) \parallel Subject(d') \wedge$$
$$Action(d) \doteq Action(d'))$$

where C denotes a topic. $Subject(d)$ and $Action(d)$ represent the subject set and the action set of d, respectively. Here, we use the symbol "$\doteq$" to represent the similarity relationship between action sets.

3 Problem Statement

We can define the problem in this study as follows.

Input: a set of documents $D = \{d_1, ..., d_N\}$ and a document d_i in D
Output: a totally ordered set $(D, \leq)$ for d_i

where any pair of documents in the set D are compared under the coordinate relationship.

In other words, given a set of documents under a certain topic and a document in this set as the input, we want to compute a ranking list for the given document such that the documents in the list are ordered by their degrees of coordinate relationship.

4 "Similar but Different" Document Detection

As we mentioned above, in this paper, we target at documents with similar actions but different subjects, viz. articles describing the same development phase but different events. We can tackle this problem from these two aspects. We define two functions as follows.

$CoordSub(d_i, d_j)$: Given two documents d_i and d_j, this function returns the coordinate subject degree between them, which is a value between $[0, 1]$. Note that when $i = j$, its value is 0.
$SimAct(d_i, d_j)$: Given two documents d_i and d_j, this function returns the similar action degree between them, which is a value between $[0, 1]$.

Based on the assumption discussed above, we can combine the coordinate subject degree and the similar action degree via a weighted harmonic mean to compute the coordinate degree between the two documents. This formula is given below.

$$Coord(d_i, d_j) = \frac{1}{\alpha \cdot \dfrac{1}{CoordSub(d_i, d_j)} + (1 - \alpha) \cdot \dfrac{1}{SimAct(d_i, d_j)}} \tag{1}$$

where α is the weight. When $\alpha = 1$, only the subjects are considered when calculating the coordinate score; and when $\alpha = 0$, only the actions are considered.

We know that the problem turns to be two sub-problems: a comparison between subject sets and a comparison between action sets. Because subjects are presented by proper nouns and actions are presented by verbs, the two sub-problems are:

(1). Given two proper noun sets N_i and N_j that are extracted from d_i and d_j, respectively, we want to compute the coordinate degree between these two sets.

(2). Given two verb sets V_i and V_j that are extracted from d_i and d_j, respectively, we want to compute the similarity between these two sets.

To make a comparison between sets, we first introduce the comparison between terms.

4.1   Term Comparison

Here, we use two methods to compare nouns based on their coordinate relationship and verbs based on their similarity relationship. $IsCoord(n_i, n_j)$ denotes the coordinate degree between the two nouns. $IsSynonym(v_i, v_j)$ denotes the similarity degree between the two verbs. The details are addressed as below.

The WordNet Method. WordNet [13] is a large English lexical database. It groups English words into sets of synonyms called synsets, and records a number of relations between these synonym sets or their members. For example, noun synsets are arranged into hierarchies that indicate the super-subordinate relation (also called hyperonymy or hyponymy). Therefore, we know the hypernyms of a term via WordNet.

As introduced in Sect. 2, two terms are coordinate if they share any common hypernyms. Therefore, given two nouns n_i and n_j, we can look up their hypernyms in WordNet and check whether they have any in common. The result is a boolean value. Therefore, $IsCoord(n_i, n_j)$ returns a value of 0 or 1.

Because WordNet groups words into synsets that have similar meaning, given two verbs v_i and v_j, we can look up them in WordNet and check whether they are in the same synset. The result is a boolean value. Therefore, $IsSynonym(v_i, v_j)$ returns a value of 0 or 1.

The Word2vec Method. Mikolov et al. introduced word2vec, a group of related models, such as the skip-gram model and the continuous bag of word (CBOW) model, to learn vector representations of words from a text corpus [11,12]. The learned word vectors can satisfactorily capture relationships between words in semantics.

In addition to the definition of the coordinate terms introduced in Sect. 2, we also consider that, if two terms are coordinate to each other, they should appear in the same, or similar contexts. Because word2vec learns the distributed representation of words by considering the surrounding words of each word, we use the cosine similarity of learned vectors to represent the coordinate degree between words. However, synonyms have high similarities. Therefore, to distinguish coordinate terms from synonyms, we empirically set a threshold θ ($\theta = 0.9$ in the experiments) and treat words whose similarity is greater than the threshold as synonyms. In this case, $IsCoord(n_i, n_j) = 0$.

Because the word2vec model can detect semantically similar words, we simply use the cosine similarity of learned vectors to compute the similarity between two verbs. Hence, $IsSynonym(v_i, v_j)$ returns a value between 0 and 1.

4.2 Calculating the Coordinate Subject Degree

Let us consider how to calculate the coordinate degree between two noun sets. Because we already know whether two given terms are coordinate, it is easy to know the number of pairs of coordinate terms between the two sets. However, to reduce the computational complexity, we do not do pairwise comparison. Instead, we think for each term in one noun set, there is at most one coordinate term in another set. If we already find a pair of coordinate terms, e.g., *the Oregon school shooting* in d_i coordinate to *the Virginia Tech shooting* in d_j, other pairs containing one term in the found pair, such as *the Oregon school shooting* in d_i coordinate to *Virginia* in d_j, are just an enhancement, because we already find a term that plays a similar role as *the Oregon school shooting* in d_j. Therefore, we keep on removing pairs of coordinate terms that have already found and making term comparison within the rest terms in both of the two sets. As a result, we can get pairs of coordinate terms and exactly the same terms. The calculation of coordinate subject degree is based on these pairs.

It is easy to understand that if two documents have many shared proper nouns, they are more likely to describe the same event rather than different ones. Consequently, we should not assign a high coordinate degree to such documents. Based on this consideration, we introduce the following three methods listed below to calculate $CoordSub(d_i, d_j)$, called *minS1*, *minS2*, *minS3*, respectively.

$$CoordSub(d_i, d_j) = \frac{\sum_{n_m \in N_i, n_n \in N_j} IsCoord(n_m, n_n)}{min\{|N_i|, |N_j|\} + |N_i \cap N_j|} \tag{2}$$

$$CoordSub(d_i, d_j) = \frac{\sum_{n_m \in N_i, n_n \in N_j} IsCoord(n_m, n_n)}{min\{|N_i|, |N_j|\}} \cdot (1 - \frac{|N_i \cap N_j|}{min\{|N_i|, |N_j|\}}) \tag{3}$$

$$CoordSub(d_i, d_j) = \frac{\sum_{n_m \in N_i, n_n \in N_j} IsCoord(n_m, n_n)}{min\{|N_i|, |N_j|\} + e^{|N_i \cap N_j|}} \tag{4}$$

The *minS1* method penalizes sets that have the same proper nouns, the *minS2* method adds the ratio of the same ones to eliminate their effects, and the *minS3* method enhances the penalty of the same ones.

In addition, we find that, if the size difference between N_i and N_j is very large, the larger set tends to contain more common proper nouns by chance. Consequently, we should take the size difference into consideration. As a result, compared to the above methods considering the smaller size of the two sets, we introduce methods considering the average size, or the larger size as follows.

$$CoordSub(d_i, d_j) = \frac{\sum_{n_m \in N_i, n_n \in N_j} IsCoord(n_m, n_n)}{avg\{|N_i|, |N_j|\} + |N_i \cap N_j|} \tag{5}$$

$$CoordSub(d_i, d_j) = \frac{\sum_{n_m \in N_i, n_n \in N_j} IsCoord(n_m, n_n)}{avg\{|N_i|, |N_j|\}} \cdot (1 - \frac{|N_i \cap N_j|}{avg\{|N_i|, |N_j|\}}) \tag{6}$$

$$CoordSub(d_i, d_j) = \frac{\sum_{n_m \in N_i, n_n \in N_j} IsCoord(n_m, n_n)}{avg\{|N_i|, |N_j|\} + e^{|N_i \cap N_j|}} \tag{7}$$

$$CoordSub(d_i, d_j) = \frac{\sum_{n_m \in N_i, n_n \in N_j} IsCoord(n_m, n_n)}{max\{|N_i|, |N_j|\} + |N_i \cap N_j|} \tag{8}$$

$$CoordSub(d_i, d_j) = \frac{\sum_{n_m \in N_i, n_n \in N_j} IsCoord(n_m, n_n)}{max\{|N_i|, |N_j|\}} \cdot (1 - \frac{|N_i \cap N_j|}{max\{|N_i|, |N_j|\}}) \tag{9}$$

$$CoordSub(d_i, d_j) = \frac{\sum_{n_m \in N_i, n_n \in N_j} IsCoord(n_m, n_n)}{max\{|N_i|, |N_j|\} + e^{|N_i \cap N_j|}} \tag{10}$$

where Formula (5)–(7) denote methods that are called *avgS1*, *avgS2* and *avgS3*, respectively. Formula (8)–(10) denote methods that are called *maxS1*, *maxS2* and *maxS3*, respectively.

4.3   Calculating the Similar Action Degree

Let us consider how to calculate the similarity degree between two verb sets. Because we already know whether two given verbs are similar, it is easy to know the number of verbs that are the same or similar in the two sets[2]. Similarly, we do not do pairwise comparison. Instead, we keep on removing synonym pairs that have already found and making term comparison with the rest terms in both of the two verb sets. The similarity degree between the two verb sets are

---

[2] Note that verbs are compared in their base form.

Table 1. Illustration for 5 datasets.

Topic	Event
School shooting	Red Lake shooting Virginia Tech shooting West Nickel Mines School shooting
Earthquake	Bam earthquake Indian Ocean earthquake Kashmir earthquake
Heat wave	2003 European heat wave 2006 North American heat wave 1995 Chicago heat wave
Terrorist attack	Bali bombings Madrid train bombings Mumbai train bombings
Accounting scandal	Enron scandal WorldCom scandal Freddie Mac scandal

computed based on the number of verbs that are the same and similar in the two sets.

$$SimAct(d_i, d_j) = \frac{|V_i \cap V_j| + \sum_{v_m \in V_i, v_n \in V_j} IsSynonym(v_m, v_n)}{avg\{|V_i|, |V_j|\}} \qquad (11)$$

5 Experiments

In this section, we outline the details of our experiments.

5.1 Datasets

We manually created our datasets, containing 5 datasets (shown in Table 1), for evaluation. Each dataset corresponds to a topic, which means we suppose documents in each dataset are the search results of a keyword query that indicates the topic. For better comparison, there are 3 different events in each dataset. For each event in each topic, we surveyed on the Web and extracted related news articles from the New York Times Annotated Corpus. Because the corpus only contains news articles published by the New York Times, there are not so many articles found for each event. Besides, we manually removed noises from each dataset, e.g., news articles summarized the news in the past period. Finally, we got 60 ∼ 90 news articles for each topic.

Table 2. Combination of methods used in the experiments.

Methods for term comparison	weight α	Methods to calculate $CoordSub(d_i, d_j)$
WordNet	0.7	minS3, avgS3, maxS3
word2vec	0.5	minS3, avgS2, maxS2

5.2   Experimental Setting

We used Stanford POS Tagger[3] to do POS (Part-of-Speech) tagging. Therefore, we got the tagger for each term. Based on these taggers, we extracted proper nouns (or proper noun phrases) and verbs, respectively.

Since we mentioned before that we employ the word2vec model for term comparison, we trained the model on the New York Times Annotated Corpus with article publication time from 2002 to 2007.

Because of the space limitation and numerous combinations of the methods, we cannot show all experimental results. We did a preliminary experiment to choose the combinations. We found when using the WordNet to compare two terms, a good choice for the weight α of harmonic mean in both Formula (1) is 0.7. And the methods *minS3*, *avgS3* and *maxS3* perform better. When using the word2vec model, a good choice for α is 0.5 and the methods *minS3*, *avgS2* and *maxS2* perform better. The combinations of methods used in the experiments are listed in Table 2.

5.3   Experimental Results

Two baseline methods are employed for better comparison.

Sim. We employ vector space model [17] and represent each article by a TF/IDF vector. Similarity between two articles is computed by cosine similarity of their feature vectors. We denote the *sim* method a ranking based on the similarity to the query article.

MMR. Maximal Marginal Relevance (MMR), a document summarization method proposed by Carbonell and Goldstein [3], is widely used when diversity needs to be considered. Since we aim at finding documents with the same topic but talking about different events, it is also a diversity problem. When the method is used to select desired documents, it considers both relevance of each selected document and diversity of the whole output. That is, the output should not contain similar documents even if they are relevant.

We randomly select 10 news articles in each dataset and regard each of them as an input. Therefore, we evaluate the proposed methods on 50 queries.

---

[3] http://nlp.stanford.edu/software/tagger.shtml.

Table 3. Precision at different k.

@k	WordNet			word2vec			sim	MMR
	minS3	avgS3	maxS3	minS3	avgS2	maxS2		
1	0.400	**0.800**	0.400	0.600	0.200	0.200	0.400	0.340
2	0.400	**0.500**	**0.500**	0.400	0.300	0.300	0.300	0.310
3	0.400	0.400	**0.467**	0.400	0.267	0.267	0.333	0.267
4	0.400	0.350	**0.450**	0.400	0.250	0.250	0.300	0.295
5	**0.400**	0.360	0.400	0.320	0.240	0.240	0.280	0.200
6	**0.400**	0.30	0.367	0.267	0.233	0.267	0.300	0.167
7	**0.371**	0.314	0.314	0.229	0.229	0.257	0.314	0.143
8	**0.375**	0.325	0.325	0.225	0.200	0.225	0.300	0.250
9	**0.422**	0.356	0.3556	0.200	0.200	0.244	0.267	0.222
10	**0.440**	0.380	0.360	0.220	0.220	0.240	0.260	0.296

It is a time-consuming and expensive process involving human beings to assess relevance of each article in the ranking list by given one as the input. In information retrieval, it is usual for relevance to be assessed only for a subset. *Pooling* is the most standard approach to reducing the burden. Therefore, we first take a subset of the collection that is formed from the top k ($k = 10$) articles returned by the proposed methods and two baseline methods. Then we manually evaluate articles in the pooled set under the criterion that they state the same development phase of different news events (compared with the query article).

We use precision and recall, two traditional evaluation metrics in information retrieval, for evaluation.

Table 3 shows the performances of the proposed methods and two baseline methods, using precision for evaluation. It details the precision for each method at different k. From the table, we know that

(1) using the WordNet method to compare terms can get a better precision score than using the word2vec method. Besides, all the three methods *Word-Net+minS3*, *WordNet+avgS3* and *WordNet+maxS3* outperform both of the two baseline methods (*sim* and *MMR*), no matter what k is. Especially, the methods *WordNet+avgS3* and *WordNet+maxS3* significantly improve the precision when $k \leq 5$.
(2) the performance of the method *WordNet+minS3* is quite stable, which means the precision does not change a lot with the increase of k.
(3) using the word2vec method to compare terms is less than satisfactory. Only *word2vec+minS3* is competitive with the baseline method *sim*.
(4) the precision for the *sim* method does not decrease a lot with the increase of k, while the precision for the *MMR* method changes differently.

The precision scores of various methods at different k are used to calculate the statistical significances between the performance differences of the methods.

Table 4. Result of t-tests between the precision of various methods.

P value	WordNet+ avgS3	WordNet+ maxS3	word2vec+ minS3	word2vec+ avgS2	word2vec+ maxS2	sim	MMR
WordNet+minS3	**0.874**	**0.726**	**0.099**	2.62E−07	1.72E−07	0.0002	2.29E-05
WordNet+avgS3		**0.750**	0.008	0.006	0.012	0.024	0.002
WordNet+maxS3			**0.059**	4.74E−07	1.31E−05	0.002	2.58E−05
word2vec+minS3				0.040	**0.101**	**0.512**	0.032
word2vec+avgS2					0.021	0.002	**0.499**
word2vec+maxS2						0.010	**0.999**
sim							0.019

Table 5. Recall at different k.

@k	WordNet			word2vec			sim	MMR
	minS3	avgS3	maxS3	minS3	avgS2	maxS2		
1	0.029	**0.065**	0.040	0.052	0.012	0.012	0.037	0.040
2	0.059	**0.081**	**0.081**	0.065	0.050	0.050	0.051	0.058
3	0.083	**0.096**	0.108	0.091	0.075	0.075	0.077	0.080
4	0.112	0.111	**0.138**	0.117	0.087	0.087	0.091	0.093
5	0.142	0.137	**0.151**	0.117	0.099	0.099	0.106	0.117
6	**0.168**	0.137	0.163	0.117	0.112	0.124	0.131	0.146
7	**0.181**	0.165	0.163	0.117	0.125	0.137	0.158	0.167
8	**0.208**	0.190	0.189	0.128	0.125	0.137	0.183	0.176
9	**0.273**	0.241	0.239	0.128	0.137	0.163	0.183	0.188
10	**0.323**	0.292	0.276	0.165	0.174	0.175	0.197	0.231

Table 4 shows the two-tailed p values of t-tests, where a blank cell indicates a comparison with itself, or a duplicate comparison. The general trends indicated by the tests are discussed next.

There are statistical significances between the precisions of our methods which use the WordNet method to compare terms and the two baseline methods, because the p values are all smaller than 0.05. However, there are no statistical significances within these three methods, because the p values are close to 1. For example, the p value between *WordNet+minS3* and *WordNet+avgS3* is 0.874. We also find that our methods which use different ways to compare terms are almost statistically significant.

Table 5 shows the performances of the proposed methods and two baseline methods, using recall for evaluation. It also details the recall for each method at different k. We can find similar phenomenon to that of the precision. Using the WordNet method to compare terms can get a better recall score than using the word2vec method. Especially, the three methods *WordNet+minS3*, *Word-Net+avgS3* and *WordNet+maxS3* significantly improve the recall when $k \geq 9$. And unfortunately, using the word2vec method to compare terms cannot make

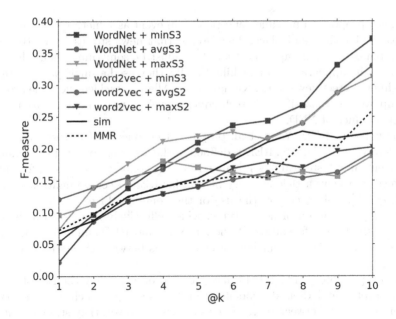

Fig. 1. Performance evaluated by F-measure.

any improvement in recall, compared to either the baseline method *sim* or the baseline method *MMR*.

To consider both the precision and the recall, we employ F-measure, one of the other traditional evaluation metrics in information retrieval, for evaluation. It can be interpreted as a weighted harmonic mean of the precision and the recall, where an F-measure score reaches its best value at 1 and worst at 0. Figure 1 shows the performance of our proposed methods and the two baseline methods, evaluated by F-measure. From this figure, we can point out that almost all methods using WordNet for term comparison, except for *WordNet+minS3* when $k = 1$, outperform both of the two baseline methods *sim* and *MMR*. However, when using the word2vec model to compare terms, the performance turns to be bad. Only the method *word2vec+minS3* performs better than both *sim* and *MMR* when $k \leq 5$.

To conclude, compared to the two baseline methods only considering similarity, our proposed methods employing WordNet for term comparison can significantly improve both precision and recall. Besides, we also get a big increase in F-measure. These findings illustrate the importance of coordinate relationship to find similar but different documents.

6   Related Work

Allan et al. introduced the concept of new event detection (NED) [1]. NED identifies news stories that discuss an event that has not been reported in the past. They proposed a possible definition of an event as something that happens at a particular time and place. They found that news stories about the same event often occur in clumps, and that there must be something about the story that makes its appearance worthwhile. Finally, they used a single pass clustering algorithm to detect new events. Kumaran and Allan [8] tackled the same problem and employed text classification techniques as well as named entities to improve the performance of NED.

Compared to NED, Yang et al. proposed the concept of retrospective news event detection (RED) [19]. RED is defined as the discovery of previously unidentified events in a historical news corpus. Both the contents and time information contained in a news article are very helpful for RED. Because multiple studies, including [19], only focus on the use of the contents, Li et al. [9] considered a better representation of news events, which effectively models both the contents and the time information. Although NED and RED can detect and track news events in some way, but lack of connections between events to show their relationships.

Several previous works [5, 6, 14] have studied on capturing the rich structure of news events and their dependencies on a news topic, such as causality or temporal-ordering between pairs of news events. However, they still concentrate on the development of a single news event and do not consider relationships (between news articles) across different news events.

Ohshima et al. [16] introduced methods of searching Web pages that are similar in theme but have different content from the given sample pages. This is similar to our objective to find similar but different documents. However, the methods were implemented by computing the "common" and "unique" feature vectors of the given sample pages, which requires at least two sample pages as the input, while we aim at finding similar but different documents from a single document that indicated by users.

7   Conclusion

We propose a method to find similar but different documents of a user-given one. Especially, we target at documents with the same topic as that of the given document, but describing different events or concepts. To accomplish this goal, we introduce the concept of "coordinate relationship" between documents. Experimental results verify the effectiveness of our method and illustrate the importance of coordinate relationship to find similar but different documents.

Acknowledgment. This work was supported in part by the following projects: Grants-in-Aid for Scientific Research (Nos. 16H02906, 15H01718 and 24680008) from MEXT of Japan.

References

1. Allan, J., Papka, R., Lavrenko, V.: On-line new event detection and tracking. In: Proceedings of SIGIR, pp. 37–45 (1998)
2. Bao, S., Xue, G., Wu, X., Yu, Y., Fei, B., Su, Z.: Optimizing web search using social annotations. In: Proceedings of the 16th International Conference on World Wide Web, WWW 2007, pp. 501–510 (2007)
3. Carbonell, J., Goldstein, J.: The use of MMR, diversity-based reranking for reordering documents and producing summaries. In: Proceedings of SIGIR, pp. 335–336 (1998)
4. Erkan, G., Radev, D.R.: Lexrank: graph-based lexical centrality as salience in text summarization. J. Artif. Intell. Res. **22**, 457–479 (2004)
5. Feng, A., Allan, J.: Finding and linking incidents in news. In: Proceedings of CIKM, pp. 821–830 (2007)
6. Feng, A., Allan, J.: Incident threading for news passages. In: Proceedings of CIKM, pp. 1307–1316 (2009)
7. Haveliwala, T.H.: Topic-sensitive pagerank: a context-sensitive ranking algorithm for web search. IEEE Trans. Knowl. Data Eng. **15**(4), 784–796 (2003)
8. Kumaran, G., Allan, J.: Text classification and named entities for new event detection. In: Proceedings of SIGIR, pp. 297–304 (2004)
9. Li, Z., Wang, B., Li, M., Ma, W.Y.: A probabilistic model for retrospective news event detection. In: Proceedings of SIGIR, pp. 106–113 (2005)
10. Mihalcea, R., Tarau, P.: Textrank: bringing order into texts. Proc. EMNLP **2004**, 404–411 (2004)
11. Mikolov, T., Chen, K., Corrado, G., Dean, J.: Efficient estimation of word representations in vector space. In: Proceedings of ICLR Workshop (2013)
12. Mikolov, T., Sutskever, I., Chen, K., Corrado, G.S., Dean, J.: Distributed representations of words and phrases and their compositionality. In: NIPS, pp. 3111–3119 (2013)
13. Miller, G.A.: Wordnet: a lexical database for english. Commun. ACM **38**(11), 39–41 (1995)
14. Nallapati, R., Feng, A., Peng, F., Allan, J.: Event threading within news topics. In: Proceedings of CIKM, pp. 446–453 (2004)
15. Ohshima, H., Oyama, S., Tanaka, K.: Searching coordinate terms with their context from the web. In: Aberer, K., Peng, Z., Rundensteiner, E.A., Zhang, Y., Li, X. (eds.) WISE 2006. LNCS, vol. 4255, pp. 40–47. Springer, Heidelberg (2006). doi:10.1007/11912873_7
16. Ohshima, H., Oyama, S., Tanaka, K.: Sibling page search by page examples. In: International Conference on Asian Digital Libraries, pp. 91–100 (2006)
17. Salton, G., Wong, A., Yang, C.S.: A vector space model for automatic indexing. Commun. ACM **18**(11), 613–620 (1975)
18. Snow, R., Jurafsky, D., Ng, A.Y.: Semantic taxonomy induction from heterogenous evidence. In: Proceedings of the 21st International Conference on Computational Linguistics and the 44th Annual Meeting of the Association for Computational Linguistics, ACL '44, pp. 801–808 (2006)
19. Yang, Y., Pierce, T., Carbonell, J.: A study of retrospective and on-line event detection. In: Proceedings of SIGIR, pp. 28–36 (1998)

Information Extraction and Analysis

Rule-Based Page Segmentation for Palm Leaf Manuscript on Color Image

Papangkorn Inkeaw[1], Jakramate Bootkrajang[1], Phasit Charoenkwan[2], Sanparith Marukatat[3], Shinn-Ying Ho[4], and Jeerayut Chaijaruwanich[1(✉)]

[1] Department of Computer Science, Faculty of Science,
Chiang Mai University, Chiang Mai, Thailand
{papangkorn_i,jakramate.b,jeerayut.c}@cmu.ac.th
[2] College of Arts, Media and Technology, Chiang Mai University,
Chiang Mai, Thailand
ple@dr.com
[3] National Electronics and Computer Technology Center, Pathum Thani, Thailand
sanparith.marukatat@nectec.or.th
[4] Institute of Bioinformatics and Systems Biology,
National Chiao Tung University, Hsinchu, Taiwan
syho@mail.nctu.edu.tw

Abstract. Palm leaf manuscripts are important source of history and ancient wisdom. Large number of manuscripts have been already digitized in the form of folio images. To extract useful information, an optical character recognition (OCR) is often considered to be the first step towards text mining. Unfortunately, folio images contain multiple unsegmented palm leaf images, making it difficult to manage in OCR process. This motivates us to propose a new page segmentation method for palm leaf manuscripts. This method consists of two main steps, first of which is the detection of objects in folio images using Connected Component Labeling method in a transformed L*a*b* color space. The second step is rule-based selection of objects as either palm leaf or not palm leaf. The experiments performed on 20 publicly available palm leaf manuscripts composed of 384 folio images demonstrated that the proposed method effectively segmented folio images into separate palm leaf images, with 99.86 % precision and 96.67 % recall scores.

Keywords: Palm leaf manuscripts · Page segmentation · L*a*b* Color Space · Rule-based selection

1 Introduction

Palm leaf manuscript is a document made from dried palm leaves (see examples in Fig. 1). Palm leaves were primarily used as writing material in South Asia and South-East Asia in ancient times. The manuscripts are an important source of religion, history and ancient wisdom. During the last hundred years, the manuscripts have been damaged. Many organizations have since started to

© Springer International Publishing AG 2016
A. Morishima et al. (Eds.): ICADL 2016, LNCS 10075, pp. 127–136, 2016.
DOI: 10.1007/978-3-319-49304-6_16

survey manuscripts in local communities in order to preserve and to archive these manuscripts. A lot of valuable manuscripts had been recovered, especially in Lao, Burma, Sri Lanka, India and Thailand. At the beginning, palm leaf manuscripts were archived using a microfilm. Once the digital camera was invented, the microfilm was replaced by digital photographs.

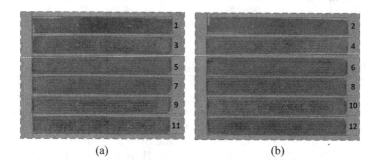

Fig. 1. Examples of a folio image of a palm leaf manuscript. (a) a folio image contains odd page number of palm leafs. (b) a folio image contains even page number of the same palm leafs in (a)

Page ordering of palm leaf manuscript is similar to that in modern books. A palm leaf contains two pages of content. One page is on one side of the leaf and the consecutive page is on the other side of the same leaf. To reduce the cost of digitizing these manuscripts, several palm leaves were put into a single image, called a folio. It is then impossible to put two pages from the same palm leaf in the same folio. As shown in Fig. 1), odd pages are in folio (a) while even pages are in folio (b).

The way the folio was constructed have been shown to greatly impacts the automated processing of the digitized manuscripts. For example, a typical Optical Character Recognition (OCR) system would fail to correctly operate on the folio compared to the case when a single palm leaf image was given as an input to the system [1,2].

Due to the problem, each palm leaf image has to be segmented from the folio. Separated page images can be passed to the OCR system. In addition, the segmented images can later be reordered to provide user-friendly archives to readers. To date, much of the efforts have been made to manually segment the palm leaf images. Although it is the straightforward approach to complete the task, manual segmentation turns out to be too laborious. And this motivated us to develop a new algorithm to automatically segment the palm leaf images from a folio image.

In document image analysis, page segmentation is a task of separating an input image into homogeneous components e.g., group of text blocks or group of figures [3]. In this context, a folio image can be considered as a page with highly overlapping layout and palm leaf images in that folio are components that need to be singled out. As shown in Fig. 1), dashed border rectangle is considered as a layout of picture while solid border rectangles are considered as a component contained in the picture layout. The reason that a folio exhibits overlapping layout is because there is no clear distinction between the foreground which is the actual palm leaf and the background of the folio. There are several page segmentation methods developed for pages with overlapping layout both in unsupervised and supervised manner [3]. In this work, the unsupervised segmentation approach was adopted. The advantage of the unsupervised method is that there is no need for a labeled training set, which is costly to obtain. One of the unsupervised methods for page segmentation was proposed by Jain and Bhattacharjee [4]. The method employs eight Gabor filters with two radial frequencies namely $32\sqrt{2}$ and $64\sqrt{2}$ in each of the four directions: $0°$, $45°$, $90°$ and $135°$. Eight filtered images are generated using these filters and are then used as features vectors for each pixel. A clustering algorithm was later applied to cluster all pixels into 3 clusters namely, uniform regions, boundaries of uniform regions and text regions. Another work presented by Acharyya and Kundu [5] applied 2D M-band wavelet to generate feature vector for each pixel. The k-mean clustering algorithm was then used to cluster all pixels into two groups corresponding to text and uniform region.

Despite competitive results reported by the authors, the two methods are not directly applicable to our problem. Partly because both methods operate on gray image, while most of the available palm leaf folio images are in color. Discarding color information in palm leaf image might affect the segmentation performance. In addition, the characteristics of the folio being considered namely image contrast, background color, occlusion and gap between palm leaves image cannot be addressed using existing algorithms adequately. Motivated by the fact that many color-based image segmentation methods [6–8] achieved high performance by processing on an L*a*b* color space. It is then interesting to apply their idea to our page segmentation problem. Further, by incorporating prior knowledge on the shape and size of the palm leaf pages to be segmented, we expect to get even better segmentation results.

In this work, we propose an automatic method for segmenting palm leaf on color image. The proposed method consists of two major steps namely object detection and object selection. In the object detection step, the folio is transformed into L*a*b* color space [9]. The k-mean clustering algorithm is then applied to cluster all the pixels, which are now represented by a* and b*, into k groups. By using cluster number as a label, objects can then be detected via the Connected Component Labeling algorithm. In object selection step, a rule-based selector was constructed under the assumptions about the shape and the size of the palm leaves. The selector is expected to identify palm leaves from all objects by considering objects rectangularity [10], objects width and objects height. Once the selection is completed, the boundary of each palm leaf can be drawn, and palm leaf images can be segmented out from the folio image.

We evaluate the effectiveness of the proposed method on nine real-world datasets. The results showed that the proposed method achieved better precision

Table 1. The nine different characteristics of folio images on each dataset.

Dataset	Characteristics				Number of pages
	Image contrast	Background color	Occlusion	Gap between leafs	
I	High (≈3.27)	Uniform	No	High (≈0.05)	154
II	Low (≈1.89)	Uniform	Yes	High (≈0.03)	32
III	High (≈3.06)	Non-uniform	Yes	High (≈0.03)	158
IV	High (≈3.19)	Non-uniform	No	High (≈0.02)	609
V	High (≈3.10)	Non-uniform	No	Low (≈0.00)	355
VI	Low (≈1.97)	Non-uniform	Yes	Low (≈0.01)	546
VII	High (≈4.44)	Non-uniform	Yes	Low (≈0.01)	182
VIII	Low (≈1.98)	Uniform	No	High (≈0.02)	17
IX	High (≈4.77)	Uniform	Yes	High (≈0.02)	76

and recall scores compared to existing page segmentation algorithms presented in [4] and [5].

The rest of the paper are organized as follows. Section 2 describes how the folio images were produced. The description of materials that we used in this work and the details of our proposed method are presented in Sect. 3. Section 4 demonstrates the effectiveness of our proposed method while Sect. 5 concludes the study.

2   Materials

In this section we will describe a general procedure for obtaining a palm leafs manuscript folio. A folio image containing multiple of palm leafs was photographed by a specialized equipment. The equipment consists of three parts namely a background plate, a monopod and a digital camera. Line markers and labels might be put on the background plate. The line markers are used to control the alignment of palm leafs, while the labels were used to identify the title of the document, the volume as well as the page number. Unfortunately, during the process of digitization, the environment might not be properly controlled. This directly effects the quality of the folio images.

In this work, folio images were collected from five repositories namely Lanna manuscripts collection of Chiang Mai University [11], Digital Library of Lao Manuscripts [12], LACMA [13], Harvard Art Museums [14] and Old Mon Manual Script [15] resulting in 384 high resolutions (≥ 300 dpi) color images. Since the folio in each of the datasets were digitized in possibly different environment, i.e., different illumination, we have divided them into nine set of data based on four characteristics: image contrast, background color, occlusion and gap between two consecutive leafs. We categorize the datasets into high and low image contrast using the Global Contrast Factor (GCF) [16]. The datasets were categorized as high contrast if its GCF is more than 2.00. Next characteristic is the background color. The images which its background is irregular were

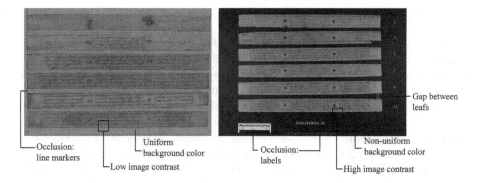

Fig. 2. Illustration of the four characteristics of folio images.

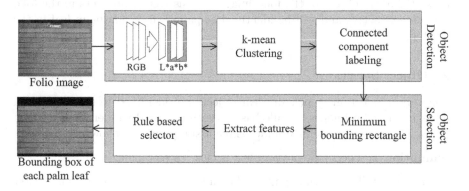

Fig. 3. The system flow of the proposed method.

classified to non-uniform background color, otherwise classified as uniform background color. Line markers and labels in the image is considered as occlusions. Lastly, a ratio of gap between two consecutive leafs to image height was calculated. The resulting value is used to categorize the dataset into high (the ratio exceeding 0.01) and low gap, otherwise. Table 1 summarizes the characteristics of folio images in each of the datasets considered, while Fig. 2 illustrates the four characteristics of folio images.

3   The Proposed Method

In this section, we describe a systematic method for segmenting palm leaf images from folio images. The proposed method contains two main steps namely object detection step and object selection step. The system flow of the proposed method is shown in Fig. 3. The details of the two steps are described as follows.

3.1 Object Detection

In object detection step, all objects in a folio image are detected. First, the image in RGB color space is transformed into L*a*b color space. The L*a*b* color space represents the color with respect to human visual sense. It composes of 3-axis color system with dimension L* for illumination and a* and b* for expressing color [9]. In order to avoid the effect of different illumination, only a* and b* are considered. All pixels represented by a* and b* are clustered into k groups. In this work, k-mean clustering was used. The value of parameter k depends on the variance of color in the image. In this work, we cluster pixels into two group, e.g. $k = 2$. Next, the labeled image I is generated by using cluster number as a label of a pixel (x, y). Then, the connected component labeling algorithm [17] is applied on the image I. Each connected component is represented as an object in the folio image. In this step, all objects in the folio image are extracted, and will be identified as palm leaf or non-palm leaf in the next step.

3.2 Object Selection

In the object selection step, palm leaf objects are identified from all detected objects in the folio images. A rule-based selector is used to identify palm leaf objects. The rules were defined under three assumptions as follows.

Assumption 1. The shape of palm leaf is close to rectangle.

Assumption 2. The width of palm leaf on a folio image is equal to or is greater than ϵ of the width of the folio image, where ϵ, which takes value between 0 and 1, is an expected ratio between the width of palm leaf and the width of folio image. The value of $\epsilon = 0.5$ translates to the situation where the width of palm leafs is more than a half of the width of the folio image.

Assumption 3. The height of all palm leafs in the same book is not significantly different.

The rectangularity of an object is calculated by using minimum bounding rectangle method [10]. The rectangularity takes a value between 0 and 1. The shape of an object is considered close to rectangle when its rectangularity is close to 1. To estimate the rectangularity of an object, a minimum bounding rectangle (MBR) is fitted to the object by minimizing the difference of area between the rectangle and the object. The rectangularity is the ratio of the area of the object to the area of its MBR. In addition, the width and height of MBR is taken as object's width and height, respectively.

As a consequence, an object O_i is identified as a palm leaf image in folio image F_j that is contained in collection M if it complies with the following three rules.

Rule 1. The rectangularity of O_i is equal to or more than the rectangularity threshold r, where $0 \leq r \leq 1$.

Table 2. The comparison of precision, recall and F-measure between three methods applied in each nine different characteristics of folio images.

Measurement	Precision			Recall			F-measure		
Method	RBPS	GF	WF	RBPS	GF	WF	RBPS	GF	WF
Dataset I	1.0000	0.8966	0.1930	1.0000	0.8125	0.3438	1.0000	0.8525	0.2472
Dataset II	0.9870	0.2843	0.0055	0.9870	0.1883	0.0065	0.9870	0.2266	0.0059
Dataset III	1.0000	0.4444	0.0581	1.0000	0.1519	0.1139	1.0000	0.2264	0.0769
Dataset IV	1.0000	0.6676	0.0339	1.0000	0.4049	0.0837	1.0000	0.5041	0.0483
Dataset V	1.0000	0.0851	0.0852	0.9831	0.0227	0.1690	0.9915	0.0359	0.1133
Dataset VI	1.0000	0.0000	0.4137	1.0000	0.0000	0.5842	1.0000	-	0.4844
Dataset VII	1.0000	0.0000	0.3943	1.0000	0.0000	0.5330	1.0000	-	0.4533
Dataset VIII	1.0000	0.6364	0.0000	1.0000	0.4118	0.0000	1.0000	0.5000	-
Dataset IX	1.0000	0.0000	0.0067	1.0000	0.0000	0.0132	1.0000	-	0.0088
Average	**0.9986**	0.3349	0.1323	**0.9967**	0.2213	0.2053	**0.9976**	0.3909	0.1798
SD	±0.004	±0.341	±0.165	±0.006	±0.276	±0.227	±0.004	±0.300	±0.191

RBPS = The proposed method, GF = The Gabor filters method presented in [4].
WF = The wavelet features method presented in [5].
Note, the F-measure cannot be calculated if precision and recall is equal to 0.

Rule 2. The width of O_i is equal or more than ϵ of the width of F_j, where $0 \le \epsilon \le 1$.

Rule 3. The height of O_i is between $\mu - \alpha \cdot \mu$ and $\mu + \alpha \cdot \mu$, where μ is the average height of all palm leafs on M, and α is the ratio of an acceptable deviation from μ. The value of α is between 0 and 1.

In this work, we used $r = 0.75$, $\epsilon = 0.75$, and $\alpha = 0.33$. These parameters were optimized among multiple evaluation.

4   Experimental Results

In this section we present the segmentation results from a battery of datasets described in Sect. 2. All samples in each dataset were used to evaluate the proposed method. We also compare the proposed method to the methods based on Gabor filtering and Wavelet features presented in [4] and [5], respectively. Table 2 summarizes the segmentation performances in terms of precision, recall and F-measure [18]. These measurements were defined as follows:

$$precision = \frac{|\{retrieved\ palm\ leaf\ objects\}|}{|\{totally\ retrieved\ objects\}|} \qquad (1)$$

$$recall = \frac{|\{retrieved\ palm\ leaf\ objects\}|}{|\{actual\ palm\ leaf\ objects\}|} \qquad (2)$$

$$F - measure = 2 \cdot \frac{precision \cdot recall}{precision + recall} \qquad (3)$$

We can see from the results that the proposed method achieved the highest possible precision score on 8 out of 9 datasets tested. The precision score of 1.0 indicates that the proposed algorithm achieves perfect segmentation, it did not mistakenly identify non-palm leaf objects as palm leaf.

We continue to demonstrate the sensitivity of the proposed method as measured by recall score. It is worth mentioning that, the performance of the proposed method on Dataset II and Dataset V are slightly lower. This is because both of the datasets are more challenging. Indeed, Dataset II is composed of extremely low contrast images while the gap between two palm leafs in Dataset V is very tight. Since the precision and recall score cannot be used to compare the performance of any different methods. The F-measure was calculated in order to compare the performance of the proposed method to the two competing algorithms. The results show that our algorithm still outperformed the two competing algorithms on these datasets. The two methods under comparison cannot deal with the low contrast image and non-uniform background color well. In addition, occlusion on image and small gap between palm leafs also caused the two methods to misidentify the actual palm leaf.

Apart from performance measurements, it is also interesting to see the actual outcome of the algorithm. Figure 4 illustrates an example of the results obtained from object detection step (Fig. 4(b)) and object selection step (Fig. 4(c)). A working system of the proposed method is available at http://202.28.248.55: 5001. The system does not only accurately segment palm leaf images from folio images but also automatically put palm leaf pages into correct order. The system is currently being used by Lanna palm leaf manuscripts preservation group of Chiang Mai university, Thailand.

Overall, based on the empirical evidences we can conclude that the proposed framework is an effective method for segmenting palm leaf images from folio images.

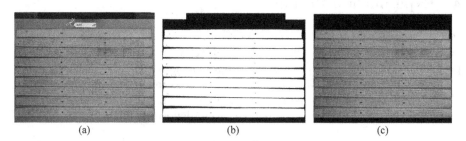

(a)   (b)   (c)

Fig. 4. A result image produced by the proposed method in each step. (a) An folio image. (b) The result of object detection step. (c) The result of object selection step.

5   Conclusions

We presented a method for segmenting palm leafs from folio images. The proposed method contains two major steps namely object detection step and object selection step. In object detection step, a* and b* dimensions on L*a*b* color space of the folio images were extracted and were used to represent a pixel of the folio image. The k-mean clustering algorithm was then applied to cluster all pixels into two group in order to label each pixel on the color image. The connected component labeling algorithm is then applied to detect objects in the labeled image. In object selection step, a rule-based selector was constructed under the assumptions about the shape and the size of a palm leaf. The selector was then used to single out palm leaf objects from all objects detected in the first phase. The experimental results show that the proposed method achieved highest average precision and recall scores of 99.86 % and 99.67 %, respectively. It also provided highest F- measure compared to the Gabor filters method and the method using wavelet features.

Acknowledgments. This study was funded under the Royal Golden Jubilee Ph.D. Program by the Thailand Research Fund. We would like to thank Faculty of Science and Lan na Studies, Chiang Mai University, Thailand, for financial support and collection of digital Lanna archives, respectively.

References

1. Inkeaw, P., Chueaphun, C., Chaijaruwanich, J., Klomsae, A., Marukatat, S., (eds.): Lanna dharma handwritten character recognition on palm leaves manuscript based on wavelet transform. In: IEEE International Conference on Signal and Image Processing Applications (ICSIPA); 19–21 Oct.; Kuala Lumpur, Malaysia (2015)
2. Thammano, A., Pravesjit, S.: Recognition of archaic Lanna handwritten manuscripts using a hybrid bio-inspired algorithm. Memetic Comput. **7**(1), 3–17 (2015)
3. Doermann, D., Tombre, K.: Handbook of Document Image Processing, Recognition. Springer, Heidelberg (2014)
4. Jain, A.K., Bhattacharje, S.: Text segmentation using gabor filters for automatic document processing. Mach. Vis. Appl. **5**(3), 169–184 (1992)
5. Acharyya, M., Kundu, M.K.: Document image segmentation using wavelet scale-space features. IEEE Transactions on Circuits and Systems for Video Technology. **12**(12), 1117–1127 (2002)
6. Baldevbhai, P.J., Anand, R.S.: Color image segmentation for medical images using L*a*b* color space. IOSR J. Electron. Commun. Eng. **1**(2), 24–45 (2012)
7. Recky, M., Leberl, F., (eds.): Windows detection using K-means in CIE-lab color space. In: 2010 20th International Conference on Pattern Recognition (ICPR), 2010 23–26, August 2010
8. Zhang, Q., Chi, Y., He, N.: Color image segmentation based on a modified k-means algorithm. In: Proceedings of the 7th International Conference on Internet Multimedia Computing, Service; Zhangjiajie, Hunan, China. 2808538: Observation of strains. Infect Dis Ther. 3(1), 35–43. ACM (2015). pp. 1–4 (2011)
9. Fairchild, M.D.: Color appearance models. Wiley, United Kingdom (2013)
10. Rosin, L.P.: Measuring rectangularity. Mach. Vis. Appl. **11**(4), 191–196 (1999)
11. The collection of Lanna Manuscripts [Internet]. Chiang Mai University (2015). http://library.cmu.ac.th/lanna_ebook/
12. Digital Library of Lao Manuscripts [Internet]. National Library of Laos (2009). http://www.laomanuscripts.net/

13. The Collections of Palm Leaf Manuscripts [Internet]. Los Angeles County Museum of Art. http://www.lacma.org/

14. The collections of palm-leaf manuscripts [Internet]. Harvard Art Museums. http://www.harvardartmuseums.org/

15. Old Mon Palm Leaf Manuscripts Collections [Internet]. Mon Language. http://www.monlanguage.net/

16. Matkovi, K., Neumann, L., Neumann, A., Psik, T., Purgathofer, W.: Global contrast factor - a new approach to image contrast. In: Proceedings of the First Eurographics Conference on Computational Aesthetics in Graphics, Visualization, Imaging; Girona, Spain. 2381242: Observation of strains. Infect Dis Ther. 3(1), 35–43: Eurographics Association; 2005. pp. 159–67 (2011)

17. Samet, H., Tamminen, M.: Efficient component labeling of images of arbitrary dimension represented by linear bintrees. IEEE Trans. Pattern Anal. Mach. Intell. **10**(4), 79–86 (1988). doi:10.1109/34.3918

18. Baeza-Yates, R.A., Ribeiro-Neto, B.: Modern Information Retrieval. Addison-Wesley Longman Publishing Co. Inc., United States (1999)

Exploiting Synonymy and Hypernymy
to Learn Efficient Meaning Representations

Thomas Perianin[1,3(✉)], Hajime Senuma[2], and Akiko Aizawa[2,3]

[1] Université Pierre et Marie Curie, Paris, France
thomas.perianin@gmail.com
[2] The University of Tokyo, Bunkyo, Tokyo, Japan
{senuma,aizawa}@nii.ac.jp
[3] National Institute of Informatics, Chiyoda, Tokyo, Japan

Abstract. Word representation learning methods such as word2vec usually associate one vector per word; however, in order to face polysemy problems, it's important to produce distributed representations for each meaning, not for each surface form of a word. In this paper, we propose an extension for the existing AutoExtend model, an auto-encoder architecture that utilises synonymy relations to learn sense representations. We introduce a new layer in the architecture to exploit hypernymy relations predominantly present in existing ontologies. We evaluate the quality of the obtained vectors on word-sense disambiguation tasks and show that the use of the hypernymy relation leads to improvements of 1.2 % accuracy on Senseval-3 and 0.8 % on Semeval-2007 English lexical sample tasks, compared to the original model.

Keywords: Sense embedding · Semantic relation · Auto-encoder · Hypernymy · Word-sense disambiguation

1 Introduction

1.1 Distributed Representations

Distributed representations for words, or word embeddings, are often used as inputs of machine learning systems for a wide range of Natural Language Processing (NLP) applications, such as sentiment classification [11] or machine translation [1]. It is however possible to learn vector representations for different linguistic units like senses or morphemes [8].

Embeddings are generally real vectors containing semantic information. For example, the Skip-Gram and CBOW models (word2vec) [4] are able to capture underlying semantic relations from big text corpora and encode them into word representations.

This work was supported by JSPS KAKENHI Grants Number 15H02754 and 16K12546.

A. Morishima et al. (Eds.): ICADL 2016, LNCS 10075, pp. 137–143, 2016.
DOI: 10.1007/978-3-319-49304-6_17

1.2   Semantic Knowledge

While many existing methods produce embeddings using only text corpora, it's also possible to incorporate ontological information within a learning system. Knowledge graphs such as WordNet [5] have shown to enhance the quality of word vectors [12].

Rothe and Schütze (2015) [10] propose AutoExtend, an auto-encoder that relies mainly on the synonymy relations present in WordNet to learn embeddings for synsets and lexemes. In WordNet, a *synset* is a group of synonyms that form a sense unit; each word is defined as a set of meanings. A *lexeme* represents an association between a word and one of the synsets to which it belongs.

In AutoExtend, a neural network containing lexemes and synsets layers is built, while the synonymy relations are utilised to configure links between each layer. Other semantic relations, such as hypernymy and antonymy are considered to define a similarity constraint added to the objective function for the neural network optimisation. Their parameter analysis shows that this constraint doesn't have much impact on the quality of synsets embeddings for WSD tasks.

However, while synsets constitute the main structure of WordNet, hypernymy is the most frequent relation beetween synsets. Around 42 % of the synsets in Wordnet are linked to one or more hyponyms. Because of its importance, we investigate in this paper how to use this relation to learn embeddings by additive composition instead of similarity constraint.

1.3   Motivation and Contribution

We show that we can modify the AutoExtend model to take different semantic relations into consideration. More generally, our goal is to prove that we can exploit several relations by introducing additional layers to the neural network. Our model is a direct extension of their work, utilising the hypernymy relation to define the link configuration of the network. By doing so, we impose more constraints on the trained vector that reflects hypernymy defined in Wordnet.

Comparing the embeddings obtained by the enhanced and the original AutoExtend models, we show that the synsets embeddings learned using the hypernymy relation are more efficient for the English lexical sample WSD tasks of Senseval-3 [3] and Semeval-2007 [7].

2   Related Work

Although the problem of polysemous words is present in many usual NLP tasks, the literature about representations for word senses is recent.

Reisinger and Mooney (2010) [9] first propose a clustering method: they represent all occurrences of words by vectors of their co-occurrences in some window, and then cluster all vectors for a word to obtain meaning representations.

Jauhar et al. (2015) [2] propose a probabilistic approach by building a Markov network containing words linked to their different senses. They also develop an adaptation of the Skip-Gram model from word2vec, as Neelakantan et al. (2015) [6] to learn meaning embeddings. There is a similar approach in the work of Qiu et al.(2014) [8], who adapt the CBOW model to learn morphemes embeddings by extracting morphemes from context words and using them to infer the morpheme from the targeted word.

3   Proposed Model

3.1   Architecture

We refer to words as $w_i \in \mathbb{R}^d$, lexemes as $l_{i,j} \in \mathbb{R}^d$, synsets as $s_j \in \mathbb{R}^d$, and hypernyms as $h_j \in \mathbb{R}^d$ for $i = 1, ..., W$ and $j = 1, ..., S$ where d, W, $S \in \mathbb{N}$. In our experiments, $d = 300$.

The first two layers are identical to the AutoExtend model: we view a lexeme as a multiplication of its word vector and a synset as the sum of its lexemes. Namely,

$$l_{ij} = \theta_{i,j} \circ w_i \quad and \quad s_j = \sum_i l_{i,j} \,, \tag{1}$$

where $\circ$ denotes the pointwise multiplication and $\theta_{ij} \in \mathbb{R}^d$.

Our contribution is the introduction of a new layer of representations, linking each synset embedding with its hypernyms; we view hypernyms as the sum of their hyponyms. With $\gamma_{i,j} \in \mathbb{R}^d$, let

$$h_j = \sum_{i \in hypo(j)} \gamma_{i,j} \circ s_i \,. \tag{2}$$

A decoding part of the model is defined in an identical way. The final architecture of the auto-encoder is shown in Fig. 1.

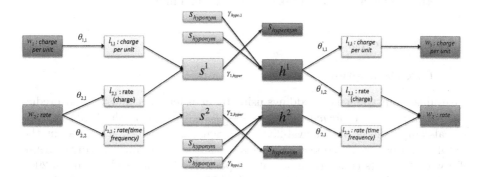

Fig. 1. Subgraph of the model architecture for the words *rate* and *charge per unit*.

We experiment two versions of our model: in the first *SimpleAdd* model, the synsets are simple sums of their hyponyms, which means that $\forall i, j, d, \gamma_{i,j}^d = 1$

and that $\gamma_{i,j}^d$ is never updated during training. In the second *WeightedAdd* model, the weights are updated. The idea is to investigate a model where hypernyms are weighted sums of their hyponyms.

3.2   Normalisation

As a word is viewed as the sum of its lexemes and an hypernym as the sum of its hyponyms, we define the following normalisation constraints:

$$\sum_j \theta_{i,j}^d = 1, \ \forall i, \ d \quad and \quad \sum_j \gamma_{i,j}^d = 1, \ \forall i, \ d \ . \tag{3}$$

We normalise the weights for a given word and a given hypernym at each iteration and proceed to experiments with and without this option.

3.3   Ressources and Complexity

We use the 49,700 hypernymy links between synsets provided by WordNet 3.0, and the word2vec vectors from the CBOW model as inputs. The corpus provides 300-dimensional vectors for 3 millions words and sentences, and WordNet indexes 117k synsets. The intersection between these two corpora gives us a total of 54k word inputs.

The transformation from one representation to another is basically a pointwise multiplication, unlike in usual neural networks where projections are products between vectors and full matrices of parameters. This choice is justified by technical reasons: otherwise, the size of the model would make the training extremely difficult to implement. The total number of parameters would be multiplied by d, while the gradient weight is already around 10 gigabytes.

We use the algorithm of batch gradient descent to train our models. Depending on the model, an iteration takes about 40 s to 1 min.

4   Experiments

4.1   Task Description

We evaluate our trained embeddings using them as features, and by their predictive performance ($Accuracy = \frac{true\ positive + true\ negative}{total}$) on the WSD english-lexical-sample tasks of Semeval-2007 and Senseval-3, which was used in the AutoExtend paper. The objective of this tasks is to determine the correct sense of a word given its context, among all its possible meanings. The Semeval-2007 datasets contains respectively 22,274 and 8,022 training samples, and 4,849 and 3,944 testing samples, all provided with context, for 158 different words. The training samples are words with already disambiguated lemmas in context, and contexts are given by surrounding words.

4.2   Sense Disambiguation

We adopt a supervised learning strategy and use a framework for english WSD presented in [13] to train a support vector machine (SVM) for each lemma in the dataset and predict its correct sense.

We use our embeddings to compute the cosine distance between each meaning representation of a targeted word and the centroid vector of its context. Sense vectors are obtained from the hypernyms layer of our model while the centroid is simply the addition of all the word2vec representations of its words. The resulting cosine distances are used as inputs features for the SVM.

4.3   Quantitative Analysis

We also investigate a word2vec baseline in order to show that the improvements are not only due to the information encoded in the word2vec vectors. We follow Rothe and Schütze (2015) and compute a synset representation as the sum of the word2vec representations of its words.

Table 1. Results on Senseval-3 and Semeval-2007

	Senseval-2007	Senseval-3
Word2vec	80.92	58.75
AutoExtend	80.94	61.05
WeightedAdd	80	58.22
WeightedAdd + norm	81.38	61.31
SimpleAdd	81.21	61.56
SimpleAdd + norm	**81.72**	**62.22**

The experimental results in Table 1 show that the SimpleAdd model with simple addition show better performance on both datasets. The WeightedAdd shows inferior results because of overfitting; the normalization feature helps to prevent this as the weights are constantly re-normalised and shows improvements for both models. The accuracy ameliorations of around 1 % are small but correspond to a gain of around 40 well classified examples for each dataset.

4.4   Discussion

We show that adding a layer of representations allows us to encode semantic knowledge via additive composition, and that the hypernymy relation improves the WSD accuracy. For example, the disambiguation of the word *rate* in the Semeval-7 dataset was successfully performed because of this extra knowledge. Moreover, the difference between the two models suggests that a simple additive composition performs better than a weighted additive composition.

5   Conclusion and Future Work

We extended the model from Rothe and Schütze (2015) [10] by adding an additional layer corresponding to the hypernymy relation present in the WordNet Corpus. We show that providing the hypernymy information in that way can improve the quality of embeddings for the task of Word-Sense Disambiguation.

A further work is to extend the idea to any many-to-one synset relation, such as meronymy in WordNet. Such relation could be used to define a new layer, which could be added in the current model.

However, the small size of the datasets only allows us to evaluate a few embeddings compared to the large amount that we produce; we learn over 100k meaning representations and only evaluate around 1.217 for Semeval-2007 and 558 for Senseval-3. To develop a method for more comprehensive evaluation is also left for future study.

References

1. Devlin, J., Zbib, R., Huang, Z., Lamar, T., Schwartz, R.M., Makhoul, J.: Fast and robust neural network joint models for statistical machine translation. In: ACL (1), pp. 1370–1380. Citeseer (2014)
2. Jauhar, S.K., Dyer, C., Hovy, E.: Ontologically grounded multi-sense representation learning for semantic vector space models. In: Proceedings NAACL, vol. 1 (2015)
3. Mihalcea, R., Chklovski, T.A., Kilgarriff, A.: The senseval-3 english lexical sample task. In: Association for Computational Linguistics (2004)
4. Mikolov, T., Sutskever, I., Chen, K., Corrado, G.S., Dean, J.: Distributed representations of words and phrases and their compositionality. In: Advances in neural information processing systems, pp. 3111–3119 (2013)
5. Miller, G.A.: WORDNET: A lexical database for english. In: Human Language Technology, Proceedings of a Workshop held at Plainsboro, New Jerey, USA, March 8–11, 1994. http://acl.ldc.upenn.edu/H/H94/H94-1111.pdf
6. Neelakantan, A., Shankar, J., Passos, A., McCallum, A.: Efficient non-parametric estimation of multiple embeddings per word in vector space (2015). arXiv preprint: arXiv:1504.06654
7. Pradhan, S.S., Loper, E., Dligach, D., Palmer, M.: Semeval-2007 task 17: English lexical sample, srl and all words. In: Proceedings of the 4th International Workshop on Semantic Evaluations, pp. 87–92. ACL (2007)
8. Qiu, S., Cui, Q., Bian, J., Gao, B., Liu, T.Y.: Co-learning of word representations and morpheme representations. In: COLING, pp. 141–150 (2014)
9. Reisinger, J., Mooney, R.J.: Multi-prototype vector-space models of word meaning. In: Human Language Technologies: The 2010 Annual Conference of the North American Chapter of the Association for Computational Linguistics, pp. 109–117. Association for Computational Linguistics (2010)
10. Rothe, S., Schütze, H.: Autoextend: Extending word embeddings to embeddings for synsets and lexemes. In: Proceedings of the ACL (2015)
11. Turney, P.D., Littman, M.L.: Measuring praise and criticism: Inference of semantic orientation from association. ACM Trans. Inf. Syst. **21**(4), 315–346 (2003). http://doi.acm.org/10.1145/944012.944013

12. Xu, C., Bai, Y., Bian, J., Gao, B., Wang, G., Liu, X., Liu, T.Y.: Rc-net: A general framework for incorporating knowledge into word representations. In: Proceedings of the 23rd ACM International Conference on Conference on Information and Knowledge Management, pp. 1219–1228. ACM (2014)

13. Zhong, Z., Ng, H.T.: It makes sense: A wide-coverage word sense disambiguation system for free text. In: Proceedings of the ACL 2010 System Demonstrations, pp. 78–83. Association for Computational Linguistics (2010)

Entity Linking for Mathematical Expressions in Scientific Documents

Giovanni Yoko Kristianto[1]([✉]), Goran Topić[2], and Akiko Aizawa[1,2]

[1] The University of Tokyo, Bunkyo, Tokyo, Japan
giovanni@nii.ac.jp
[2] National Institute of Informatics, Chiyoda, Tokyo, Japan
{goran_topic,aizawa}@nii.ac.jp

Abstract. This paper addresses the challenge of determining the identity of math expressions in scientific documents by linking these expressions to their corresponding Wikipedia articles. Math expressions are frequently used to denote important concepts in scientific documents, yet several of them, for example, famous equations, often have minimal explanation in the documents. This task will allow us to obtain an additional explanation from Wikipedia regarding these math expressions. This paper proposes an approach to this challenge, where the structures and surrounding text of math expressions are used for math entity linking. Our initial evaluation shows that a balanced combination of math structures and textual descriptions is required to obtain reliable linking performance.

Keywords: Knowledge acquisition · Math entity linking · Math expression similarity · Wikification

1 Introduction

Entity linking is the task of linking entity mentions in text to corresponding entities in a knowledge base. One variant of entity linking is wikification [2, 3,5,6], which identifies a set of entity mentions in each document and then locates the most accurate mapping from mentions to Wikipedia articles. Current works on wikification have focused on natural language mentions, which are often expressed in the form of noun phrases. Such an approach, however, may not be sufficient for the wikification of scientific documents.

Important concepts in scientific documents are often found not only in the form of natural language text, but also mathematical expressions. Therefore, to *wikify* all important concepts in scientific documents, especially those from Science, Technology, Engineering, and Mathematics (STEM), we need to consider both forms. To the best of our knowledge, no study has attempted to wikify

This work was supported by JSPS Kakenhi Grant Number 14J09896, and CREST, JST.

A. Morishima et al. (Eds.): ICADL 2016, LNCS 10075, pp. 144–149, 2016.
DOI: 10.1007/978-3-319-49304-6_18

math expressions found in scientific documents. Hereinafter, we will refer to the task of wikifying math expressions as math entity linking (MEL).

The possible applications of MEL include computer-assisted learning, unsupervised concept graph generation [1], and document representation [7]. In the area of computer-assisted learning, MEL enables us to develop an educational application that can suggest supplementary information for math formulae unknown to a reader. In unsupervised concept graph generation, one of the challenges is to identify informative concepts in documents. We suggest that the important concepts in a scientific document are often denoted as math expressions, thus we can exploit math expressions to identify these concepts.

Because of their abstract notation, the semantics of mathematical expressions are often difficult to identify from their surface level representations. This makes their wikification particularly difficult for existing methods. In this paper, we propose using techniques developed for mathematical formula search to address the MEL challenge. The contributions of this paper are as follows:

– We introduce the novel challenge of MEL, that is, linking math expressions in scientific documents to corresponding Wikipedia articles.
– We propose an initial framework based on the combination of math and text similarity measures to address the MEL challenge.

2   Math Entity Linking Framework

Figure 1 shows an overview of our framework. The three main tasks performed in the framework are as follows: (i) detection of math expression mentions, (ii) candidate generation for each mention, and (iii) disambiguation of the candidates.

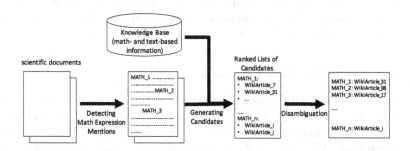

Fig. 1. Overview of math entity linking framework

2.1   Mention Detection

The first task in MEL is to identify math expressions in a given document that will be wikified. For instance, given a piece of text as displayed in Fig. 2, we extract the math formula $p(t_n, H_T, H_W) = \frac{P(t_n, t_{n-2}, t_{n-1})P(w_n, t_n)}{P(t_n)}$ and consider

... Note that the usual HMM tagging model is given by

$$p(t_n, H_T, H_W) = \frac{P(t_n, t_{n-2}, t_{n-1})P(w_n, t_n)}{P(t_n)}$$

which has the form of a maximum entropy model ...

Fig. 2. An example of a math mention in a document

it as the math mention to wikify. Additionally, we extract contextual information for each math mention, that is, noun phrases found in the paragraphs surrounding the mention (containing the paragraph together with one preceding and following paragraph). Each extracted noun phrase is accompanied by a proximity score (the closer the noun phrase to the mention, the higher this score), which as shown by [8] can be used to identify the noun phrase defining a math mention. Both the math mention and noun phrases are used as a query in the next candidate generation module.

2.2   Candidate Generation

The second task in MEL is to identify Wikipedia articles that correspond to each math mention. For each math mention, the second module outputs a ranked list of Wikipedia articles that contain math expressions similar to the query math mention. For this purpose, we encode the math expressions in both the query and Wikipedia articles. The similarity between math expressions is calculated using path-based and subtree-based math representation that were introduced by the math search system MCAT [4]. Additionally, we take into account the text similarity between the noun phrases surrounding the math mention and words in each Wikipedia article (title, summary, anchor text, weighted keywords [9], and text surrounding the math expressions found in the article). The scoring and ranking in our framework is based on the tf-idf similarity.

2.3   Disambiguation by Unification

The disambiguation module uses a unification technique to recalculate the scores of the selected candidate articles. Given two math expressions, we consider them unifiable if they become the same after substituting variables with other variables or constants. We use the SWI-Prolog[1] implementation for unification. The score recalculation in our current system uses a rather ad hoc approach, that is, if a Wikipedia article contains math expressions (or any of their subexpressions) that can be unified with the query math mention, we simply double the math similarity score of the article. Then, the disambiguation module selects the Wikipedia article with the highest similarity score as the final MEL result.

---

[1] http://www.swi-prolog.org/.

3 Preliminary Experiment

3.1 Dataset and Evaluation Method

In our preliminary evaluation of the proposed MEL framework, we used four papers from ACL Anthology[2]. From these papers, we extracted 46 math expressions that appeared in an equation-type environment (i.e., appeared on their own lines). We believe that such expressions are usually more important than in-line equations, each of which often consists of only a single identifier. As the ACL papers were originally in PDF format, we first converted them into XML format using InftyReader[3]. Then, we manually postedited the obtained MathML and extracted the 46 math expressions. Moreover, we used the Wikipedia dataset from NTCIR-12 MathIR-Wikipedia Task [10] as the knowledge base for this MEL task. The Wikipedia articles were initially in MediaWiki format. The NTCIR organizers extracted the math expressions by first converting the MediaWiki math templates to LaTeX and then converted them together with LaTeX formulae demarcated by < math > tags in the articles to MathML format using LaTeXML[4].

We applied our proposed MEL method to link the 46 math expressions to the Wikipedia articles, then manually checked the links using following guidelines:

– A *link is highly relevant* if the returned article explains the concept represented by the math mention.
– A *link is partially relevant* if the returned article explains either a concept that is related to the concept represented by the math mention OR a concept that is not related to the math mention, but the article contains math expressions that are similar to the math mention.

3.2 Results

The results show that the proposed method returns seven correct, highly relevant links (15.22 % precision) and 10 additional partially relevant links (36.96 %). We found that this outperforms the results obtained when we used only math expressions (one relevant (2.17 %) and three partially relevant links (6.52 %)) for generating candidates. On the other hand, using only surrounding noun phrases delivers similar results: eight relevant (17.39 %) and seven partially relevant links (32.61 %). This suggests that in our method, the similarity score of each returned link is dominated by the text similarity.

Table 1 shows examples returned by our method. In the table, examples #1 and #2 are judged to be highly relevant. These math mentions contain conventional notation, such as *cos* for cosine similarity and H for entropy. Moreover, the textual mentions are appropriate as descriptions of the math mentions. Examples #3 and #4 are judged as partially relevant. Although the math expressions in

---

[2] https://aclweb.org/anthology.

[3] http://www.inftyreader.org.

[4] http://dlmf.nist.gov/LaTeXML/.

Table 1. Examples of the output of MEL.

No.	Math mention and its meaning in the documents	Corresponding Wikipedia article (formula hit and article title)
Relevant Links		
1	$cos(\theta(u,v)) = \frac{|u.v|}{|u||v|}$	$soft\_cosine_1(a,b) = \frac{\sum_{i,j}^N s_{ij} a_i b_j}{\sqrt{\sum_{i,j}^N s_{ij} a_i a_j}\sqrt{\sum_{i,j}^N s_{ij} b_i b_j}}$
	"cosine similarity"	Cosine_similarity
2	$\bar{H}(T|n,q) = P(q(H) = True|n)\bar{H}(T|n,q(H)=True)) + \ldots$	$H(Y|X) \equiv \sum_{x\in X} p(x)H(Y|X=x) = \ldots$
	"conditional entropy"	Conditional_entropy
3	$P(D(T(f))) = \prod_{u\in D(T(f))} P(u)$	$P(X_k|o_{1:t})$
	"prior probability of tree decomposition"	Forward-backward_ algorithm
4	$\sum_{i=1} M z_{iA0} \le 1$	$\sum_{i=1}^n p_i x_i \le W$
	"constraint in linear programming"	Budget_constraint
False Links		
5	$score(i) = p_i = \frac{e^{act_i}}{\sum_{1\le j\le e^{act_j}}}$	$BS = \frac{1}{N}\sum_{t=1}^N (f_t = o_t)^2$
	"posterior estimation for class i"	Brier_score
6	$P(y|h_0(e_i,f_j),h_1(e_i,f_j)\ldots h_n(e_i,f_j)) = \frac{1}{Z}exp(\sum_k \lambda_k h_k(e_i,f_i) + \lambda_s)$	$h(n) = max\{h_1(n),h_2(n),\ldots,h_i(n)\}$
	"MaxEnt model to interpolate heuristics function h_i"	Heuristic_function

the corresponding Wikipedia articles are similar, the topics of the query mention and Wikipedia article do not match well. Examples #5 and #6 are not correctly wikified by our system. They should be linked to the articles about the softmax function and maximum entropy, respectively. According to our analysis, such errors occur because most of the terms in the textual mention are not quite relevant to the math mentions. For instance, within the text surrounding mention #6, the term "heuristic" has a higher frequency than "maximum entropy."

3.3   Analysis: MEL with Annotated Descriptions

Based on the above observation, we performed an additional experiment by first manually annotating the exact textual descriptions of each math mention and then using these descriptions (instead of all noun phrases found in the surrounding paragraph) as a textual mention in our MEL system. The evaluation result shows that this approach returns 11 highly relevant links (23.91 %) without any partially relevant links. This approach now returns the correct link for mention #5, but still provides a false link for mention #6.

In this experiment, we also obtained an interesting relevant linking:

$D(p||\tilde{p}) = \sum_{t,H_T,H_W} p(t,H_T,H_W)log\frac{p(t,H_T,H_W)}{\tilde{p}t,H_T,H_W}$

(Kullback information) links to *"Conditional_mutual_information"*

We consider this to be interesting because the ideal answer should be a linking to the "Kullback-Leibler_divergence" article, but our system returns an alternative answer that is also relevant. In this alternative article, the formula hit is $I(X;Y|Z) = D_{KL}[p(X,Y,Z)||p(X|Z)p(Y|Z)p(Z)]$, which is described as "Kullback-Leibler divergence." There are two parts of the given math mention that allow our system to obtain this linking:

- the description of the mention that matches perfectly with the description of the formula hit, and
- a segment of the math mention, that is, $D(p||\tilde{p})$, which is structurally similar to a segment of the hit, that is, $D_{KL}[p(X,Y,Z)||p(X|Z)p(Y|Z)p(Z)]$.

From this initial evaluation, we conclude that MEL requires the structures of math mentions and their textual descriptions to perform a good link. For further development, we need to apply NIL detection, that is, the identification of math mentions with no corresponding article, because not all scientific concepts have corresponding Wikipedia articles.

4 Conclusion and Future Work

In this paper, we proposed the task of MEL and introduced our MEL framework, which used an existing math search technique. Our initial evaluation conducted on a small dataset produced the precision of 15.22 % for relevant and 36.96 % for partially relevant linkings. Several aspects to address in the further development of MEL include preprocessing math mentions (splitting long math mentions around the equation symbol), extracting short but informative textual information for each mention, tuning the scoring function to obtain a better balance between math and text similarity, and NIL detection.

References

1. Agrawal, R., Gollapudi, S., Kannan, A., Kenthapadi, K.: Data mining for improving textbooks. SIGKDD Explor. Newsl. **13**(2), 7–19 (2012)
2. Cheng, X., Roth, D.: Relational Inference for Wikification. In: Proceedings of EMNLP (2013)
3. Cucerzan, S.: Large-scale named entity disambiguation based on wikipedia data. In: Proceedings of the Joint Conference of EMNLP-CoNLL (2007)
4. Kristianto, G.Y., Topić, G., Aizawa, A.: The MCAT math retrieval system for NTCIR-12 MathIR task. In: Proceedings of the 12th NTCIR Conference (2016)
5. Mihalcea, R., Csomai, A., Wikify!: Linking documents to encyclopedic knowledge. In: Proceedings of the 16th ACM CIKM (2007)
6. Milne, D., Witten, I.H.: Learning to link with wikipedia. In: Proceedings of the 17th ACM CIKM (2008)
7. Ni, Y., Xu, Q.K., Cao, F., Mass, Y., Sheinwald, D., Zhu, H.J., Cao, S.S.: Semantic documents relatedness using concept graph representation. In: Proceedings of the 9th ACM WSDM (2016)
8. Pagel, R., Schubotz, M.: Mathematical language processing project. In: Work in Progress Track at CICM (2014)
9. Rose, S., Engel, D., Cramer, N., Cowley, W.: Automatic Keyword Extraction from Individual Documents. Applications and Theory, In Text Mining (2010)
10. Zanibbi, R., Aizawa, A., Kohlhase, M., Ounis, I., Topić, G., Davila, K.: NTCIR-12 MathIR task overview. In: NTCIR, National Institute of Informatics (NII) (2016)

Improved Identification of Tweets that Mention Books: Selection of Effective Features

Shuntaro Yada[✉] and Kyo Kageura

Graduate School of Education, The University of Tokyo,
7-3-1 Hongo, Bunkyo-ku, Tokyo 113-0033, Japan
{shuntaroy,kyo}@p.u-tokyo.ac.jp

Abstract. In this paper, we assessed the effectiveness of different types of features for the identification of tweets on Twitter that mention books among tweets that contain the same strings as full book titles. In the previous work, the bag-of-words based features were taken from the context of individual tweets. While performance was reasonable, we identified room for improvement in terms of the extraction of features. We proposed additional types of features such as words appearing in the profiles of tweet authors, POS tags of mentioned book titles, and bibliographic elements within tweets, e.g. authors and publishers. We conducted a grid search for all combinations of the above feature sets, and observed performance improvements suitable for practical applications.

Keywords: Book title identification · Text classification · Named entity recognition · Twitter · Machine learning

1   Introduction

In this paper, we assessed the effectiveness of different types of features for the identification of tweets on Twitter that mention books (henceforth TMB).

We are currently developing an online book recommendation system that aims to simulate the situation where an individual discovers books by chance through daily informal conversation with friends [4]. This is intended to replicate, in the digital world, the experience of physical exposure to books. Though this experience may substantially contribute to the reading habits of individuals, it is shrinking due to the growing popularity of e-books, the decreasing number of local bookstores, and the growing habit of buying books online. The system we are developing will provide users with recommendations for some books that have been mentioned or alluded to by their friends on SNSs (among which we are focusing on Twitter) via gentle and relevant ways of notifications with casual intervals.

TMB identification constitutes one of the essential modules of our system. For the moment, our focus is on Japanese books and Japanese Twitter[1], but the

---

[1] The number of local bookstores is rapidly decreasing in Japan. In 1999, there were 22,296 bookstores in Japan, and the number had fallen to 13,488 by 2015.

© Springer International Publishing AG 2016
A. Morishima et al. (Eds.): ICADL 2016, LNCS 10075, pp. 150–156, 2016.
DOI: 10.1007/978-3-319-49304-6_19

method of TMB identification as well as the book recommendation system can be applied to other languages with some modifications to the language-specific processing parts.

An informal survey we conducted revealed that books are referred to on Twitter in different ways, e.g. by full titles, by abbreviated titles, or by author names with additional specifications (i.e. "the latest book by Fuminori Nakamura"). Here, we focused on TMBs containing full book title strings because they would be the primary case for sharing one's reading habits in daily situations. The identification of tweets that contain full book titles can be regarded as a named entity recognition task. As an up-to-date, comprehensive list of book titles is available, we can identify tweets that contain the same strings as full book titles. The main difficulty of identifying TMBs among the tweets that contain full book title strings lies in distinguishing between those which really mention books and those which do not (which we call *noise*). This difficulty is caused by the fact that a substantial portion of book titles consist of ordinary phrases or expressions, such as *Kidnapping* or *A Night in Paris*. Therefore, our task can be defined as a classification task, i.e. classifying tweets containing the strings as book titles into TMBs and *noise* tweets.

As we will see in Sect. 2 is work in TMB identification, but the performance is not good enough for practical use [5]. The methods we examine in this paper can be regarded as an extension of this previous work in terms of data size, learning methods, and especially feature extraction.

2   Related Work

There is much work in terms of tweet classification in general. For instance, Theodotou, et al. (2015) classified tweets into predefined categories with external features such as words from linked URLs, mentioned user profiles, and Wikipedia articles as well as tweet texts [2]. They reported that the former two features improved the performance.

There are also studies on tweet classification for the identification of specific information most typically represented by named entities, including the identification of useful information related to software products [1] and the health conditions of Twitter users [3]. While these studies are related to our task, there has been little work so far that addresses the identification of TMBs.

We are tackling a TMB identification task mainly from the work [5], the performance of which has an F1 score of about 0.7. This may be good as a starting point for experimental research, but is not satisfactory for our practical applications. Upon analysing the results, we noticed three directions for improving the performance: (i) *extending the dataset*: the training data used in [5] is insubstantial and skewed, even if we consider the fact that the gross number of TMBs is not large; (ii) *enriching features*: features used in [5] are taken from body texts in tweets, and other features which can be taken from twitter are not used; (iii) *learning algorithms*: while [5] adopts several standard algorithms, there are other possibilities. Taking these into account, we established and experimented an enhanced TMB identification method. As stated in Sect. 1, we will mainly focus on (ii) the effect of features for the performance improvement of TMB identifications.

3   Method

3.1   Data Set

First, we collected tweets containing book title strings through Twitter Streaming API from 30th April to 5th May 2015, and obtained 436 TMBs and 5,563 instances of *noise* through the manual annotation [5]. In order to augment the TMBs in a simple and automatic manner, secondly, we selected five book-related keywords from a set of words appearing much more frequently in the TMBs, and searched on Twitter for tweets containing these keywords in addition to the same strings as the book titles on 25th April 2016, and regarded them as TMBs. We obtained 4,376 tweets containing at least one of the following five keywords: "読了 (finished reading)," "読む (read),"[2] "再読 (re-read)," "読破 (read through a book)," "読み応え (worth reading)." The data set for this research, thus, contains 4,812 TMBs and 5,563 *noise* tweets.

3.2   TMB Classifier Settings

In the work [5], four different ML algorithms were compared for the TMB identification task, and the Support Vector Machine performed best. Under the same experiments with our augmented TMB data set, however, we found that the Maximum Entropy Modelling (MaxEnt) outperformed other methods in terms of the balance of scores and the training speed. Since our interest in this paper is on selecting features, we will only report the results obtained by using MaxEnt, which is provided by the `scikit-learn` library (0.17.1) for Python, or $\min_{w,c} ||w||_1 + C \sum_{i=1}^{n} \log (\exp (-y_i x_i^T w) + 1)$, where w is a weight to learn, C is a constant for regularisation strength (we set this to 10.0), x_i is the ith feature vector extracted from the ith input tweet, and y_i is a label (TMB or *noise*) of the ith tweet.

3.3   Features

Baseline Features. The baseline features we adopted are the same as those used in [5]: *Words in tweet body texts, URL host names appeared in tweet texts,* and *Name of Twitter client application.* As in [5], we use these tokens as bag-of-words (BoW) features in applying ML methods to TMB identification tasks.

---

[2] This is the only verb among the five keywords; all the others are nouns.

Augmented Features. As mentioned earlier, we observed that features other than words within tweets could be more effective and useful in improving the performance of TMB identification. While it is possible to make use of a wider range of information extractable from the information given in tweets, we can make generalised features from tokens by means of abstraction.

Words in profile texts (`profile`): Frequent readers often declare in their Twitter profile description that they read many books, which should provide positive weight to the possibility that the strings in their tweets which take the same form as book titles actually are book titles. In the experiment, we observed the effect of this feature by applying learning algorithms (a) without using this feature set (`off` state), (b) by combining the tokens extracted from the profile texts with baseline features (`on` state), and (c) by providing this feature set (`diff` state) separately.

Words in web pages linked from tweets (`link`): This feature set is generated from the main textual content of web pages linked from tweet texts. Some TMBs contain URLs linked to book-related web pages such as the descriptions of the book or book reviews[3]. As with `profile`, we observed the effect of this feature in the `off`, `on`, and `diff` states.

POS tags of book titles (`title_ness`): As mentioned before, many book titles consist of ordinary expressions that can be used in different contexts as non-book titles. However, it is also true that a non-negligible amount of book titles have expressions and forms that do not tend to occur in usual informal conversation in Twitter. We introduce occurrences of Part-of-Speech (POS) tags within a mentioned book title as features that can possibly represent this information.

Abstraction of bibliographic elements (`bib`): If any words in a TMB matches the bibliographic elements (other than book titles) of a mentioned book, the words are abstracted into the corresponding names of the bibliographic elements. For example, if "Haruki" and "Murakami" appear in a TMB that mentions the book *1Q84* (for which the bibliographic information indicates that the author is Haruki Murakami), these two tokens will be converted into "`%CREATOR%`." We consider the following six bibliographic elements: creators (authors), publisher, edition, volume, publication year, and titles of short stories if the mentioned book is a collection.

In all of these features, we calculate the TFIDF values for the individual words and the POS tags.

3.4 Experimental Setup

For all combinations of the feature sets introduced in Sect. 3.3, we conducted TMB identification tests with three-fold cross validation (CV), or a *grid search.*

---

[3] We utilised the `readability` algorithm of arc90.

We observed the performance by using the mean F1 measure of a three-fold CV, which is the harmonic mean of Precision and Recall, because the application we have in mind requires balance between them[4].

After we obtained the scores, we carried out statistical tests in order to assess which feature set is effective in TMB identification. Due to the numbers of feature providing states, we apply the t-test to `bib` and `title_ness` features (for two states), and ANOVA (analysis of variance) to the `profile` and `link` features (for three states).

4   Result

In this section, we will first report the descriptive aspects of the results. While the TMB classifier with baseline features scored 0.879 (F1 measure), the one with `diff` state of `profile` and `link` in addition to the `on` state of `title_ness` performed best (0.915 F1 measure). Table 1 summarises the mean F1 measures, focusing on each one of the feature sets, instead of our showing all scores. We observed that all feature sets are possibly effective individually, and that the `diff` state of `profile` contributes best. However, the contributions of other settings are relatively small.

We can assess such contributions in further detail from the p values in Table 1 that shows the results of statistical tests to the differences of mean F1 scores between each state of providing features. These values mean that the features

Table 1. Descriptive statistic values and p values of statistic tests of each state for augmented features. In "State" column, '-' denotes `off` and 'o' means `on`. The values in the "Mean" to "Max" columns are the corresponding descriptive statistic values of the F1 measures. The p values in the `profile` and `link` rows are provided by ANOVA while those in the other rows are generated by t test.

Setting	State	Count	Mean	SD	Min	Max	p value
`profile`	-	12	0.885	0.003	0.879	0.890	2.06×10^{-24}
	o	12	0.872	0.004	0.865	0.879	
	diff	12	0.910	0.002	0.907	0.915	
`link`	-	12	0.887	0.017	0.865	0.911	0.761
	o	12	0.889	0.016	0.868	0.911	
	diff	12	0.892	0.017	0.873	0.915	
`title_ness`	-	18	0.888	0.017	0.865	0.915	4.45×10^{-4}
	o	18	0.890	0.016	0.869	0.912	
`bib`	-	18	0.887	0.017	0.865	0.912	1.93×10^{-8}
	o	18	0.891	0.016	0.871	0.915	

---

[4] Taking into account the fact that the number of TMBs is not so great, recall is important. However, the lack of precision greatly hampers the mission of the system.

Table 2. Tukey HSD tests on the states of providing `profile` features with the significance level set to 5 %. symbols in the "Group" columns are the same as in Table 2. The "Lower" and "Upper" column shows bounds of the range of significance.

Group 1	Group 2	Mean diff	Lower	Upper	Reject
-	○	−0.012	−0.0143	-9.80×10^{-3}	True
-	diff	0.0256	0.0233	0.0278	True
○	diff	0.0376	0.0354	0.0399	True

other than `link` have a statistically strong significance in TMB classification. As for `profile`, we conducted multiple comparisons using the Tukey HSD test in order to evaluate the differences between each pair of the states of this feature setting, the results of which are shown in Table 2. This indicates that the differences between all of the pairs are statistically significant. Comparing other settings, we can conclude that the `diff` state of `profile` setting improved our TMB identifier relatively substantially. On the other hand, the `on` state of the setting seems rather to spoils the performance.

5 Conclusion

In this paper, we improved the TMB identification task, which is a book titles recognition task with text classification, using four additional feature sets extracted from tweets containing the same strings as book titles, namely words in profile texts (`profile`), words in linked web pages (`link`), POS tags of book titles (`title_ness`), and abstraction of bibliographic elements (`bib`). Through a grid search for all combinations of above feature sets, we found `profile`, `bib` and `title_ness` settings improve the performance of our TMB identifier with statistical significance.

We can also note that the contribution of `profile` features separately added against other features was outstanding. This implies that users' self descriptions of themselves are related to the topics of their tweets within the context of *mentioning books*. It has also been suggested that we can apply `profile` features to such tasks as tweets mentioning music titles, movie titles, and other media titles as well.

Part of the reason why `link` does not improve the performance could be the parsing error of web pages. However, due to the too much variation in linked web pages in tweets, it may be costly to optimise the performance.

In this paper, we focus not on interaction among multiple feature sets, but on the effects of individual feature sets. Thus, we obtained the result that the maximum scored combination of settings did not correspond to such individual settings that have statistical significance between the `on` and `off` states. We need to conduct N-way ANOVA in order to clarify the point.

Acknowledgement. This work was supported by JSPS KAKENHI Grant Number JP 16K12542.

References

1. Prasetyo, P.K., Lo, D., Achananuparp, P., Tian, Y., Lim, E.P.: Automatic Classification of Software Related Microblogs. In: 28th International Conference on Software Maintenance, pp. 596–599. IEEE (2012)
2. Theodotou, A., Stassopoulou, A.: A system for automatic classification of twitter messages into categories. In: Christiansen, H., Stojanovic, I., Papadopoulos, G.A. (eds.) CONTEXT 2015. LNCS (LNAI), vol. 9405, pp. 532–537. Springer, Heidelberg (2015). doi:10.1007/978-3-319-25591-0_44
3. Tuarob, S., Tucker, C.S., Salathe, M., Ram, N.: An ensemble heterogeneous classification methodology for discovering health-related knowledge in social media messages. J. Biomed. Inf. **49**, 255–268 (2014)
4. Yada, S.: Development of a book recommendation system to inspire "Infrequent Readers". In: Tuamsuk, K., Jatowt, A., Rasmussen, E. (eds.) ICADL 2014. LNCS, vol. 8839, pp. 399–404. Springer, Heidelberg (2014). doi:10.1007/978-3-319-12823-8_43
5. Yada, S., Kageura, K.: Identification of Tweets that Mention Books: an experimental comparison of machine learning methods. In: Allen, R.B., Hunter, J., Zeng, M.L. (eds.) ICADL 2015. LNCS, vol. 9469, pp. 278–288. Springer, Heidelberg (2015). doi:10.1007/978-3-319-27974-9_30

A Visualization of Relationships Among Papers Using Citation and Co-citation Information

Yu Nakano, Toshiyuki Shimizu$^{(\boxtimes)}$, and Masatoshi Yoshikawa

Graduate School of Informatics, Kyoto University, Kyoto 606-8501, Japan
ynakano@db.soc.i.kyoto-u.ac.jp, {tshimizu,yoshikawa}@i.kyoto-u.ac.jp

Abstract. When we conduct scholarly surveys, we occasionally encounter difficulties in grasping the vast amount of related papers. Because academic papers have relationships, such as citing and cited relationships, we considered utilizing them for supporting scholarly surveys. In this paper, we propose a method for visualizing relationships among papers, and we construct *paper graphs* using two types of relationships, namely, citation and co-citation. Moreover, we quantify the strengths of citations and co-citations based on their frequency and the positions of co-citations, and show both types of relationships together in a graph. We constructed paper graphs using papers in the database field and discussed their usefulness.

Keywords: Scholarly survey · Co-citation analysis · Citation graph

1 Introduction

Researchers examine academic papers related to their research field and acquire knowledge for their own research. This process is called scholarly surveys, and many researchers use academic search engines, such as Google Scholar[1]. Because the number of academic papers has recently been increasing, it is impossible to read all the related papers. Therefore, how efficiently and comprehensively we understand them is one of the problems in scholarly surveys.

A possible approach to overcome this issue is to visualize relationships among papers [1,2]. Understanding relationships among papers makes it easy for researchers to grasp the insistence of each paper and to obtain insights into their research field. Therefore, analyzing and visualizing relationships among papers supports scholarly surveys. In this paper, we show a graph of relationships among papers, aiming to help researchers conduct scholarly surveys more efficiently.

There are many types of research that use citations to analyze relationships among papers [3,4]. This is because by citing their related papers, researchers describe the similarities and differences of their research and make its contributions clear when writing papers; thus, in this paper, we use citations as it was done in previous research.

---

[1] https://scholar.google.co.jp.

© Springer International Publishing AG 2016
A. Morishima et al. (Eds.): ICADL 2016, LNCS 10075, pp. 157–163, 2016.
DOI: 10.1007/978-3-319-49304-6_20

In addition to citations, we also focus on co-citations. A co-citation is a situation in which two papers are cited in the same paper. Some research indicates that co-citation provides relationships such as similarities among papers [3,5].

After we extract relationships among papers, we have to consider how understandably we should show the relationships. There are many types of research about visualizing relationships among papers by using citations, which is known as a citation graph [1,2,6]. In this paper, we considered visualizing relationships among papers by using not only citations but also co-citations. We constructed *paper graphs* using the frequency of citations, frequency of co-citations, and positions of co-citations. By obtaining information on citations and co-citations simultaneously, we believe that researchers can understand their research field more effectively.

2   Relationships Among Papers

We visualize the relationships of a given set of papers using a directed graph. We call this directed graph a *paper graph*. We assume that a given set of papers is related to each other, such as the search results of academic search engines. In paper graphs, a node represents a paper, and an edge is a relationship between two papers.

In this paper, we utilize citations and co-citations as relationships among papers. After quantifying the strengths of the two types of relationships, we visualize both of them in the same graph. We can observe citation information and co-citation information from the paper graph simultaneously. From the citation information, we can identify a paper cited from many other papers. Similarly, from the co-citation information, we can grasp how strongly papers are related.

In this section, we describe which papers we should connect in the given paper set considering citations and co-citations and its strength. We also describe how to arrange nodes when visualizing paper graphs.

2.1   Strength of Edge

In this section, we explain which edges we show in paper graphs based on citing and cited relationships in the papers. We assume that two papers are related if they have a citation relationship or co-citation relationship and we describe how to visualize these two types of relationships in paper graphs.

In Case of Citation. Two papers that have a citing and cited relationship are related, but one paper typically cites many papers; therefore, if we show all edges of citations in a paper graph, it becomes too complicated to describe the graph. Therefore, we show the edge of citations if a cited paper has a strong relationship to a citing paper. We considered that there is a strong relationship between two papers if a paper cites another paper in the text many times.

We quantify the strength of citing and cited relationships based on the frequency of citations. Let the (i, j)th entry m_{ij}^{cite} in matrix M^{cite} be the strength of a citing and cited relationship between paper p_i and paper p_j; we define m_{ij}^{cite} as follows.

$$m_{ij}^{cite} = \frac{\text{citation frequency of } p_j \text{ in } p_i}{\text{total citation frequency in } p_i} \tag{1}$$

If m_{ij}^{cite} is greater than the threshold $\alpha(i)$, then we connect an edge of citation from p_i to p_j. The threshold α is a function, as follows.

$$\alpha(i) = \text{the value of top } r_\alpha\% \text{ of } i\text{-th row of } M^{cite} \tag{2}$$

The variable r_α is a parameter. When $r_\alpha = 100$, in the paper graph, there are all edges of citations in the given papers. As r_α becomes smaller, there are fewer edges of citations in the paper graph, and there are no edges of citations when $r_\alpha = 0$.

In Case of Co-Citation. Two papers that have co-citation relationships are related, but showing all co-citations in a paper graph has the same problem as with citations; thus, we show strong relationships even in this case.

When quantifying the strength of co-citations, we can utilize the positions of co-citations. Eto [5] calculates similarities between two papers using the positions of co-citations, and he shows that the closer the positions where two papers are cited, the more similar the two papers are.

We attempted to quantify the strength of co-citation relationships based on the frequency and the positions of co-citations. Let the (i, j)th entry m_{ij}^{cocite} in matrix M^{cocite} be the strength of co-citation relationships between p_i and p_j, and let P be a given set of papers that cite both p_i and p_j; then, we define m_{ij}^{cocite} as follows.

$$m_{ij}^{cocite} = year\_coef_{ij} \times \sum_{p_x \in P} cocite\_pos(i, j) \text{ in } p_x \tag{3}$$

In this definition, $cocite\_pos(i, j)$ in p_x is the positions of two papers that have co-citation relationships, and we define the following formula based on Eto [5].

$$cocite\_pos(i, j) = \begin{cases} 1 & \text{(enumeration)} \\ 0.75 & \text{(same sentence)} \\ 0.25 & \text{(same section)} \\ 0 & \text{(across sections)} \end{cases} \tag{4}$$

If there are multiple co-citations in one paper, then we regard the position of them as the closest one and ignore other co-citations for simplicity.

The definition of $year\_coef_{ij}$ is a coefficient, as follows.

$$year\_coef_{ij} = \left(\frac{year_i + year_j - (start - 1) * 2}{interval * 2} \right)^2 \tag{5}$$

Here, $year_i, year_j$ are the publication years of p_i, p_j, respectively; *start* is the earliest year in the given papers; and *interval* is the difference between the last year and earliest year in a given paper set. The value of *year_coef* becomes larger for newer papers. The intuition of the formula (3) is that if two papers that have co-citation relationships are new, then they are more related than older ones which have the same frequency and the positions of co-citations. The reason why we introduce *year_coef* is that older papers tend to have more co-citation relationships because of its nature.

If m_{ij}^{cocite} is greater than the threshold β, then we connect an edge of co-citation between p_i and p_j. The threshold β is as follows.

$$\beta = \text{the value of top } r_\beta\% \text{ of non-zero elements of } M^{cocite} \qquad (6)$$

The variable r_β is a parameter. When $r_\beta = 100$, in the paper graph, there are all edges of co-citations in the given papers. As r_β becomes smaller, there are fewer edges of co-citations in the paper graph, and there are no edges of co-citations when $r_\beta = 0$.

2.2 Arrangement of Nodes

When observing paper graphs, it is difficult to obtain useful information if the nodes in the paper graphs are disordered. We arranged papers in paper graphs in chronological order. This helps researchers estimate the history of their research topic. This method is generally used in research of visualizing citations [1,2,6].

3 Preliminary Experiment

3.1 Dataset

We constructed paper graphs using the proposed method described in Sect. 2. The outline is presented below.

1. define a group of papers as a dataset D
2. retrieve papers D_q by searching with a query q we choose on Google Scholar
3. select target papers D_t which are included in both D and D_q
4. construct a paper graph of the top-k papers of citation count in D_t

The dataset D we used is made of papers published in SIGMOD[2], VLDB[3], and ICDE[4] from 2000 to 2015. The reason why we selected these conferences is because they are top conferences in the database field and papers published there are expected to be strongly related, which is a suitable situation to obtain relationships among papers.

---

[2] http://www.sigmod.org/.
[3] http://www.vldb.org/.
[4] http://www.icde.org/.

We extracted 201,404 citations and 1,664,014 co-citations from 6,977 papers in the dataset. Citations and co-citations that both of two papers are in the dataset are 47,716 and 100,355, respectively. We used ParsCit [7] to extract citing and cited relationships.

Using this dataset, we constructed paper graphs of three queries, namely, "skyline", "top-k queries" and "uncertain data". We set the parameters k, r_α and r_β to various values. Parameter k is the value described in the outline of the method, that is, the top-k papers of citation count in retrieved papers. Parameters r_α and r_β are the values appearing in the formulas (2) and (6), respectively. We used Graphviz[5] to visualize the paper graphs.

3.2   Results and Discussion

Figure 1 is a paper graph of a query "skyline" with parameters $(k, r_\alpha, r_\beta) = (15, 5, 20)$. In this figure, one node is one of the papers in the dataset and it has information such as its ID, published conference and published year. While black edges represent citation relationships, blue edges represent co-citation relationships. In other words, a black edge from node A to node B means that paper A cites paper B, and a blue edge between two papers means that the two papers are cited together in another paper. Moreover, the width of edges indicates the strength of relationships.

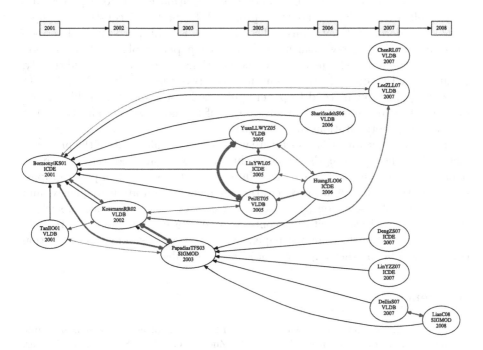

Fig. 1. $q =$ "skyline", $k = 15, r_\alpha = 5, r_\beta = 20$ (Color figure online)

---

[5] http://www.graphviz.org/.

From this figure, for example, we can understand the fact that because papers BorzsonyiKS01 and PapadiasTFS03 are frequently cited by other papers, the two papers strongly affect other papers. When looking at the edges of co-citations, we can estimate that because the four papers YuanLLWYZ05, LinYWL05, Pei-JET05, and HuangJLO06 or the three papers BorzsonyiKS01, KossmannRR02, and PapadiasTFS03 are connected to each other by blue edges, they form one cluster of similar topics. We can observe these two results by focusing only on either of the two relationships, but from Fig. 1, we can find out which papers affect a cluster and how two clusters influence each other. We observe this advantage in paper graphs of the other two queries as well.

As r_α/r_β increase, the number of edges of citations/co-citations increase. While the increase of the edges of citations allows us to examine relationships among papers in more detail because more edges are connected to one node, the increase of the edges of co-citations allows us to observe paper graphs in a larger scale because the cluster size becomes larger. However, the increase of the edges makes a paper graph complicated; thus we need to adjust the parameters according to how much detail we want to observe in the paper graph.

4   Conclusion and Future Work

In this paper, to help researchers understand relationships among papers and support efficient scholarly surveys, we proposed the method of constructing *paper graphs* considering both citations and co-citations. For this purpose, we described some information that we can use to construct paper graphs, such as citation frequency, co-citation frequency, and the positions of co-citations. Additionaly, we attempted to quantify the strength of the two relationships. Moreover, we actually applied our method to papers published in the database field, and we discussed the advantages and disadvantages of the proposed visualization, that is, visualizing both citations and co-citations.

There are some directions for future work, that is, evaluations of the proposed method such as the strength of relationships that we quantified; the use of more papers published in other conferences; improvement of visualizing paper graphs; and so forth. Although we used citation frequency, co-citation frequency, and the positions of co-citations, it is worth considering other information, such as the position of citation, citation contexts, and citation functions [8]. To fully understand relationships among papers, visualization of summaries of citation contexts will be another improvement of paper graphs.

References

1. Shogen, S., Shimizu, T., Yoshikawa, M.: Enrichment of academic search engine results pages by citation-based graphs. In: Zuccon, G., Geva, S., Joho, H., Scholer, F., Sun, A., Zhang, P. (eds.) AIRS 2015. LNCS, vol. 9460, pp. 56–67. Springer, Heidelberg (2015). doi:10.1007/978-3-319-28940-3_5

2. Nanba, H., Abekawa, T., Okumura, M., Saito, S.: Bilingual PRESRI-integration of multiple research paper databases. In: RIAO, pp. 195–211 (2004)
3. Small, H.: Co-citation in the scientific literature: a new measure of the relationship between two documents. J. Am. Soc. Inf. Sci. **24**(4), 265–269 (1973)
4. Nanba, H., Okumura, M.: Towards multi-paper summarization using reference information. In: IJCAI, pp. 926–931 (1999)
5. Eto, M.: Evaluations of context-based co-citation searching. Scientometrics **94**(2), 651–673 (2013)
6. Shahaf, D., Guestrin, C., Horvitz, E., Leskovec, J.: Information cartography. Commun. ACM **58**(11), 62–73 (2015)
7. Councill, I.G., Giles, C.L., Kan, M.: ParsCit: an open-source CRF reference string parsing package. In: LREC (2008)
8. Teufel, S., Siddharthan, A., Tidhar, D.: Automatic classification of citation function. In: EMNLP, pp. 103–110 (2006)

Education and Digital Literacy

A Lecture Slide Reconstruction System Based on Expertise Extraction for e-Learning

Yuanyuan Wang[1(✉)] and Yukiko Kawai[2]

[1] Graduate School of Sciences and Technology for Innovation, Yamaguchi University,
Ube, Japan
y.wang@yamaguchi-u.ac.jp
[2] Faculty of Computer Science and Engineering, Kyoto Sangyo University, Kyoto,
Japan
kawai@cc.kyoto-su.ac.jp

Abstract. MOOC has brought many benefits to e-learning systems as students are able to obtain various educational presentation slides through digital libraries. These presentation slides provide varying levels of knowledge to specific students. On the other hand, students usually have different levels of knowledge. Thus, it is important to detect expertise levels of lecture slides for specific students, and supplement the lecture slides with related information automatically for different knowledge levels of students. Therefore, we developed a novel automatic slide reconstruction system for digital libraries in e-learning, it generates new lecture contents from one original content related to users' interests and knowledge levels by adding and removing slides, in order to enable users to learn the reconstructed slides that they do not need no more searching. Our system first extracts topics and groups slides on topics to detect the expertise level of an original content by considering the context in the presentation. The system then searches other necessary contents and determines unnecessary original slide groups based on users' interests and knowledge levels. Through this, the system can automatically reconstruct lecture slides by classifying them into four groups based on expertise of lecture slides. Those groups are: basic contents for beginners, basic or specialized contents for intermediate students, and specialized contents for advanced students. As a result, users can satisfy and joyfully learn the newly reconstructed slides that are suit to their interests and knowledge levels. In this paper, we discuss our automatic slide reconstruction system to deal with different knowledge levels of students for content understanding, knowledge deepening, and interest-expanding, and verify its effectiveness.

Keywords: Slide reconstruction · Expertise · Lecture slides · e-Learning

© Springer International Publishing AG 2016
A. Morishima et al. (Eds.): ICADL 2016, LNCS 10075, pp. 167–179, 2016.
DOI: 10.1007/978-3-319-49304-6_21

1   Introduction

In recent years, digital libraries have been a rapid growth in MOOC, such as Coursera[1] and SlideShare[2], students can learn lecture slides whenever they want to learn. While learning lecture slides, students are probably interested in some contents in the slides and search related information through the Web. For example, students may search specialized knowledge appeared in an academic presentation or check details of basic concepts in an introductory lecture content. However, since lecture slides have various topics and they provide different levels of knowledge to specific students, when searching the Web, students possibly spend more time and the large number of search results returned will make it difficult for the students to find the information appropriate to their levels of understanding. For example, beginners may want a summary of basic knowledge of image processing, while others may be more interested in 3DCG using thermal image processing. In other words, there can be different knowledge levels and demands when students learn the same lecture slides about image processing, and they have to refer to other lecture slides or resources for the wanted information such as prior knowledge of image processing or advanced image processing techniques. Therefore, it is necessary to extract expertise levels of lecture slides for specific students, and supplement them automatically with related information.

In this work, we aim to develop a novel automatic slide reconstruction system for digital libraries in e-learning, to generate new lecture contents based on users' interests and knowledge levels. The system integrates new slides that are created by using other related contents (e.g., Wikipedia pages, figures) into an original content, and it also removes unnecessary original slides based on expertise of original slides on related topics. To achieve our goal, we first extract topics and group slides on topics to detect the expertise level of an original content by considering the context in the presentation. Then, we extract expertise of the whole original content and its each slide group by calculating the number of links in Wikipedia, because Wikipedia is an encyclopedia providing a vast amount of structured world knowledge. Therefore, we can determine how to generate four kinds of new lecture contents based on users' interests and knowledge levels. In this paper, we create new slides to add into the original content by summarizing the content and figures of related Wikipedia pages searching from Google search engine. As a result, different knowledge levels of students can satisfy and joyfully learn the reconstructed slides for digital libraries in e-learning.

The next section provides an overview of our system and reviews related work. Section 3 explains how to detect topics and their slide groups of lecture slides. Section 4 describes our research model for generating new lecture contents. Experimental results and conclusions are given in Sects. 5 and 6, respectively.

---

[1] https://www.coursera.org/.

[2] http://www.slideshare.net/.

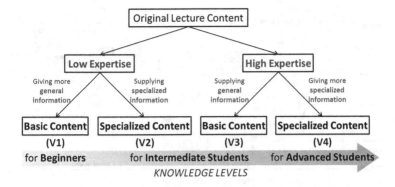

Fig. 1. Four kinds of lecture contents based on expertise of an original lecture content.

2   System Overview and Related Work

2.1   Slide Reconstruction System

The system generates four kinds of lecture contents based on the expertise of an original lecture content (see Fig. 1). This will help different users to learn lecture contents that suit their interests and knowledge levels. The generated lecture contents from one lecture content are defined as follows:

- **V1**: a basic content for beginners
- **V2**: a specialized content for intermediate students
- **V3**: a basic content for intermediate students
- **V4**: a specialized content for advanced students

They are classified into four kinds by determining expertise of the whole original content and each slide group in the original content. If the expertise of the whole original content is low, in order to generate **V1**, the system adds new related slides after original slide groups that are with low expertise for providing more information about basic points, simultaneously, the system removes original slide groups that are with high expertise. On the contrary, in order to generate **V2**, the system adds new related slides after original slide groups that are with high expertise for giving explanations about specialized knowledge, simultaneously, the system removes original slide groups that are with low expertise. If the expertise of the whole original content is high, in order to generate **V3**, the system adds new related slides after original slide groups that are with low expertise for giving explanations about basic points, simultaneously, the system removes original slide groups that are with high expertise. On the contrary, in order to generate **V4**, the system adds new slides by using other related contents after original slide groups that are with high expertise for providing more information about specialized knowledge, simultaneously, the system removes original slide groups that are with low expertise. Moreover, additional new slides are created by summarizing the content and figures in related Wikipedia pages that are acquired from Google search engine.

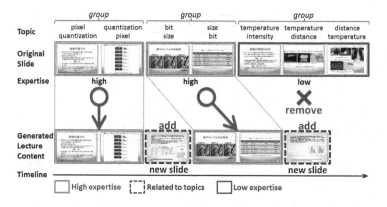

Fig. 2. Conceptual diagram of generating **V4** from a high expertise content.

An example is shown in Fig. 2. This figure depicts an overview of generating a lecture content (**V4**) from a high expertise content. Slide groups with high or low expertise are detected by extracting topics from an original content. Double line frames denote original slide groups with high expertise. Dashed line frames denote additional slides related to topics of original scene groups with high expertise. A single line frame denotes an original slide group with low expertise, which will be removed from the original presentation. In this manner, if an original content is with high expertise and students have higher knowledge want to gain more information about their interested topics, they can learn a specialized content for advanced students (**V4**), and they can also learn a basic content for intermediate students (**V3**) that is easier to understand than **V4**.

2.2 Related Work

Over the past few decades, a considerable number of studies have been conducted on the retrieval of presentation slides through digital libraries. In order to improve the efficiency of slide retrieval, several techniques have been developed for retrieving users' desired slides by utilizing slide structure information ([2,9]). On the other hand, many recent research efforts have focused on extracting important slides using an image processing technique by considering color distribution and animation occurrence in slides ([3,10]). Sakuragi et al. [5] proposed a slide retrieval system based on the meanings for groups of shapes by analyzing relations between shapes in slides. These studies focused on analysis of structural information and visual information in order to extract slides. In this work, we aim to automatically generate new lecture contents from one original content for satisfying users' interests and knowledge levels by creating new related slides and removing unwanted slides. Therefore, our system extracts the topics by considering the context in the presentation based on the slide structure information, and detects slide groups corresponding to the extracted topics.

As in related studies about the slide reconstruction of various presentation slides. Many recent applications address the need to capture the complex relationships among content items, and assist in crafting compelling narratives. NextSlidePlease [7] is a novel slide reconstruction tool for authoring and delivering slideware presentations. This tool addresses issues of content integration, presentation structuring, time-management, and flexible presentation delivery. iPoster [8] reconstructs slides into a structured layout to help users grasp an overview of the presentation, and it uses a ZUI to navigate elements of slides moving from an overview to details. Several research efforts have focused on generating new presentations by reusing elements in the original slides ([6,12]). They can retrieve a variety of elements in slides based on a similarity search over the text and images. On the other hand, Edge et al. [1] and Pschetz et al. [4] proposed presentation editing tools for laying out slides or elements. In this work, while our proposed slide reconstruction system is similar to these works for browsing support, we aim to generate lecture contents are not only for the same knowledge levels of users, but also for different knowledge levels of users.

3 Topic Extraction and Slide Group Detection

3.1 Extracting Topics of Slides

In general, topics can be considered as high frequency terms or slide titles. Since it may lose the context of presentation, a topic can be described as a learning point with multiple nouns that frequently appears at different levels (i.e., bullet points) in neighboring slides by considering the context in the presentation. The topics that appear at the title of a slide and the body of other slides can be considered to indicate its context in a presentation. Then, we extract topics of the whole presentation with our proposed method in our previous work [8] by locating the same noun phrases in different slides, at varying levels based on itemized sentences of bullet points in the slide text. If a noun phrase k appears at the different indentation levels in every two slides s_i and s_j in serial order of the presentation, then k is a candidate for being one of the topics T in the presentation. i and j denote the slide number of the presentation. In this way, if a noun phrase appears at the body of only one slide and the titles of other serial slides, it also can be a candidate of topics.

$$T = \{k | l(k, s_i) \neq l(k, s_j), k \in s_i, k \in s_j\} \tag{1}$$

Here, T is a bag of noun phrases that can be considered as candidates for topics. $l(k, s_i)$ is a function that returns the highest level of k in the slide s_i. When the highest level is the title, e.g., the 1st level of s_i, then $l(k, s_i)$ returns 1; and when the highest level is the 3rd level of s_j, then $l(k, s_j)$ returns 3. When k appears at different levels, k is determined as a candidate for topics provided $l(k, s_i)$ is not equal to $l(k, s_j)$. Then, the weight of k in T is defined using the levels of k, and the distance between slides s_i and s_j, as follows:

$$I(k) = \frac{1}{l(k, s_i)} + \sum_{k \in T} \left(\Delta \cdot \frac{1}{dt(s_i, s_j)} \right) \tag{2}$$

$$\Delta = \left| \frac{1}{l(k, s_j)} - \frac{1}{l(k, s_i)} \right| \tag{3}$$

Here, Δ indicates the context of k in s_i and s_j, and it denotes variation of the highest levels of k in both s_i and s_j by Eq. (3). $dt(s_i, s_j)$ corresponds to the relevance between s_i and s_j, and it denotes the distance between s_i and s_j, that is a number of slides between them. Thus, if k appears at the high levels in s_i and s_j, and the distance between s_i and s_j is short, the weight $I(k)$ of k is high.

3.2   Detecting Slide Groups

In this work, we consider that one slide group is the collection of topics. We then divide slide groups if the cosine similarity between every two adjacent slides except a cover along the timeline of one presentation, exceeds a threshold value α. α is defined as the average cosine similarity of all slide pairs except the cover of the presentation. However, if a slide contains only a figure or a table, it is determined to belong to the previous slide. In order to calculate the cosine similarity, we normalize the weights of all topics, and we use topics and their normalized weights to generate the feature vector of each slide. The cosine similarity of two adjacent slides x and y by using the following formula:

$$Sim(\overrightarrow{x}, \overrightarrow{y}) = \frac{\sum_{n=1}^{|V|} x_n \cdot y_n}{\sqrt{\sum_{n=1}^{|V|} (x_n)^2} \cdot \sqrt{\sum_{n=1}^{|V|} (y_n)^2}} \tag{4}$$

$\overrightarrow{x}$ denotes the feature vector of slide x, and $\overrightarrow{y}$ denotes the feature vector of slide y. $|V|$ is the number of dimensions of the feature vector.

4   Slide Reconstruction Based on Expertise

4.1   Extracting Expertise of Slide Groups

In order to extract expertise of each slide group, we determine the total expertise of all important words that appear in the slide group. If a word is high expertise, it may low generality and it has not been recognized by many people. In this work, we focused on Wikipedia that is a large-scale encyclopedia, users can freely edit it. In Wikipedia, if knowledge items are well-known to many people, there are a large number of links to them; and if knowledge items are not well-known to many people, there are less links to them. Then, we consider that Wikipedia can determine whether any knowledge item is recognized by many people. In other words, we can determine the expertise of each word by counting the number of links on it. If the number of links is large, the expertise of the word is determined to be low; and if the number of links is less, the expertise of the word is determined to be high.

For this purpose, important words of each slide group are extracted by scoring words using word frequency with the indentation positions in each slide [11].

$$Weight(k, s_i) = \sum \left(\frac{1}{l(k, s_i)} \cdot f(k, s_i) \right) \tag{5}$$

Here, $l(k, s_i)$ returns the highest level of k in slide s_i by Eq. (1). $f(k, s_i)$ returns the number of occurrences of k in s_i. If a word appears frequently at the high level, the weight of this word is high. We set a threshold value of Eq. (5) at 0.6 in the preliminary experiment. Then, k can be determined as an important word in s_i, when $Weight(k, s_i)$ is more than 0.6.

In this work, we first acquire the number of links of each important word in each slide group by using the MediaWiki action API[3]. Next, we calculate the average number of links of important words in each slide group. Therefore, we determine the expertise of each slide group as follows:

$$\begin{cases} \frac{\text{total \#links of important words in each group}}{\text{total \#important words in each group}} \geq \beta, \text{low expertise} \\ \frac{\text{total \#links of important words in each group}}{\text{total \#important words in each group}} < \beta, \text{high expertise} \end{cases} \tag{6}$$

Here, β is defined as the average number of links of all important words in an original content.

4.2   Creating Additional Slides

We first detect low frequency words in an original content from important words of each slide groups. Because these low frequency words are not described in detail, supplements of them are needed. Next, we use the low frequency words of each slide group as a query to acquire top ranked Wikipedia pages by searching the Web. Therefore, we summarize the acquired Wikipedia pages using a Japanese Dependency Analysis by Yahoo! Japan Developer Network[4].

As an example in Fig. 3, a single line frame denotes an abstract on the top of a Wikipedia page by using a query (low frequency words of a slide group); a

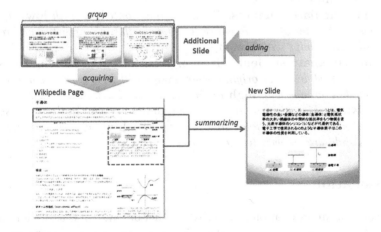

Fig. 3. An example of additional slide creation.

[3] https://www.mediawiki.org/wiki/API:Main_page.
[4] http://developer.yahoo.co.jp/webapi/jlp/da/v1/parse.html.

dashed line frame denotes a figure on the top of the Wikipedia page. Then, the abstract and the figure are summarized in the bottom right slide as an additional slide, and it will be added after the original slide group. If the Wikipedia page does not include any figure, we will acquire related figures from Google Images; and if no Wikipedia pages describe the query, we will acquire top-5 web pages from Google Search and summarize them to create a new slide.

4.3   Generating New Lecture Contents

In order to generate new lecture contents from an original content, we first determine the expertise of the whole original content as determination of the expertise of each slide group is described in Subsect. 4.1. Then, we extract the expertise of the whole original content by calculating the average number of links of slide groups as follows:

$$
\begin{cases}
\frac{\text{total \#links of slide groups}}{\text{total \#slide groups}} \geqslant \gamma, \text{low expertise} \\
\frac{\text{total \#links of slide groups}}{\text{total \#slide groups}} < \gamma, \text{high expertise}
\end{cases} \tag{7}
$$

γ is defined as the average value of the maximum and the minimum number of links of slide groups in an original content.

Therefore, in this work, new lecture contents can be generated based on the expertise of the whole original content and the expertise of each slide group in the original content with the following conditions.

V1 for beginners. If *an original content is with* **low** *expertise* then *add new slides after original slide groups with* **low** *expertise and remove original slide groups with* **high** *expertise.*

V2 for intermediate students. If *an original content is with* **low** *expertise* then *add new slides after original slide groups with* **high** *expertise and remove original slide groups with* **low** *expertise.*

V3 for intermediate students. If *an original content is with* **high** *expertise* then *add new slides after original slide groups with* **low** *expertise and remove original slide groups with* **high** *expertise.*

V4 for advanced students. If *an original content is with* **high** *expertise* then *add new slides after original slide groups with* **high** *expertise and remove original slide groups with* **low** *expertise.*

5   Evaluation

The purpose of this evaluation is to verify whether our system is useful for helping different knowledge levels of students to learn generated lecture contents.

5.1   Experimental Dataset

We used four actual lecture contents of digital libraries and generated four types of lecture contents **V1~V4**.

1. Original lecture content (L1): Computer Literacy -Lesson #1-
2. Original lecture content (L2): Image Processing -Lesson #2-
3. Original lecture content (L3): Cognitive Science -Lesson #2-
4. Original lecture content (L4): Image Processing -Lesson #3-

Table 1 shows the generated lecture contents in the evaluation. Here, '+' denotes 'added' and '-' denotes 'removed.' The expertise of original lectures (L1, L3) determined by the system is low; and the expertise of original lectures (L2, L4) determined by the system is high. Furthermore, we prepared eight patterns of generated lecture contents for beginners, intermediate students, and advanced students. The number of slide groups detected by the system is 9 for L1, 22 for L2, 10 for L3, and 7 for L4. The average number of slides in each detected slide group is approximately 2.6. In addition, we determine the expertise of each detected slide group by setting a threshold value of $\beta = 270$.

Fifteen college students completed the following 4 items (**Content Understanding**: $Q1$, **Knowledge Deepening**: $Q2$, **Interest-Expanding**: $Q3$) in a questionnaire after browsed original lecture contents and generated lecture contents from other original lectures. Moreover, before completing the questionnaire, all subjects are required to write down their knowledge levels (B: beginner, I: intermediate, or A: advanced) of each original lecture after confirmed its title.

- $Q1$: Could understand lecture contents.
- $Q2$: Deepened knowledge of lecture contents.
- $Q3$: Felt that expanding interests about lecture contents.
- $Q4$: Write down words that you felt they are specialized words.

Table 1. Generated four kinds of lecture contents **V1~V4**

	Expertise	Knowledge level	#Slides	+#Slides	-#Slide groups
L1	Low	—	24	—	—
V1	Low	Beginners	20	3	3
V2	High	Intermediate students	9	1	6
L2	High	—	43	—	—
V3	Low	Intermediate students	38	9	9
V4	High	Advanced students	23	8	13
L3	Low	—	33	—	—
V1	Low	Beginners	18	3	5
V2	High	Intermediate students	21	3	5
L4	High	—	25	—	—
V3	Low	Intermediate students	19	4	3
V4	High	Advanced students	13	3	4

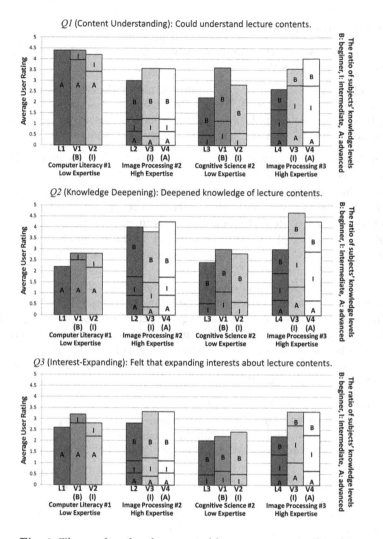

Fig. 4. The results of each generated lecture content in $Q1 \sim Q3$.

5.2 Effectiveness of Lecture Content Generation

Figure 4 illustrate the ratings of $Q1 \sim Q3$ based on a five-level Likert scale. High user ratings indicate good results. The results and findings are shown as follows:

- Except **V1** and **V2** generated from L1, $Q1$ for other generated lecture contents gain higher ratings than their original lecture contents.
- $Q2$ for lecture contents generated from L1, L3, and L4, reach higher ratings than their original lecture contents. **V3** generated from L2 is rated low. Because L2 explains a processing flow of images about "input" → "output" → "processing", **V3** does not explain "output" in the processing flow of images, it is difficult to provide enough knowledge to beginners.

Table 2. Specialized words written by subjects

Word (#Links)				
LSI (90)	silicone (199)	cylinder model (0)	single-plate type (0)	additive color mixture (1)
chip (96)	half-toning (0)	piezo element (5)	sampling theorem (96)	CIE-xyz color system (0)
rod(4)	hexamodel (0)	RGB color space (3)	uniform color space (0)	arithmetic logic unit (100)
HSB (5)	volatility (100)	supercomputer (0)	electronic shutter (1)	color mixing system (4)
DLP (105)	hard disk (424)	visible light (215)	reduction theory (0)	central processing unit (1)
DMD (7)	processor (300)	color matching (0)	tristimulus values (0)	piezoelectric element (121)
pixel (92)	photodiode (669)	architecture (134)	cogito proposition (1)	color appearance system (6)
traffic (0)	data center (173)	OLED display (6)	substance dualism (0)	von Neuman type compute (0)
CIE (7)	I/O devices (4)	spectral energy (0)	logical positivism (185)	mind-body problem (110)
monism (232)	turing test (0)	broad band (210)	integrated circuit (802)	munsell color system (9)
drive (241)	HIS space (0)	interlaced scan (0)	piezoelectric effect (9)	philosophical thinking (0)
TFlops (0)	principia (15)	dither method (0)	gamma correction (11)	subtractive color mixture (1)
CMOS (251)	distortion (36)	user interface (15)	alignment layer (0)	photosensitive drum (0)
holism (25)	descartes (23)	control unit (117)	phenomenology (440)	CIE-RGB color system (0)
memory (345)	program (246)	pixel amplifier (0)	comatic aberration (25)	error diffusion method (0)
fusing (0)	Harvard (28)	germanium (356)	alias distortion (0)	mind-body dualism (26)
HSV (4)	conic solid (29)	multiple core (254)	microcontroller (302)	photo-electric effect (0)
RGB (544)	transistor (499)	FOVEON sensor (0)	euclidean distance (35)	spherical aberration (31)
CCD (35)	geometry (722)	color system (16)	microprocessor (714)	pinhole camera model (0)
X-ray (901)	CCD sensor (0)	functionalism (39)	three-plate type (0)	perspective projection (8)
moire (39)	Aristotle (1124)	CMOS sensor (0)	dot impact printer (0)	Discourse on the Method (51)
server (1149)	Alexandros (40)	multispectral (0)	pinhole camera (156)	general-purpose computer (49)
CPU (1810)	software (3829)	global shutter (0)	optical aberration (40)	standard luminosity function (1)
GPU (90)	—	—	—	—

- $Q3$ for **V1∼V4** are rated higher than their original lecture contents, because additional slides provide more related information, they are able to expand subjects' interests and can help subjects learn the lecture contents.
- In $Q4$, the specialized words written by subjects are shown in Table 2, the average number of links of these words in Wikipedia is 157.9, it is appropriate that we assumed the specialized words have a few links in Wikipedia. How-

ever, for lecture contents containing a lot of specialized words, this method should not only involve the use of links in Wikipedia, but also include such aspects as the use of domain-specific dictionaries.

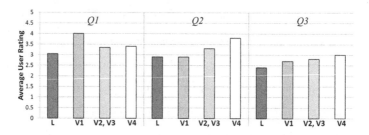

Fig. 5. The results of $Q1{\sim}Q3$ for original lecture contents (L), generated contents for beginners (**V1**), for intermediate students (**V2**, **V3**), and for advanced students (**V4**).

As discussed above, the experimental results are rated good. In particular, $Q1$ for **V1** and $Q2$ for **V4** reach high ratings. In $Q3$, although all generated lecture contents are higher than their original contents, we need to analyze the relevance between additional slides and original contents. Since there are mismatches of the expertise of several lecture contents and knowledge levels of subjects, the experiment will be carried out for different knowledge levels of more subjects.

In summary, Fig. 5 illustrates the overall ratings of **V1**$\sim$**V4** in $Q1{\sim}Q3$. The average rating of **V1**$\sim$**V4** is 3.3, it is higher than that of original lecture contents (2.8), we confirmed that our system is useful for generating four kinds of lecture contents to suit different users' interests and knowledge levels. In particular, $Q1$ for **V1** and $Q2$ for **V1** gain high ratings. In $Q3$, although all generated lecture contents are higher than their original lecture contents, we need to improve their low ratings. In the future, it is necessary to consider how to show additional slides about their insert positions or the number of additional slides.

6   Conclusions and Future Work

In this paper, we developed a novel automatic slide reconstruction system for digital libraries in e-learning, which automatically generates four kinds of lecture contents from one original content by adding new related slides and removing original slides, based on users' interests and knowledge levels. Finally, we conducted an evaluation, and the results revealed that our system can help users learn generated lecture contents suit their interests and knowledge levels.

In the future, we plan to improve the method for selecting additional contents of other types (e.g., voice, video clips, microblogs). Another future direction is to extend the usability of the system. For example, the system can allow users to decide whether and how to present the supplementary information.

Acknowledgments. This work was partially supported by JSPS KAKENHI Grant Numbers 26280042, 15K00162, 16H01722.

References

1. Edge, D., Gulwani, S., Milic-Frayling, N., Raza, M., Saputra, R.A., Wang, C., Yatani, K.: Mixed-initiative approaches to global editing in slideware. In: Proceedings of CHI 2015, pp. 3503–3512 (2015)
2. Hayama, T., Nanba, H., Kunifuji, S.: Structure extraction from presentation slide information. IEICE Trans. Inf. Syst. **J92-D**(9), 1483–1494 (2009)
3. Liew, G.M., Kan, M.-Y.: Slide image retrieval: a preliminary study. In: Proceedings of JCDL 2008, pp. 359–362 (2008)
4. Pschetz, L., Yatani, K., Edge, D.: Turningpoint: narrative-driven presentation planning. In: Proceedings of CHI 2014, pp. 1591–1594 (2014)
5. Sakuragi, Y., Aoyama, A., Kimura, F., Maeda, A.: A method for estimating meanings for groups of shapes in presentation slides. Int. J. Comput. Theory Eng. **8**(1), 74–79 (2016)
6. Sharmin, M., Bergman, L., Lu, J., Konuru, R.: On slide-based contextual cues for presentation reuse. In: Proceedings of IUI 2012, pp. 129–138 (2012)
7. Spicer, R., Lin, Y.-R., Kelliher, A., Sundaram, H.: Nextslideplease: authoring and delivering agile multimedia presentations. ACM Trans. Multimedia Comput. Commun. Appl. **8**(4), 53:1–53:20 (2012)
8. Wang, Y., Kawai, Y., Sumiya, K.: iposter: interactive poster generation based on topic structure and slide presentation. Trans. Japan. Society Artif. Intell. **30**(1), 112–123 (2015)
9. Wang, Y., Sumiya, K.: A browsing method for presentation slides based on semantic relations and document structure for e-learning. J. Inf. Process. (JIP) **20**(1), 11–25 (2011)
10. Watanabe, Y., Wu, Y., Yokota, H.: Digesting online multimedia presentation archives based on visual effects. In: Proceedings of SMDMS 2010, pp. 477–482 (2010)
11. Yokota, H., Kobayashi, T., Okamoto, H., Nakano, W.: Unified contents retrieval from an academic repository. In: Proceedings of LKR 2006, pp. 41–46 (2006)
12. Zhang, J., Xiao, C., Watanabe, T., Ishikawa, Y.: Content-based element search for presentation slide reuse. IEICE Trans. Inf. Syst. **E97-D**(10), 2685–2696 (2014)

Developing a Mobile Learning Application with LIS Discipline Ontology

Chao-Chen Chen, Wei-Chung Cheng[✉], and Yi-Ting Yang

Graduate Institute of Library and Information Studies,
National Taiwan Normal University, Taipei, Taiwan
joycechaochen@gmail.com, weichung1222@gmail.com,
ytyang729@gmail.com

Abstract. For university students stepping into learning of the professional field or even graduate students that have engaged in learning of such a field for many years, they are often unable to grasp the big picture of "the scope of professionalism", neither do they have a clue how to engage in self-learning. Therefore, how to construct the discipline-oriented ontology from the learner's standpoint to enable the learner to grasp the whole picture of the discipline as well as developing a learning APP for young people to use are important issues that facilitate self-learning. In this study, library and information science was used as the example for developing discipline-oriented LIS Ontology. In addition, the ORCID system API was employed to integrate teachers' English publications included in the Scopus database and Chinese publications included in the CLISA database in order to develop a learning APP for the discipline, allowing students to search departments, teachers, curriculums, research projects, knowledge scope, and other information of the discipline and link to the full-text database via their mobile phone, so that they can plan their own learning map and path.

Keywords: Domain ontology · Mobile application · Library and information science · Learning system · ORCID

1 Introduction

With the rise of knowledge engineering and human-computer interaction research in the 1990s, how to effectively share and reuse domain knowledge has become an important issue. Hence, how to develop ontology that presents the knowledge content and the relationships has come to focus [1]. In 2001, the Semantic Web promoted by Berners-Lee, Hendler, and Lassila [2] has added to the importance of ontological development and has closely facilitated links with the online world. Semantics used to express ontology have also been developed into XML and RDF-based SKOS(Simple Knowledge Organization System)and OWL(Web Ontology Language)syntax. At present, ontology has been applied in various fields, with diverse application modes. For instance, in the field of life science, ontology is vastly applied to link genetic codes, full-text papers or link biological names or codes to richer records and carry out inter-database search through ontology [3, 4].

A. Morishima et al. (Eds.): ICADL 2016, LNCS 10075, pp. 180–187, 2016.
DOI: 10.1007/978-3-319-49304-6_22

In the field of education, Cornell University also adopted RDF and Ontology technology as the basis for establishing an open scholar-VIVO system. In 2012, Chen et al. used the VIVO open program to construct TLIS VIVO [5]. In 2013, ORCID was applied to further integrate TLIS VIVO and Scopus data, enabling local data and global data to be combined [6]. However, the open scholar systems are mainly established for researchers rather than students. For not only university students who just step into the professional field but also the graduate students who have engaged in such a field for many years, the big picture of the scope of professionalism often fails to be grasped, neither do they have a clue how to engage in self-learning. Therefore, developing the discipline-oriented ontology from the learner's standpoint and developing a mobile learning APP which is used for retrieving discipline-related literatures for young people are important issues that facilitate self-learning. Studies related to discipline ontology are scarce. Only Stricker [7] briefly covered it by using teaching projector slides. This study used library and information science as an example for developing discipline-oriented ontology and implementing a learning APP for the discipline, allowing students to search departments, teachers, curriculums, research projects, and knowledge scope of LIS discipline via their mobile phone and link to relevant literatures through discipline ontology.

2 Related Works

What is a "discipline"? According to the definition of DBpedia, "an academic discipline, or field of study, is a branch of knowledge that is taught and researched at the college or university level." [8] Obviously, a discipline usually refers to partial knowledge of a specific field; it may even be composed of cross-disciplinary knowledge. Discipline and domain knowledge have a high degree of overlap, but they are not necessarily the same. Domain knowledge is not bound by university instructions or the scope of research and discipline ontology should still be based on domain ontology. The development of domain ontology usually starts from extracting vocabulary, defining semantic relations among words and is represented through standard syntax, and forming the knowledge architecture [9]. Vocabulary is generally extracted from two approaches: top-down and bottom-up. It's not possible to include the latest knowledge development through existing classification alone, and also it is difficult to define semantic relations among vocabularies with automatically extracting them from websites. Chen, Yeh, and Sie [10] once assisted the government in establishing policy implementation ontology for the Executive Yuan, and these two methods were conjunctively used. The former refers to selecting government policy implementation related vocabulariess from the existing classification and establishing hierarchical relations; the latter refers to researchers' extraction of words from website contents of respective ministries through skills of word segmentation and n-gram, which supplement the former.

A number of studies on domain ontology as the learning design basis are available. Gascueña, Fernández-Caballero, and González [11] believe that it will enhance users' learning efficiency through integrating "sharability" and "structure" contained in ontology into the learning system, enabling users to flexibly know the domain knowledge details or understand a wide range of domain knowledge. Panagiotopoulos, Kalou, Pierrakeas, and Kameas [12] through cooperation with domain knowledge experts and ontology engineers and targeting different instructors, established personal ontology. It is then integrated with a more complete field of ontology. Alrifai, Gennari, Tifrea, and Vittorini [13] established an adaptive learning system with learning objects as the orientation. Yarandi, Jahankhani, and Tawil [14] also adopted users' learning ability as the core to establish different levels of teaching activities and principles. Through domain ontology, an adaptive learning system was developed, enabling users to engage in learning activities via their mobile phone according to their capabilities. In 2013, Soualah-Alila, Mendes, and Nicolle [15] defined learning domain and supporting learning context through ontology and established standardized learning object meta-data. However, the abovementioned learning systems mainly target K-12 students, and univeristy student-centered learning designs are relatively rare.

On the other hand, with the popularization of science and technology, mobile phones have become essential information devices in everyday life. Due to the advancement of network technology, a variety of mobile applications have emerged. Users no longer need to open the browser and enter a URL in a conventional manner; instead, they can open an APP and directly connect to the website for access of resources needed, thus substantially changing people's information use behavior. Gikas and Grant [16] believe that users can directly interact with information contents with the features of mobile learning, which indirectly enhances learning motivation and effectiveness. However, relevant studies have also pointed out that the major limitations of learning through a mobile phone are that hardware performance inadequacy [17] or the learner's needs fails to be catered to in actual situations [18]. Therefore, if features of ontology can be brought into play and not only apply it in mobile phone learning, but also consider them as means to strengthen contents instead of overly relying on hardware conditions. It should help the learner to achieve the most effective learning.

3   Purpose of Research

Over the past, the open scholar system established by the education field through ontology mainly targeted researchers rather than students as service targets. Not only university students who initialize their learning in a professional field, but also experienced graduate students are often unable to clarify "the scope of professionalism", neither do they have a clue how to engage in self-learning. Therefore, how to develop the discipline-oriented ontology from the learner's standpoint to enable the learner to grasp the whole picture of the discipline and implement a learning APP for young people are important issues.

Specifically, this study used the discipline of library and information science as an example, develop the ontology of library and information science and implement a learning App for the discipline. However, in non-English speaking countries such as Taiwan, in addition to collecting articles published in English by researchers, researchers' articles published in Chinese must also be integrated in order to collect learning resources. Therefore, the Name-Authority File in Chinese and English is the priority issue to be dealt with when building discipline-based databases. Chen, Liang, and Sie [19] once used Scopus Author Identifiers, ORCID and Google Scholar Citations to organize authority for library and information science domain in Taiwan. The study also designed an application program model through Linked Open Data technology to effectively link researchers and their publications. Based on the model, this study added teachers' (authors') service units, courses commenced, topic domain, and research projects to develop library and information science domain ontology and to integrate the complete discipline ontology of library and information science.

4   Learning Application Design of LIS

4.1   Framework of Discipline-Oriented Ontology

For students of library and information science, in order to understand the scope of the discipline, there are two main perspectives to consider: One perspective is related to what schools/departments the domain belong to, which departments teachers belong to, which curriculums are taught by instructors, which research projects are executed, and which articles are published; the other perspective is the knowledge framework of the discipline, which is the domain ontology. In short, discipline ontology with leaners as the starting points mainly consists of five parts: domain ontology, schools/departments, instructors, curriculums, and research projects. From these five search points, relevant literatures can be found and interconnected, enabling the learner to grasp the whole picture of the discipline. The relations of the five parts are as shown in Fig. 1.

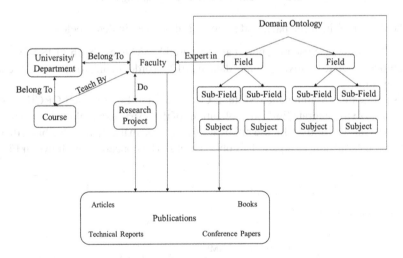

Fig. 1. LIS discipline ontology

4.2   LIS Learning APP Design

System Framework.   To the user, the above-mentioned discipline ontology is also the front-end search function of the learning system. Thus, in order to achieve the five search points and their interconnection function, the back-end system need to include three main parts: LIS Open Scholar System, LIS Publication Maintenance System, and LIS Domain Ontology Maintenance System. The complete system framework is as shown in Fig. 2.

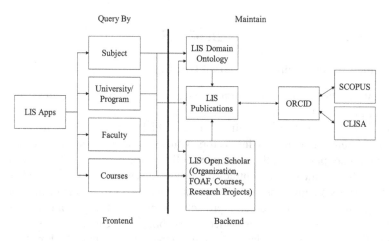

Fig. 2.   System structure of LIS learning APP

The design of the three back-end systems is described in detail below:

- LIS Open Scholar System: Chen et al. once used VIVO to establish TLIS VIVO, and employed RDF to archive Scholars data in 2012, in order to link to other open scholar systems [5].
- LIS publication Maintenance System: Chen, Ko, and Lee [6] used ORCID system API in 2013 to integrate English publications of the instructors included in the Scopus database, as well as the Chinese publications included in the CLISA database, thereby quickly establishing complete LIS publications. The concept is as shown in Fig. 3.

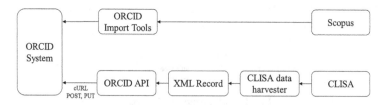

Fig. 3.   Publications harvesting via ORCID (Source: LNCS 8279, p. 114)

- LIS Domain Ontology Maintenance System: The Ontology Editing System mainly includes maintenance of knowledge tree and thesaurus. Each node in the knowledge tree can be linked to the thesaurus and the detailed function is as shown in Fig. 4.

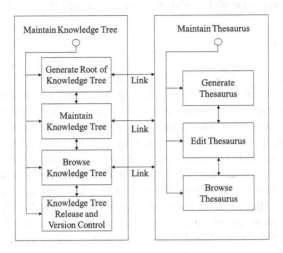

Fig. 4. Domain Ontology maintain system

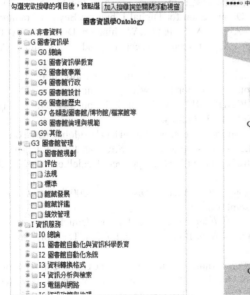

Fig. 5. System interface

Mobile Phone Search Interface. The mobile APP mainly developed in this study allows users to commence search and read literatures at any time and any place. The back-end ontology interface and mobile phone search frame are as shown in Fig. 5. The evaluation of the system usability will be processed in the future.

5   Conclusion

Over the past, the open scholar system established by the education field through ontology mainly targeted researchers rather than learners as service targets. Many ontology-based learning systems adopt K-12 as targets. Those that adopt university learners as targets are scarce. The researcher once established the open scholar system and ontology system at different time settings. This study is in continuation to previous studies of researchers and systems developed. However, the greatest difference between the system in this study and those developed in the past is that this study is learner-oriented and that discipline-oriented ontology has been developed. It not only expresses domain ontology with discipline knowledge as the scope, but also develops learning APP intended for young people to use, which facilitates self-learning. Furthermore, the LIS Discipline Ontology developed in this study is an ontology that can be shared. As far as discipline development is concerned, it shall serve as a very important basis.

References

1. Gruber, T.R.: A translation approach to portable ontology specifications. Knowl. Acquisition **5**(2), 199–220 (1993)
2. Berners-Lee, T., Hendler, J., Lassila, O.: The semantic web. Sci. Am. **284**(5), 35–43 (2001)
3. Hodge, G.: Systems of Knowledge Organization for Digital Libraries: Beyond Traditional Authority Files. 1755 Massachusetts Ave., NW, Suite 500, Washington, DC 20036 (2000)
4. Klischewski, R.: Semantic web for e-Government-a research agenda. AIS SIG SEMIS Newsletter (2004)
5. Chen, C.-C., Chen, C.-H., Lai, C.-C., Lu, C.-H., Yu, C.-Y.: Implementation of open scholar platform and integration of open resources in national Taiwan normal university (NTNU). In: Chen, H.-H., Chowdhury, G. (eds.) ICADL 2012. LNCS, vol. 7634, pp. 344–346. Springer, Heidelberg (2012). doi:10.1007/978-3-642-34752-8_46
6. Chen, C.-C., Ko, M.W., Lee, V.T.-Y.: Migrating researcher from local to global: using ORCID to develop the TLIS VIVO with CLISA and scopus. In: Urs, S.R., Na, J.-C., Buchanan, G. (eds.) ICADL 2013. LNCS, vol. 8279, pp. 113–116. Springer, Heidelberg (2013). doi: 10.1007/978-3-319-03599-4_13
7. Stricker, M.: Developing an Ontology for Academic Disciplines (2008). http://owd.hu-berlin.de/pdf/OntologyAcademicDisciplines.pdf
8. DBpedia. (n.d.): academic discipline. http://dbpedia.org/ontology/academicDiscipline
9. Jacob, E.K.: Ontologies and the semantic web. Bull. Am. Soc. Inf. Sci. Technol. **29**(4), 19–22 (2003). doi:10.1002/bult.283
10. Chen, C.-c., Yeh, J.-h., Sie, S.-h.: Government ontology and thesaurus construction: a Taiwanese experience. In: Fox, E.A., Neuhold, E.J., Premsmit, P., Wuwongse, V. (eds.) ICADL 2005. LNCS, vol. 3815, pp. 263–272. Springer, Heidelberg (2005). doi: 10.1007/11599517_30

11. Gascueña, J.M., Fernández-Caballero, A., González, P.: Domain ontology for personalized e-learning in educational systems. In: 6th IEEE International Conference on Advanced Learning Technologies (2006)
12. Panagiotopoulos, I., Kalou, A., Pierrakeas, C., Kameas, A.: An ontological approach for domain knowledge modeling and management in e-learning systems. In: Iliadis, L., Maglogiannis, I., Papadopoulos, H., Karatzas, K., Sioutas, S. (eds.) AIAI 2012. IAICT, vol. 382, pp. 95–104. Springer, Heidelberg (2012). doi:10.1007/978-3-642-33412-2_10
13. Alrifai, M., Gennari, R., Tifrea, O., Vittorini, P.: The user and domain models of the TERENCE adaptive learning system. In: Vittorini, P., et al. (eds.) International Workshop on Evidence-Based TEL. AISC, vol. 152, pp. 83–90. Springer, Heidelberg (2012)
14. Yarandi, M., Jahankhani, H., Tawil, A. R.: An ontology-based adaptive mobile learning system based on learners' abilities. In: 2012 IEEE Global Engineering Education Conference (EDUCON) (2012)
15. Soualah-Alila, F., Mendes, F., Nicolle, C.: A context-based adaptation In Mobile Learning. In: IEEE Computer Society Technical Committee on Learning Technology (TCLT) (2013)
16. Gikas, J., Grant, M.M.: Mobile computing devices in higher education: Student perspectives on learning with cellphones, smartphones & social media. Internet High. Educ. **19**, 18–26 (2013)
17. Godwin-Jones, R.: Emerging technologies mobile APPs for language learning. Lang. Learn. Technol. **15**(2), 2–11 (2011)
18. Pernas, A.M., Diaz, A., Motz, R., Oliveira, J.P.M.D.: Enriching adaptation in e-learning systems through a situation-aware ontology network. Interact. Technol. Smart Educ. **9**(2), 60–73 (2012). doi:10.1108/17415651211242215
19. Chen, C.C., Liang, H.S., Sie, S.H.: Transforming publication list of LIS TW in author identification services to open linked data for mobile application. In: Tuamsuk, K., et al. (eds.) ICADL 2014. LNCS, vol. 8839, pp. 423–427. Springer, Switzerland (2014)

Heuristic Evaluation of an Information Literacy Game

Yan Ru Guo[✉] and Dion Hoe-Lian Goh

Wee Kim Wee School of Communication and Information,
Nanyang Technological University, Singapore, Singapore
{W120030,ashlgoh}@ntu.edu.sg

Abstract. Libraries have tapped on the popularity of digital game-based learning to promote information literacy (IL) education to students. However, among the many IL games that have been developed, evaluations have mostly relied on anecdotal quotations, or procedures which were neither systematic nor rigorous. This study fills in this gap by adopting the heuristic evaluation method with end-users to evaluate *Library Escape*, an IL game for tertiary students. Participants identified problems with the game according to the Heuristic Evaluation of Playability (HEP) framework. Useful feedback was gathered, as well as suggestions on how to improve it. We proposed to extend the HEP framework by including two more categories on characters/graphics and pedagogical effectiveness. Implication and limitations of this study are discussed, and directions for future work are pointed out.

Keywords: Digital game-based learning · Game design · Information literacy · Heuristic evaluation · Heuristic Evaluation of Playability

1 Introduction

With the explosion of digital information, information literacy (IL) skills have become more important, especially to students. There is a widespread acknowledgement that students need to be supported in the development of their IL skills. Here, a development that has significantly influenced learning is the use of digital games. Digital game-based learning (DGBL), refers to the use of digital games for learning purposes [1]. Digital games have found a broad audience, particularly for youth. In particular, DGBL affords a highly interactive medium with sophisticated pedagogical attributes [2]. Libraries have tapped on the popularity of DGBL to promote IL education to students [3].

However, in the rush to produce fun and educational games, many such initiatives failed [2]. DGBL requires effective delivery of educational content and enjoyable game-play experiences, and it is not easy to weave the two concepts together in a coherent and holistic manner [4]. To ensure success, DGBL designers need to adopt iterative design and evaluation approaches informed by user input [5]. Currently, most user evaluations of IL games have relied on anecdotal quotations (e.g., *The Information Literacy Game* [6]), or procedures which were neither systematic nor rigorous (e.g., *LibraryCraft* [7]). Therefore, this paper addresses this gap by demonstrating how heuristic evaluation with users can be employed as a systematic and effective way to evaluate an IL game.

© Springer International Publishing AG 2016
A. Morishima et al. (Eds.): ICADL 2016, LNCS 10075, pp. 188–199, 2016.
DOI: 10.1007/978-3-319-49304-6_23

Compared with interviews and surveys, heuristic evaluation is fast and inexpensive, and it offers clear, concrete and specific rules that can be used to refine the game and implement changes directly [8]. By separating the heuristics into different categories, heuristic evaluation provides enough information to enable evaluators to judge all major problems of a system. Further, heuristic evaluation with end-users (i.e., students) makes it possible for them to communicate their ideas and concerns to librarians, game designers and developers. We used the Heuristic Evaluation of Playability (HEP) as a framework to evaluate an IL game that was previously developed.

2   Related Work

2.1   Digital Game-Based Learning in Information Literacy Education

Many academic libraries have tapped on DGBL to encourage students to acquire IL knowledge. For example, the University of North Carolina reported success of *Information Literacy Game*, a graphically-simple online board game [6]. Carnegie Mellon University designed two IL games: *Within Range* and *I'll Get It* [3]. *Within Range* asks the players to sort three shelves of books into the correct order. *I'll Get It* puts the player in the role of a librarian at a busy university library help desk. Players need to prioritize the students so that no one is waiting too long and gives up, and fulfill their information requests by selecting the most appropriate resources.

Students are recruited to playtest the IL games evaluate their effectiveness. For example, Utah Valley University developed two IL games: *Get a Clue* and *LibraryCraft* [7]. *Get a Clue* follows a detective through the steps of solving a crime. Students can tour around the physical library building using the clues. In the initial evaluation, almost half of the participants were confused about the gameplay. The library hence revised the game. Over three hundred students played the revised game and completed a short survey. The results indicated the game reached students who had minimal exposure to the library, and most students agreed the game was easy to follow. The second game, *LibraryCraft*, aims to get students familiar with the library's website and digital resources. A short survey was attached to the game for evaluation purposes. Among the 52 students who completed *LibraryCraft*, a majority agreed that they learnt something useful, and the game was fun. Moreover, the University of Michigan designed *BiblioBouts* to help students produce a higher-quality bibliography in their assignments [2]. Students can check the sources that other players contribute, to discover sources they would not have found otherwise. To evaluate *BiblioBouts*, students were invited to play the game over a two-week period. The extensive evaluation process involved game diary forms, pre-and post-game questionnaires, immediate focus group interviews, follow-up interviews four or more months later, pre- and post-game individual interviews, and game activity logs. While most students reported positive learning experiences during gameplay, some failed to grasp its educational values.

As shown, existing user evaluations of IL games with short surveys and interviews were too generic to be of much use, and they failed to offer insights on how to further improve the games. Hence in the next section, we present an evaluation method commonly used in the software development community: heuristic evaluation.

2.2 Heuristic Evaluation

To ensure success, game designers need to involve end-users to elevate the game's usability. Various methods have been devised for identifying usability problems in both early designs and more mature prototypes. One technique that has the potential to be useful here is heuristic evaluation with experts. Heuristics are those "rules of thumb" that define key aspects in software design [9]. Compared with other methods such as laboratory usability studies or user interviews, expert-based heuristic evaluation uses simple questions to examine different aspects of the software and find usability problems or violations that may have a deleterious effect on the users' interaction with the software [10]. Heuristic evaluation is an intuitive, efficient, analytical and low-cost usability method; it has become the ideal method in iterative development environments commonly found in the software design industry [5, 11, 12].

Heuristic evaluation has been used to in various situations, from medical websites, to e-learning applications and commercial video games. For example, [12] analyzed four mobile games using the heuristic evaluation method with two experts. The playability heuristics helped them identify problems with commercially successful games and the areas in which the games could improve, such as on mobility and usability. Heuristic evaluation has also been used to assess DGBL. In another example, primary school teachers were invited in the heuristic evaluation of *MathQuest*, a role-playing game that teaches mathematics [13]. The authors used the usability problems highlighted from the heuristic evaluation and developed a new version of the game, which was positively received by students.

However, one criticism of expert-based heuristic evaluation approach is that experts may not fully understand the context of the IL game and predict user expectations, so they are not able to identify issues from the end-users' perspective [14]. Few studies have involved end-users in the heuristic evaluation of DGBL. One of the few such studies is reported by [15]. They designed, *Socialdrome*, an educational game to teach social skills to young children. Twelve primary school children were invited to evaluate the game. The authors reported that the heuristics were found to be effective in providing structure and as scaffolds to support game evaluation with children.

2.3 Heuristic Evaluation of Playability

The HEP was built on prior studies [16]. The authors invited several playability experts and game designers to verify the framework. We chose HEP as the framework for the present study as it focuses not only on usability but also on playability, fun and enjoyment, factors closely connected to user experience in DGBL.

The HEP comprises four categories: game play, game story, mechanics, and usability. Specifically, *game play* refers to the players' interaction with the game system. Example heuristics include challenging and positive game experiences, varying game activities to minimize players' fatigue, appropriate pacing, immediate feedback and meaningful rewards. *Game story* includes all plots and character development in the game. Good game stories should be consistent, interesting, and emotion-intriguing. *Mechanics* is concerned with providing an interactive structure and environment. For example, the control should be initiative, customizable and consistent. *Usability* refers to the degree to which the players are able to interact with the game. Example heuristics include easy-to-understand tutorials, pleasing visual design, meaningful auditory cues, and so on.

Further, the HEP has been validated by others in game evaluations. For example, the HEP was assessed with eight professionals from the game industry and academia [17]. Results indicated that the HEP excelled in providing short and compact descriptions that are clear and understandable to users. Furthermore, the HEP was adopted to evaluate eight commercial games and investigate the design factors that influence players' continuous engagement [18]. The HEP has been used together with qualitative questionnaires, system logs and focus group interviews, to identify problems and issues in a game prototype [19].

3 Library Escape

The game to be evaluated is briefly introduced here. More information can be found in [4]. *Library Escape* is a role-playing game that belongs to the room escape genre, where the protagonist Tom, has to escape from a haunted library within an hour. The game starts with a comic strip to introduce the backstory when the protagonist is shocked to have gotten a D for his IL module. He consults the instructor, Professor Senka, who suggests that he should go to a special library. She leads Tom to a haunted library and pushes him in. The game begins.

The game comprises six missions in six locations of the library, and walks players through an academic information search process. Different objects are scattered in each mission where useful IL knowledge is hidden. Each mission aims to teach IL-related topics, from foundational concepts such as what is IL and why is IL important, to practical skills such as how to search for information systematically, and how to evaluate information for academic purposes. Players have to answer three to five quiz questions at the end of each mission before proceeding to the next. The questions take various forms, such as fill-in-the-blanks, single-choice, multiple-choice, and sorting questions (see Fig. 1 for an example).

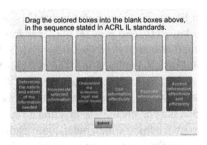

Fig. 1. Quiz question   **Fig. 2.** Feedback from librarian

Mr. Babbage, the guardian of the library, helps players along the way. Scripted feedback from Mr. Babbage is provided when players successfully find an object, and after they submit answers in the quizzes (see Fig. 2). Players are given two chances to answer each question, and they cannot progress to the next mission without answering correctly. There are also obstacles in the game that players have to overcome, such as an evil ghost and a computer virus. After Mission Six, Mr. Babbage thanks them for finding the magic wand, and gives a certificate as the reward, showing that they have finished the game. Afterwards, Mr. Babbage shows their performance on the quiz questions, which is calculated based on their answers and differs from individual to individual.

Mission One takes place in the closed stacks. It introduces background knowledge about IL. Players need to find the relevant objects to reveal the content (see Fig. 3), for example, the definition of IL behind a dictionary, the IL standards behind a scale. Mission Two takes place in the open shelves, where the evil ghost sleeps and wakes up occasionally. Players need to stop moving when the ghost wakes up to avoid being attacked. This mission teaches players how to select a topic, as well as what library anxiety is, its causes, and how to overcome it. Mission Three takes place in the reference section, where the ghost constantly moves and the players need to avoid touching it. It presents the scholarly publication cycle. Different sources of scientific literature are also included, especially journals, to help students understand the range of sources they can refer to when working on academic projects.

Fig. 3. Tom walks in Mission One   **Fig. 4.** Evil ghost in Mission Five

Mission Four brings the players to the digital library with a computer virus inside. Players need to quickly find objects hidden with knowledge to prevent the virus from infecting the entire digital library. Practical information search strategies are introduced here, including building blocks, pearl growing, and successive fractions. The evil ghost becomes furious in Mission Five and spews out fire to burn down the library (see Fig. 4). Players need to put out the fire in a timely manner. Here, some objects can only be activated after others have been found. For example, the players have to first find a piano that plays a piece of music, in order to entertain an owl, behind which hides some useful information. This mission requires players to evaluate the information retrieved, and to reflect on their information seeking process. Two ghosts roam around in the café in Mission Six, and the players have to be strategic in their movements. Mission Six concludes the game by listing the roles and responsibilities of an author, plagiarism, and the importance of making citations.

4 Research Method

Heuristic evaluations are usually conducted among five to seven experts. Some scholars argue that since heuristic evaluations are conducted with experts, it cannot provide attitudinal or behavioral data from actual users, hence this method should be supplemented with user playtesting and other usability studies [9]. Evaluation with users is the benchmark of any playability evaluation, since designers can never completely predict user behavior [16]. Further, studies found that while experts are good at identifying general heuristic violations, students can point out more specific issues with the game design [14]. Hence we involved end-users in the heuristic evaluation.

Participants were recruited from a major local university and participation was voluntary. All students were introduced to the heuristic evaluation method and the HEP framework. The game file compressed in a CD, together with the content form and heuristic evaluation questionnaire, were distributed to those who agreed to take part in this study. They were asked to install the game on their own computers, complete the game, and fill in the heuristic evaluation questionnaire.

The heuristic evaluation questionnaire consisted of three sections. The first section contained 43 heuristics from HEP. Participants were asked to play the game while focusing on how it supported or violated each heuristic on a 5-point Likert-type scale (4: strongly agree, 3: agree, 2: disagree, 1: strongly disagree, and 0: not applicable). The second section gathered participants' subjective feedback on the top and bottom two heuristics in each of the four HEP categories that the game fulfilled or violated, and how to improve the game. The last section collected demographic information such as gender, age, gaming experience game play frequency and genre preference.

5 Results

In total, 39 students played the game and completed the heuristic evaluation questionnaire. The sample is fairly balanced in terms of gender, with slightly more male (56.4 %) than female students; a majority of participants were below 30 years old (82.1 %). In terms of gaming experience, around half of them had been playing computer games for more than two years (64.1 %), with two participants without any experience. Among the different types of games, mobiles games are most popular, with a majority playing at least once a month (84.6 %), followed by standalone PC games at 35.9 %. While there are 43 heuristics in the HEP framework, we will focus on the top and bottom two heuristics in each category due to space constraints.

- **Game Play:** The top rated heuristics are that the game provides clear goals, present overriding goal early and short-term goals throughout play ($M = 3.21$), and the first player action is obvious and result in immediate positive feedback ($M = 3.19$). The two most violated heuristics are: the game is enjoyable to replay ($M = 1.97$), and player's fatigue is minimized by varying activities and pacing ($M = 2.31$).

- **Game Story:** The top rated heuristic in this category is that the player understands the storyline as a single consistent vision ($M = 3.41$). The second highest rated heuristic is that player experiences fairness of outcomes ($M = 2.93$). However, the lowest rated heuristics are: the player spends time thinking about possible story outcomes ($M = 2.22$), and player is interested in the storyline ($M = 2.34$).

- **Mechanics:** The most supported heuristics are: a player should always be able to identify their score/status and goal in the game ($M = 3.43$); and the game should react in a consistent way to the player's actions ($M = 3.16$). Players mostly disagree with the heuristics that mechanics actions have consistently mapped and learnable responses ($M = 2.69$), and players should be given controls to learn quickly yet expandable for advanced options ($M = 2.70$).

- **Usability:** The two highest rated heuristics are: sounds from the game provide meaningful feedback or stir a particular emotion ($M = 3.45$), and players do not need to use a manual to play game ($M = 3.42$). The lowest rated heuristics are: the player can easily turn the game off and on, and be able to save games in different states ($M = 1.78$); and the player should experience the menu in the game ($M = 2.35$).

6   Discussion

6.1   Top and Bottom Heuristics

Game Play. The clear goals of *Library Escape* were rated positively by participants. The goals are presented at the start: help the librarian find the magic wand and escape. Participants understood the goals very well, which is confirmed by this comment: *"the game clearly establishes the main goal early: to rid the librarian of the ghost. The intermediate goals of finding the clues and completing the quiz are also clearly presented and obvious"*. Further, the game starts in an easy manner: players just need to use the arrow keys to move the protagonist, which is obvious and intuitive to players. Participants welcomed the easy start. An example comment is that *"the game is easy to start and manipulate; it is difficult to complete the goals at the end"*.

On the negative side, there are some aspects of game play that frustrated the players, such as making them repeat the mission if they cannot answer the questions correctly, and inadequate game scenarios and outcomes. Participants remarked that *"The game had lots of repeatable steps: finding the objects from the start again and again was very tiring and irritating"*. The repetition led to a decrease in their learning motivation. Typical comments include: *"While the storyline and game goals are presented consistently, the linear storyline with lack of different possible outcomes made it less engaging"* and *"I no longer yearn to learn the knowledge"*. To improve on this aspect, one participant suggested providing rewards to keep players going in each mission: *"Player should not be asked to start finding the hidden objects over and over. There should be rewards to motive the player to go through all the activities"*.

Game Story. The simple and consistent storyline in *Library Escape* was rated favorably. The storyline is simple: to find the magic wand by acquiring IL knowledge, and to battle the evil ghost along the way. Many participants praised the simplicity and consistency of the storyline in *Library Escape*. For example, one noted that "*the storyline of the game is very simple and easy to understand. I was able to grasp the story just after a minute of the gameplay start*", and "*The game story and goals are consistent*". However, other participants found this too simplistic and not interesting. This is suggested by comments such as "*The story is very simple. It's a no brainer to the players, and doesn't make the players think much*".

The outcome of *Library Escape* is strictly based on the answers to the quiz questions, so it is fair. At the same time, it is binary: correct and incorrect. Participants expected divergent storylines and various potential outcomes based on their different actions in the game. In this aspect, some lamented that "*There is only one way to complete the game and it doesn't provide the player the element of surprise or challenge, which is what makes player come back*", and "*The story outcomes are the same for every level and I just need to find the items without interrupting the ghost. And then I need to answer the quiz correctly at the end.*"

Mechanics. Participants rated highly on the immediate feedback in *Library Escape*, one of which is the countdown timer. To help players concentrate on the educational content, the countdown timer in *Library Escape* pauses when players are reading. It is a deliberate design decision so that players do not need to hurry or panic when learning. This was noticed and praised by participants: "*Timer is accurate as it stops while content is being explained. It only drains while game is ongoing*". The game provides frequent feedback for players to determine progress towards objectives, and helps players concentrate on the tasks at hand. For instance, one participant wrote that "*No matter which level I am on, I can find the score in the top right corner so that I can clearly know how many items I still need to find on this level*".

As *Library Escape* is a simple game, there are no complicated mechanics. The simple and intuitive mechanics have some merits. For example, participants remarked that "*the controls are intuitive and I feel in control throughout the gameplay*", and "*Though there is a lack of customizability of controls, it is not a big concern for this game genre as the controls are already simplistic enough*". However, some hardcore game players were disappointed, and one lamented "*There is no setting. It doesn't provide user with additional sense of control*". In some missions, players need to move carefully to avoid colliding with the evil ghost. Participants found it stressful. Some complained that "*It is very frustrating and demoralizing, especially when I was penalized by being caught by the evil ghost. After a few attempts, I lost my interest.*" To improve the game, some rules may be modified to enhance enjoyment. For example, the game could allow players to find ways to kill the evil ghost, through acquiring the IL content, or answering questions correctly and quickly.

Usability. Participants liked the immediate auditory cues and easy start. This is confirmed by comments such as "*Each time I find an object, instantaneous sound effect is provided. And I will know that's the object I need*", and "*the player does not have to* *use a manual to play the game, the game is very intuitive in its design*". Further, the sounds are consistent with the overall game experience to create the haunted library feeling, which impressed the players. This is implied by comments such as "*The background sound matches game very well, I feel scared when ghost is approaching me quickly*".

However, the game lacks important functions such as save, using "ESC" to quit the game, or using the mouse to move the protagonist on screen. It caused some initial confusion and anxiety among participants. Many participants complained about the lack of these functions. They complained that "*I cannot skip levels, cannot turn off the unnecessary disruptions, and when I accidentally hit the "Esc" button, it resets everything*", and "*the lack of save ability was a big annoyance as players had to dedicate a substantial amount of time and risk losing all progress*".

6.2   Possible Extensions to HEP

This section proposes two possible extensions to HEP, together with the detailed heuristics in each category, that emerged from participants' comments (see Table 1).

Table 1.   Two new categories for HEP

Characters/Graphics	• Players have a sense of control over their characters (HEP) • Players are interested in the characters (HEP) • The non-player characters can stir up emotional feelings • The graphics are meaningful, and not distractive • The animations are attractive and realistic
Pedagogical effectiveness	• The educational content is presented in an interesting manner to attract players' attention • Players can exercise what they have learnt • Educational knowledge is related to storyline and game progression • The game provides options to accommodate different learning styles from players

Supplementary Category: Characters/Graphics. HEP has two heuristics on character design: the player has a sense of control over their character and is able to use tactics and strategies; as well as the player is interested in the characters because they are like me, or they are interesting to me, or the characters develop as action occurs. We propose to move these two heuristics to the new category on characters/graphics, while adding three new heuristics.

These two heuristics only focus on player characters, and there are no heuristics on the non-player characters. Thus the first heuristic is on non-player characters: that they can evoke emotions to heighten players' experience. In *Library Escape*, the antagonist (evil ghost) stirred up negative emotions from participants. One participant expressed how he became emotional when battling the evil ghost. He said that "*I feel scared when ghost is approaching me quickly*". This indicates that players were immersed in the game and enjoyed playing it since flow experience can include heighten positive and negative experience.

To provide a richer and more immersive game environment, the second heuristic is that the graphics in the game are meaningful, and not distracting to players. The graphics in *Library Escape* were received positively. This is affirmed by commented such as *"The graphics are fun and inspiring. A good amount of effort seems to be put in to create it"*, and *"Interface and graphics are not intrusive at all, they connect well with the game"*. Participants commented that the art and graphics in the game are an important aspect, and should be recognized easily. For example, one noted that *"I think it is important to match the drawing and the characters. So the players will not be confused with the graphics and spend much time to understand the graphics"*.

The third heuristic concerns the animation work, which is attractive and realistic to help keep the player engrossed in the gameplay, enhancing the motivational appeal of the educational game. Some participants commented on the character animation in *Library Escape*, which was actually simple. They noticed that the facial expressions from the protagonist identified with their own feelings. One participant wrote: *"Whenever I feel scared, the character also changed: it sweats and expresses the emotions similar to how I was feeling"*.

Complementary Category: Pedagogical Effectiveness. Given that the purpose of this game is to teach IL knowledge, we propose one complementary category to HEP, on pedagogical effectiveness. This category specifies how the educational content should be combined with gameplay experience in DGBL. Informed by participants' input, we propose four heuristics in this category.

First, the educational content is presented in an interesting manner to attract players' attention. In Library Escape, the players need to equip themselves with adequate IL knowledge to rescue the librarian and escape from the haunted library. Many participants liked the idea of learning IL from a game and found it innovative. For example, they stated that *"It is fun playing the game while gaining some good knowledge"*, and *"I can learn some information theories which are good for me. I think I will not read articles to learn the knowledge. But learning from game is a cool idea."* The use of affective feedback also increased their learning motivation. This is confirmed by comments such as *"I was very happy to get immediate feedback and felt encouraged after completing each task and progressing through the next levels"*.

The second heuristic is that the educational content is relevant to players, and players should be allowed to exercise what they have learnt in the game. Although the IL content in Library Escape is useful to players, many participants wanted to relate the content to their prior knowledge level. For example, one participant suggested providing customized learning plans based on prior test performance. He stated that *"players can take a test about IL in the game at first. Based on the test result, the game can suggest different lessons for players to study. Then the game can ask the player to take a test again at the end"*.

The third heuristic is that the acquisition of educational knowledge is related to the game storyline, and useful for game progression. Some participants were focused on enjoyable play experience, and complained that the IL knowledge and quiz questions distracted them from enjoying the game. Typical comments include *"The quiz is* disrupting", and "*After a few failed attempts, I just go through the motion without gaining additional knowledge from the repeated actions.*" Some participants suggested making do with incorrect answers, so that they can continue the gameplay. One wrote: "*The Q&A can be less important, so the scores are still tracked, but level advancement is possible with incorrect answers*".

Finally, the game provides options to accommodate different learning styles from students. This can be achieved by providing options of single or multiple players, competitive or collaborative gameplay, and auditory cues. For example, some of our participants liked to socialize and compete with other players in the game. One wrote that "*we can have an option to play together with other players, in an online version. This would bring out player's competitiveness so that player can study the content and be serious about the learning*". Other participants commented that auditory cues should be provided to reduce cognitive workload. They argued that "*The materials can be read to us and we can listen like normal lectures*".

7   Conclusion

This study engaged end-users in the heuristic evaluation of *Library Escape*, an IL game for tertiary students. The HEP was adopted as the heuristic evaluation framework for participants to identify how the game fulfilled or violated these heuristics. We proposed to extend the HEP framework by including two categories on characters/graphics and pedagogical effectiveness for DGBL evaluation.

This study has several implications. On the theoretical front, we combined a user-centered design approach with a traditionally expert-based heuristic evaluation. By giving end-users a voice and using a systematic heuristic evaluation, specific issues have been identified. We proposed a supplementary category on characters/graphics and a complementary category on pedagogical effectiveness increases the usefulness of HEP framework in evaluations of a broader range of computer games, including educational ones. On the practical front, the involvement of students to contribute to the design process may lead to a sense of ownership in them, and result in better buy-in for the IL game. These findings will empower designers to develop educational games more efficiently. The development of better educational games will in turn fuel more research in DGBL.

Nonetheless, using homogeneous participants could have reduced the generalizability of our findings. Hence a follow-up study that involves users with more varied profiles from diverse backgrounds of different ages could help broaden our understanding of DGBL design. Moreover, the heuristics in the additional two categories proposed in this study emerged from users' comments for this game. Future researchers can validate them in other educational games. Finally, future research can explore other evaluation methods, such as the empirical evaluation method to triangulate findings from this study.

References

1. Gee, J.P.: What video games have to teach us about learning and literacy. Comput. Entertainment **1**(1), 20 (2003)

2. Markey, K., Leeder, C., Rieh, S.Y.: Designing Online Information Literacy Games Students Want to Play. Rowman & Littlefield, Lanham (2014)
3. Beck, D., Callison, R., Fudrow, J., Hood, D.: Your library instruction is in another castle: developing information literacy based video games at Carnegie Mellon University. In: Harris, A., Rice, S.E. (eds.) Gaming in Academic Libraries: Collections, Marketing and Information Literacy, pp. 135–148. Association of College and Research Libraries, Chicago (2008)
4. Guo, Y.R., Goh, D.H.-L.: The Design of an Information Literacy Game. In: Tuamsuk, K., Jatowt, A., Rasmussen, E. (eds.) ICADL 2014. LNCS, vol. 8839, pp. 354–364. Springer, Heidelberg (2014). doi:10.1007/978-3-319-12823-8_37
5. Baxter, K., Courage, C., Caine, K.: Evaluation methods. In: Baxter, K., Courage, C., Caine, K. (eds.) Understanding Your Users, 2nd edn, pp. 430–446. Morgan Kaufmann, Boston (2015)
6. Rice, S.: Education on a Shoestring: Creating an Online Information Literacy Game. Association of College and Research Libraries, Chicago (2008)
7. Smith, A.-L., Baker, L.: Getting a clue: creating student detectives and dragon slayers in your library. Ref. Serv. Rev. 39(4), 628–642 (2011)
8. Choi, J., Bakken, S.: Web-based education for low-literate parents in Neonatal Intensive Care Unit: development of a website and heuristic evaluation and usability testing. Int. J. Med. Informatics 79(8), 565–575 (2010)
9. Köffel, C., Haller, M.: Heuristics for the evaluation of tabletop games. In: Workshop at the 2008 Conference on Human Factors in Computing Systems. ACM, New York (2008)
10. Carmody, K.W.: Exploring serious game design heuristics: a delphi study (Doctor of Education). Northeastern University, Boston, Massachusetts (2012)
11. Federoff, M.A.: Heuristics and usability guidelines for the creation and evaluation of fun in video games (Master of Science). Indiana University (2002)
12. Ponnada, A., Kannan, A.: Evaluation of mobile games using playability heuristics. In: International Conference on Advances in Computing, Communications and Informatics, pp. 244–247. ACM, New York (2012)
13. Shafie, A., Ahmad, W.F.W.: Design and heuristic evaluation of mathQuest: a role-playing game for numbers. Procedia Soc. Behav. Sci. 8, 620–625 (2010)
14. Yen, P.-Y., Bakken, S.: A comparison of usability evaluation methods: heuristic evaluation versus end-user think-aloud protocol-an example from a web-based communication tool for nurse scheduling. In: American Medical Informatics Association Symposium, pp. 714–718. PubMed, Bethesda (2009)
15. Tan, J.L., Goh, D.H.-L., Ang, R.P., Huan, V.S.: Participatory evaluation of an educational game for social skills acquisition. Comput. Educ. 64, 70–80 (2013)
16. Desurvire, H., Caplan, M., Toth, J. A.: Using heuristics to evaluate the playability of games. In: CHI Extended Abstracts on Human Factors in Computing Systems, pp. 1509–1512. ACM, New York (2004)
17. Korhonen, H., Paavilainen, J., Saarenpää, H.: Expert review method in game evaluations: comparison of two playability heuristic sets. In: 13th International MindTrek Conference: Everyday life in the Ubiquitous Era, pp. 74–81. ACM, New York (2009)
18. Febretti, A., Garzotto, F.: Usability, playability, and long-term engagement in computer games. In: CHI Extended Abstracts on Human Factors in Computing Systems, pp. 4063–4068. ACM, New York (2009)
19. Jegers, K.: Investigating the applicability of usability and playability heuristics for evaluation of pervasive games. In: Third International Conference on Internet and Web Applications and Services, pp. 656–661. IEEE, New York (2008)

Models and Guidelines

Guideline for Digital Curation for the Princess Maha Chakri Sirindhorn Anthropology Centre's Digital Repository: Preliminary Outcome

Sittisak Rungcharoensuksri[✉]

Princess Maha Chakri Sirindhorn Anthropology Centre (SAC),
20 Borommaratchachonnani Rd., Bangkok, Taling Chan 10170, Thailand
sittisak.r@sac.or.th

Abstract. This research will examine the development of the guideline for digital curation by demonstrating a case study from digital repository of the SAC. This institution is an interesting case study because the historical background and the digital resources that have been produced by the centre are very unique. However, during the work process, the SAC's databases have faced several problems about data management because the centre has not provided any guideline for its staffs. In order to solve the problems, the centre has planned to develop the guideline for digital work process. Therefore, this research is part of an attempt to accrete the digital curation guideline for the SAC.

Keywords: Digital curation · Digital repository · Digital Curation Life-cycle Model · Digital guideline

1 Introduction

1.1 The Changing Role of Repository in the Digital Age

Over the last two decades, the development of information technology has had a considerable impact on the work process of academic institutions. The general public have preferred searching for information on websites to visiting those institutions. As a result, the academic institutions have changed their roles from storing documents to being digital repositories and aimed to be the hub of learning, teaching and researching for global audience. They have begun classifying and converting their materials (e.g. documents, photographs, and videos) to the digital items. However, during the transformation, many institutions have found some technical and working problems. Hence, to solve the problems, many institutions have started listing the digital guidelines for their work process based on international standards and their organizational cultures.

The academic institutions in Thailand have also faced the same situation as their colleagues around the world have. According to Klungthanaboon et al. [6], the IRs in Thailand are currently at the beginning stage and might be challenged by four issues. The first issue is that they need a *time-consuming work process*.

© Springer International Publishing AG 2016
A. Morishima et al. (Eds.): ICADL 2016, LNCS 10075, pp. 203–211, 2016.
DOI: 10.1007/978-3-319-49304-6_24

To elaborate, for some authors, to deposit their work and assign metadata by themselves are an extra workload other than their routine jobs. As a result, they are likely to ignore to upload their works to the repositories. Secondly is the issue of *copyright management* due to the fact that some printed materials belong to the publishers or the funding sponsors. Thus, some authors have hesitated to submit their research output to the system out of the concern over copyright infringement. The third one is the issue of *commitment.* To elaborate, the continuous support from stakeholders, such as, authors, publishers, and university administrators is very important to the management and maintenance of digital repositories. Although, the budget and man-hour to create the digital project might not be high in the beginning, these stakeholders have to sacrifice their money and time to sustain the system for the long-term service. Lastly is the issue of *digital preservation,* of which main question is: How can the IRs preserve and ensure the long-term accessibility to the digital materials? Though, many institutions have designed and applied archival standards and strategic plans to preserve their digital items, *there are inconclusive national standards in Thailand, especially, an effective practice guide for digital repositories.* These four recommendations have also been supported by Wipawan and Wanna [10]. From their study, the lacks of policy, quality and technical standards, general information, and legal enforcement have obstructed the development of digital repositories in Thailand.

The Princess Maha Chakri Sirindhorn Anthropology Centre (SAC) was established in 1991 with the primary objective of being a bank of anthropological data and information in related fields. Information is made accessible to scholars, students, and the general public through online databases (www.sac.or.th) such as Ethnic Identity Research Database, Local Museums Database, and Anthropological Archives Database. Nevertheless, during the work process, each database has encountered several problems about digital materials management as the centre has not provided any guideline for its staffs.

1.2   Research Objective, Benefits, Methodology, and Outline

Therefore, this research will examine the development of the guideline for digital curation by demonstrating a case study from digital repository of the SAC. This institution is an interesting case study because the historical background and the digital resources that have been produced by the centre are very unique. However, during the work process, the SAC's databases have faced several problems about data management because the centre has not provided any guideline for its staffs. In order to solve the problems, the centre has planned to develop the guideline for digital work process [1]. Therefore, this research is part of an attempt to accrete the digital curation guideline for the SAC. There are two benefits from this research as follows:

1. The SAC can understand the situations and problems of digital repositories in the world context[1], in Thailand, and of itself.
2. The SAC can apply the Digital Curation Lifecycle Model and further suggestions from this research to develop its own digital curation guideline.

There are four procedures to investigate the questions for this research. The first one is *literature review* which has aimed to understand the situations of digital repositories in the world context and in Thailand. The second procedure is the *online questionnaire* which is based on the Data Asset Framework (DAF) and Digital Curation Lifecycle Model. This stage has aimed to understand the current situations of the SAC digital work process. The third procedure is *focus group discussion* with the SAC staffs with the aims to acquire the knowledge about data management of the staffs, and to seek for the process to adapt the digital curation concept to the SAC work process. The fourth one is the *analysis stage* which will bring the results from the online questionnaire and a focus group discussion to analyse and compare with the Sequential Actions of Digital Curation Lifecycle Model. Furthermore, some suggestions about the situations and how to start a digital curation project with the SAC are also included in this procedure.

This paper discusses preliminary results from the first and second procedures of the project. There are four parts in this paper. Section 1: Introduction provides brief situation and problems of digital repositories in the world context, history and definition of digital curation. This part also includes research objectives, benefits, methodology, and outline. Section 2: Digital Curation Overviews explains the definitions and benefits of the digital curation and the eight stages of Digital Curation Lifecycle Model. Section 3: The current situations of the SAC provides the result from the Survey of the SAC digital work process and some brief comments from the staffs. The last Sect. 4 is the Conclusion.

2 Digital Curation Overview

2.1 History and Definition of Digital Curation

In order to understand the definition of digital curation, it seems important to understand the historical background of this term which is related to the UK digital repositories work process. This term was first used in 2001 at the *Digital Curation: digital archives, libraries, and e-science seminar*. In this seminar, the archivists, librarians, information management specialists, and data management in e-science came to discuss and establish the scope and definition of digital curation across their areas of studies. They agreed to use this term for their preservation and maintenance of the collections and databases as well as adding value and knowledge to them [2, p. 4].

---

[1] Mainly, the digital curation concept has been applied to the digital work process by the scholars in Europe (especially in the UK) and the United States. However, because of the time limitation this research has only focused on the digital curation activities in the UK.

Then, many researchers and institutions have brought the digital curation concept to interpret in their work. For instance, according to Lee and Tibbo [7], digital curation involves the management of digital objects over their *entire lifecycle*, ranging from pre-creation activities wherein systems are designed, and file formats and other data creation standards are established, through ongoing capture of evolving contextual information for digital assets housed in archival repositories. Whereas, according to Harvey [3, p. 7], digital curation is a more inclusive concept than either digital archiving or digital preservation. It addresses the whole range of process applied in digital objects over their *lifecycle*. Digital curation begins before digital objects are created by setting standards for planning data collection that results in curation ready digital objects that are in the best possible condition to ensure that they can be maintained and used in the future. And lastly is from the Digital Curation Centre (DCC), digital curation involves maintaining, preserving and adding value to digital research data throughout its *lifecycle*[9].

Consequently, *to understand and to curate the whole lifecycle stages of digital objects for the long-term usage seem to be the main purposes of digital curation*. As a result, a lifecycle model is designed to explain the steps of curating digital materials. Each stage is connected by the *information lifecycle*, that is, the information from the previous stages will have an effect on the actions of managing and preserving in the following stages of life cycle. Furthermore, the lifecycle model is useful for the work process of digital repositories. They can use this model for their digital curation activities, as well as for identifying the specific actions, technologies, standards, and skills required at each stage, and even adding or deleting from it where required [3, p. 34].

2.2 The Importance of Digital Curation and Digital Curation Lifecycle Model

After the introduction of digital curation in 2001, this concept has been applied in many digital projects because the academic institutions have been realising the importance of data management and preservation for the future use and reuse. According to Harvey [3, p. 12], there are four reasons why data creators should pay attention to digital curation. Firstly, digital curation *improves the quality of data accession*. To elaborate, the procedure of digital curation leads to the continual, speedy, and reliable access to the data. Secondly, it helps *improve data quality*, that is, the procedure of digital curation helps to improve the quality of data, and data trustworthiness, and helps certify the credibility of the data as a formal record (legal evidence). Thirdly, it *encourages data sharing and reuse* in that the common standards and information about the context and provenance of the data are applied to digital data which have aimed to encourage data sharing and reuse throughout its life time. Lastly, digital curation *helps protect data*. That is, the procedures of protecting and preserving data are adapted to the digital data with an aim to prevent technology obsolescence and data loss.

After the benefits of digital curation have been comprehended, the next question is: *How can we apply this idea to our digital repository?* In order to understand this question, the Digital Curation Lifecycle Model should be unfolded and investigated in details. *Fundamentally, the digital curation concept has aimed to address the whole lifecycle of data. The lifecycle model is designed to explain the steps of curating digital materials.* There are three sets of action in the Digital Curation Lifecycle Model. The first one is Full Lifecycle Actions which has four levels, namely, Description and Representation Information, Preservation Planning, Community Watch and Participation, and Curation and Preservation. The second one is Sequential Actions which locates in the outer ring of the model. This loop represents the key actions for digital curation through their lifecycle, namely, Conceptualise, Create or Receive, Appraise and Select, Ingest, Preservation Action, Store, Access, Use, and Reuse, and Transform. First, Conceptualise aims to develop and plan data creation procedures and outcomes in mind. Second, Create or Receive aims to associate description and representation information of the data for data curation and also includes external sources. Third, Appraise and Select aims to evaluate the data determination before keeping them in the long term. Fourth, Ingest aims to prepare data for the addition to the digital archive. Fifth, Preservation action aims to ensure long-term data preservation and data retention. However, in some actions, the process of transferring data to a different format (i.e. migration) is included in this stage. Sixth, Store aims to secure description and representation information in appropriate way. Seventh, Access, Use, and Reuse aims to make sure that data can be accessed by authorized users for the use and later reuse. Eighth is the action of Transform in which original data will be created to the new data by generating a subset of data. The last one is Occasional Actions which may not apply to all data, and will be used when specific conditions occur; so, this loop has only two actions: Dispose and Reappraise [3, 9, p. 34–35].

3 The Current Situation of the SAC

3.1 The Survey Report of the SAC Staffs Digital Work Process

In order to understand the current situation of the SACs digital work process, the online questionnaire was designed by adapting the set of questions from Data Asset Framework [4, 5] and Digital Curation Lifecycle Model with the aim to survey the working behaviour of the SAC staffs. In the first place, the questionnaire was distributed to 58 staffs who are from the Office of Academic Affairs and Information of the centre. However, only 39 people or 67 % responded to the questionnaire and the other 19 people or 33 % made no response. The questionnaire is divided into four parts. Firstly, the *introduction part* aims to give the general information and the objectives of the questionnaire to the intended respondents. The second part is *general information of the participant* which aims to know the position, job description, and the current responsibility of the respondents. Thirdly is the *current situation of SAC's digital work process* which aims to understand the working behaviour and the general knowledge about data management of the staffs. For instance, what types of materials and file formats which they have been created? How often do they back up their data and where do they store them? How do they create and receive data? Fourthly is the set of questions which were designed to conform with the eight stages of Sequential Actions in Digital Curation Lifecycle Model. For example, how do they participate in the digital project during the Conceptualise stage? Do they apply any Appraisal or Selection criteria to their data before Ingest them to the long-term storage? [8]

According to the survey [8], there are two interesting points that we should interpret in details. The first point is the *interest and knowledge* of the respondents which may be broadly divided into three groups. Group 1: Interested and has some knowledge, most of the respondents belonging to this group are the staffs from the Database Division[2]. They are familiar with the technical terms about data management and able to explain the limitation of their current work process rather well, because digital objects management is included in their job descriptions. Group 2: Interested but lack of knowledge, those respondents in this group are interested in digital curation concept and would like to apply these processes to their project. However, because of the lack of data management skills, they are at risk of data loss. Furthermore, it is found that they are relatively confused about the utility of Information Management and Information Technology (IT) but somehow believe in the potential of the technology tools that can easily help solve the problems from digital mistakes. However, the Data Management Plan (DMP) is the heart of data administration because the data preparation that begins at the Conceptualise stage is an effective way to prevent data loss. Group 3: Not interested, the respondents in this group are not interested in digital curation because this kind of work is not included in their job descriptions. The second point is the *roles and activities of the respondents in each stage of Digital Curation Lifecycle Model* (Fig. 1). Overall, all of the staffs from the Office of Academic Affairs and Information involve in digital curation activities. The intensity of their involvement in each stage depends on their job descriptions. For instance, the man-hour of the database administrators and the librarians have focused in Create or Receive, Appraise and Select, Ingest, and Preservation actions data of the project. On the other hand, the programmers and audiovisual staffs have participated in Preservation actions and Store data from the project by applying technology tools. However, it is interesting to highlight the role of researchers in the curation activities. Fundamentally, the researchers are the managers of the SAC's projects and, thus, have to set the concept and workflow of the projects. Furthermore, they involve in digital curation activities more than half of the actions in the Digital Curation Lifecycle Model (Create or Receive, Appraise and Select, Ingest, Preservation actions, Access, Use, and Reuse data of the project). In short, these researchers are the key figures to propel the digital work process of the SAC's project since they have to manage and maintain both the data and the staffs who have involved in the projects. These two interesting points from the survey have disclosed the

---

[2] There are four divisions in the Office of Academic Affairs and Information of the SAC, namely, Research, Database, Knowledge Communication and Network Relations, IT and Audiovisual, and Library.

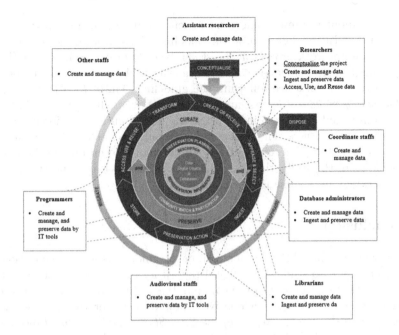

Fig. 1. The relations between the SAC's staffs and Digital Curation Lifecycle Model

notions and relations of the SAC's staffs with digital curation idea. The next question is: *How do we apply digital curation concept to the SAC digital work process?*

3.2 How to Apply Digital Curation Concept to the SAC Digital Work Process: A Brief Comments from the Survey

Some interesting comments from the survey have indicated the possibility of applying the digital curation concept to the SAC digital work process. However, the centre should impose three measures for setting the stages for success in digital curation guideline. First, *to create awareness and encourage knowledge about digital curation*, the centre should demonstrate the benefits of data management and damages caused by the lack of best practice for data management to the stakeholders, especially, for the researchers who have played the key role in the project. After that, the centre should provide the staffs with the knowledge about digital curation at the appropriate levels, taking their positions and responsibilities into consideration in order to make them aware and acknowledge the relations between their work process and the Digital Curation Lifecycle Model in each stage. Second, *to adapt the guideline in an appropriate way and establish effective communication*, the centre should take the users' behaviours and the levels of staffs' knowledge about digital curation into consideration before applying the digital curation idea to the SAC digital curation guideline. The policy makers should clearly and effectively communicate with the stakeholders about the importance and benefits of data management processes in compliance with the digital curation guideline. Furthermore, the centre must include the digital work process in the staffs' Key Performance Indicator (KPI) since this might help persuade and encourage the staffs to change their working routine to the best practice following the guideline. Third, *to provide support from the policy makers*, the role and the support from the policy makers are the most important factors to incorporate the digital curation guideline to the work process of the centre. The policy makers should declare the digital curation as part of the SAC's project objectives. Furthermore, to encourage the digital curation skills to the staffs, the policy makers should devise an effective human resource strategy in compliance with this idea.

4   Conclusion

This paper has examined the development of the guideline for digital curation by demonstrating a case study from digital repository of the SAC. Although, this concept is rather well known in the communities of library, archive, and record management in the UK, it is a relatively new concept for the Thai scholars. The result from the *Survey Report of the SAC Staffs' Digital Work Process* has shown their lack of knowledge about data management. However, some of the respondents of this survey have started to realise the importance of best practice for data management, and they have made a demand from the policy makers to support and apply the digital curation concept to the centre's work process.

In conclusion, the result from this paper is not the complete answer of the digital curation guideline for the SAC. Alternatively, it is the starting point to deal with data management problems of the centre that have accumulated for nearly a decade. As a result, the next procedures of the research (focus group discussion and analysis stage) are the following steps to acquire the answer for this research.

References

1. SAC, "SAC strategy review seminar for 2017 (8–10 June)," SAC, Prachuap Khiri Khan (2015). (Unpublished document)
2. Beagrie, N.: Digital curation for science, digital libraries, and individuals. Int. J. Digital Curation **1**(1), 3–16 (2006)
3. Harvey, R.: Digital Curation: A How-To-Do-It-Manual. Neal-Schuman Publishers Inc., New York (2010)
4. DAF, "Data Asset Framework: Implementation Guide" (2009)
5. Jones, S., Ross, S., Ruusalepp, R.: Data Audit Framework Methodology. HATII, Glasgow (2009)
6. Klungthanaboon, W., Leelanupab, T., Moss, M.: Institutioanl repositories for scholary communities in Thailand. KMTL Inf. Technol. J. **1**(1) (2012). https://www.researchgate.net/publication/231513559_Institutional_Repositories_for_Scholarly_Communities_in_Thailand

7. Lee, C.A., Tibbo, H.R.: Digital curation, trusted repositories: steps toward success. Digital Curation and Trusted Repositories **8**(2) (2007). https://journals.tdl.org/jodi/index.php/jodi/article/view/229/183

8. Rungcharoensuksri, S.: The Suvey Report of the SAC's Staffs Digital Work Process. The Princess Maha Chakri Sirindhorn Anthropology Centre, Bangkok (2016). (Unpublished document)

9. DCC, "What is digital curation?" http://www.dcc.ac.uk/resources/curation-lifecycle-model. Accessed 1 April 2016

10. Wipawin, N., Wanna, A.: Institutional repositories in Thai Universities. In: Tuamsuk, K., Jatowt, A., Rasmussen, E. (eds.) ICADL 2014. LNCS, vol. 8839, pp. 385–392. Springer, Heidelberg (2014). doi:10.1007/978-3-319-12823-8_41

Describing Scholarly Information Resources with a Unified Temporal Map

Robert B. Allen[✉], Hanna Song, Bo Eun Lee, and Jiyoung Lee

Yonsei University, Seoul, South Korea
{rballen,hnsong,belee}@yonsei.ac.kr, jiyoung.lee@simmons.edu

Abstract. We consider the use of procedures for providing structured descriptions of information resources such as scholarly works and of their contents. This goes beyond the usual view of metadata as discrete elements. For instance, we consider mapping the structured and interdependent activities in the publication of Ulysses. We discuss some specific representations and discuss the development of structured scholarly guides. Finally, we consider how the activities associated with publication, along with other historical activities, can be positioned on a unified temporal map. Ultimately, there should be a unified framework for the description of individual information resources and collections of information resources across periods and technologies.

Keywords: Archives · Metadata · Scholarly records · Structured continuum · Structured scholarly guides · Threads

1   Procedures and Information Artifacts

Formal modeling of processes and procedures goes back at least to Herbert A. Simon's research on business decision making and human cognition. That work led to studies of office and organizational processes and eventually to the development of object-oriented programming languages. Petri Nets are a specific modeling technique that are the key to many formal approaches to modeling procedures. Petri Nets set conditions for the gating of transitions in a procedure and generally require that all conditions are met before a procedure can proceed. Thus, Petri Nets provide a way to specify and manage flow control. They are the foundation of tools such as UML Activity Diagrams and workflow specifications such as Taverna.

There would be many advantages to combining a powerful content ontology with computer-based procedure specification. [4] attempted to reconcile the notion of Procedures derived from the programming language community with the notion of Process from the Basic Formal Ontology (BFO) [6]. That work extended the BFO notion of Process, which is conceived of as a sequence of present participles (e.g., racing, running, walking), to include descriptions of how the transitions are connected. Procedures are viewed as Processes which include some sort of condition, contingency, or gating. This broader perspective considers interaction with other entities in the context of Scenarios

© Springer International Publishing AG 2016
A. Morishima et al. (Eds.): ICADL 2016, LNCS 10075, pp. 212–217, 2016.
DOI: 10.1007/978-3-319-49304-6_25

and attempts to specify the causes of the transitions within and across Processes and Procedures.

The production, publication, and use of information resources follow many procedures. Capturing these procedures, using them to organize the materials, and then using them to support access should be have substantial benefits over current approaches. The procedures would weave together what might otherwise appear as disjoint events. When supported with rich historical knowledge sources and powerful inferencing tools, the procedures should provide a useful perspective for many different levels of scholarship.

The earliest formal work for procedures associated with information resources was by [18] who used Petri Nets to model the procedures for the "office of the future". While there can be difficulties in taking office procedures too literally [15], such specifications are now fairly common. An emphasis on business processes also became established as a core principle in the archives community, which argued that archival records should be organized by their business or organizational purpose. However, the descriptive systems that have been developed for records management were based on static metadata models [12]. Some recent work is beginning to address the preservation of the temporal aspects of business processes. [1] gives an example using a business Role Activity Diagram (RAD) to structure and then support visualization of project-management records. The notable and extensive work of Rauber and colleagues (e.g., [10, 11]) describes preservation of templates for business processes and scientific workflows along with consideration of the reuse of those procedures.

In many cases, procedures have a simple path and straightforward results. In other cases (e.g., a student who juggles schoolwork, family, and a job), there may be many interacting procedures in which some of the procedures may be blocked and suspended and then restarted later. We can distinguish these as closed and open worlds from which the models are drawn. We see both situations in descriptions of scholarly activity. The prototype procedure for processing conference or journal papers assumes a closed world while post-hoc descriptions, which are typical of scholarly editions or other histories, are open worlds with many interacting factors. Just as Petri Nets can be used to coordinate the parts of an individual procedure, they may also be helpful in post-hoc descriptions of interacting procedures.

2 Scholarly Records and Modeling Scholarly Activity

Like other complex human activities, scholarly authoring, publishing, and commentary are threads across time (e.g., [13]). Systems for organizing individual scholarly works and collections of works should go beyond traditional metadata and capture these temporal threads or events. This approach should allow us to describe a wide variety of technologies and media and to provide richer data than traditional approaches that deliver decontextualized metadata.

We believe that procedure descriptions should be used to develop a new generation of scholarly description. The production of scholarly materials is, generally, highly sequential and routine. It should be helpful to capture that routine. When there are failures in the routine or other exceptions, we can highlight them by contrasting them to the expected procedures.

Consider the possible variations in the route of a modern research article before it is "published" in a journal. Descriptions of the research may appear as a technical report, be posted on an open-access repository, and/or be presented at a conference. Even within the context of a journal, the article may appear in an online repository long before it appears in print and arrives on a subscriber's desk or in a library. In short, the very meaning of publication and publication date are increasingly broadened. Yet, accurate records are, ultimately, essential for the credibility of scholarship.

Scholarly records are used in many ways. The most common is to assign appropriate credit to the discoverers of new insights and ideas. In other cases, we want to better understand the nuances and creative pressures in works. This has often been done retrospectively through scholarly editions. Scholarly editions are an important resource for research. There are extensive recommendations for the development of scholarly editions[1] and a recent statement about the development of digital scholarly editions[2] but systematic approaches have not been proposed.

Beyond publication of scholarly texts, there is an increasing number of other scenarios with a temporal or causal component (e.g., performance or of new musical works) that are important for scholarly records, which may benefit from a systematic approach. Literature, for example, is an area in which complex publication histories are common. The novel *Ulysses* by James Joyce has a particularly complex history. There were many editions with many revisions. Moreover, its distribution was disrupted by court battles. This is an example of publication in an open-world context in which many, sometimes unexpected, procedures interact.

3 Next Steps

3.1 Standard Sets of Procedures

Scholarly description has separate traditions and approaches across archives, literary studies, intellectual history, librarianship, and even genomics [8] that all have common traits. For instance, both archives and literary theory place great emphasis on understanding the context (i.e., "original order") in which works are created. We believe that especially with the many similarities across the fields both conceptual frameworks and specific procedures should be better coordinated.

Our emphasis on standardization comes from an information science perspective rather than a humanities perspective. However, just as there are clear benefits from

---

[1] Modern Language Association, Guidelines for Editors of Scholarly Editions. Last revised 29 June 2011, https://www.mla.org/Resources/Research/Surveys-Reports-and-Other-Documents/Publishing-and-Scholarship/Reports-from-the-MLA-Committee-on-Scholarly-Editions/Guidelines-for-Editors-of-Scholarly-Editions.

[2] MLA Statement on the Scholarly Edition in the Digital Age, MLA Committee on Scholarly Editions, May 2016, https://www.mla.org/content/download/52050/1810116/rptCSE16.pdf.

accepting the EAD and TEI standards, we believe there would be benefits from adoption of standard descriptions of scholarship based on procedures. Moreover, once standard frameworks are developed, they could be populated with data and would become valuable resources in their own right.

There are many procedures involved in the production and publication of a scholarly work. We would need to categorize then and develop a flexible framework for coordinating those variations. There is an even greater challenge in developing a broad set of procedures for an open-world approach. For the immediate future, guidelines could be proposed for developers to use initially while a standard set of procedures is developed to cover general cases. Ultimately, a flexible framework such as coordination theory [9] could be applied to less structured situations even including the process of authoring.

3.2 From Scholarly Editions to Scholarly Guides

There may be many scholarly editions of a single work. Many works are published in a traditional bound paper format and in multiple electronic formats. One web site with an ad hoc list of cholarly electronic editions has 399 entries[3]. As noted above, there is no standard structure even for the core elements of a scholarly edition. Some editions have many types of material beyond the annotations to the text itself. Moreover, this additional material is unstructured. The situation with scholarly editions seems analogous to archival finding aids before the EAD [7] was introduced. The EAD has proven extremely useful in the coordination of archival materials by providing an XML DTD that provides a common structure across finding aids. We believe there would be similar benefits in standardizing scholarly editions with consistent sections and data structures. We call these standardized versions of scholarly editions Structured Scholarly Guides. Once a general framework is established, it could be applied to support applications such as structuring digital articles and guides, such as Wikipedia, about books and scholarly works.

3.3 Unified Temporal Map and Interactive Services

An important aspect of our proposal is that procedures could be mapped into a single over-arching framework. Not only would the creation and production of scholarly works be mapped but post-publication events such as reviews and citations could all be included. This may be thought of as providing a Continuum approach [16, 17] rather than a finite lifecycle approach to records about scholarly publishing.

Beyond enabling viewing histories of individual works, a unified temporal map could allow coordinated views of several works by the same author, by the same publisher, or by authors working in a specific media or in specific geographical regions. Indeed, a broad range of other historical events and procedures could all be coordinated into one view (e.g., [3]). In addition, the temporal knowledgebase could be linked to other factors such as genres, technologies, and cultural and intellectual trends that may be only

---

[3] A catalog of Digital Scholarly Editions, v 3.0, snapshot 2008ff, compiled by P. Sahle, last change 2016/05/19, http://www.digitale-edition.de/.

indirectly based on temporal factors. Views of individual works could be implemented as threads which are highly interconnected sub-sets of sub-views of the broader map.

The rich models proposed here should be able to support several types of structured interaction. For instance, scholarly procedures could be mapped onto interactive time-lines (e.g., [2]). In addition, there has been considerable discussion about the possibility of interactive digital scholarly editions (e.g., [14]). Our approach suggests some services that should be useful for such editions. In addition, as we noted above, there are similarities between archival finding aids and structured scholarly guides. Interactive versions of those guides could be implemented which would be analogous to the interactive archival finding aids proposed by [5].

4   Conclusion

We have proposed the use of procedures for the description of information resources that goes far beyond scholarly editions and requires a broader integration of approaches. We have proposed initial steps toward a new structure for organizing descriptions of scholarly material. Rather than having bibliographic description as a set of disjoint and decontextualized metadata categories, we propose focusing on the continuity and the inter-relatedness of activities. Our solution is to provide process-based descriptions that allow richer structures. If needed, those richer descriptions could be reverted to basic category labels. Evidence and argumentation about evidence could be supported with "structured applied epistemology" [3]. Based on the structured description of processes, we foresee a unified framework for the description of individual information resources and collections of information resources that covers different periods and technologies.

References

1. Allen, R.B.: Using information visualization to support access of archival records. J. Archival Organ. **3**, 37–49 (2005). doi:10.1300/J201v03n01_04
2. Allen, R.B.: Visualization, Causation, and History. In: iConference (2011). doi: 10.1145/1940761.1940835
3. Allen, R.B.: Issues for the Direct Representation of History. In: Morishima, A., Rauber, A., Liew, C.L. (eds.) ICADL 2016. LNCS, vol. 10075, pp. 218–224. Springer, Heidelberg (2016)
4. Allen, R.B., Chu, YM.: Architectures for complex semantic models. In: IEEE Conference on Big Data and Smart Computing, pp. 254–261 (2105). doi:10.1109/35021BIGCOMP. 2015.7072809
5. Anderson, S., Allen, R.B.: Malleable Finding Aids. TPDL, pp. 402–407 (2012). doi: 10.1007%2F978-3-642-33290-6_43
6. Arp, R., Smith, B., Spear, A.D.: Building Ontologies with Basic Format Ontology. MIT Press, Cambridge (2015). http://purl.obolibrary.org/obo/bfo/Reference
7. DeRose, S.J.: Navigation, access, and control using structured information. Am. Archivist **60**, 298–309 (1997). doi:10.17723/aarc.60.3.0777u1361u62tqp6
8. Huntley, R.P., Sawford, T., Martin, M.J., O'Donovan, C.: Understanding how and why the Gene Ontology and its annotations evolve: the GO within UniProt, GigaScience, 3 (2014). doi:10.1186/2047-217X-3-4

9. Malone, T.W., Crowston, K.: The interdisciplinary Study of coordination. Comput. Surv. **26**, 87–119 (1994). doi:10.1145/174666.174668

10. Mayer, R., Antunes, G., Caetano, A., Bakhshandeh, M., Rauber, A., Borbinha, J.: Using ontologies to capture the semantics of a (business) process for digital preservation. Int. J. Digital Librar. **15**, 129–152 (2015). doi:10.1007/s00799-015-0141-7

11. Mayer, R., Proell, S., Rauber, A.: On the Applicability of Workflow Management Systems for the Preservation of Business Processes, iPres (2012). http://www.ifs.tuwien.ac.at/~mayer/publications/pdf/may_ipres12-workflows.pdf

12. McKemmish, S., Acland, G., Ward, N., Reed, B.: Describing Records in Context in the Continuum: the Australian Recordkeeping Metadata Schema, Archivaria, (48) (1999)

13. Rico, F.: Scholarly editions and real readers. Variants **5**, 1–13 (2006)

14. Robinson, P.: Current Directions in the Making of Digital Editions: Towards Interactive Editions. Ecdotica **4**, 176–191 (2007)

15. Suchman, L.: Plans and Situated Action. Cambridge U. Press, Cambridge (1987)

16. Upward, F.M.: Structuring the Records Continuum, Part One: Postcustodial Principles and Properties. Archives and Manuscripts 25 (1997). http://www.infotech.monash.edu.au/research/groups/rcrg/publications/recordscontinuum-fupp1.html

17. Upward, F.M.: Structuring the Records Continuum, Part Two: Structuration Theory and Recordkeeping. Archives and Manuscripts, 25 (1997). http://www.infotech.monash.edu.au/research/groups/rcrg/publications/recordscontinuum-fupp2.html

18. Zisman, M.D.: Representation, Specification and Automation of Office Procedures. Ph.D. thesis, University of Pennsylvania Wharton School of Business, Pennsylvania (1977)

Issues for the Direct Representation of History

Robert B. Allen[✉]

Yonsei University, Seoul, South Korea
rballen@yonsei.ac.kr

Abstract. We propose that representations for structured models of human and social history need to go beyond traditional ontologies to the combination of rich semantic ontologies with programming languages. We base our approach on the Basic Formal Ontology (BFO) and then consider how to extend it beyond traditional approaches to ontology with higher-level structures. For instance, we propose the need for composite entities that allow transitions in the configuration of component entities. We then explore the relationship of these composite entities to notion of systems and consider how they may provide a definition of "causal unity" and be related to models of social systems. We identify some challenges in defining the nature of social entities. Finally, we introduce structured applied epistemology as a framework for managing historical evidence, analysis, and argumentation.

Keywords: Causal unity · Conditionals · Community models · Composite reference entity · Historical newspapers · Late binding · Scenarios · Systems

1   Introduction

Ontologies can be applied to the description of history [12]. However, histories go beyond typical applications of ontologies, in having extended interactions of complex instances across many different contexts. In addition, consider the difficulty that traditional search engines have in indexing the broad range of stories in historical newspapers. Individuals, institutions, and locations may be closely coordinated in some articles but are found in very different settings in other articles. We propose that higher-level structures and semantic search are needed. Such higher-level structures could support a wide range of new interactive services ranging from games to educational and scholarly applications. Semantic search may greatly enhance performance for searches of the full range of historical newspaper articles. We have termed the use of rich semantics to organize content from digitized historical newspapers – and by extension all historical material – as developing semantic "community models" [5].

We adopt the Basic Formal Ontology (BFO) [8] as the basis for modeling history. BFO is an upper ontology that is widely used in biology. BFO is an appropriate choice because it supports "realist" modeling and there should be value in working toward a unified framework that has the potential to be integrated across different domains. While BFO is relatively well developed with respect to the description of natural science entities, it is still a work in progress and important aspects of it are still open. Here, we

© Springer International Publishing AG 2016
A. Morishima et al. (Eds.): ICADL 2016, LNCS 10075, pp. 218–224, 2016.
DOI: 10.1007/978-3-319-49304-6_26

discuss some high-level structures that might be developed to facilitate the representation of history. Several of these issues have been discussed in our earlier work such as developing complex entities and basing representations on object-oriented programming languages (e.g., [4]).

2   Rich Semantics

2.1   Continuants and Composite Entities

As an upper ontology, BFO specifies different types of entities. These different types of entities are coordinated through different types of relationships to form descriptions of complex entities. For instance, an ontology would likely specify that Continuant Material Entities (e.g., Objects) would have the Dependent Continuant Quality of Mass. If Mass were not specified in a given ontology of physical properties, then it cannot be used for descriptions based in that ontology.

It would be useful to have greater ability to examine and evaluate configurations of composite Entities. Such configurations could be developed as schemas. Indeed, there could be several types of schemas. A Composite Reference Entity would be a schema of all the relevant parts of a non-instantiated composite entity. There could be inheritance from the Composite Reference Entity. The Composite Reference Entity could be one part of a Reference Ontology [8, p39]. The Composite Reference Entities could also be instantiated, what we term Instantiated Composites. In the example above, the Reference Entity would have a Mass and, possibly, a range of acceptable values for that Mass, but only Instantiated Composites will have would have a specific value for Mass.

An Instantiated Composite could have a long existence. Consider if the Instantiated Composite represented a person. In the course of a lifetime, that individual could have a vast range of experiences. One hand the potential for those experiences may have been present in the original person Reference Entity. On the other hand, there is such a broad range of outcomes for an individual; it does not seem plausible associate every possible outcome with the original Reference Entity. Rather, some outcomes (e.g., Roles associated with a person) would have to be attached to the Instantiated Composite across time. In In terminology of object-oriented programming, this is known as late binding [4].

2.2   Occurrents and Transitions

A classic paradox for ontologies is to distinguish between the sense in which a river is a fixed entity and the sense in which it is continually being renewed. In BFO, this paradox is addressed by allowing the river to be both a Continuant and an Occurrent. They are entities that change through time in the sense that a river is always changing. Occurrents are composed of the "present participle" form of verbs (e.g., the running done by a Continuant across a time region) [8, p. 121]. In BFO, Occurrents include Processes, Process Boundaries, and Temporal Regions (i.e., intervals and periods). One specific type of Process is a History, which according to BFO is composed of the processes that occur in the Temporal Region covered by that Material Entity [8, p122]. While such definitions are clearly useful for describing different types of biological activities, the BFO definition of a History might more accurately be called a chronology. We also note the similarity of a Temporal Region to the historical notion of an era or events that extend across time.

We believe it is also useful to identify Transitions. A Transition is any change in the structure of an Composite Entity. We can distinguish between transitions of individual Material Entities (BFO:Object) and Transitions across Reference Composites or Instantiated Composite. Transitions are due to Processes. Because the Processes are related to Transitions, they should specify a Domain and Range. Moreover, the relationship between Processes and Material Entities is said to be analogous to the relationship of a Specifically Dependent Continuant to a Material Entity [8, p. 121]. This linkage is notably similar to the linkage of classes and methods in Java. It implies that Material Entities can have both quality-like processes and "realizable" Processes. Thus Processes like breathing could be considered as part of the definition of an Independent Continuant. This is a very low level of modeling and is consistent with our call for a programming-language approach to rich semantics. In the example above, it considers both the river and the changes in the river's molecules. Another high-level structure is a Scenario [2, 4]. The Scenario is the relevant context for a collection of entities. We can say that, a Transition between parts of a Process is caused by other Entities in the Scenario (cf. [7]).

A Procedure is a prescription whose execution can cause Transitions in a Process. A Procedure is different from a Process in having gates or contingencies. It is usually controlled by a third party. For instance, in Gibbon's "The Decline and Fall of the Roman Empire" we find:

> Those princes, whom the ostentation of gratitude or generosity permitted for a while to hold a precarious sceptre, were dismissed from their thrones, as soon as they had performed their appointed task of fashioning to the yoke the vanquished nations. The free states and cities which had embraced the cause of Rome were rewarded with a nominal alliance, and insensibly sunk into real servitude.[1]

According to the passage, the princes were permitted by Rome to hold their thrones until "they had fashioned a yoke". Computer programs are artifacts that specify Procedures.

2.3 Structure and Function

Structure is the relationships among the parts of a composite entity. For instance, the chapters of a book form the structure of the book. Structure is often contrasted with function. Across many academic disciplines, insights are gained by considering complexity in terms of both structure and function. Consider anatomy (structure) versus physiology (behavior and function).

In BFO, Functions are Dispositions that are Realizable Entities. Functions specify potential Transactions [14]. For example, a hammer has the function "to drive in nails"

---

[1] From E. Gibbon, Decline and Fall of the Roman Empire, Chap. 1: The Extent of the Empire In The Age Of The Antonines.—Part III. http://www.gutenberg.org/files/731/731-h/731-h.htm#link22HCH0002.

[8, p 103] and a Continuant with a Function can have Agency (though not intention). A structured set of interacting entities forms a System (e.g., [4]) and a full description would include the entire set of sub-systems that constitute the overall system. We believe that such systems provide a definition of "causal unity".

Both structure and function may provide useful perspectives to societal models. A range of sociological "grand theories" has been developed applying the different approaches. There are structuralists such as Levi-Strauss, functionalists such as Malinowski and structural-functionalists such as Parsons. The different approaches to societal models employ different assumptions and tools. Our approach, which is grounded in object-oriented modeling, seems most compatible with structure-functionalism as an approach to social systems.

Many aspects of historical models involve social entities. However, social entities are contentious and difficult to model. They are based on an unpredictable and even chaotic foundation – the needs of individuals. Social systems may be self-organizing and different cultures at different times have found their own ways of balancing these factors. We consider some outlines that appear useful to explore further. We might develop an ontology of human Needs based on the work of Maslow [11]. Presumably, Needs are grounded in biological processes that could be linked back into BFO. Even without being able to model the mechanisms in detail, we can see that relatively stable social structures (e.g., religions, governments) may develop. Work on Social Ontologies which is related to BFO has explored deontic entities (i.e., rights and obligations). Particular attention is paid to document acts (laws, regulations, records, etc.) [13]. One of government's major activities is establishing frameworks for document acts and enforcing their commitments.

3 Example Application

We have been exploring community models to support access to digitized historical newspapers (e.g., [5]). As a specific example to illustrate some of the points explored here, we selected an individual essentially at random and found a set of news reports about him: D.C. O'Connor, who appeared in the newspapers of Norfolk, Nebraska over several years primarily in his role as Superintendent of Schools of Norfolk, Nebraska. He moved from Superintendent of Schools for the town of Madison to Norfolk. O'Connor worked in Norfolk until 1905 when he resigned and became Superintendent of Schools for the Panama Canal Zone. During the years he was in Norfolk, there are numerous reports in the newspapers of his activities for the School Board such as making reports and participating in professional organizations. There are also reports of his participation in local social activities. In one news item,[2] a teacher (McCoy) resigned to

---

[2] *The Norfolk Weekly News Journal* (Norfolk, Neb.), 29 March 1900. *Chronicling America: Historic American Newspapers*. Library of Congress. http://chroniclingamerica.loc.gov/lccn/sn95070060/1900-03-29/ed-1/seq-7/
The Norfolk Weekly News-Journal. (Norfolk, Neb.), 04 Sept. 1903. *Chronicling America: Historic American Newspapers*. Library of Congress. http://chroniclingamerica.loc.gov/lccn/sn95070058/1903-09-04/ed-1/seq-6/.

take a position in a different school district and the Superintendent needed to replace him. We can model this particular development with Entities such as the School District and the Roles of the School Superintendent and Teacher (cf., [9]) as well as implementing Transitions for hiring, resigning, and traveling. We interpreted employment as a type of Role attachment. Thus, hiring is implemented as a transition in which the Role (e.g., Teacher or School Superintendent) becomes linked to the Person. Constraints could be included such as requiring an employee to be of a certain age. Instances could be created for the school entities of the local towns, the individuals involved (O'Connor and McCoy) and their initial roles. In terms of narrative structures, this could thought of as defining the Setting.

As a first transition, O'Connor resigned from the Madison School District. A second transition was his hiring by the Norfolk School District. These transitions are directly connected and might be thought of as forming a thread, episode, or scenario. A second set of related transitions starts with McCoy's resignation as a Teacher. The vacancy created by McCoy's resignation triggers an activity associated with O'Connor's Superintendent Role, a recruiting trip. Unlike the other transitions in these passages, the transition between McCoy's resignation and O'Connor's trip is best characterized as a causal relationship. In response to the vacancy, O'Connor's obligation to find a replacement is triggered and to fulfill that obligation, he makes a trip to find a replacement teacher. We could implement that trip with the Motion frame.

The news item ends with the description of O'Connor on the train without reporting the results of the trip. We may believe that he succeeded in recruiting a new teacher and thus filled the vacancy but we need to mark that as a speculation. We can also be confident that the positions of Superintendent and Teacher include specific activities in a job description though we can probably never know the details of those job descriptions. A common challenge for these implementations is gaps in knowledge. The use of plausible inference is common to compensate. The formal structure highlights the number of such inferences that are required and the need for explicit placeholders to show that some details are unknown.

4   Coordinated Collections of Historical Resources and Structured Applied Epistemology

[3] called for coordinated, large-scale repositories of historical resources. We renew that call and add that material could be enriched in several ways. We could create rich social and historical domain ontologies for descriptions. For that, the approach of the OBO Foundry for BFO-based biological domain ontologies could be extended to the development of social and historical domain ontologies. A related project could develop collections of standard procedures and policies (e.g., job descriptions), geographic locations, train schedules, as well as census and economic data. These could be linked into collected texts. Moreover, the texts, reviews about them as well as facts about their authors, and their publication histories could be positioned on a broad temporal map (see [6]).

The texts could also be enriched as analysis or argumentation structures. The texts may provide evidence for claims about history. The evidence could be a quotation from another text. The links into the texts could be thought of as comparable to footnotes in narrative and analytical histories [1, 3].

Epistemology is usually distinguished from ontology in focusing on criteria for how we can be said to know something. Structured applied epistemology is concerned with providing support for belief and knowledge about claims based on semantic models. This could also be considered structured semantic abduction where abduction is defined as determining the best explanation given the evidence. These analyses could consider the plausibility alternative semantic models of scenarios. The scenarios could be evaluated at several levels starting with whether they meet basic physical constraints. For instance, two Material Entities cannot to occupy exactly the same Spatio-Temporal Region. The scenarios should also be supported by evidence linked to specific aspects of the scenario with structures reflecting the traditional criteria for the evaluation of historical claims [10]. For instance, the reliability of the source of a quotation used as evidence could be critiqued. If there were disagreement about the evidence and warrants, the differing viewpoints could be explored with argumentation structures.

References

1. Allen, R.B.: Model-oriented information organization: part 2, discourse relationships. D-Lib Mag. (2013). doi:10.1045/july2013-allen-pt2
2. Allen, R.B.: Repositories with Direct Representation, NKOS Workshop, Seoul (2015) arXiv: 1512.09070
3. Allen, Robert, B., Chu, Y.: Towards a full-text historical digital library. In: Tuamsuk, K., Jatowt, A., Rasmussen, E. (eds.) ICADL 2014. LNCS, vol. 8839, pp. 218–226. Springer, Heidelberg (2014). doi:10.1007/978-3-319-12823-8_22
4. Allen, R.B., Chu, Y.M.: Architectures for complex semantic models. IEEE Big Data Smart Comput. (2015). doi:10.1109/35021BIGCOMP.2015.7072809
5. Allen, R.B., Japzon, A., Achananuparp, P., Lee, K.-J.: A framework for text processing and supporting access to collections of digitized historical newspapers. HCI Int. Conf. (2007). doi: 10.1007/978-3-540-73354-6_26
6. Allen, R.B., Song, H., Lee, B.E., Lee, J.Y.: Describing scholarly information resources with a unified temporal map. In: Morishima, A., et al. (eds.) ICADL 2016. LNCS, vol. 10075, pp. 212–217. Springer, Heidelberg (2016)
7. Allen, Robert, B., Wu, Y., Luo, J.: Interactive causal schematics for qualitative scientific explanations. In: Fox, Edward, A., Neuhold, Erich, J., Premsmit, P., Wuwongse, V. (eds.) ICADL 2005. LNCS, vol. 3815, pp. 411–415. Springer, Heidelberg (2005). doi: 10.1007/11599517_50
8. Arp, R., Smith, B., Spear, A.D.: Building Ontologies with Basic Formal Ontology. MIT Press, Cambridge (2015)
9. Chu, Y., Allen, Robert, B.: Formal representation of socio-legal roles and functions for the description of history. In: Fuhr, N., Kovács, L., Risse, T., Nejdl, W. (eds.) TPDL 2016. LNCS, vol. 9819, pp. 379–385. Springer, Heidelberg (2016). doi:10.1007/978-3-319-43997-6_30
10. Howell, M.C., Prevenier, W.: From Reliable Sources: An Introduction to Historical Methods. Cornell U. Press, Ithaca (2001)
11. Maslow, A.: Theory of human motivation. Psychol. Rev. **50**, 370–396 (1943)

12. Meroño-Peñuela, A., Ashkpour, A., van Erp, M., Mandemakers, K., Breure, L., Scharnhorst, A., Schlobach, S., van Harmelen, F.: Semantic technologies for historical research: a survey. Semant. Web **6**, 539–564 (2015)
13. Smith, B.: Document Acts, Conference on Collective Intentionality, Basel (2010). http://ontology.buffalo.edu/smith/articles/document-acts.pdf
14. Spear, A.D., Ceusters, W., Smith, B.: Functions in Basic Formal Ontology, Applied Ontology, 11 (2016, in press)

Preserving Containers – Requirements and a Todo-List

Klaus Rechert[1]([✉]), Thomas Liebetraut[1], Dennis Wehrle[1], and Euan Cochrane[2]

[1] University of Freiburg, Freiburg, Germany
{klaus.rechert,thomas.liebetraut,dennis.wehrle}@rz.uni-freiburg.de
[2] Yale University Library, New Haven, USA
euan.cochrane@yale.edu

Abstract. Container technology has been quickly adopted as a tool to encapsulate and share complex software setups, e.g. in the domain of computational science. With growing significance of this class of complex digital objects their longevity is also of growing importance. In this paper we analyze requirements for long-term maintenance and preservation of containers in memory institutions.

1 Introduction

Driven by the demand for reproducible computational science, virtualization and container technologies have been quickly adopted by researchers [1,2]. Container technologies are becoming particularly popular, as containers are more lightweight compared to a full hardware virtualization approach (i.e. virtual machines). Containers are able to encapsulate a software environment, like an application or a complex tool-chain, including specific settings, into a single, portable entity. For instance, the setup of a complex scientific computational model is done once (by a specialist) and the configured environment can be shared, deployed and re-used independently of its original creation environment.

With the growing significance of this class of complex digital objects, memory institutions with focus on research data management, but not limited to these, have to develop a policy on how this kind of objects (containers) should be treated, and, if these objects are to be preserved, what kind of procedures and infrastructure are required. Apparently, containers offer a set of features convenient for the preservation of (complex) software setups. When using containers, software as well as all their dependencies are already resolved and encapsulated such that only a dependency on the container runtime remains mainly an operating system capable of executing container. While there are various container flavors currently available (most prominently Docker[1], but also LXC[2] or rkt[3]) all provide similar functionality differing only in assisting tools and their run-time convenience layer.

---

[1] Docker Container, https://www.docker.com/.

[2] Linux Containers, https://linuxcontainers.org/.

[3] rkt/CoreOS, https://coreos.com/rkt/.

A. Morishima et al. (Eds.): ICADL 2016, LNCS 10075, pp. 225–230, 2016.
DOI: 10.1007/978-3-319-49304-6_27

In order to make scientific methods accessible, usable and citable in the long-term, the longevity of containers themselves needs to be ensured. This paper analyzes requirements to compile an initial todo-list for long-term maintenance and preservation of containers in memory institutions. We investigate two essential properties for functional long-term preservation: portability and longevity. In particular, we provide a detailed analysis on the portability constraints of containers, applicable as a pre-ingest checklist for archives that may be accepting or proposing to accept containers for ingest and preservation, and providing structural guidelines for creating preservable containers. Second, we lay out the infrastructure requirements necessary to keep containers functional in the long-term.

2 Demystifying Container Technology

Container technology (also called operating system virtualization) is promoted as a lightweight alternative to virtual machines, requiring less resources while maintaining portability. In contrast to the way virtual machines provide real hardware virtualization, containers utilize the abstraction of the underlying operating system. Instead of virtualizing specific hardware features like CPU and hard disks, container technology virtualizes operating system features like file access, running applications or managing a network connection, and the corresponding programming interfaces. For Linux-based container implementations, the virtualization of programming interfaces is built on a specific feature set of the Linux kernel that provide isolated environments – namespaces [3] and (process) control groups (cgroups) [4]. Namespaces allow users to create multiple isolated views on the operating system's interfaces. Anything running inside a namespace is separated from other namespaces, i.e. other containers or the underlying host system. *cgroups* are able to control and limit access to system resources shared with the host and among other containers.

Due to the strict isolation, containers need to be self-contained, i.e. all software dependencies (libraries, applications etc.) have to be included within the container. Therefore, one part of a container consists of an archive containing a self-contained filesystem with installed and configured software components depending only on (virtualized) operating system features to be provided at runtime. The second container component is a runtime configuration defining, for instance, (data) mappings and an entry point (e.g. a start-script) to the container or the container's network environment. Even though, all container flavors operate on the same technological base, their representation of the runtime configuration differs significantly.

3 Preservation Risks

Based on the aforementioned technical analysis of container technology, these objects already provide an important property for preservation, access and reuse: portability, i.e. being able to run a container in any (unknown) technical environment. By definition, only a well-defined runtime environment is required to *render* these type of complex objects.

Therefore, the first risk-assessment step is identifying additional (external) dependencies required to maintain the functionality of a container instance. The container's runtime configuration may add additional dependencies explicitly, e.g. if it requires access to specific hardware or by defining if and how the container should be able to use the network. Unfortunately, in addition to these explicit dependencies, there are two other classes of (implicit) dependencies that need to be investigated. Firstly, specific software dependencies on kernel version, e.g. utilizing specific kernel features which are only present from a certain release and similar hardware dependencies on a special CPU instruction set, e.g. optimized scientific software compiled for a specific CPU version. A second class of (implicit) dependencies are the containers' *expectations* on an external (technical) environment, e.g. the availability of network services such as licensing servers or data to be available at a certain address. These kind of (implicit) external dependencies pose not only the highest preservation risk for an individual container, but require specific effort and infrastructure to be identified and are expensive to monitor.

The second major preservation risk is the availability of the container runtime in the long-term, i.e. keeping the container runtime useable. A container's *technical runtime* is composed of two components: a hardware component (the computer) and a software component consisting of an operating system with installed tools and infrastructure required to run containers. The software component is usually a disk (image) attached to hardware. If we assume that the software component is a fixed setup, the long-term preservation risk of containers can be reduced to the availability of hardware required to host the software component, i.e. providing necessary hardware supported by the Linux kernel version used as software runtime. When compatible physical hardware becomes unavailable, virtual hardware can be used by means of emulation. In this case, specific properties of containers come handy again. Typically, software running within containers has only a very basic, heavily abstracted view on its underlying hardware, to make them as portable a possible (see discussion above). Furthermore, Linux operating systems support a wide range of hardware. Both properties ease the process of replacing physical hardware.

4   Requirements

Based on the aforementioned technical and risk-analysis, preservation tasks and infrastructure ensuring long-term availability of containers can be broken down into three fields of work: analysis of the containers' runtime configuration and possibly management of additional technical dependencies, maintaining the availability of a container software runtime and finally, the container's data and software management.

Runtime configuration & dependency identification: While there are different container flavors available, in a first step it is desirable to unify container packaging and runtime configuration into a open, standardized and well documented format to simplify long-term maintenance. One potential goal would be to migrate a container's runtime configuration to a generic runtime like $runC$ [4].

A second task is then to analyze the runtime configuration for external dependencies, e.g. specific hardware requirements or expected data mappings. For typical scientific computing scenarios the strict isolation of all of an experiment's content within a container is impractical, especially if computational methods are stored independently from data sets to support re-use of the method separately from the data. In such cases, processing software components require access to the external (from the container's view) input data in order to produce a desired output. The runtime configuration defines how a container expects data to be "mapped", a mechanism to inject files and directories from the host computer into the container at runtime. Management of the data to be made available to a container is discussed in the *Data Management* section. Similar mechanisms exist for accessing hardware through interfaces provided by operating system drivers. If for instance, a containerized application needs access to the hosts GPU hardware, the device nodes need to be mapped into the container e.g. `--device /dev/nvidia0:/dev/nvidia0`.

Finally, the container should be tested in a restricted and controlled environment, i.e. by using the memory institution's runtime, to uncover (implicit) external dependencies (e.g. dependencies on specific network resources or restrictions imposed by installed software components). Based on the nature of the external dependency found, its long-term risks need to be assessed. Furthermore, the environment's version used for a successful test run should archived and added to the container's technical meta-data.

Maintaining the Availability of a Technical Runtime: Preservation of the technical runtime can be divided into two tasks. The first task focuses on managing the software container runtime. For some operations specific operating system features are necessary, even though the software setup within a container is self-contained. In particular, to facilitate reproducibility, changes to the operating system API should be tracked, i.e. different versions should be kept available. Fortunately, the software installation is typically very basic and small[5] and there are usually no specific hardware requirements. Furthermore, Linux supports a wide range of computer hardware and also keeps supporting hardware for long periods of time. This makes it easy to maintain different versions of the software runtime on the same (carefully chosen) hardware configuration.

The second preservation problem is maintaining the necessary hardware, which will be obsolete at some point. Due to the rather generic nature of the software runtime and the non-specific hardware requirements, the technical runtime is the prime target for an emulation-based preservation strategy. Using an emulation-based preservation strategy, the focus is on maintaining the availability of a suitable hardware replacement (the emulator) to keep a number of

---

[4] The Open Container Initiative, runC, http://runc.io.
[5] The boot2docker installation is only about 27 MB, http://boot2docker.io/.

container runtime environments and a large number of containers accessible and usable.

Data Management: To combine a computational software-based process with a scientific data set, the data has to be made available to the container. In a preservation scenario, the scientific data set is assumed to be preserved independently in specialized (domain-specific) data-repositories and to be accessible through a persistent identifier (PI) e.g. DataCite[6]. Upon re-enactment of the archived containerized process, this data has to be made available to the container, e.g. via a simple file download.

One potential solution is to delegate the retrieval task to the container, e.g. a direct download into the container, allowing the container directly to interact with a data repository and to verify the right data format. Such an approach, however, is difficult to maintain in the long-term, as technical interfaces to data repositories may change over time and thus, the container would require adaptation. A more flexible and sustainable approach would be to make data available in the host computer's file system. Once the data set is available on the host system, the container runtime is able to make this data available to the software within the container, i.e. the runtime configuration maps data into the container at startup or even during runtime.

For instance, the nucleotid.es project[7] provides access to a large collection of genome assembler algorithms that are encapsulated in Docker containers. Each algorithm takes some input data and produces output in an output directory. The nucleotid.es Image API[8] specifies that all algorithms have to take three command line arguments. The first specifies a predefined algorithm configuration and the other two specify the input and output paths, respectively. Furthermore, the data files have to be in a specific file format. As all containers adhere to these simple rules, automatically managing different containers and many sets of input data becomes feasible.

If the data retrieved is not in the format expected by the scientific process, additional conversion steps have to be performed. The container might expect the data input to be represented by several files but upon archiving, the data was consolidated into a single file archive, e.g. as ZIP, TAR, BagIt or any similar archive format. In this case, the previously retrieved file from the repository has to be unpacked first.

In order to facilitate these tasks in an automated way, it is necessary to describe expected file formats usable with a specific container instance and how they these files should be made available within a specific container instance. Furthermore, a service that re-enacts containers with data-sets needs to implement and monitor data retrieval interfaces for PI and repository implementations.

Software Management: Many scientific organizations make regular and substantial use of proprietary software applications as part of computation-

---

[6] DataCite, http://www.datacite.org.

[7] nucleotid.es, a genome assembler catalogue http://nucleotid.es.

[8] The nucleotid.es Image API, http://nucleotid.es/image-api/.

dependent science that they undertake. Such proprietary software applications do not readily lend themselves inclusion into containers due to the Digital Rights Management (DRM) technologies the application developers use to enforce compliance with software license parameters in order to protect their intellectual property. Such DRM technology can bind instances of software to specific hardware instances, preventing the software from being reused on other hardware configurations.

As with the method for enabling access to external data dependencies of containers that was described above, a solution for the problem of hardware-constrained proprietary software should be implemented through the "transclusion" of software applications through the use of references to external software resources and software configurations from within a container. Such an approach would be similar to the concept from the digital archiving community called a "holey bag"[9]. Holey bags are archival packages of data that can be defined and shared without formally including the data files in the "bag" or data package, and instead by referencing the locations of the data to be shared. Such an approach, however, requires additional infrastructure to resolve required software packages, identify its configuration, and to be able to reference a canonical instance of that software but would allow to be able to manage rights and to simplify usage of proprietary software in portable containers.

5   Conclusion

Containers are and will be interesting research topic in the domain of digital preservation, both because of their widespread use and their technical characteristics. This initial study suggests, that if the long-term preservation of containers focuses on their technical runtime, e.g. by structured archival of the software runtime and an emulation-based strategy for their hardware dependencies, the preservation risks seem to be manageable in a (cost) efficient way (compared to the number of objects to be preserved). For many practical scenarios, i.e. usage of restricted software, novel concepts and infrastructure are required.

References

1. Meng, H., Kommineni, R., Pham, Q., Gardner, R., Malik, T., Thain, D.: An invariant framework for conducting reproducible computational science. J. Comput. Sci. **9**, 137–142 (2015)
2. Boettiger, C.: An introduction to docker for reproducible research. SIGOPS Oper. Syst. Rev. **49**(1), 71–79 (2015)
3. Biederman, E.W., Networx, L.: Multiple instances of the global linux namespaces. In: Proceedings of the Linux Symposium, vol. 1, pp. 101–112 (2006)
4. Menage, P.B.: Adding generic process containers to the linux kernel. In: Proceedings of the Linux Symposium, vol. 2, pp. 45–57 (2007)

---

[9] http://digital.library.unt.edu/ark:/67531/metadc29802/m2/1/high_res_d/ Phillips-2010-Chronopolis_MetaArchiv%20[presentation].pdf).

Development of Imaginary Beings Ontology

Wirapong Chansanam[1] and Kulthida Tuamsuk[2(✉)]

[1] Chaiyaphum Rajabhat University, Chaiyaphum, Thailand
wirapongc@cpru.ac.th
[2] Information and Communication Department, Khon Kaen University, Khon Kaen, Thailand
kultua@kku.ac.th

Abstract. A knowledge organization system is the key element of knowledge engineering. Ontology provides a fundamental framework for the development of the Semantic Web. This paper presents a building method for an imaginary beings' knowledge base. According to the approach, we established an ontological structure including primitive and contemporary imaginary beings' information. Combining the existent creature knowledge, we have applied the idealized cognitive models: ICM to build the knowledge system. Based on the introduction of ontology theory, we use Hozo of the Osaka University, for the construction, editor, and maintenance tool of ontology, to design and complete the imaginary beings' knowledge, based on ontology. The resulting ontology, Imaginary Beings Ontology (IBO), covers concepts derived from old as well as contemporary information. The system is applied to semantic web technology. The validity of IBO was evaluated by eight professional experts—three ontology engineers and five comics experts; this system makes significant improvements in the key techniques including the scope determination, classes definition, properties definition, instance definition, and future development and application. Finally, we describe our results that the system could resolve many problems in the field of imaginary beings' knowledge engineering.

Keywords: Imaginary beings · Ontology development · Semantic web · Knowledge-based systems

1 Introduction

There is much out there on imaginary beings, by folklorists, ethnologists and by others, which attempts to approach this topic both sensitively, by regarding people's beliefs, and comprehensively, by studying what defines the imaginary beings, and not by some external criteria. Perhaps it is time for new literature on imaginary beings' studies. Certainly, the delicate path of cross-cultural comparison can be stepped more lightly than this. Borges' book fails in terms of the description, analysis, and synthesis. It is a throwback to a time of cultural heritage study one hoped had long ago been overshadowed. Despite the rare reference to corpus introductions in semantics literature, one can classify information specialists' opinions in this connection into three approaches. Some believe that it is the duty of the corpus maker to provide the users with all the information they need at the point of entry, because these users rarely refer to their corpus

© Springer International Publishing AG 2016
A. Morishima et al. (Eds.): ICADL 2016, LNCS 10075, pp. 231–242, 2016.
DOI: 10.1007/978-3-319-49304-6_28

introductions [1–3]. One can interpret Borges's strange story in many ways or not at all. Here, we'll call it a fable, and attach my own harsh meaning to it: unless we increase our imagination to better take entity of the realities of other forms of being as well as our own, we miss our main task.

Our previous studies on imaginary beings have shown that the imaginary being information involves a lot, including content on old and contemporary beings around the world, thus, to build an imaginary beings semantic search platform must depend on the ontology in this field. Furthermore, the imaginary beings' knowledge on the web is dynamic and ever changing, so knowing how to guarantee the updates and accuracy of the imaginary beings' knowledge is of great importance, and it is considerably significant to look into the ontology construction in the imaginary beings' field.

Although both old and contemporary imaginary beings' knowledge has been well documented in textbooks and many electronic resources, it is often presented in flat knowledge form, i.e., lack of depth in taxonomies and hierarchy [4], and not well organized. Currently, most of all creatures' websites use web 2.0 technology that have been implemented against a relational database system. These systems also contain a tremendous amount of data that could not serve very useful in a complicated relation type analysis for their owners. Additionally, these websites may have multiple systems that use different database technologies.

The topic and content in the textbooks are only used as a frame of reference. In an imaginary beings' knowledge domain, the relationships between real beings or imaginary beings with semantic are still unclear. In terms of knowledge management, old and contemporary imaginary beings' knowledge should deploy a more well-organized form regarding the next generation of information requirement [5]. This will enable imaginary beings' knowledge to be reusable, sharable, and permitted to interoperate between knowledge domains.

Ontology is an explicit description of a domain, including concepts, properties and attributes of concepts, constraints on properties and attributes, and often includes individuals. With ontology, one can define a common vocabulary and a shared understanding of a domain [6]. Ontology engineering means defining concepts in the domain (classes), arranging the concepts in a hierarchy (superclass-subclass hierarchy), defining which attributes and properties classes can have and constraints on their values, as well as defining individuals and filling in values. Analysis and evaluation is one of the main research issues in ontology engineering. Ontologies have been realized as the key technology to shaping and exploiting information for the effective management of knowledge and evolution of the Semantic Web. Ontologies establish a common vocabulary for community members to interlink, combine, and communicate knowledge, shaped through practice and interaction among community members, binding the knowledge processes of creating, importing, capturing, retrieving and using knowledge [7].

This paper gives an improved ontology construction method, and utilizes this method to implement the construction of an imaginary beings' ontology knowledge domain. With these terminologies and relations, it defines the regulations of these vocabularies' extension, and ontologically describes them with the OWL language. In the end, it verifies and evaluates the created ontology in an instance and to develop its application as a semantic search system, in order to provide an effective imaginary beings semantic search for exploration of contemporary knowledge. The system is expected to increase the efficiency of search results by providing more relevant results.

2   System Conceptual Framework

The system conceptual framework, as shown in Fig. 1, consists of modules for the knowledge base, ontology, database and user interface. The ontology technology was used in building the conceptual knowledge for the imaginary beings' knowledge domain. The imaginary beings' database was originally created using MySQL. In constructing the knowledge base, the database data was integrated with the ontology to create the knowledge base in the Resource Description Framework (RDF) by using the Ontology Application Management (OAM) framework [8]. RDF is a standard model for data interchange. It facilitates data merging between different schemas. In this study, it facilitated the ontology schema and instance of data to be stored in the OAM. After implementing all these steps, the user can perform the querying process on top of the provided SPARQL query facility. This article focuses on the scope of domain knowledge necessary in answering the relevant queries in imaginary beings' ontology.

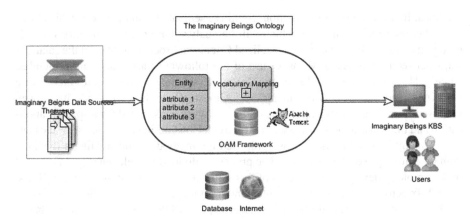

Fig. 1.   System conceptual framework

From Thesauri to Ontology.   Thesauri is defined as: "a terminology control tool that transforms the document indexing or the user's natural language into a standardized language; it is a constantly replenished and standardized vocabulary composed of the terminology concepts with semantic relations" [9, 10]. Thesauri is a structured text with the rich concepts of the domain terms, and, three kinds of semantic relations, such as equivalence, hierarchical, and associative relations, have been used in the thesauri. These characteristics are helpful for ontology construction, and this is also the reason why thesauri have been frequently used for the ontology construction.

Thesauri can be understood, even if there are not entirely logical relationships because it is read by people, but the ontology is the basis of semantic logic and has the strict logical requirement, so one must build strict logic for it, so that the computers can process the correct semantic reasoning. In the converted process from thesauri to ontology, it is required to overcome the semantic flaws.

3   Materials and Methods

Materials: We constructed imaginary beings' ontology using an ontology editor tool named Hozo (http://www.hozo.jp/), which is based on fundamental theories of ontology engineering for capturing the essential conceptual structure of the target world. Hozo has more than 1,500 users around the world, and it has been used to implement various ontologies for functional design, oil refinery plants, genomics, medicine, learning and instructional theories, and so on. The features of Hozo include: (1) supporting role representation [11], (2) visualization of ontologies in a friendly GUI, and (3) distributed development based on the management of dependencies between ontologies [12]. Hozo's native language is an XML-based framework language, and ontologies can be exported into OWL and RDF('s) [13]; Ontology Application Management (OAM), developed by the Language and Semantic Technology Laboratory, National Electronics and Computer Technology Center (NECTEC) [14]; and MySQL 5.0.

Methods: In this ontology construction, cognitive semantics will be used for this objective. The three main constructs which will be analyzed are corpus definitions, terminology meanings, diverse kinds of Idealized Cognitive Models (ICM) and the relationships between them. An ICM makes use of the following four structuring principles, namely, [15] (a) propositional structure, (b) image schematic structure, (c) metaphoric mappings, and (d) metonymic mappings. Almost all of these methods have been proposed in specific projects. Such ontology is always constructed for a specific application and the construction processes are different. Considering the wide use of thesauri and so many indexed literatures, we proposed the method of constructing a dynamic domain ontology based on thesauri. The process is divided into eleven steps. The steps of the ontology development process of this study are shown and described as follows.

All sixteen concepts have been implemented in the system. Some of them were based on the work by an imaginary beings' thesaurus [16], while others were directly based on the meaning of OWL DL operators. Some of these concepts are explained in detail below. This design decision was taken to allow the tool to be generic: it can be applied to any knowledge domain without the previous preparation or the construction of a high level ontology about that domain. As will be seen from the titles of the steps below, most concepts map directly to OWL constructs. So, for each question the user answers affirmatively, a fact is generated in the imaginary beings' database with all the details that must be saved in the resulting OWL ontology.

Step 1 Define classes, individuals and relations. These concepts are extremely simple and just suppose that every linking phrase is a candidate relation and that every concept that is connected to a linking phrase may be a class or an individual. They work mostly as a fallback if no other heuristic can generate a supposition about that element. The suppositions generated by these concepts are presented to the user as the last ones.

Step 2 Identify inverse properties. This cognitive looks for the map for linking phrases that are oriented exactly opposite from each other, namely, the arrows point towards reverse directions and every concept that is on the right side of one of them must be on the left side of the other, and vice versa. These linking phrases are considered possible inverse properties. It should be noted that complete agreement between the concepts on the left side of one relation and those on the right side of the other relation is necessary for these concepts to work.

Step 3 Define transitive properties. This concept looks for transitive relations definitions.

Step 4 Define enumerations. Some classes may be defined by enumeration. These concepts look for these cases by inspecting the text of the linking phrases and using a vocabulary of words that may signal an enumeration.

Step 5 Define generalization and instantiation. According to concept maps own creators, the relationship that is most easily represented in concept maps is the taxonomic relationship [17, 18]. So, some concepts that were found for this kind of relationship were implemented. Basically, these concepts check if the text of the linking phrase corresponds to a word in a vocabulary of words with a generalized meaning and if both sides of the linking phrase are candidates for classes. To account for the possibility of a linking phrase, meaning an instantiation relation, a vocabulary for this case has also been created. Because these vocabularies overlap, sometimes the user may have to decide if a given relation represents a specialization, an instantiation or none of them.

Step 6 Identify noun phrases. This concept looks for concepts in the concept map that are noun phrases which may hint at a taxonomic relationship. [19]

Step 7 Determine functional properties. Functional properties are usually used to describe objects attributes and are often used as part of more complex expressions to describe classes [20]. The concept used to find these properties is quite simple and uses a dictionary to find linking phrases that may denote a functional property, such as "has".

Step 8 Specify different individuals. Since the unique name assumption is not valid in OWL, it is necessary to specify explicitly when individuals are in fact different. This concept treats this case. This is one of the concepts that does not generate a yes or no question. Instead, it presents the user with a list of individuals and the user has to check those that are different among themselves.

Step 9 Specify disjoint classes. This one is equivalent to the previous concepts, except that it deals with classes instead of individuals.

Step 10 Determine mereologic relationships. Mereologic relationships are also important relationships in concept maps, especially in some domains, such as technical ones [21]. This paper used the work by Rector et al. [22] as a guideline to implement the description of mereologic relations. The concepts that searches for mereologic relations also uses a dictionary, but it differs from the aforementioned ones in that it does not show the user a yes/no question, but a list of possible concepts in the concept map that were found to be possible components of the concept being described. The user can select the ones that make sense. This approach, which is different from the general rule used with other relations, is used because, as a more detailed meaning is given to the relation, the expert may find that some of the concepts that he/she defined as "part of" another concept cannot, under this stricter interpretation, be considered parts. A second concept has also been implemented that, after a mereologic relation has been declared, questions the user if every individual composed of the same parts defined in that mereologic relation is also a member of the defined class. For example, if the user defines that "garuda have wings", the system would ask him/her something like, "Should I consider that every individual that has wings is a garuda?".

Step 11 Define dictionaries and corpus. As was cited in the description of some concepts, dictionaries were used to identify some special kinds of relationships. By "dictionary" it is meant a list of regular expressions matching possible linking phrases. The original vocabulary was created by analyzing existing concept maps. This was done mainly in English and the expressions were then translated into Thai. Afterwards, the vocabulary was expanded with an analysis of some of the maps in Thai. The application has a feature that allows an advanced user to expand the vocabulary. This part of the application can be translated quite simply to other languages, given that there is a collection of maps to create the vocabulary.

IBO consists of 16 major classes: Imaginary Beings, Imaginary Process, Imaginary Objects, Place, Capable Activity, Discipline, Imaginary Domain, Origins, Symbolic

Table 1. The important concepts in IBO

Concepts	Description
Imaginary Beings	A creature of the imagination; a person that exists only in legends, contemporary, myths or fiction
Imaginary Process	A process of the imagination; a mental sequence of events or states that you are not directly aware of
Imaginary Objects	An item of the imagination; a discrete item that provides a description of virtually anything known to an intangible
Place	An abstract mental location
Capable Activity	Having the skills and qualifications to do things well
Discipline	A system of rules of conduct or methods of practice
Imaginary Domain	The content of a particular imaginary field of knowledge
Origins	The source of something's existence or from which it derives, or is derived
Symbolic Meaning	Something visible that by association or convention represents something else that is invisible
Power Source	A source of primary energy, an energy form found in nature that has not been subjected to any conversion or transformation process
Enemy	An opposing military force
Habit	An automatic pattern of behavior in reaction to a specific situation; may be inherited or acquired through frequent repetition
Role	The actions and activities assigned to, or required, or expected of a human
Born From	A coming into being
Gender	The properties that distinguish organisms on the basis of an imaginary beings' reproductive role
Costume	The attire characteristic of an imaginary being (including accessories and hair style as well as garments)

Meaning, Power Source, Enemy, Habit, Role, Born From, Gender, and Costume. These classes are described as follows (Table 1):

(1) The Imaginary Beings class represents the imaginary beings use for the major conceptual purpose defined in the definition according to the old and contemporary imaginary beings' definition in the book of imaginary beings [23] and electronic resources around the world. The main component of the imaginary beings is the type of beings. It represents information of each imaginary beings' genre including human-like imaginary being, animal-like imaginary being, plant-like imaginary being, and multiple mixed imaginary being. This class as shown in Fig. 2.

(2) Imaginary Process class was defined according to the entity process. Here the process entity is classified according to three sub classes. The class hierarchy of the imaginary process is shown in Fig. 3.

(3) The Imaginary Objects class represents all creature objects by imagination. The relation between intangible objects and imaginary beings are represented as their properties.

(4) The Place class is the imaginary place. It aims to represent any place was creature by human in each story. This class serves as a connecting class of important concepts in imaginary beings.

(5) The Capable Activity class aims to conceptualize the capability of a process, existing in or produced by nature or supernatural (rather than by the intent of human beings).

(6) The Discipline class represents groups of a system of rules of conduct or method of imaginary beings practice.

(7) The Imaginary Domain class represents the scope of people in general; especially a distinctive group of people with some shared interest in an unusual activity or creativity. This class as shown in the visualization style in Fig. 4.

(8) The Origins class represents the source of something's existence, or from which it derives, or is derived.

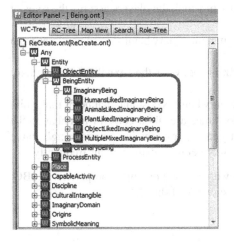

Fig. 2. Imaginary beings class

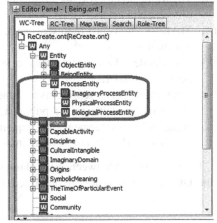

Fig. 3. The imaginary process class

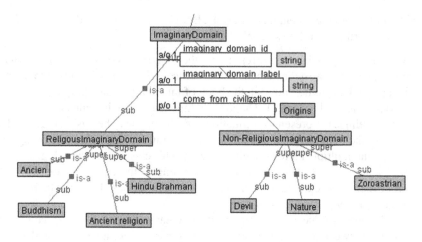

Fig. 4. The imaginary domain class visualization style

(9) The Symbolic Meaning class represents the serving as a visible symbol for something abstract. The message that is intended, expressed or signified of an imaginary being.

(10) The Power Source class represents a source of power for each imaginary being, such as by birth or by practice; their powers include flight, super strength, x-ray vision, invulnerability, speed, heat vision, freezing breath, super flare (a recently added huge heat blast that obliterates anything within a quarter mile radius), and superhuman senses.

(11) The Enemy class represents the imaginary beings have a recurring person who is extremely hostile or opposed to someone or something. At least one of these super villains will be the imaginary beings' archenemy.

(12) The Habit class represents a settled or regular tendency or practice of each imaginary being, especially a character that is hard to give up.

(13) The Role class represents a type of duty in which the players assume the roles of different characters.

(14) The Born From class represents an original imaginary beings' born or comes from a particular place.

(15) The Gender class represents a separation between the sexuality of imaginary beings by gender.

(16) The Costume class represents an imaginary being's costume that helps make him or her recognizable to the public. Costumes are often colorful to enhance the character's visual appeal and frequently incorporate the imaginary being's name and theme. Many features of an imaginary being's costume recur frequently.

The relationships between these classes were defined by object properties. In IBO, important object properties are described as shown in Table 2.

Table 2. The important object properties in IBO

Object properties	Description
hasDomainOfImaginaryBeings	Provides any creature information regarding members of imaginary beings' domain.
hasPowerOfSupernatural	Relates the power with the potential of the action to show with the Capable activity.
hasGivenRole	Relates to the actions and activities assigned to, or required, or expected of a particular social setting with the imaginary beings.
hasHabit	Relates the pattern of behavior in reaction to a specific situation; may be inherited or acquired through frequent repetition with the Imaginary beings.
hasBelieveThings	Relates to being confident about something with the being entities.
hasEncodedMeanings	Relates to a meaning that is not expressly stated but can be inferred with the symbolic meaning.
hasPowerSource	Relate power source originates causes or initiates something with the Source of power.
hasImaginaryObjects	Relates to a tangible and visible entity; an entity that can cast a shadow with the beings' entities.

4   Ontology Evaluation

To evaluate the method to construct the IBO proposed above, a study was conducted with eight professionals, to check their reaction to the method and test if the method would be accepted by experts working in ontology engineering. Also, some other impressions from the domain experts were measured. These are presented below.

The evaluation assessed the quality of the ontology by drawing upon semiotic theory [24], taking some metrics into consideration for assessing the syntactic, semantic, and pragmatic aspects of ontology quality. The validity of classes, sub classes, vocabularies and relationships identification are tested. The experts include three professional ontology engineers and five comics experts.

The evaluation criteria consisted of 5 categories: Determine Scope; Define Classes; Define Properties; Define Instance; and Future Development and Application. Overall opinions of the experts in both groups strongly agreed with IBO (86.00 % score). Comparing across the 5 categories, the most strongly agreed category is Future Development and Application, 93.40 % and 92.00 % in the ontology engineers and comics experts, respectively. The opinions in the other categories strongly agreed with the IBO in both groups (more than 80 %) in Determine Scope, Define Classes, Define Properties, and Define Instance, as illustrated in Fig. 5. Based on the results, IBO is generally acceptable and valid in terms of ontology development for construction of an imaginary beings' knowledge base.

Imaginary Beings Ontology Evaluation Result

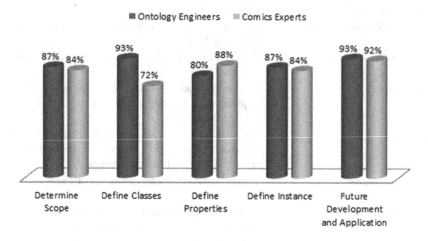

Fig. 5. Ontology evaluation result total score

4.1 Application Performance Evaluation

We developed a Semantic Web application for querying imaginary beings' information to demonstrate the application of IBO. The standard evaluation approach to a knowledge retrieval system revolves around the notion of relevant and non-relevant documents [24]. With respect to a user-context information requirement, a document in the test collection is given a binary classification as either relevant or non-relevant. This decision is referred to as the gold standard, or ground truth judgment of relevance. The test document collection and suite of information needs to be of a reasonable size; they need to provide average performance over fairly large test sets as results are highly variable over different documents and contextual information needs. As a rule of thumb, 80 % of the contextual information needs have usually been found to be a sufficient minimum. The accuracy of the application using the developed ontology is shown in Table 3.

Table 3. Knowledge retrieval efficiency results

		Relevant		
	Semantic searching	Relevant meaning	Non-relevant meaning	Overall meaning
Retrieved	Able	210	0	218
	Unable	0	20	

$$Recall = 0.9633$$
$$Precision = 0.8824$$
$$F - Measure = 0.9211$$

The results of the knowledge retrieval showed that the Semantic Web application was effective regarding values of Recall, Precision, and F-Measure. The application demonstrates that IBO has been developed consistently with both the physical resources and electronic resources of imaginary beings, with both old and contemporary information. Thus, readers and audiences around the world who are interested, can benefit from adopting and reusing this ontology. It provided functions of a concept-based search system which improved efficiency of the information query, by excluding non-relevant information items during the query answering process.

5   Conclusion

In this paper, the imaginary beings' knowledge-based system (IBKBS) was built based on ontology, and is introduced into the construction of imaginary beings' resources, with both old and contemporary information. With eleven-steps as a guide, we used the structured development method in knowledge engineering to design a general imaginary domain using the ontology construction method. Finally, in order to illustrate the method, we construct an ontology for knowledge engineering major. The construction method has strong universality and portability, and can be used as a reference for construction of other ontology domains.

To extend the content in ontology, we plan to use this in various information systems, including: belief Semantic Web, cultural heritage Semantic Web, comics/cartoon Semantic Web. More applications based on the developed ontology will be implemented, such as a recommendation system and a question–answer smart system.

Acknowledgement. This research is funded by the Digital Humanities Research Group of Khon Kaen University, Thailand.

References

1. Hornby, A.S., Cowie, A.P., Gimson, A.C.: Oxford Advanced Learner's Dictionary of Current English, 3rd edn. Oxford University Press, Oxford (1973)
2. Wiegand, G.E.: Two new genera of calcareous nanofossils from the Lower Jurassic. J. Paleontol. **58**, 1151–1155 (1984)
3. Berkov, V.P.: A Modern Bilingual Dictionary-Results and Prospects. Akademiai Kiado, Budapest (1990)
4. Bamber, S. Trope and taxonomy: an examination of the classification and treatment of illness in traditional Thai medicine [dissertation]. Australian National University, Canberra (1987)
5. Kitamura, Y., Qu, Y., Mizoguchi, R. (eds.): Semantic Technology, pp. 306–312. Springer, Heidelberg (2012)
6. Noy, F., McGuinness. L.: Ontology Development 101: A Guide to Creating Your First Ontology. http://protege.stanford.edu/publications/ontology_development/ontology101.html

7. Wielinga B.J., Schreiber A. T., Wielemaker J., Sandberg, J.A.C.: From thesaurus to ontology. In: Proceedings of the International Conference on Knowledge Capture, pp. 194–201. ACM Press (2001)

8. Tungkwampian, W., Theerarungchaisri, A., Buranarach, M.: Development Thai herbal medicine knowledge base using ontology technique. Thai J. Pharmaceutical Sci. (TJPS), **39**(3), 64–126 (2015)

9. Jidong, Z., Yisheng, Y.: Construction and research of ontology based on thesaurus. In: Document, Information & Knowledge (2006)

10. Steinberger, R., Pouliquen, B., Hagman, J.: Cross-lingual document similarity calculation using the multilingual thesaurus EUROVOC. In: Gelbukh, A. (ed.) CICLing 2002. LNCS, vol. 2276, pp. 415–424. Springer, Heidelberg (2002)

11. Mizoguchi, R., Kozaki, K., Sano, T., Kitamura, Y.: Construction and deployment of a plant ontology. In: Dieng, R., Corby, O. (eds.) EKAW 2000. LNCS (LNAI), vol. 1937, pp. 113–128. Springer, Heidelberg (2000). doi:10.1007/3-540-39967-4_9

12. Kozaki, K., Kitamura, Y., Ikeda, M., Mizoguchi, R.: Hozo: an environment for building/using ontologies based on a fundamental consideration of "Role" and "Relationship". In: Gómez-Pérez, A., Benjamins, V.R. (eds.) EKAW 2002. LNCS (LNAI), vol. 2473, pp. 213–218. Springer, Heidelberg (2002). doi:10.1007/3-540-45810-7_21

13. Kozaki, K., Sunagawa, E., Kitamura, Y., Mizoguchi, R.: Distributed construction of ontologies using hozo (2007). http://www.www2007.org/workshops/paper_19.pdf. Accessed 10 May 2010

14. Buranarach, M., Thein, Y.M., Supnithi, T.: A community-driven approach to development of an ontology-based application management framework. In: Takeda, H., Qu, Y., Mizoguchi, R., Kitamura, Y. (eds.) JIST 2012. LNCS, vol. 7774, pp. 306–312. Springer, Heidelberg (2013). doi:10.1007/978-3-642-37996-3_21

15. Lakoff, G.: Cognitive models and prototype theory. In: Neisser, U. (ed.) Concepts and Conceptual Development: Ecological and Intellectual Factors in Categorization, pp. 63–100. Cambridge University Press, New York (1987)

16. Chansanam, W., Tuamsuk, K.: Development of an imaginary beings knowledge structure. In: Allen, R.B., Hunter, R., Zeng, M.L. (eds.) ICADL 2015. LNCS(LNAI and LNBI), vol. 9469, pp. 291–293. Springer, Heidelberg (2015). doi:10.1007/978-3-319-27974-9

17. Novak, J.D.: Learning, Creating and Using Knowledge: Concept Maps as Facilitative Tools in Schools and Corporations. Lawrence Erlbaum Associates, Mahwah (1998)

18. Derbentseva, N., Safayeni, F., Cañas, A.A.: Experiments on the effects of map structure and concept quantification during concept map construction. In: Proceedings of the First International Conference on Concept Mapping, vol. 1. Universidad Pública de Navarra, Pamplona (2004)

19. Bird, S., Klein, E., Loper, E.: Natural Language Processing with Python. O'reilly & Associates Inc., Sebastopol (2009)

20. Borgida, A., Brachman, R.J.: Conceptual modeling with description Logics. In: Baader et al. (eds.) The Description Logic Handbook: Theory, Implementation and Applications, pp. 359–381. Cambridge University Press, Cambridge (2002). (Chap. 10)

21. Stokes, M. (ed.): Managing Engineering Knowledge. ASME Press, New York (2001)

22. Rector, A., Welty, C., Noy, N., Wallace, E.: Simple Part-Whole Relations in OWL Ontologies, August 2005

23. Borges, J.L., Guerrero, M.: The book of imaginary beings. Dutton, New York (1969)

24. Belew, R.K.: Finding out About: A Cognitive Perspective on Search Engine Technology and the www. Cambridge. Cambridge University Press (2000)

Open Access and Data

MathDL: A Digital Library of Mathematics Questions

Chu Keong Lee[1]([✉]), Joan Jee Foon Wee[1], and Don Tze Wai Chai[2]

[1] Nanyang Technological University, Singapore, Singapore
{ascklee,joanwee}@ntu.edu.sg
[2] Singtel, Singapore, Singapore
donchai@gmail.com

Abstract. The open-access movement is a global effort to make available scientific and scholarly research articles online for free. Today digital content is readily available beyond the full texts of articles, from raw and semi-raw data to images, audio, video, multimedia, and software. However, to date, no open access database of mathematics questions exists. This paper describes the current status of the development of MathDL, a digital library that provides access to mathematics questions useful to high school and pre-university students. MathDL provides the highest level of openness, allowing the author not just to reuse, but also to remix, revise and redistribute the questions. The benefits of MathDL are discussed, along with the possibility of using it to transform the way mathematics textbooks are published. Finally, the future plans for MathDL are presented.

Keywords: Mathdl · Mathematics questions · Open access · Open educational resources · Wordpress

1 Introduction

The open access movement has so far aimed to provide the public with unrestricted and free access to scholarly research – much of which is publicly funded. The argument is that making research publicly available to everyone without price and permissions restrictions will allow authors to reach a larger number of readers and accelerate the pace of scientific progress. The reality of shrinking library budgets and the fact that universities in many developing countries cannot afford to pay the subscriptions required to access toll access literature has fueled the pace of the movement, and today, we have a good number of open access journals, repositories, educational resources, software, images, videos and multimedia content.

Even though much progress has been made in the past two decades, one type of content that has been neglected by the open access community is mathematics questions. In fact, up to now, it seems that the concept of open access applies mainly to scholars. Little emphasis has been paid to students, specifically students at the secondary and pre-university levels. The community of students at these levels are unlikely to benefit from unfettered access to scholarly research or raw research data. What students require is access to learning materials. For the case of mathematics, students need questions.

© Springer International Publishing AG 2016
A. Morishima et al. (Eds.): ICADL 2016, LNCS 10075, pp. 245–250, 2016.
DOI: 10.1007/978-3-319-49304-6_29

For this reason, at the Nanyang Technological University, we have started a project with the sharp focus of providing open access to mathematics question. This project started as a result of the analysis of some 100 mathematics textbooks for secondary and pre-university students from 15 countries. These textbooks can be categorized into three groups. Some of these textbooks were copyright expired, some not copyright expired, but long out-of-print, and the remainder, not copyright expired, and still in print. Whatever group they belonged to, we noted that there is a significant overlap in the topics covered in the curriculum of the different countries. Some of the similarities stems from historical reasons. For example, the mathematics curriculum in Malaysia, Singapore, Australia and Hong Kong are very similar because they were all at one time, British colonies, and inherit the British curriculum. However, we also noted the similarities of the curriculum in the countries which have been independent throughout their history, for instance, Thailand and Japan.

In addition, we noted that questions in many of the textbooks were similar. The practice of recycling mathematics questions is unsurprising because textbooks, such as Euclid's *The Elements* on geometry, started to be written some 2,000 years ago. Even textbooks on more recent mathematical innovations, e.g. calculus, were already available by 1696, over 300 years ago [1]. The recycling of question either represents unnecessary repetition, where the authors skims older textbooks to "locate" questions he likes), or reinvention of the wheel, where the author creates questions from scratch, which he could have obtained from other books. Either way, the author's time can be more productively spent.

We also noted that many of the textbooks today are extremely bulky and costly. For example, the 13th edition of *Thomas' Calculus* is 1,194 pages [2], and retails for US $229.89 on Amazon.com! Anecdotal evidence from conversations we had with the university bookstore, students from the engineering faculty and instructors indicated that students were finding the price of textbooks prohibitively high and a chore to lug around, and were avoiding to buy them unless absolutely necessary.

An analysis of our collection of textbooks indicated that some 30–40% of the textbook were devoted to examples and questions. Removing these from textbooks and placing them in a central, open access repository can potentially reduce the number of pages by that amount. This will lower the bulk of the textbook, and publishers may even be persuaded to lower the price. This was what we set out to do – create a database to store mathematics questions so that anyone who needs them – authors, teachers, students or researchers – could retrieve them from this single, central source.

2   Related Work

Neither the digitization of educational resources, nor making them available freely is an uncommon activity. In 2006, thirty Nigerian university libraries cooperated to digitize their collection of past question papers, theses and dissertations. Their efforts were stymied by the lack of funds, appropriate facilities, skilled manpower, and an unreliable electricity supply. Nevertheless, they persisted as library users were anxious to have the services to commence because of their importance in facilitating teaching, learning and research [2]. Earlier, the University of Birmingham reported the digitization of 1,500 examination paper, amounting to a total of 1,500 A4-sized pages. They decided against digitizing the papers into the HTML format due to the high cost involved, and scanned them into the PDF format, one exampaper per PDF file [3]. In both cases, scanning was done at the level of examination paper. We decided we would go down to the level of individual questions, i.e., one question per WordPress post. We also decided that we would not would use the PDF format, but encode the questions in HTML. This raised the amount of effort required as each question had to be manually keyed in.

Organizations like FlatWorld Knowledge and the CK-12 foundation have started to publish open textbooks, textbooks that have been funded, published, and licensed to be freely used, adapted, and distributed. Textbooks are especially important to improving learning outcomes in developing countries because of the preponderance of large class sizes, a high proportion of unqualified teachers, and a shortage of instructional time. Unfortunately, developing countries are also faced with connectivity barriers that need to be overcome to access open textbooks [4].

Merlot is both a community of mostly faculty members and a collection of teaching and learning resources. It is a community of staff, volunteers, and members who work together in various ways to provide users of Open Educational Resource teaching and learning materials with a wealth of services and functions that can enhance their instructional experience. Since 1997, it has made available a collection of tens of thousands of discipline-specific learning materials, learning exercises, and Content Builder web pages, together with associated comments, and bookmark collections, all intended to enhance the teaching experience of using a learning material [5].

3   The Mathematics Digital Library

We call our digital library the Mathematics Digital Library (MathDL; http://mathematics-dl.org/). It is sharply focused on mathematics questions. Working with the constraint of time and expertise, we decided that the delivery vehicle for the questions would be WordPress, a popular blogging and website content management system. The QuickLatex plugin, by Pavel Holoborodko was used to render the mathematical questions. We realize that although digitizing the questions in HTML and LaTex for the mathematical equations would be very time consuming, this was the path we would take because that would make each question searchable, and this would also enable us to assign metadata to each question. We also made a conscious decision that the focus of the project would be the content, and not the development of the platform. What motivated us was the fact that once a question was posted, we had essentially unlocked the question. We had, in a sense made it visible again.

To date, we have keyed in 6,000 questions, and we aim to have another 4,000 questions keyed in by the end of 2016. A problem unique to mathematics questions is brevity. Most questions have a single-word instruction, the most common ones being, solve, integrate, differentiate, expand, calculate, factorize, proof and show. This brevity makes it difficult to search. The word "integrate" retrieves nearly a thousand posts.

4   Benefits of the Mathematics Digital Library

Unlock the Contents of Old Textbooks. Many established academic libraries have an impressive collection of old textbooks, build up over many years. Some of the textbooks have been heavily used in the past because they were the adopted textbook of a course, but have since been forgotten. Because of a low number of people borrowing them, librarians typically transfer them to the closed stacks, where they not only lay unused, but also impossible to discover serendipitously. The contents in such books are still relevant, and MathDL unlocks this content. The questions are made visible and available again, this time to even the remotest parts of the world.

Drive Down the Cost of Textbooks. The cost of textbooks has skyrocketed over the last two decades, outpacing the rate of inflation [6]. Part of the high cost is due to the bulk of the textbooks: calculus textbooks typically have more than 700 pages. The exorbitant price of textbooks has spawned several creative workarounds. Some publishers have started to reprint the classics, and selling them at a fraction of the price, such as the Ishi Press' reprinting of Taylor's (1959) *Calculus with Analytic Geometry*. With MathDL, publishers can point their readers to questions on MathDL, from the textbook's website, eliminating the pages previously devoted to questions and examples. reduces the number of pages by some 30–40%.

Reduce the Reinvention of Wheels (Questions). The questions: Evaluate $\int \sin^2 x dx$, Prove that $\sqrt{2}$ is irrational, and thousands of others appear in countless textbooks. MathDL makes them available, one and for all. This reduces the recreation of these questions. Recreation is a waste of time, time that authors can spend on creating original content. Instructors can prepare sets of tutorial questions by pointing to questions on MathDL.

Make Available Local Material. Much material useful for learning mathematics remain local (the country in which it was created), and can be difficult to obtain outside the country of origin. Local materials are important because they allow students around the world to benchmark themselves against students in other countries. Policy makers can start to understand the different mathematics curriculum around the world, and to see how the differences affect the performance of the different countries in international benchmarks like TIMSS. MathDL makes three categories of local material available:

- **Textbooks:** The mathematics curriculum in different countries differ in various ways – structure, framework (which captures the philosophy and believes of what should be done in the mathematics classroom, and pedagogical approach), and order of content [6, 7]. These differences are reflected in the textbooks. Making questions from textbooks around the world will acquaint educators with the different ways mathematics is taught around the world.
- **National Competition Questions:** Many countries hold mathematical competitions. These are often published in local mathematical journals, which may be difficult to obtain outside their country of origin. For example, the Singapore Mathematical Olympiad is an annual event organized by the Singapore Mathematical Society.

The Singapore Inter-School Mathematical Competition questions have been made available through *The Mathematical Medley*, the society's journal. Competition questions are interesting because a "mathematical problem" is one that is non-routine, for which a solution or a method of solution is not immediately forthcoming to the solver [8]. Attempting problems from mathematical Olympiads complements school mathematics lessons. This is because by problems from Olympiads stretch students by introducing them to questions beyond their curriculum. Currently, competition questions are available only through specialist publishers, and not easy to access. MathDL makes them more accessible.

- **National and Examination Papers:** Many countries have national examinations. Singapore, for example, has the annual A-Levels examinations, in which mathematics is tested at three levels (Higher 1, Higher 2 and Higher 3). Individual schools have their own examination papers, and in Singapore, such papers can be downloaded from websites like TestPapers.com.sg and Singapore-Exam-Papers.com. Questions from such examination papers may be of interest to students of other countries, and with international participation, and MathDL can be a repository of questions from different countries.

Provide Students with a Large Stock of Question. Mathematics is a participation sport. A student of mathematics cannot merely read about mathematics, or watch a video on how to solve a particular question. He has to get his hands dirty, and attempt to solve questions himself. For this to happen he has to have access to a rich stock of questions, which MathDL supplies. Khan Academy and YouTube has a large number of videos related to the solution of mathematics problems, but after watching, students need to be able to attempt related questions.

Facilitate Seamless Learning. The questions available from MathDL offers opportunities for teachers to expose their students to a greater repertoire of question types. As MathDL is mobile friendly, it also an element in the mobile realm of seamless learning, a learning notion that emphasizes the bridging of different learning efforts across a variety of learning settings, ideally by leveraging mobile technology to assist individual students in carrying out cross-space learning on a 24×7 basis. Students learn differently, and MathDL allows students to acquire mathematical knowledge through different pathways.

Promote Individualized Instruction. Students have different needs, interests, abilities, aspirations and motivational levels. There are students who need a great deal of guidance and handholding, and students who are very independent; students who love to read and others who would rather tinker and make something; students who are full of ideas and those who can carry out the ideas of others. The diversity of students is easy to observe. Yet, a majority of educators have tended to teach as though all students were alike. They assign the same questions to the entire class they teach. MathDL makes individualized instruction possible.

5 Future Work

As teachers have begun to use MathDL, they have provided some feedback, most of which we intend to address in next phase of development. First, we will be focusing on enabling registered users to contribute questions and the solutions to the questions. Second, the database is "calculus heavy", and so, we intend to increase the number of questions from other topics in mathematics. To standardize the look-and-feel of the posts, we will be creating a style manual.

To improve the searchability of the questions, we will be evaluating the 2010 Mathematical Subject Classification to see if it can be used to classify the questions. This classification scheme is organized into three levels, and we are also evaluating the granularity to which we should classify the questions. In addition, we will also be evaluating the typology of questions to see if they can be used for tagging the questions [9].

References

1. US Bureau of Labor Statistics. Databases, Tables & Calculators by Subject (2015). http://data.bls.gov/timeseries/CUUR0000SSEA011?output_view=pct_3mths
2. Thomas Jr., G.B., Weir, M.D., Hass, J.R.: Thomas' calculus, 13th edn. Pearson, London (2015)
3. Hampson, A., Pinfield, S., Upton, I.: The digitization of exam papers. Electron. Libr. **17**(4), 239–246 (1999)
4. Yaya, J.A., Adeeko, K.: Digitization of educational resources in Nigerian academic libraries: Prospects, challenges and the way forward. Int. J. Inf. Res. Rev. **3**(1), 1594–1600 (2016)
5. Alhaji, I.U.: Digitization of past question papers, dissertations and theses: A case study of 30 Nigerian university libraries. Int. Inf. Libr. Rev. **39**(3–4), 228–246 (2007)
6. Lee, N.H.: Singapore Maths – A coherent structure, an eclectic approach: A conversation with Dr Lee Ngian Hoe. EduNation **9**, 4–12 (2015)
7. Aharoni, R.: The real benefit of learning mathematics: A conversation with Ron Aharoni. EduNation **10**, 28–30 (2016)
8. Toh, T.L.: How can students benefit from Mathematical Olympiads. Math. Medley **36**(1), 15–22 (2010)
9. Fan, L., Zhu, Y.: An analysis of the representation of problem types in Chinese and US mathematics textbooks. In: Paper presented at the 10th International Congress on Mathematics Education. Copenhagen, Denmark (2004)

Interleaving Clustering of Classes and Properties for Disambiguating Linked Data

Takahiro Komamizu[(✉)], Toshiyuki Amagasa, and Hiroyuki Kitagawa

University of Tsukuba, Tsukuba, Japan
taka-coma@acm.org, {amagasa,kitagawa}@cs.tsukuba.ac.jp

Abstract. As Linked Data (or LD) increasingly expands its capacity, ambiguity in vocabularies on LD has become more problematic. This paper deals with a part of the ambiguity, namely, class ambiguity and property ambiguity. In this paper, we propose a novel clustering method, CPClustering, which clusters synonymous classes and properties in an interleaving manner. CPClustering groups classes by their related properties, and, inversely, groups properties by their related classes. CPClustering iteratively clusters classes and properties, and updates their representations in terms of immediate clustering results.

Keywords: Interleaving clustering · Class disambiguation · Property disambiguation · Linked Data

1 Introduction

Linked Data (or LD) has pervaded in a large varieties of domains. LD is a paradigm for connecting data on the Web in order to utilize published datasets. LD is accessible via various means like downloadable dumps (or archives), and SPARQL endpoints for querying through SPARQL query [4]. Reusability of data motivates data holders to publish their data and to connect their data with existing data.

LD datasets are a crucible of various ontologies which are used for representing entities and relationships among entities in the dataset. A typical and largest LD dataset, DBpedia[1], contains OWL[2], FOAF[3], and so forth. Such heterogeneity makes confusions of class and property usage, that is, it is not obvious which classes (or properties) are appropriate to represent an entity (or a relationship). For example, person entities can belong to the following two classes: foaf:Person[4] and dbo:Person[5]. A few works, such as [2,5], attempt to solve this ambiguity problem. Zhang et al. [5] detect synonymous properties having high *synonymity scores*. A synonymity score of a pair of properties is based on (1) overlapping

---

[1] http://dbpedia.org/about.
[2] http://www.w3.org/TR/owl-ref/.
[3] http://xmlns.com/foaf/spec/.
[4] http://xmlns.com/foaf/0.1/Person.
[5] http://dbpedia.org/ontology/Person.

© Springer International Publishing AG 2016
A. Morishima et al. (Eds.): ICADL 2016, LNCS 10075, pp. 251–256, 2016.
DOI: 10.1007/978-3-319-49304-6_30

triples, and (2) relative ratio of cardinalities of triples having that properties. The clustered properties based on the synonymity scores are considered to be synonymous. Morzy et al. [2] propose a frequent pattern mining approach for finding substitutive items among transactions.

In this paper, we attempt to disambiguate classes and properties using clustering. Clustering is a typical approach to find groups of similar items. For the clustering, designing features is an important task. This paper proposes feature deigns for both classes and properties. This paper characterizes classes by relevant properties, and characterizes properties by relevant classes. On one hand, a class can be characterized by properties contained in the class, and/or properties referring to objects of the class. On the other hand, a property can be characterized by classes on object positions on triples containing the property, and/or classes on subject positions on triples containing the property. In real LD datasets, classes and properties are highly correlated each other. Thus, it is not reasonable to perform clustering using only one of them (i.e., class or property). The clusters of classes have an influence on those of properties, and vice versa.

In this paper, we propose a novel interleaving clustering approach, **CPClustering**, to cluster classes using properties as features, and vice versa. Firstly, we perform clustering over classes and properties individually. We arrange the representations of classes and properties in accordance with the clustering results. Again, we perform clustering using the arranged class and property representations. In this paper, we apply the proposed algorithm to classes and properties in DBpedia.

2   Interleaving Clustering of Classes and Properties

CPClustering is an interleaving clustering of classes and properties, and utilizes classes and properties for characterizing each other. If two classes have similar set of properties, these classes are considered to have similar features and thus they are synonymous. If two properties are associated with a similar set of classes, these properties are considered to be synonymous. Based on these observations, we characterize classes by properties, and vice versa. Formally, given a set C of classes and a set P of properties, a class c in C is represented as a vector in the P space, $\mathbf{c} = (w_1, w_2, \ldots, w_{|P|})$, and a property p in P is represented as a vector in the C space, $\mathbf{p} = (w_1, w_2, \ldots, w_{|C|})$.

2.1   Class and Property Representation

The relationship from classes to properties can be classified into two categories. In one case, instances of a class appear in the subject position and properties are in the predicate position. The other case is that instances of a class appear in the object position. The former implies that properties are attributes of the class, and we call it **Internal Property Representation** (or **IPR**). On the other hand, the latter implies how instances of the class are used, and we call it **External Property Representation** (or **EPR**).

IPR: Each weight in class vector **c** is proportional to the number of triples which subjects are of c and properties are the corresponding property. Formally, the weight w_i for the corresponding property p_i in class c is calculated as IPR as $\frac{|D(c,p_i,*)|}{|D(c,*,*)|}$, where $D(\cdot)$ is the triples in the dataset matching with the given condition. $D(\cdot)$ with condition $(c, *, *)$ means that triples which subject is of class c, and another condition $(c, p_i, *)$ means triples which subject is of class c and predicate is p_i.

EPR: Each weight in class vector **c** is proportional to the number of triples whose objects are of c and properties are the corresponding property. Formally, the weight w_i for the corresponding property p_i in class c is calculated as EPR as $\frac{|D(*,p_i,c)|}{|D(*,*,c)|}$. $D(\cdot)$ with condition $(*, *, c)$ means that triples whose object is of class c, and another condition $(*, p_i, c)$ means triples whose object is of class c and predicate is p_i.

The relationship from properties to classes can also be classified into two categories, that is, instances of the classes are in subject position or object position. The former means that a property is characterized by the classes which instances use the property as predicate, and we call it **Source Class Representation** (or **SCR**). The latter means that a property is characterized by the classes which instances are used by the property as predicate, and we call it **Destination Class Representation** (or **DCR**).

SCR: Each weight in property vector **p** is proportional to the number of triples which properties are p and classes on subject position are of the corresponding class. Formally, the weight w_i for the corresponding class c_i in property p is calculated as SCR as $\frac{|D(c_i,p,*)|}{|D(*,p,*)|}$. $D(\cdot)$ with condition $(*, p, *)$ means that triples which predicate is p, and another condition $(c_i, p, *)$ means triples which predicate is p and subject is of class c_i.

DCR: Each weight in property vector **p** is proportional to the number of triples which properties are p and classes on object position are of the corresponding class. Formally, the weight w_i for the corresponding class c_i in property p is calculated as DCR as $\frac{|D(*,p,c_i)|}{|D(*,p,*)|}$. $D(\cdot)$ with condition $(*, p, c_i)$ means triples which predicate is p and object is of class c_i.

2.2   Clustering Algorithm: CPClustering

Given representations of classes and properties, CPClustering clusters them one by one in an interleaving manner. First, classes are clustered. Then, representation of properties are updated according to the class clustering. This process enables similar features can be merged. Using the updated representations, properties are clustered. Similar to above, representations of classes are updated. These procedure continues until updates do no change representations. This procedure is summarized in Algorithm 1.

Classes and properties in the datasets are represented in the vector space model, thus, most of clusterings (e.g., agglomerative clustering, k-means and

---

Algorithm 1. CPClustering algorithm.

Input: Classes $C^{(0)}$, Properties $P^{(0)}$
Output: Clusterings $C^{(*)}$, $P^{(*)}$
1: $t \leftarrow 0$
2: **while** $(C^{(t-1)} \neq C^{(t)}$ and $P^{(t-1)} \neq P^{(t)})$ or $t = 0$ **do**
3:     $C^{(t+1)} \leftarrow clustering(C^{(t)})$
4:     $P^{(t)} \leftarrow update(P^{(t)}, C^{(t+1)})$
5:     $P^{(t+1)} \leftarrow clustering(P^{(t)})$
6:     $C^{(t+1)} \leftarrow update(C^{(t+1)}, P^{(t+1)})$
7:     $t \leftarrow t + 1$
8: **end while**
9: $C^{(*)} \leftarrow C^{(t)}$, $P^{(*)} \leftarrow P^{(t)}$

DBSCAN) can be performed with any similarity measurements based on vector space model (e.g., cosine similarity [1]). We simply employ cosine similarity. The function $update(A^{(t)}, B^{(t+1)})$ maps A which is based on clustering $B^{(t+1)}$. Objects in $A^{(t)}$ are updated by aggregating weights according with the clustering $B^{(t+1)}$. That is, for a cluster $B_j^{(t+1)} \in B^{(t+1)}$, the weights of the members of the cluster are aggregated (i.e., summing up), and the aggregated value is set to the weight in the updated object. Formally, $\mathbf{a}_j^{(t)} \leftarrow \sum_{i \in B_j^{(t+1)}} \mathbf{a}_i^{(t)}$.

3   Experimental Evaluation

This section tries to prove the effectiveness of CPClustering using real and largest LD data, DBpedia. The number of triples is about 438 million, that of classes is about 0.3 million, and that of properties is about 64 thousand. We randomly selected 1000 classes and 10,000 properties for evaluation. For the individual clusterings, in this experiment, we use agglomerative clustering.

3.1   Evaluating Clustering via Purity

Purity [1] is one of evaluation methods for clusterings. Given clustering and labels of members, purity of the clustering is calculated as average ratio of the largest number of labels in each cluster. In order to obtain the labels, we conduct a user study which asks users group functionally similar items in a cluster. Then, we consider the groups as labels, and calculate the purity with the largest groups.

The evaluation results are shown in Fig. 1. Two charts depicts purities of class clusterings and property clusterings for each combination of representations (i.e., IPR & SCR, IPR & DCR, EPR & SCR, and EPR & DCR). The purities on class clustering are over 0.65, while those on properties are various top-2 purities are above 0.6 but others are in 0.45 to 0.55.

Evaluation results show that the best combinations of representations for class clustering is IPR & SCR and IPR & DCR, while that for property clustering is IPR & DCR and EPR & DCR. These indicate that, for class clustering, IPR

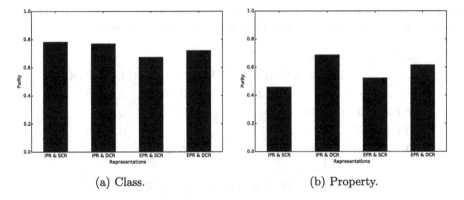

(a) Class.   (b) Property.

Fig. 1. Purities of clusterings w.r.t. representations (i.e., IPR and EPR for class, and SCR and DCR for property). The graphs are higher better, that is, better clusterings have higher purities.

represents functionalities of classes more appropriately than EPR. While, for property clustering, DCR represents functionalities of properties more than SCR. Indeed, the combination of IPR and DCR performs best for overall clustering.

3.2   Observing Relationships Among Clusterings

This paper proposes a various representations, here we observe relationships among clusterings based on different representations. If clusterings of different representations are overlapping, clustering higher purity is always superior to the others. Conversely, overlaps of clusterings are less, the combinations of different clusterings may improve clustering accuracy.

To measure overlapping of clusterings, we employ Adjusted Rand Index (ARI) [3]. ARI evaluates whether co-occurrences of objects in a clustering also appears in the other clustering. That is, the larger ARI, the more overlapping.

Table 1(a) and (b) respectively show ARIs for clusterings with different representations for classes and properties. For class clustering, IPR & SCR and EPR & SCR have the highest value, indicating that these clusterings are similar. This may be caused by the representation, SCR, of properties. Even the two best purity clusterings (IPR & SCR, and IPR & DCR) have relatively smaller ARI value (i.e., 0.30679). This indicates that, when to cluster classes, properties should be represented both SCR and DCR.

For property clustering, IPR & DCR and EPR & DCR have the highest values. This indicates that property representation, DCR, provides similar clusterings. The best purity property clustering, IPR & DCR, have smaller ARI with others with SCR property representation. Thus, it looks possible to improve clustering accuracy by combining features over SCR property representations.

Table 1. Adjusted Rand Index for class clusterings and property clusterings of different representations. The table is symmetric as is for adjusted Rand Index.

(a) Class clusterings

	IPR & SCR	IPR & DCR	EPR & SCR	EPR & DCR
IPR &SCR	-	0.30679	0.51389	0.26819
IPR &DCR	0.30679	-	0.31785	0.25950
EPR &SCR	0.51389	0.31785	-	0.27820
EPR &DCR	0.26819	0.25950	0.27820	-

(b) Property clusterings

	IPR & SCR	IPR & DCR	EPR & SCR	EPR & DCR
IPR &SCR	-	0.23138	0.14902	0.24907
IPR &DCR	0.23138	-	0.03130	0.81658
EPR &SCR	0.14902	0.03130	-	0.02909
EPR &DCR	0.24907	0.81658	0.02909	-

4   Conclusion

This paper has proposed an interleaving clustering algorithm, CPClustering, which clusters classes and properties of a Linked Data dataset alternatively. In CPClustering, classes and properties are characterized each other, that is, classes are represented by properties and properties are represented by classes. Thus, clustering of classes effect the of properties, and vice versa. The empirical study implies the usability of CPClustering.

Acknowledgement. This research was partly supported by the program *Research and Development on Real World Big Data Integration and Analysis* of the Ministry of Education, Culture, Sports, Science and Technology, and RIKEN, Japan.

References

1. Manning, C.D., Raghavan, P., Schütze, H., et al.: Introduction to Information Retrieval, vol. 1. Cambridge University Press, Cambridge (2008)
2. Morzy, M., Ławrynowicz, A., Zozuliński, M.: Using substitutive itemset mining framework for finding synonymous properties in linked data. In: Bassiliades, N., Gottlob, G., Sadri, F., Paschke, A., Roman, D. (eds.) RuleML 2015. LNCS, vol. 9202, pp. 422–430. Springer, Heidelberg (2015). doi:10.1007/978-3-319-21542-6_27
3. Steinley, D.: Properties of the hubert-arable adjusted rand index. Psychol. Methods **9**(3), 386 (2004)
4. W3C: SPARQL Query Language for RDF (2008). https://www.w3.org/TR/rdf-sparql-query/
5. Zhang, Z., Gentile, A.L., Blomqvist, E., Augenstein, I., Ciravegna, F.: Statistical knowledge patterns: identifying synonymous relations in large linked datasets. In: Alani, H., et al. (eds.) ISWC 2013. LNCS, vol. 8218, pp. 703–719. Springer, Heidelberg (2013). doi:10.1007/978-3-642-41335-3_44

A Framework for Linking RDF Datasets for Thailand Open Government Data Based on Semantic Type Detection

Pattama Krataithong[1,2(✉)], Marut Buranarach[1], Nattanont Hongwarittorrn[2], and Thepchai Supnithi[1]

[1] Language and Semantic Technology Laboratory,
National Electronics and Computer Technology Center (NECTEC), Pathumthani, Thailand
{pattama.kra,marut.bur,thepchai.sup}@nectec.or.th
[2] Department of Computer Science, Faculty of Science and Technology, Thammasat University,
Pathumthani, Thailand
nth@cs.tu.ac.th

Abstract. Most of datasets in open government data portals are mainly in tabular format in spreadsheet, e.g. CSV and XLS. To increase the value and reusability of these datasets, the datasets should be made available in RDF format that can support better data querying and data integration. Our previous work proposed a semi-automatic framework for generating RDF datasets from existing datasets in tabular format. In this paper, we extend our framework to support automatic linking of the RDF datasets. One of the important steps is mapping some literal values that appear in a dataset to some standard URIs. Several previous researches use semantic search API such as DBpedia or Sindice for URI mapping. However, this approach is not appropriate for the datasets of Thailand open data portal (Data.go.th) because there is insufficient data for Thai name entities. In addition, a name may match with more than one URI, i.e. word ambiguity. For example, the name "Bangkok" may match with those referenced by URIs of a province, a hospital or a university. To resolve these issues, our framework proposes that finding semantic types is essential to resolve word ambiguity in retrieving a proper URI for a name entity. This paper presents a framework for finding semantic types and mapping name entities to URIs, i.e. URI lookup. A Name Entity Recognition (NER) technique is applied in finding semantic type of a column in a CSV dataset. The results are used for creating ontology and RDF data that include the URI mappings for name entities. We evaluate two approaches by comparing the performance of a semantic search API, i.e. Wikipedia and the NER technique using some datasets from the Data.go.th website.

Keywords: Finding semantic types · Name Entity Recognition (NER) · Automatic ontology creation · Automatic linked dataset creation

1 Introduction

Open Government Data initiatives are widely adopted in many countries in order to increase the transparency, public engagement and the channel of communication between government and their citizens. Data.go.th is the national open government data

© Springer International Publishing AG 2016
A. Morishima et al. (Eds.): ICADL 2016, LNCS 10075, pp. 257–268, 2016.
DOI: 10.1007/978-3-319-49304-6_31

portal of Thailand, which was initiated in 2014. As of July 2016, there are over seven hundred datasets available on this portal in various formats (e.g. XLS, CSV, etc.). Data.go.th also promotes applications and innovations that are created based on the content published on the portal. One of the applications created based on the datasets is the Thailand Government Spending website[1].

Based on the 5-star open data model[2], to increase the value and reusability of these datasets, the datasets should be made available in the Resource Description Framework (RDF) format that can support better data querying and data integration. Specifically, the RDF data allows data querying via SPARQL endpoint. In addition, RDF uses URI as a means for referencing data in different RDF datasets, i.e. Linked Data. We previously proposed a semi-automatic framework [1] in transforming tabular data in spreadsheet format, i.e. CSV, to RDF format. The framework provides a support system[3] for the users in creating an RDF dataset, i.e. 4-star open data, from an existing dataset without the required knowledge of RDF. The system also provides the data as a service via RESTFul APIs for every RDF dataset published on this portal. Figure 1 demonstrates the dataset publishing service on Demo-api.data.go.th and access to the datasets as RDF datasets and RESTFul APIs for the datasets.

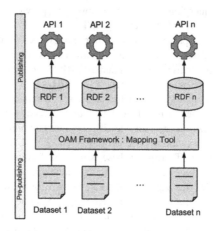

Fig. 1. Layers of Dataset Service API at Demo-api.data.go.th

In this paper, we describe our ongoing effort to create a framework to support automatic linking of the RDF datasets, i.e. 5-star open data. The framework focuses on finding columns that contain some common name entities that appear across different datasets and link them to the same referenced URIs for the name entities. One of the important steps is mapping some literal values that appeared in a dataset to some standard URIs, i.e. URI lookup process. Our framework proposes to apply a Name Entity Recognition (NER) technique for finding semantic type of a column in a CSV dataset.

---

[1] http://govspending.data.go.th/.

[2] http://5stardata.info/en/.

[3] http://demo-api.data.go.th/.

The results are used for creating ontology and RDF data that include the URI mappings for name entities. We evaluate the performance of the proposed NER technique by comparing with the results of a semantic search API, i.e. Wikipedia, using some datasets from the Data.go.th website.

This paper is structured as follows. Section 2 focuses on the problem and motivation using a real-world example. Section 3 describes a framework for generating linked RDF datasets for Data.go.th. Section 4 provides some evaluation results. Section 5 describes some related work. Section 6 provides a summary and discussion.

2   A Motivating Example

One of the important steps in linking RDF datasets is mapping some literal values for name entities that appear in a dataset to some standard URIs, i.e. URI mapping for name entities or URI lookup process. Several previous researches use semantic search API such as DBpedia[4] or Sindice[5] for URI mapping. However, this approach is not suitable for the datasets of Thailand open data portal (Data.go.th) because there is insufficient data for Thai name entities. In addition, a name may match with more than one URI, i.e. word ambiguity. For example, the name "Bangkok" may match with those referenced by URIs of a province, a hospital or a university. Figure 2 shows an example of using the term "กรุงเทพ" (Bangkok) for URI lookup via the Wikipedia API[6].

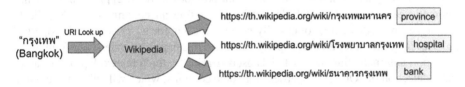

Fig. 2. Example of word ambiguity problem in URL lookup for a name entity

Another common problem for URI lookup is the multiple word representation problem. The same thing can be represented by multiple words that make it difficult to identify the same things and mapping them to the same URI. For example, the term "Bangkok" in Thai can be represented by multiple terms such as กรุงเทพ", "กรุงเทพฯ", "กรุงเทพมหานคร", "กทม".

To resolve these issues, we propose that finding semantic types is essential to resolve the word ambiguity in retrieving a proper URI for a name entity. In this paper, we present a framework for finding semantic types in a dataset in tabular form, i.e. CSV format. The semantic type information will be used in the URI lookup process of Demo-api.data.go.th that will allow mapping of the related name entities to URIs in the resulted RDF dataset. Figure 3 shows an example of using semantic type information to resolve

---

4   http://wiki.dbpedia.org/projects/dbpedia-lookup.

5   http://www.sindice.com/.

6   https://th.wikipedia.org/w/api.php?action=query&prop=revisions&rvprop=content& format=json&titles=กรุงเทพ&rvsection=0.

word ambiguity problem in URI lookup. The proposed method for automatic semantic type detection is based on applying NER technique over column headers and column data values in CSV dataset.

Fig. 3. Example of using semantic type information to resolve word ambiguity in URI lookup

3   A Framework for Generating Linked RDF Datasets for Demo-api.data.go.th

In this section, we describe our ongoing effort in creating a framework to support automatic linking of the RDF datasets for some datasets of Data.go.th. The framework focuses on finding columns that contain some common name entities that appear across different datasets and link them to the same referenced URIs for the name entities. This framework takes one input: a tabular data file such as CSV, Excel. Then it generates RDF and OWL files from the tabular data. Our previous work [1, 2] proposed the semi-automatic generation of a RDF dataset by converting all columns of a CSV file to "Datatype Properties". It automatically generates URIs for all subjects and properties and uses literal form for all the property values. In this paper, we extend our framework to support automatic linking of RDF datasets. Basically, the framework provides automatic detection of "Object Properties" for some columns, which will allow the column values to be mapped to some URIs in the RDF data. The two important steps that are focused on in this paper are the process for semantic type detection and URIs look up for name entities.

3.1   Generating CSV to Linked RDF Dataset Workflow

The workflow for generating a linked RDF dataset from a CSV file for Demo-api.data.go.th is shown in Fig. 4.

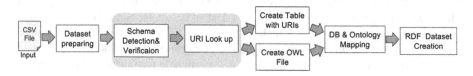

Fig. 4. Workflow for generating linked RDF datasets for Demo-api.data.go.th

The RDF dataset generations consist of seven processes as follows:

(1) **Dataset Preparing:** the datasets must be cleaned and arranged to a structured form that should follow the canonical model of tabular data[3] before uploading to Demo-api.data.go.th.

(2) **Schema Detection and verification:** there are three sub-processes including data type detection, nominal type detection and semantic type detection. These steps are necessary for URIs look up process. The system-detected schema is presented to the users for verification.

(3) **URIs Lookup:** this step uses schema and semantic type information from the previous process to lookup URIs for name entities to generate linked RDF dataset.

(4) **Create Database Table with URIs Alignment:** the system will create a database table and add new columns with URI lookup results for the columns with the nominal type.

(5) **Create OWL File:** this step uses the schema and semantic type information to automatically generate OWL file.

(6) **Database schema to Ontology Mapping:** the system will create an RDB to RDF mapping file between database schema and ontology.

(7) **RDF Dataset Creation:** the datasets are transformed from tabular data to RDF datasets by using Apache Jena, D2RQ and TDB triples storage.

3.2 Schema Detection Process for a Dataset

The schema detection process for a dataset consists of three steps including data type detection, nominal type detection, and semantic type detection as shown in Fig. 5.

(1) **Data type detection:** the system will automatically detect the data types for each column. Data types of a column can be categorized into two main groups that are string and numeric. String type can be categorized into three sub-groups including literal, date, and nominal types. Numeric type can be categorized into three sub-groups including integer, float, and nominal types

(2) **Nominal type detection:** columns with nominal types are transformed to object properties in the ontology and are possible for both string and integer. Nominal type detection needs to use the information from data values and column headers in each column [1].

(3) **Semantic type detection:** columns with nominal types are further analyzed for their semantic types. We pre-define a set of known semantic types such as "province", "district", and "company", etc. The system will use the column headers and column data values to check whether a column has the known semantic types. If matched, the system will define the semantic type of this column.

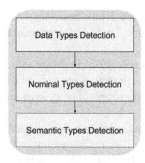

Fig. 5. Dataset schema detection process

3.3 Semantic Type Detection Based on Name Entity Recognition

In our framework, a Named Entity Recognition (NER) technique is applied in the semantic type detection process. Generally, Thai name entities can be classified into five groups including person, organization, place, abbreviation and ambiguous/cross-types as follows [4]:

(1) *Person Name* - person name may include first name, last name, title name, nick-names, and alias names.
(2) *Organization Name* – organization name refers to a group of people that act of forming or establishing something or an institution that have a structure or activity like an organization such as ministry, hospital, museum, school, etc.
(3) *Place Name* – place name refers to a building, natural place, cities, country, region such as province, tourist attraction, etc.
(4) *Abbreviation* – abbreviation is typically used to indicate organization name or place name.
(5) *Ambiguity or cross-type of entities.*

Currently, we only focus on two groups of name entities: organization and place names. Our NER technique to identify the semantic types of each column is based on an observation that many Thai name entities founded in CSV dataset starts or ends with a common noun that can refer to the category of name entities such as "ประเทศไทย" (Thai *country*), "วัดพระแก้ว" (Wat Phra Kaew *temple*) [7]. Rule-based boundary recognition is a simple process for identifying the category of a Thai name entity [7, 8]. Front or tail boundary of a name label can refer to a semantic type of the name entity. For example, two simple rules for recognizing organization names may be defined as:

(1) If the front boundary term is "บริษัท" ("company") and the tail boundary term is "จำกัด" ("ltd."), then the semantic type of this name entity is concluded as a company such as "บริษัทการบินไทยจำกัด" (Thai Airways International Public Company Ltd.)
(2) If the front and tail boundary terms are "ศูนย์" ("center") and "แห่งชาติ" ("national") respectively, then the semantic type of this name entity is a government agency such as "ศูนย์อิเล็กทรอนิกส์และคอมพิวเตอร์แห่งชาติ" (National Electronics and Computer Technology Center).

The detailed process of semantic type detection for a CSV dataset is shown in Fig. 6.

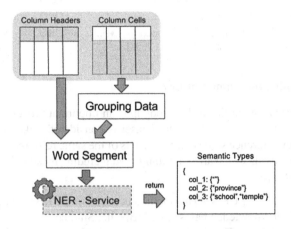

Fig. 6. Semantic type detection process for a CSV dataset

The steps for semantic type detection for a CSV dataset are described as follows:

(1) Reading column headers and column cells from a tubular data.
   - For column headers, the system checks whether the string appeared in the column header is matched with a set of NER entities. For example, a column header "ชื่อโรงพยาบาล" ("Hospital Name") is submitted to NER-service API and the semantic type of "hospital" is returned.
   - For column cells, there are three sub-steps as follows:
     - Grouping all data values of a column as a list of distinct values.
     - Analyzing each distinct value by splitting a prefix of literal.
     - Sending the extracted prefix to the NER-service API. For example, for the segmented words "ร.พ.| แพทย์รังสิต" ("Rangsit", "Hospital"), the prefix "ร.พ." ("Hospital") is submitted to NER-service API and the semantic type of "hospital" is returned.

(2) Data values of a column may match more than one semantic type. The system keeps all the detected semantic types and the proportion of data values for each type to the total distinct values of the column. If a detected semantic type for a column has the proportion value of more than 30 percent, the system will define it as a semantic type of the column.

Examples of synonyms and abbreviations representing some semantic types that are used by the NER- service are shown in Table 1.

Table 1. Examples of terms representing some semantic types used by the NER- service

Semantic Type	Terms	Abbreviations	Tag	Nominal
Province	province, จังหวัด	จ.	PLACE	yes
School	school, โรงเรียน	ร.ร.,รร.	ORG	yes
Company	Company, บริษัท,ห้างหุ้นส่วน	บจ.,หจก.,ห.จ.ก., Co.,ltd	ORG	yes

3.4 URI Mapping for Name Entities

URI mapping for name entities or URI lookup is an important process for linking data across different RDF datasets. An RDF dataset is considered linked to another RDF dataset when they reference some common URIs of the same resources. There are some URIs mapping methods which are commonly used including reusing the exist URIs and creating new URIs [6]

(1) Reusing the existing URIs – This method uses existing URIs of entities defined on some semantic knowledge bases, e.g., DBpedia, Sindice.
(2) Creating new URIs – This method creates new URIs programmatically based on a pattern of URI and primary ID of an entity.

Our framework uses the second approach because there is insufficient data for Thai name entities in the existing knowledge bases. After the semantic types of a column were detected and verified, the next step is to lookup the proper URIs for the data values appeared in the column. We created a URI lookup service for Demo-api.data.go.th. The URI lookup service takes a literal value and semantic type as an input and returns the standard URI for the value. Figure 7 shows an example of the URIs lookup and alignment process. The URIs mapping for name entities in our approach consists of two parts: URI lookup and URI alignment which are exemplified as follows.

(1) **URI lookup:** The table lookup method is used for getting information about a dataset that contains the standard URIs for a semantic type. For example, in Fig. 7, for the "province" semantic type, the standard URIs for this semantic type are located in the "thai_location" dataset, whose IDs are in the "province_id" column and labels are in the "province_name" column. In Fig. 8, the "thai_school" dataset contains the "Province" column with the "province" semantic type. Thus, the values for this column are compared with the values in the "province_name" column of the "thai_location" datasets. The standard URIs of the matched province names, which were created based on the "province_id" column, are returned. This step uses SPARQL querying via the RESTFul API of the dataset, which was created using the OAM framework [1, 9], to query the required data from dataset "thai_location".
(2) **URI alignment**: Next, we created new column called "Province_URI" in the "thai_school" dataset and stored the URI lookup results in this column. This newly created column will be used instead of the original "Province" column when transforming to the RDF format. Thus, the resulted RDF dataset of "thai_school" will reference to URIs of the "thai_location" dataset, and thus, becomes a linked RDF

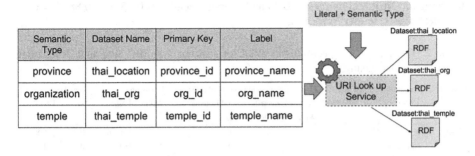

Fig. 7. Semantic type and dataset mapping for the URI lookup service

Dataset: thai_school   Semantic type = "province"   URI Look up Results

SchoolID	SchoolName	Province	Province_URI
1110100001	สตรีวรนาถ	กรุงเทพมหานคร	http://demo-api.data.go.th/.../10
1110100003	สุขุมาศพิทยาคม	กรุงเทพมหานคร	http://demo-api.data.go.th/.../10
1150100028	มงฟอร์ตวิทยาลัย	เชียงใหม่	http://demo-api.data.go.th/.../50

Dataset: thai_location

URI	province_id	province_name	province_name_en
http://demo-api.data.go.th/.../10	10	กรุงเทพมหานคร	Bangkok
http://demo-api.data.go.th/.../11	11	สมุทรปราการ	Samutprakan
http://demo-api.data.go.th/.../12	12	นนทบุรี	Nonthaburi

Fig. 8. Example of URIs lookup and alignment for province name entities

dataset. In case of the entities that cannot be found using the URI lookup service, we programmatically built new URIs based on the literal values.

4   Evaluation

We evaluate two approaches by comparing the performance of a semantic search API, i.e. Wikipedia API[7] and the NER technique using 21 datasets from the Data.go.th website. Our objective was to compare the performance of semantic type detection of a column in a CSV dataset. We focused on two groups of semantic types: organization (ORG) and place (LOC). The 21 datasets consist of the total of 186 columns. The categories of the datasets include government, location, travel, culture and statistics categories.

Table 2 shows the results of semantic type detection by comparing two approach as following: The average precision for using the Wikipedia API was 1 and average recall was 0.28 (P = 1, R = 0.17 for ORG, P = 1, R = 0.37 for LOC). The average precision

---

[7] https://th.wikipedia.org/w/api.php.

for using the NER technique was 0.94 and average recall was 0.85 (P = 0.88, R = 0.97 for ORG, P = 1, R = 0.75 for LOC).

Table 2. Comparison of precision and recall for semantic type detection approaches using datasets from Data.go.th

Group	Semantic Types	Total columns	Detected Semantic types (Columns)				Precision (P)		Recall (R)	
			Correct Detected		Total Detected		Wiki	NER	Wiki	NER
			Wiki	NER	Wiki	NER				
ORG	government	5	1	4	1	6	1	0.66	0.2	0.8
	company	6	0	6	0	6	–	1	0	1
	hospital	2	1	2	1	2	1	1	0.5	1
	factory	1	0	1	0	2	–	0.5	0	1
	museum	1	0	1	0	1	–	1	0	1
	library	1	0	1	0	1	–	1	0	1
	temple	2	1	2	1	2	1	1	0.5	1
	Total/avg.	18	3	17	3	20	1	0.88	0.17	0.97
LOC	province	12	12	12	12	12	1	1	1	1
	district	8	8	8	8	8	1	1	1	1
	sub district	7	0	7	0	7	–	1	0	1
	region	1	0	1	0	1	–	1	0	1
	road	5	2	5	2	5	1	1	1	1
	natural attractions	1	0	1	0	1	–	1	0	1
	bus stop	1	0	0	0	0	–	–	0	0
	bike-routes	1	0	0	0	0	–	–	0	0
	Total/avg.	36	22	34	22	34	1	1	0.37	0.75
Total/Avg.		54	25	51	25	54	1	0.94	0.28	0.85

In summary, semantic type detection using the Wikipedia API has higher precision and lower recall than using the NER technique. The low recall was primarily due to insufficient data for Thai name entities in Wikipedia. In addition, some name entities in some datasets are provided as short names or abbreviations, which do not match with those provided by Wikipedia.

Although the NER technique approach has good precision and recall, an incorrect detection will occur when a header name in column is ambiguous. For example, the dataset "bicycle routes in Thailand" has a header name "เส้นทาง/ถนน" ("route"), which our algorithm incorrectly suggested the semantic type of this column as "road".

5 Related Work

There are several research approaches for linking a RDF dataset. Varish M. et al. developed an automatic tool for converting tabular data to RDF. They proposed a semantic type prediction algorithm that provides mapping between column headers and ontology class by using query to find the semantic types on Wikiology. It uses four vocabulary database consisting of DBpedia, Ontology, Freebase, WordNet, and Yago [5]. The Karma system is a semi-automatic tool that allows users to define a semantic type of each column header. Then, the system will learn labels of semantic types from the users using the condition random field (CRF) technique and suggests the learned semantic types to the next users [10]. Miel Vander S. et al. proposed a lightweight tabular to RDF conversion tool. In the process of concept matching, they use string and lexical matching approach for finding the relations between header columns and concepts of ontology. Context graph is created for every column and then uses a Steiner tree algorithm for finding an optimal path in graph [11]. Fadi M. et al. develops an extension for Google Refine called "RDF Refine". The tool aims to find a corresponding URI from existing knowledge bases (e.g. DBpedia, Europeana) for linking a RDF dataset. RDF Refine provides an instance matching service based on Freebase, a collection of some well-known name entities. The result of matching instance is used to suggest types for the data value in the column. Users can choose the appropriate type from a list of suggestions [6].

6   Conclusion

In this paper, we describe our ongoing initiative to provide support for automatic linking of RDF data generated from some datasets of the Thailand open government data portal. We propose a unique approach for automatic detection of semantic types and mapping name entities to URIs, which are important steps for creating linked RDF datasets. An NER technique is applied in finding semantic type of a column in a CSV dataset. Our approach can improve coverage of mapping Thai name entities and can resolve a problem of word ambiguity that are two main problems in identifying the proper URIs for name entities, i.e. URI lookup. We evaluated two approaches by comparing the performance of a semantic search API, i.e. Wikipedia, and the NER technique using some datasets from the Data.go.th website. Our evaluation results with 21 datasets showed that the NER technique generally has better recall with comparable precision compared with using the Wikipedia API. Our future work will focus on improving and assessing the effectiveness of the URI alignment process and extending the coverage of the known semantic types.

Acknowledgement.   This project was funded by the Electronic Government Agency (EGA) and the National Science and Technology Development Agency (NSTDA), Thailand.

References

1. Krataithong, P., Buranarach, M., Hongwarittorrn, N.: Semi-automatic framework for generating RDF dataset from open data. In: Proceedings of the 11th International Symposium on Natural Language Processing (SNLP2016), February 2016
2. Krataithong, P., Buranarach, M., Supnithi, T.: RDF dataset management framework for data.go.th. In: Proceedings of the 10th International Conference on Knowledge, Information and Creativity Support Systems (KICSS 2015), November 2015
3. Ermilov, I., Auer, S., Stadler, C.: User-driven semantic mapping of tabular data. In: Proceedings of the 9th International Conference Semantic System - I-SEMANTICS 2013. 105 (2013)

4. Tirasaroj, N., Aroonmanakun, W.: Thai named entity recognition based on conditional random fields. In: 2009 Eighth International Symposium Natural Language Processing, pp. 216–220 (2009)
5. Mulwad, V., Finin, T., Syed, Z., Joshi, A.: Using linked data to interpret tables. In: Proceedings of the First International Workshop on Consuming Linked Data (2010)
6. Maali, F., Cyganiak, R., Peristeras, V.: Re-using Cool URIs: Entity reconciliation against LOD hubs. In: Proceedings of the Linked Data on the Web Workshop 2011 (LDOW 2011), WWW 2011 (2011)
7. Chanlekha, H., Kawtrakul, A., Varasrai, P., Mulasas, I.: Statistical and heuristic rule based model for thai named entity. In: Proceedings of SNLP 2002 (2002)
8. Chanlekha, H., Kawtrakul, A.: Thai named entity extraction by incorporating maximum entropy model with simple heuristic information. In: Proceedings of the IJCNLP (2004)
9. Buranarach, M., Thein, Y.M., Supnithi, T.: A community-driven approach to development of an ontology-based application management framework. In: Takeda, H., Qu, Y., Mizoguchi, R., Kitamura, Y. (eds.) JIST 2012. LNCS, vol. 7774, pp. 306–312. Springer, Heidelberg (2013). doi:10.1007/978-3-642-37996-3_21
10. Knoblock, C.A., et al.: Semi-automatically mapping structured sources into the semantic web. In: Simperl, E., Cimiano, P., Polleres, A., Corcho, O., Presutti, V. (eds.) ESWC 2012. LNCS, vol. 7295, pp. 375–390. Springer, Heidelberg (2012). doi:10.1007/978-3-642-30284-8_32
11. Sande, M.V., De Vocht, L., Van Deursen, D., Mannens, E., Van De Walle, R.: Lightweight transformation of tabular open data to RDF. In: 8th International Conference on Semantic Systems, pp. 38–42 (2012)

An Attempt to Promote Open Data for Digital Humanities in Japanese University Libraries

Emi Ishita[1(✉)], Tetsuya Nakatoh[2], Kohei Hatano[1], and Michiaki Takayama[3]

[1] Research and Development Division, Kyushu University Library, 6-10-1 Hakozaki, Higashi-ku, Fukuoka 812-8581, Japan
{ishita.emi.982,hatano.kohei.236}@m.kyushu-u.ac.jp
[2] Research Institute for Information Technology, Kyushu University, 6-10-1 Hakozaki, Higashi-ku, Fukuoka 812-8581, Japan
nakatoh@cc.kyushu-u.ac.jp
[3] Faculty of Humanities, Kyushu University, 6-10-1 Hakozaki, Higashi-ku, Fukuoka 812-8581, Japan
takayama@lit.kyushu-u.ac.jp

Abstract. Many universities have declared open access policies in response to increasing interest in open access in the academic world. The next developments will be focused on open data. Huge data repositories are already used in specific fields. However, the discussion regarding open data in universities has just begun. We attempted to promote open data for digital humanities in a university library. University libraries hold rare collections, which are generally highly valued research resources. We selected a rare collection in a library, and then digitized and published it. We investigated additional data that aids a reader's understanding of the material. To promote the open data, we produced images of the resources and multiple types of interpretation texts. We displayed the digital images in an exhibition and obtained an evaluation using a survey of visitors.

Keywords: Open data · Digital humanities · Digital libraries · Rare collection · Open research resource · Promotion of open data

1 Introduction

Many universities have installed institutional repositories in response to a push towards open access in the academic world. The next developments will be focused on open access to scientific data. Murray-Rust [1] said that "open data is an emerging term in the process of defining how scientific data may be published and re-used without price or permission barriers". He also noted that "much of this requires advocacy and it is likely that when scientists are made aware of the value of labeling their work the movement will grow rapidly". There are already huge data repositories in specific fields. However, the discussion regarding open data in universities has just begun. University libraries contain useful humanities resources. We should consider how university libraries can promote open data resources for digital humanities in university libraries.

A. Morishima et al. (Eds.): ICADL 2016, LNCS 10075, pp. 269–274, 2016.
DOI: 10.1007/978-3-319-49304-6_32

There are few initiatives for open data in Japanese Universities, with some exceptions. Open data refers to open research data, i.e., open data created through research. Open data is common in some research disciplines. For example, the World Data System [2] contains many earth science datasets. However, there are few data repositories for open data in Japanese universities. With respect to digital humanities in Japan, the National Institute of Japanese Literature has started a project to build an international collaborative research network for pre-modern Japanese texts [3]. The SAT *Daizōkyō* Text Database [4] is a repository of Buddhist wisdom. There are some projects that promote open data in digital humanities, but most are project based not institutional.

In this paper, we attempted to promote open data for digital humanities in a university library. In digital humanities, the first step is digitization. Next, the digital images must be made freely available to the public. We digitized some humanities documents from a rare collection, provided some additional information to aid researchers, and developed a digital exhibition for promoting open data.

2 Digitization of a Rare Collection

We selected the "Kasuga Masaji & Kazuo Bunko", which was added to the special collection of the library in 2015. The Kasuga Bunko is a private collection of manuscripts and books by Masaji Kasuga and his son, Kazuo Kasuga. Both were professors at Kyushu University and contributed to the development of historical research on the Japanese language, especially in the field of *kuntengogaku*, the study of Chinese-Japanese glosses and gloss lexicon.

The collection contains approximately 400 volumes, including old manuscripts (*koshahon*) and printed books (*kohanpon*) on Japanese language and literature. In particular, the collection includes many materials for the study of *kunten* (guiding marks for rendering Chinese into Japanese) and is therefore invaluable when studying the history of Japanese orthography and literary style. Some materials were selected from the collection for digitization. They were evaluated by a committee as being highly valuable materials for research in this field.

An overhead scanner (ScanSnap SV600, Fujitsu) was used to take images of each page. This scanner cannot scan documents that are larger than A3, so larger materials were digitized using a digital camera. Most materials in the collection are book-shaped, but it also includes a scroll (*makimono*) and a folded book (*orihon*). The original pages do not have page numbers. A printed page number was displayed with each page of the book-shaped materials. After digitization, the images were published in the "Special Collection" on the library website [5], in May 2016. They include 31 volumes (107 books and materials, 5,004 images in total). The images are displayed in a Web browser, which is sufficient for public access. However, this is not adequate for research purposes, so we must consider another way to provide the open data.

3   Digital Exhibition of Materials in Humanities

We developed two kinds of digital exhibition. The first was *Konkōmyō saishō ōkyō*, which is very old, rare, and valuable manuscript. The second was *Man'yōshū*, which is very popular in Japan and is useful when learning the transition of written characters in Japanese, especially Katakana.

3.1   Konkōmyō Saishō ōkyō

Konkōmyō saishō ōkyō (Sovereign Kings of the Golden Light Sutra) was chosen as one of the source materials for the study of *kunten*. It is a Buddhist sutra translated into Chinese by the Tang-dynasty monk Yijing (Jpn. Gijo) in the 7th century, and has been revered in Japan since ancient times. The Kasuga Bunko manuscript of the sutra is one of only a few complete manuscripts copied during the Nara period (710–794 AD). *Kunten* was used during the Heian period (794–1185 AD), so it provides precious data on the Japanese language at that time.

We provided two versions of this sutra. The original text and its conversion into *kundoku*. In *kundoku*, the grammar of the original Chinese text was converted into and read as vernacular Japanese through the addition of *kunten*. Because the sutra was written in *kanbun* (literary Chinese) its meaning was difficult to understand without a specialized knowledge of *kundoku*. Therefore, it was important to add information so that the text could be read in vernacular Japanese.

Images were displayed for the two versions (*kundoku* and the enabled text). We developed a pop-up function so that a window appears when the user clicks on a line (sentence) in the image. We used an iPad to display the text and additional information. A continuous large picture is appropriate for the *orihon* content, without the concept of a page. The position of an image on an iPad is freely controllable by swiping, so the display is intuitive and natural. Furthermore, we can expand and reduce the display using pinches, so a fine verification of the contents of a display is possible. These display features offer an outstanding reference function, without touching the original text. This is very significant when inspecting a valuable book. A pop-up screen activated by a tap was used to display the native Japanese reading and free translation. Users can show and hide this information as required, which is very useful when browsing, learning, and studying. We used a general display based on a Web browser and HTML so that a valuable book could be displayed in most environments. This technology is very common, so open data based on this method has few technical barriers. We consider that this is appropriate considering the aims of open data for humanities. By displaying a picture, we can easily change the display range, and expand and reduce the resolution. To display addition information in pop-up windows, we used JavaScript called from the client-side clickable image maps. A significant part of "*Konkōmyō saishō ōkyō*" was selected for this digital exhibition. The screen displayed is shown in Fig. 1.

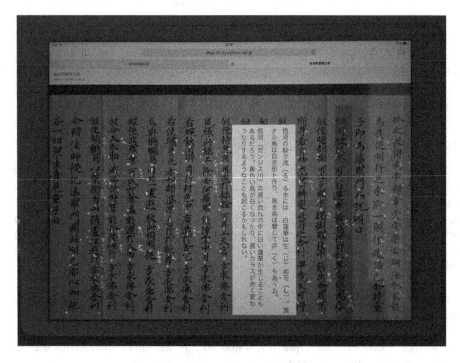

Fig. 1. Popup display on iPad

3.2 Man'yōshū

Man'yōshū is the oldest existing anthology of Japanese poetry. It consists of approximately 4500 Japanese poems written during the 350 years before the middle of the 8th century. The poems were written before the invention of Japanese syllabary (*kana*), and although they are entirely written in Chinese characters, they provide precious data on aspects of ancient Japanese language, literature, and history.

There are four main kinds of expression in the Japanese language (old and modern styles). Our display method for *Man'yōshū* poems was based on PowerPoint, by Microsoft. An illustration is shown in Fig. 2. Each slide contains four different expressions for the same poem and its modern Japanese translation (the second from the right). The first expression is written in modern Japanese characters (Chinese characters and hiragana, right). The second expression consists entirely of a subset of Chinese characters called Manyo-gana (third from the right). Manyo-gana is a set of Chinese characters chosen especially to express pronunciations in Japanese speech. The third expression is written using Manyo-gana and katakana characters (second from the left). Katakana is a set of Japanese characters made from Chinese characters. Similar to Manyo-gana, katakana characters express Japanese pronunciation. More precisely, each katakana character was created by extracting some parts of a Chinese character. Katakana is much simpler than Manyo-gana and is easy to write. Here, katakana characters are written along with Chinese characters to express the pronunciation. The final expression consists of hiragana and Manyo-gana characters (left). Hiragana is also composed from Chinese characters by simplifying shapes. Hiragana is easier to write than katanaka.

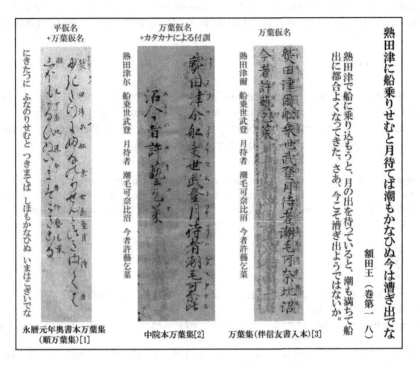

Fig. 2. Digital exhibition of *Man'yōshū* with four different expressions.

The aim of our display method was to emphasize the changes to expressions based on successively invented characters. We also attempted to provide the transition of Japanese characters and their history. This is one form of additional information that can aid a reader's understanding of the material and subject.

3.3 Evaluation of the Digital Exhibitions

A Bunko exhibition was held at the Kyushu University Library from 13th to 21th, May, 2016. The exhibition used three iPads: one displayed all the images; one (an iPad Pro) displayed the *Konkōmyō saishō ōkyō* image with other text; and one (iPad Pro) displayed *Man'yōshū*, in addition to display of original materials.

There were 548 visitors to the exhibition. Visitors were asked to reply a questionnaire, resulting in 232 respondents (42.3 %). Although the questionnaire was not developed for the digital exhibition, some respondents mentioned it in a free description field. For example, respondent A said that "the pop-up function was very interesting, because what I wanted to know popped up when I touched the line". Another respondent said "The displayed explanation helped me to more concretely understand the material". Thus, we can conclude that the digital exhibition aids understanding. Moreover, six respondents mentioned that the digital exhibition was interesting and enjoyable. We can conclude from the survey responses that digital exhibitions may be useful when promoting open data and increasing awareness of available digital data. In the future, we must conduct a survey of researchers who use these images for research purposes.

4   Conclusion

We digitized some material, designed additional data for research purposes, and developed a digital exhibition for promoting open data. We found that the digital exhibition was popular. This attempt was a first step towards open data. In the future, we plan to discuss data repository design and develop an open data flow.

Acknowledgements.   This project was supported by the Tsubasa project (Qdai-jump Research Program) at Kyushu University. We thank many librarians in the Kyushu University Library for their support. In particular, we thank Yuko Hori, Nami Hoshiko, Fumi Kaneko, and Akemi Kuhara in the library.

References

1. Murray-Rust, P.: Open data in science. Serials Rev. **34**(1), 52–64 (2008)
2. World Data System. https://www.icsu-wds.org/
3. National Institute of Japanese Literature, Project to build an international collaborative research network. https://www.nijl.ac.jp/pages/cijproject/index_e.html
4. The SAT Daizōkyō Text Database Committee, The SAT Daizōkyō Text Database. http://21dzk.l.u-tokyo.ac.jp/SAT/index_en.html
5. The Kyushu University Library. Kasuga Masaji & Kazuo Collection. https://www.lib.kyushu-u.ac.jp/en/collections/kasuga

Redesigning the Open-Access Institutional Repository: A User Experience Approach

Edward Luca[⊠] and Bhuva Narayan

University of Technology Sydney, Sydney, Australia
{edward.luca,bhuva.narayan}@uts.edu.au

Abstract. This paper details how a university library evaluated its institutional repository using a user experience design (UXD) methodology and redesigned it based on the findings. The online repository, running on DSpace, was not being utilized as expected by academics and researchers, so a detailed user evaluation and usability study was undertaken to find out the reasons why. Findings showed lack of usability and a mismatch between user expectations and system architecture. Hence, significant improvements were made to the user interface, and in communicating the status of items held in the repository (open or closed access). The authors assess the impact of these changes and argue that better usability results in greater visibility of the open-access repository, and hence, greater visibility for the university's researchers. Other challenges regarding the adoption of open access by academics and researchers at the university are also discussed.

Keywords: Open access · Institutional repositories · User experience · Usability · Digital collections · Digital libraries

1 Introduction

Institutional repositories (IRs) are a valuable proposition for universities. They showcase a university's research output, increase the visibility of their scholars' research, increase citation counts, and are a measure of an institution's prestige. They are also one of the fastest growing kinds of digital libraries, with many scholars arguing that IRs have significant potential to reshape the scholarly landscape and advance the open-access movement [1]. As a low-cost way of archiving and disseminating content, it would seem that there is a clear opportunity for IRs to break down the barriers of access to scholarly communication. Despite such promise, IRs are often under-utilized and infrequently accessed, and developing buy-in from faculty members is an especially challenging reality [2].

2 Literature Review

Academics already have numerous administrative duties that constrain their research and writing time, and the perception of IR deposits as an administrative task means that academics do not clearly understand the benefits of

© Springer International Publishing AG 2016
A. Morishima et al. (Eds.): ICADL 2016, LNCS 10075, pp. 275–281, 2016.
DOI: 10.1007/978-3-319-49304-6_33

OA repositories [3]. Bell, Foster and Gibbons argue that the issue of populating the repository with full-text materials is the most significant barrier to the success of an IR [4]. Librarians are often tasked with providing support to faculties for research data services, though many do not have sufficient training in understanding issues such as data storage, discoverability, and the workflow of researchers [5]. Librarians, often the managers or curators of these repositories, approach scholarship from a very different perspective to researchers. They see research outputs as an organizational resource to be managed [6], and are largely unaware of issues that limit academic participation in the IR, such as tenure, career development, and academic freedom. Repository software packages such as DSpace, Digital Commons, and e-Prints are often time-consuming and complicated to install and configure [7]. Koshiyama et al. conducted usability testing to correct usability and information architecture problems with their institution's repository and found that issues "such as labelling, size of source, buttons nomenclature, lack of system feedback" [11] could be identified by allowing a representative sample of users to identify issues or validate design decisions.

For a digital library to be truly useful, designers must adopt a user-centered perspective and understand who their users are, what they require of the system, and any prior knowledge that influences their behaviour [8]. While much has been written about the users of digital libraries in general, there is little research examining the accessibility and usability of institutional repositories from the end-user's perspective [9]. Aljohani and Blustein write that understanding the needs of repository users would "play a vital role in increasing the acceptability and effectiveness of the IR systems" [10]. They argue that students do not commonly use IRs because the system has not been designed with their needs in mind. To address this lack of understanding, they propose developing personas, or user profiles, to inform decision-making, refine the design of the system, and limit goals around what users actually need [10]. Despite this need for changing perceptions about institutional repositories, the process first involves an understanding of the current environment within each institution.

3   Context

The issues described in the literature review above led us to consider an approach utilizing user experience methodologies to redesign the University of Technology Sydney's (UTS) institutional repository. An archived version of the old site is located at http://web.archive.org/web/20140301103148/http://epress.lib.uts.edu.au/research. It is the second-ranked repository in Australasia (Webometric Oceania Rankings) for the size of its open-access collection, with more than 30 percent of the 35,000 publications stored available as open access. UTS uses a current research information system (CRIS) called Symplectic Elements to manage its research outputs. Researchers can log in to Symplectic Elements and 'claim' their publications if they are the authors. The system supports UTS's Open Access Policy, which mandates that all UTS research outputs must be collected and stored in the repository [14]. Nevertheless, the adoption of the system was low and the previous version of the UTS IR was very dated and unappealing to use. There was very little incentive for academics to ensure their work was made available through it, and librarians were cautious to promote a clunky and awkward system. The UTS Library team sought to address many of these issues in its redesign of their institutional repository: including findability, navigability, and overall user experience.

4 Methodology

User experience (UX) has become an increasingly valued framework for examining library technologies from the user's perspective. While the definition and scope of UX is still contested, scholars generally agree that UX is dynamic, context-dependent, and subjective [12]. Blandford and Buchanan identify "effectance" as an aspect of the user experience meaning "the user's sense of satisfaction at having achieved an interesting effect" [13]. In the context of digital libraries, a good user experience may not necessarily be about finding the perfect document, but rather about serendipity and information discovery - locating new, interesting or even surprising materials. Focusing on user experience allows us to examine more non-utilitarian qualities of the system, including meaning, affect and value. It can be difficult to translate these emotional and psychological needs into design decisions, but examining the usability, navigability, findability and accessibility of a system can inform the redesign of its features, user interface, and interaction design. This is an area that is yet to be thoroughly explored in the literature on IRs so far [2], and this paper argues that the principles of UX design can be utilized to greatly enhance the experience of using an institutional repository.

As part of this process, UTS Library conducted a user experience analysis using two complementary approaches. The first was a Heuristic Evaluation method as detailed by Jakob Nielsen [19], wherein a small set of evaluators, no more than 6–8 people [21] examine the interface and judge its compliance with recognized usability principles (the "heuristics"), which are: (1) visibility of system status, (2) match between system and the real world, (3) user control and freedom, (4) consistency and standards, and (5) error prevention. The second was the User and the Task-by-Type taxonomy by Ben Shneiderman [20], which specify that a good visualization of a digital library should provide: (1) an overview of the collection, (2) allow users to zoom in on items of interest, (3) allow users to filter out uninteresting items, (4) allow details on demand for selected items, (5) allow users to view relationships among items, (6) allow users to keep a history of actions, and (7) allow users to extract a subcollection through search parameters.

5 Results

Two Information Science researchers, two Information Science students, and two librarians, in accordance with the three stakeholder personas we were targeting, participated in the study. We conducted a paired co-discovery and analysis with dyadic participant pairs who sat down together to evaluate the system: researcher-librarian, researcher-student, librarian-researcher, and librarian-student. The user experience study included usability analysis, metadata recommendations for SEO discovery, navigability, accessibility and design recommendations. Below is a summary of the findings that relate to the redesign:

- The repository had no identity or branding and looked like a generic database.
- The interface was centered around searching rather than browsing, with a search box or basic listing of research areas as the only navigation option.
- Jargon or terminology used was never obvious or explained, for example, DSpace's *Community > Collection* structure which did not make sense to many of our researchers.
- The interface was cluttered with too much information, including a lot of metadata and statistics.
- While all of the communities and browsing categories were visible on the homepage, it was not made clear to the user what the context of these items was within the site.
- The organization of the site's content, and the way in which it was presented, gave no clear direction for the user as to where they should begin looking for content. Most users skipped straight to the search box, which impeded discovery.
- There were a number of issues flagged in terms of the handling of and display of meta-tags within the <head> of the website's code, which caused issues with search engines finding our repository's content. While it is known that Google does not rely on this metadata for indexing, it does rely on it for the display of the site's information and important subpages in a user's search results. Further to this, both OJS and DSpace display the Dublin Core metadata of indexed articles within the <head> data of the file, but this does not support the indexing of the article as stated above.
- While Dublin Core (DC) is a good schema to use as a standard recognized by all institutions, Google Scholar ignores DC terms in favor of Highwire Press Tags. Highwire Press Tags are recommended for IRs and can be enabled in both DSpace and OJS.
- According to Google Scholar's Webmaster Guidelines for indexing, it is not just the web pages that need to be optimized for indexing, but also the PDF files themselves. As academic researchers are generally responsible for adding their own research into the database (Symplectic Elements), this posed a series of issues in terms of how to get researchers to comply with recommendations for PDF optimization prior to uploading them into the system.

All of the issues identified above were subsequently addressed in the redesign of the repository.

6   Discussion and Implementation

The new interface was designed over a period of three months. An interdepart-mental collaboration was an essential part of the process, as each department (information services, IT services, eScholarship services, and graphic design), offered its own insights and perspectives into the design process. As part of this process the repository was re-branded as Open Publications of UTS Scholars (OPUS), which is now located at https://opus.lib.uts.edu.au/ and other changes were implemented as below.

6.1 Visual Design

The project team decided to implement a 'sunburst' design on the OPUS homepage and at the item level. A sunburst is where items in a hierarchy are laid out radially: the top of the hierarchy sits at the center, and deeper levels are further away. Stasko et al. found that the sunburst method is useful in conveying structure and hierarchy, and well-received by participants in their study [15]. The slices of the sunburst are categorized by the UTS Organizational Groups, which typically follows the structure of Faculty > School. The slices scale dynamically depending on the number of items, which visually communicates the size of the collection. The sunburst is also useful in orienting users who have arrived at a specific article within the OPUS collection. Users can easily 'drill up' from this point to access new materials or see related items.

6.2 Organizational System

In the previous version of the UTS eRepository, research was categorized according to Field of Research (FOR) codes, which are an Australian classification of research disciplines [16]. Although this categorization of university research was convenient for university accounting purposes, it was not always understood by the researchers themselves or by users. Hence, a decision was made to instead display the Faculty > School organizational structure of the university in OPUS to assist researchers familiar with UTS.

6.3 Terminology

Our user studies confirmed that the terminology we used for each item state were unclear to our users. This is a common issue in the design of library systems, where librarians frequently use jargon such as 'hold request', 'InterLibrary loan', and so on, which mean little to the average user. Thong, Ham and Tam argue that often there is a disconnect between the vocabulary users use to express their information needs, and the terminology of the designers of digital libraries [17]. Using natural language, elaborating or explaining confusing terms, and being consistent with terms all help to encourage correct choices by users, by reducing the cognitive barriers caused by the complexity of library resources [18].

   To address this issue, we designed a visualization of the 'Copyright Clearance Process' which not only explained the current state of an item, but also offered an indication of the process in granting access to items. By indicating some form of progression or workflow, the IR offers the user much more information about the state of objects, and also lets them know if they need to check back at a later date to access an item. The definitions of each item state were also explained in the footer of the pages. A Help page was introduced with information around how Symplectic feeds into OPUS, with a diagram explaining the workflow process for researchers.

7   Conclusion and Future Directions

Through adopting a user experience design approach and conducting a thorough usability study of our eRepository interface, we were able to redesign the DSpace interface and customize it for our institution. The resulting web interface is more intuitive and meaningful for our academics and our researchers, and also aids information discovery online for others looking for papers on any given topic through internet searches. The long-term impact of the redesign is hard to assess at this early stage, but there is some Google Analytics data to suggest that users spend more time on OPUS and download more items than in the previous version. We are unlikely to draw any substantial conclusions without a full year's worth of data. For the future, there are a number of functions on DSpace that are not implemented in OPUS which we would like to explore. These include the ability to export citations, and for digital theses, the ability to link to the supervisor's profile. We would also like to provide further statistics to the user, including download rates for publications. We plan to conduct a qualitative study using interviews to understand other factors that limit engagement by academics. Based on our current findings, academics record their research output for the purpose of their own accounting to faculty, and not to increase the visibility of their research through open access.

Acknowledgments. We thank the UTS Library for their support of this paper.

References

1. Jantz, R.C., Wilson, M.C.: Institutional repositories: faculty deposits, marketing, and the reform of scholarly communication. J. Acad. Librariansh. **34**, 186–195 (2008)
2. Betz, S., Hall, R.: Self-archiving with ease in an institutional repository: microinteractions and the user experience. Inf. Technol. Libr. **34**, 43–58 (2015)
3. Kim, J.: Motivations of faculty self-archiving in institutional repositories. J. Acad. Librariansh. **37**, 246–254 (2011)
4. Bell, S., Foster, N.F., Gibbons, S.: Reference librarians and the success of institutional repositories. Ref. Serv. Rev. **33**, 283–290 (2005)
5. MacMillan, D.: Data sharing and discovery: what librarians need to know. J. Acad. Librariansh. **40**, 541–549 (2014)
6. Armstrong, M.: Institutional repository management models that support faculty research dissemination. OCLC Syst. Serv. **30**, 43–51 (2014)

7. Körber, N., Suleman, H.: Usability of digital repository software: a study of DSpace installation and configuration. In: Buchanan, G., Masoodian, M., Cunningham, S.J. (eds.) ICADL 2008. LNCS, vol. 5362, pp. 31–40. Springer, Heidelberg (2008). doi:10.1007/978-3-540-89533-6_4

8. Van House, N.A., Butler, M.H., Ogle, V., Schiff, L.: User-centered iterative design for digital libraries: The cypress experience (1996). http://dlib.org/dlib/february96/02vanhouse.html

9. McKay, D.: Institutional repositories and their "other" users: usability beyond authors. Ariadne, 1–9 (2007)

10. Aljohani, M., Blustein, J.: Personas help understand users' needs, goals and desires in an online institutional repository. Int. J. Comput. Electr. Autom. Contr. Inf. Eng. 9, 629–636 (2015)

11. Koshiyama, D., Pinho, A.L.S., Santa Rosa, J.G.: Analysis of usability and information architecture of the UFRN institutional repository. In: Marcus, A. (ed.) DUXU 2015. LNCS, vol. 9188, pp. 197–207. Springer, Heidelberg (2015). doi:10.1007/978-3-319-20889-3_19

12. Law, EL.-C., Roto, V., Hassenzahl, M., Vermeeren, A., Kort, J.: Understanding, scoping and defining user experience. In: Proceeidngs of 27th International Conference on Human Factors in Computing System (CHI 2009), p. 719 (2009)

13. Blandford, A., Buchanan, G.: Usability of digital libraries: a source of creative tensions with technical developments. IEEE Tech. Comm. Digit. Libr. 1, 9 (2003)

14. Open Access Policy. http://www.gsu.uts.edu.au/policies/open-access.html

15. Stasko, J., Catrambone, R., Guzdial, M., McDonald, K.: An evaluation of space-filling information visualizations for depicting hierarchical structures. Int. J. Hum. Comput. Stud. 53, 663–694 (2000)

16. Australian and New Zealand Standard Research Classification (ANZSRC) (2008). http://www.abs.gov.au/ausstats/abs@.nsf/0/6BB427AB9696C225CA2574180004463E

17. Thong, J., Hong, W., Tam, K.-Y.: Understanding user acceptance of digital libraries: what are the roles of interface characteristics, organisational context, and individual differences. Int. J. Hum. Comput. Stud. 57, 215–242 (2002)

18. Kupersmith, J.: Library Terms That Users Understand. UC Berkeley Libr., 1–36 (2012)

19. Nielsen, J., Molich, R.: Heuristic evaluation of user interfaces. In: Proceedings of The SIGCHI Conference on Human Factors in Computing Systems, pp. 249–256. ACM, New York (1990)

20. Shneiderman, B.: The eyes have it: a task by data type taxonomy for information visualizations. In: Proceedings of the 1996 IEEE Symposium on Visual Languages, pp. 336–343. IEEE Computer Society, Washington, DC (1996)

21. Nielsen, J., Landauer, T.K.: A mathematical model of the finding of usability problems. In: Proceedings of the INTERACT 1993 and CHI 1993 Conference on Human Factors in Computing Systems, pp. 206–213. ACM, New York (1993)

Opinion, Sentiment and Location

Expanding Sentiment Lexicon with Multi-word Terms for Domain-Specific Sentiment Analysis

Sang-Sang Tan[✉] and Jin-Cheon Na

Wee Kim Wee School of Communication and Information, Nanyang Technological University,
31 Nanyang Link, Singapore 637718, Singapore
{tans0348,tjcna}@ntu.edu.sg

Abstract. The increasing interest to extract valuable information from networked data has heightened the need for effective and reliable sentiment analysis techniques. To this end, lexicon-based sentiment classification has been extensively studied by the research community. However, little is known about the usefulness of different multi-word constructs in creating domain-specific sentiment lexicons. Thus, our primary objective in this paper is to evaluate the performance of bigram, typed dependency, and concept as multi-word lexical entries for domain-specific sentiment classification. Pointwise Mutual Information (PMI) was adopted to select the lexical entries and to calculate the sentiment scores of the multi-word terms. With the features generated from the domain lexicons, a series of experiments were carried out using support vector machine (SVM) classifiers. While all the domain-specific classifiers outperformed the baseline classifier, our results showed that lexicons consisting of bigram entries and typed dependency entries improved the performance to a greater extent.

Keywords: Sentiment analysis · Sentiment lexicon · Machine learning · Sentiment classification

1 Introduction

The advent of Web 2.0 has brought dramatic changes to the way information is created and exchanged on the Internet. In contrast to the prior web technologies in which Internet users are merely acting as passive consumers of web content, the rapid development of web technologies that incorporate social media and other interactive platforms allows users to communicate with each other through user-generated content. Although the explosive growth of user-generated data continues to reveal new trends and opportunities to stakeholders, exploiting these data has also become more and more challenging given the enormous size of data volume and the inconsistent data quality. Therefore, sentiment analysis has been extensively studied in recent years to gather, extract, and summarize valuable information from the plethora of networked data. The development of digital libraries could also benefit from sentiment-based retrieval of digital objects with the use of sentiment-oriented recommender system and sentiment-based searching or browsing.

© Springer International Publishing AG 2016
A. Morishima et al. (Eds.): ICADL 2016, LNCS 10075, pp. 285–296, 2016.
DOI: 10.1007/978-3-319-49304-6_34

Although numerous studies have achieved acceptable performance on sentiment analysis, there are still a number of technical challenges that have yet to be fully addressed in previous studies. One problem that remains challenging to the research community is the domain adaptation issue. A sentiment classifier often suffers deterioration of performance when transferred from one domain to another [1, 2]. This issue is particularly common for lexicon-based sentiment analysis techniques, since these techniques rely on opinion expressions which often vary across domains.

By taking into consideration the sentiment scores of opinion terms, lexicon-based techniques have been proven effective in boosting the performance of sentiment classifiers (e.g., [3, 4]). Indeed, sentiment terms like "*excellent*" and "*awful*" play a crucial role in determining the sentiment polarity of text. However, not all opinions are expressed with sentiment-laden terms that contain explicit sentiment orientation. For instance, consider the sentence "*When the eyeliner dries, it forms a rubbery, latex finish material that comes off in flakes.*" While it does not contain any explicit sentiment terms, the sentence describes an undesirable fact about a beauty product. Without domain-specific knowledge, a lexicon-based sentiment classifier would most likely misclassify the sentence as neutral. In an ideal world, a lexicon that contains opinion terms for every domain would be available. Nonetheless, as pointed out by other researchers, sentiment values of terms are often domain-dependent and thus inevitably sensitive to the change of domains. In other words, the same term might have varied or even opposite sentiment values in different domains [5, 6].

Since it is extremely difficult, if not impossible, to construct a universal lexicon that caters the needs of every domain, one of the most widely accepted alternatives is to create a domain-specific lexicon that covers the commonly used sentiment terms in a studied domain. Such approach has been shown to achieve considerable improvements in domain-specific sentiment classification (e.g., [5, 7]). However, most works in this line of research have emphasized on single-word lexical entries, as opposed to creating domain lexicons that contain multi-word terms. Although single words are commonly used to indicate likes and dislikes, a lot of multi-word terms also carry sentiment which differs from that of their constituents. For instance, in a beauty product review, the sentence "*After a month, I still noticed no difference in my skin.*" should be classified as negative because the phrase "*no difference*" reveals that the product was ineffective. Apparently, if the constituents of the phrase are interpreted independently from each other, the classifier would not be able to recognize the sentiment orientation of the sentence because "*no*" and "*difference*" do not reveal any sentiment or they might contain ambiguous sentiment (i.e., the word "*difference*" by itself could be positive or negative, depending on the context).

It would thus be of interest to learn about the usefulness of multi-word terms in lexicon construction. Therefore, our study further extends this body of research by investigating the performance of distinct types of multi-word constructs in a lexicon-based, supervised sentiment classification task. Specifically, we seek to explore the potential of domain lexicons constructed using Pointwise Mutual Information (PMI) [8], with bigram, typed dependency, and concept as the lexical entries. The underlying intuition of our study is that since multi-word terms often contain additional information that cannot be captured by single-word terms, incorporating the multi-word lexical entries to generate useful features would help the performance of the sentiment classifiers.

2 Related Work

To build a robust sentiment classifier using lexicon-based approach, there are at least two critical criteria that should be satisfied: coverage and accuracy of the lexicon. Generally speaking, manually created lexicons like the MPQA subjectivity lexicon [3] normally have more accurate sentiment values compared to automatically generated lexicons like SentiWordNet [4]. However, the coverage of automatically generated lexicons is usually much more comprehensive. More importantly, to manually create new lexicons for each new domain is a labor-intensive task. This task becomes more resource demanding when dealing with dynamic and fast-moving domain data like tweets where trendy colloquial expressions appear all the time [9]. Hence, most domain adaptation techniques strive to construct domain lexicons automatically.

To further reduce the manual efforts needed in building domain lexicons, existing studies have primarily focused on unsupervised techniques, eliminating the need for labeled data. For instance, in their efforts to create lexicons for consumer reviews, Lu et al. [5] made use of various sources including a general-purpose lexicon, reviewers' ratings, thesaurus, and linguistic rules to determine the sentiment scores of terms from the unlabeled domain data. An earlier research conducted by Kanayama and Nasukawa [7] also demonstrated that domain lexicons could be built without any manual tuning and annotation of the domain corpora. Their method exploited context coherency to select lexical entries. Another common approach for automatically constructing domain lexicons is by using seed words to discover new sentiment terms in a domain. The work of Qiu et al. [6] falls under this category of research. Starting from a small list, their algorithm propagated through a large domain corpus to expand the lexicon recursively using the newly discovered features and sentiment words.

Although building domain lexicon using unsupervised techniques is less labor-intensive, the accuracy of sentiment values in the resulted lexicons might be compromised due to the inherent imperfections of the algorithms used to infer the unknown labels. To compensate for this shortcoming, a massive amount of data is often needed to achieve acceptable quality on the domain lexicons. Due to these reasons, it is also not uncommon for researchers to construct lexicons using labeled corpora, especially for domains like movie reviews and phone reviews where labeled data are easily accessible. Such approach was used by Gindl et al. [10] to resolve terms ambiguity across domains. They identified ambiguous terms based on terms frequency in labeled documents to build contextualized sentiment lexicons. A similar approach was then adopted by Weichselbraun et al. [11], but with the integration of external knowledge bases such as WordNet, ConceptNet, etc. to improve the contextualized lexicons. In the present study, we also explored the potential of multi-word constructs with a supervised approach where labeled sentences were provided to infer the sentiment scores of the lexical terms.

As mentioned in the previous section, there has been insufficient emphasis regarding the usefulness of multi-word lexical terms, yet some researchers have shown that multi-word language constructs are important in capturing contextual and domain-specific information. For example, the lexicon-based approach proposed by Ding et al. [12] not only dealt with opinion words but also with phrases and idioms. They determined the sentiment orientation of opinion terms with rules that utilized global information such as the sentiment orientation of the surrounding sentences. However, to the best of our knowledge, previous research in this field has not devoted much effort to compare the performance of different multi-word constructs in building domain lexicons. Agarwal et al. [13] evaluated various multi-word feature sets in machine learning sentiment classification but their study did not involve lexicon construction.

3   Method

3.1   Pointwise Mutual Information (PMI)

In this study, we used Pointwise Mutual Information (PMI) [8] to calculate the sentiment scores of the multi-word lexical entries. PMI has been widely used in a number of studies to compute the sentiment orientation of lexical terms (e.g., [8, 14]). Another popular method for obtaining sentiment scores is the Chi-square method. For instance, this method was used by Zhang et al. [9] in their research to build sentiment lexicons for tweets. However, in a study that explored the use of PMI and Chi-square for selecting polar phrases from a massive collection of HTML documents, PMI was found to be superior to Chi-square [15]. The latter method not only produced lower precision in most cases but also suffered low recall rates especially when the size of the lexicon was small.

Among a number of PMI variants, the implementation that we adopted is the one used by Kiritchenko et al. [14], in which no seed words are needed to infer the sentiment scores. Based on this implementation, a term is more likely to contain positive sentiment if it is frequently associated with positive sentences in relative to negative sentences, and vice versa. The sentiment score of a term w depends on its strength of association with positive sentences, i.e., $PMI(w, positive)$, and its strength of association with negative sentences, i.e., $PMI(w, negative)$:

$$score(w) = PMI(w, positive) - PMI(w, negative) \tag{1}$$

The two PMI values can be calculated as follows:

$$PMI(w, positive) = \log_2((f(w, positive) * N)/(f(w) * f(positive))) \tag{2}$$

$$PMI(w, negative) = \log_2((f(w, negative) * N)/(f(w) * f(negative))) \tag{3}$$

where $f(w, positive)$ is the frequency of w in positive sentences, N is the total number of terms in the corpus, $f(w)$ is the total frequency of w, and $f(positive)$ is the total number of terms in positive sentences. Similar definitions apply to $PMI(w, negative)$. Based on these definitions, the calculation of sentiment score for term w can be simplified as:

$$score(w) = log_2((f(w, positive) * f(negative))/(f(w, negative) * f(positive))) \quad (4)$$

When deciding whether a term should be included in a lexicon, previous studies took into account the frequency of the term in the corpus. Terms with very low frequency were usually skipped, but the thresholds varied across studies: Kiritchenko et al. [14] skipped terms that occurred less than five times whereas Kaji and Kitsuregawa [15] ignored terms that occurred less than three times. Since the present study used multi-word terms to generate lexical entries, the frequency of most of the terms were relatively low compared to those obtained in other studies. Therefore, we lowered the threshold for multi-word terms to two in order to increase the possibility of getting more entries in the lexicons. As for the unigram domain lexicons which were also created in our experiments for comparison, the threshold was set to three because single-word terms normally have higher frequencies and a lower threshold would result in too much noise in the lexicons.

Besides the frequency threshold, another factor that plays a major role in the selection of lexical entries is the sentiment score threshold, θ. While the frequency threshold aims to filter out low-frequency terms, the sentiment score threshold removes ambiguous terms that do not have strong correlations with any particular polarity. These terms usually have balanced frequencies in both polarities, so their magnitude of sentiment is weaker. In this study, we experimented with different values ($\theta = 0$ to $\theta = 4$) for the sentiment score threshold.

3.2 Multi-word Language Constructs

In the interest of generating a set of domain lexicons that capture the undisturbed semantic of phrases, we experimented with three distinct types of multi-word constructs to form the lexical entries. The multi-word language constructs are described below.

Bigram. Bigrams like *"barely enough"* and *"deal breaker"* reveal sentiment which might be missed when their constituents are interpreted in isolation. According to Wang and Manning [16], although bigram has shown mixed results in topical text classification tasks, including bigram yielded more consistent improvement in sentiment classification, presumably because bigram could capture modified verbs and nouns. Tested on ten datasets, their results demonstrated that adding bigram was often beneficial to the performance (but trigram slightly hurt the performance).

Typed Dependency. The Stanford typed dependency representation consists of pairs of words that represents the grammatical relations of words in a sentence [17]. For instance, from the sentence *"He is not an expert."*, *neg(not, expert)* is extracted as the relationship between the negation word *"not"* and the modified word *"expert"*. There are approximately 50 grammatical relations of which the full description can be found in the Stanford typed dependency manual [17]. Other dependencies include adverb modifier, conjunct, possession modifier, etc.

Concept. The focus of natural language processing has gradually shifted from word-level to concept-level [18]. Concept-level representation allows the semantic and affective information in text to be captured more precisely. Hence, it is more superior to word-level representation that often fails to capture implicit sentiment which is expressed more subtly [19]. In this study, we used Poria et al.'s [19] dependency-based concept parser to extract concepts from text. Their parser forms concepts by applying dependency rules which are triggered when certain conditions are met.

Table 1 shows the examples of bigram, typed dependency, and concept which were extracted using n-gram tokenizer, typed dependency parser, and concept parser respectively. As compared to bigram that represents the sequential relations between words, both typed dependency and concept rely on the dependency relations between words for their extraction. And yet, typed dependency and concept still differ in that the former focuses on providing syntactic or grammatical information whereas the latter focuses on extracting the semantic of text. However, since concept-level representation utilizes a smaller number of dependency rules, its ability to capture the semantic is somehow constrained by the coverage of the rules. As we can see from Table 1, although the semantic of sentence 1 was captured correctly by the concepts "*great customer service*" and "*terrible product*", the semantic of sentence 2 was missed. Besides, another distinction between typed dependency and concept in this study is that typed dependency only included direct (binary) relations, but concept involved the use of two or more words to represent the semantic of text.

Table 1. Examples of bigram, typed dependency, and concept extracted from two sentences: 1. "*Great customer service but overall terrible product.*"; 2. "*Best drugstore eyeliner I have ever laid my hands on.*"

Multi-word Construct	Sentence 1	Sentence 2
Bigram	*great customer, customer service, service but, but overall, overall terrible, terrible product*	*best drugstore, drugstore eyeliner, eyeliner I, I have, have ever, ever lay, lay my, my hand, hand on*
Typed Dependency	*service great, service customer, product but, product overall, product terrible, service product*	*eyeliner best, eyeliner drugstore, have I, eyeliner have, hand ever, hand lay, hand my, have hand, have on*
Concept	*great customer service, customer service, overall product, terrible product*	*drugstore i, lay hand*

4   Experiment

4.1   Datasets

Experiments were conducted using datasets from two diverse domains. The first dataset is the publicly available dataset introduced by Pang and Lee [20]. This dataset contains 5331 positive sentences and 5331 negative sentences collected from movie reviews. The second dataset consists of 1100 positive sentences and 1100 negative sentences obtained from reviews of beauty products. The reviews of two categories of products—eyeliners and cleansers—were collected from www.makeupalley.com, a beauty social networking site loaded with reviews of cosmetics. The reviews were then processed to remove reviewers' ratings and other information like date and reviewers' details. Only the identification numbers of the reviews were retained to allow backtracking to raw data when necessary. Stanford Parser was then used to tokenize the reviews into sentences. Two annotators involved in the manual labeling of the sentences. One of the annotators was asked to label only a total of 300 sentences, with 150 sentences from each product category, whereas the other annotator labeled all the sentences. To allow the annotators to make better judgment of the sentiment orientation, the sentences were presented in the original order in which they appeared in the reviews. Cohen's kappa was run to determine the level of agreement of the two annotators on the 300 sentences. The interrater reliability test showed high agreement between the two annotators, with $\kappa = .829$ ($p < .0005$).

4.2   Classifier and Validation

Support vector machine (SVM) was used as the basic classifier to evaluate the performance of the domain lexicons. All experiments were run on linear kernel with parameter $C = 0.1$. The presented results were obtained using 10-fold cross validation. To avoid introducing any biases into the experiments, we split the data into 10 partitions that contain the same number of sentences from each class. Specifically, each partition of the cosmetics dataset consists of 110 positive sentences and 110 negative sentences. For the movie dataset, there is one partition that contains an extra sentence from each class whereas the rests of the partitions contain 533 sentences from each class. The same partitions were used for all experiments.

In order to ensure that the test data remained completely unseen to the classifier during the training phase, we constructed 10 domain lexicons for each experiment so that domain terms were generated from all partitions except the test partition in each round of the 10-fold cross validation. When partition 1 was used as the test set, the lexicon was created from partition 2–10, and likewise for the other partitions.

Unigram and negation counts were used as the baseline features. As demonstrated in previous studies, unigram is widely accepted as one of the most common features that produces acceptable results in machine learning sentiment classification. We used binary features to indicate the presence or absence of a unigram because binary values have been shown to outperform frequency features [21]. Negation counts were obtained by counting the number of *neg* typed dependencies given by Stanford Parser.

In addition to the baseline features, we also evaluated the added benefits of having features generated from the general-purpose lexicon. The generic lexicon used in this study is the Hu and Liu's lexicon [22] which contains about 6800 single-word terms. The following lexicon-related features were used in our experiments:

Sum of Sentiment Scores. We generated three features for this feature group. The positive words and negative words from the generic lexicon were given scores of +1 and −1 respectively. For each sentence, the sentiment scores were then summed for all terms, the positive terms, and the negative terms.

Count of Terms. Three features were generated to indicate the number of positive, negative, and neutral terms in each sentence. Terms that did not appear in the lexicons were counted as neutral terms.

Similarly, to evaluate the performance of the classifier with domain knowledge incorporated, the sum and count features described above were generated using the domain lexicons. Besides the domain lexicons of multi-word terms, we also created lexicons of single-word terms with domain-specific unigrams for the purpose of comparison. Depending on the language construct used to build the lexicons (i.e., unigram, bigram, typed dependency, or concept), the same type of representation was obtained from the sentences to match the lexical entries and to generate the lexicon-related features.

5   Results and Discussion

Figure 1 shows the accuracy resulted from the domain lexicons of unigram, bigram, typed dependency, and concept terms. With varying sentiment score thresholds, there were small fluctuations in the performance of the classifiers. However, since the falling and rising of accuracy did not follow a regular pattern, the results cannot be taken as evidence to determine the optimal threshold.

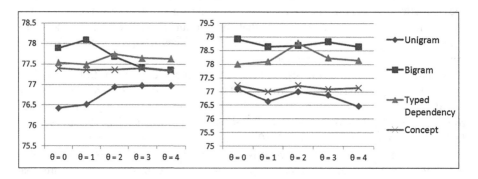

Fig. 1. The accuracy obtained on the movie dataset (left) and cosmetics dataset (right) with varying sentiment score thresholds and different types of lexical entries

Despite the irregular changes in performance within the same language construct, the results demonstrated that the bigram domain lexicons not only outperformed the unigram lexicons but also surpassed the other two types of lexicons in most cases. This finding contradicts our expectation. Theoretically, concept is able to capture the semantic in the sentences and typed dependency is better at representing the syntactic relations between words, thus they should be superior to bigram, which is simply extracted based on the sequential relations of words.

To further investigate the reason underlying this observation, we computed the size of the lexicons and the percentage of terms in the test data that also existed in the corresponding domain lexicons. The summarized results are presented in Table 2. The percentage shown in Table 2 reveals that the concept domain lexicons have a relatively lower coverage compared to other domain lexicons. As mentioned earlier in this paper, both accuracy and coverage are essential to ensure the quality of a lexicon. With the lack of coverage, most of the concepts in the test set could not be found in the domain lexicons, resulting in null values for the lexicon-related features of most sentences in the test set. As a consequence, the concept domain lexicons failed to provide discriminant information to the classifiers. However, since the coverage of a lexicon can often be improved by increasing the size of the corpus, the effectiveness of the concept-based domain lexicons might increase with a bigger volume of data.

Table 2. The number or lexical terms in the domain lexicons (*Lex. Size*) and the percentage of terms in the test data that also existed in the domain lexicons (*% Found*). The values were averaged over five sentiment score thresholds ($\theta = 0$ to $\theta = 4$).

	Movie		Cosmetics	
	Lex. Size	% Found	Lex. Size	% Found
Unigram	2333	2.62	325	2.53
Bigram	10171	3.60	1852	4.41
Typed Dependency	9269	2.64	1946	3.65
Concept	1715	0.77	322	1.30

Independent t-tests were run on the accuracy, precision, recall, and F-measure obtained from the 10-fold cross-validation. The detailed classification results are given in Table 3. For each language construct, we only present the results obtained with the sentiment score threshold that returned the best accuracy (as shown in Fig. 1).

On the cosmetics dataset, the improvements achieved using bigram lexicons and typed dependency lexicons are statistically significant but the concept-based domain lexicons fail to impact the classifier's performance. As discussed earlier, this is largely caused by the sparseness of the concept-level representation. Overall, the improvements on the cosmetics dataset are still quite promising given that the amount of data used to build the domain lexicons are not exceptionally large. If more data were available, presumably the performance of the classifier would be further improved.

On the other hand, the improvements obtained on the movie dataset are merely marginal although the size of the corpus is bigger than the cosmetics dataset. This is probably due to the wider range of vocabularies in the movie reviews because these reviews cover a number of different movie genres. However, the improvements achieved with bigram lexicons and typed dependency lexicons on the movie dataset are still statistically significant. For comparison, we also present the results obtained by other researchers on the same movie snippets dataset. With the use of bigram, typed dependency, and concept as lexical entries, our sentiment classifiers returned better accuracy than two of the three studies presented in Table 3.

Table 3. More details on the classification results with p values indicated (* $p \leq .05$, ** $p \leq .$ 01). BL: Baseline. GNR: Generic lexicon. UNI: Domain lexicon with unigram entries. BI: Domain lexicon with bigram entries. TD: Domain lexicon with typed dependency entries. CCPT: Domain lexicon with concept entries

	Movie			
	Accuracy	Precision	Recall	F-measure
BL	76.12	.762	.761	.761
BL + GNR	76.73	.768	.767	.767
BL + GNR + UNI	76.96	.770	.770	.770
BL + GNR + BI	78.09 *	.782 *	.781 *	.781 *
BL + GNR + TD	77.74 *	.778 *	.777 *	.777 *
BL + GNR + CCPT	77.40	.775 *	.774	.774
Nakagawa et al. [23]	77.30	–	–	–
Arora et al. [24]	76.93	–	–	–
Wang and Manning [16]	79.40	–	–	–
	Cosmetics			
	Accuracy	Precision	Recall	F-measure
BL	73.95	.740	.739	.739
BL + GNR	76.27	.764	.763	.763
BL + GNR + UNI	77.09	.772	.771	.771
BL + GNR + BI	78.91 **	.790 **	.789 **	.789 **
BL + GNR + TD	78.77 **	.788 *	.788 **	.788 **
BL + GNR + CCPT	77.23	.774	.772	.772

In general, the results in Table 3 indicate that by combining the use of multi-word domain lexicons, the domain-specific classifiers tend to outperform the baseline classifier which used only unigram and negation as the features for classification. In contrast to the multi-word domain lexicons, the generic lexicon and the unigram domain lexicons do not seem to have much positive effect on the performance of the classifier. The t-tests show that their results are not statistically different from the baseline results. Based on these results, there are two possible explanations for the better performance of the multi-word lexicons: First, multi-word lexical terms carry domain-specific information which could not be retrieved from the generic lexicon; second, multi-word terms could capture the additional information which is often missed by single-word domain-specific terms. Thus, our findings confirm the usefulness of multi-word terms for building domain-specific sentiment lexicons.

6   Conclusion

In this paper, we explored the use of multi-word terms as lexical entries for domain-specific lexicons. However, the findings of this study are restricted to the three multi-word language constructs examined in the experiments. It is worth noting that there are other multi-word constructs that could also be explored with the similar experimental setup. Notwithstanding its limitations, this study does suggest the feasibility and effectiveness of using multi-word sentiment terms in lexicon-based and machine learning sentiment analysis. Nonetheless, although these multi-word terms can capture the syntactic and semantic information of text to a certain extent, a more robust phrasal representation that can handle subtle affective information in text and is somehow resistant to the data sparseness problem would be the next desired advancement in sentiment analysis.

References

1. Tan, S., Cheng, X., Wang, Y., Xu, H.: Adapting naive bayes to domain adaptation for sentiment analysis. In: Boughanem, M., Berrut, C., Mothe, J., Soule-Dupuy, C. (eds.) ECIR 2009. LNCS, vol. 5478, pp. 337–349. Springer, Heidelberg (2009). doi:10.1007/978-3-642-00958-7_31
2. Aue, A., Gamon, M.: Customizing Sentiment Classifiers to New Domains: A Case Study. Technical report (2005)
3. Wilson, T., Wiebe, J., Hoffmann, P.: Recognizing contextual polarity in phrase-level sentiment analysis. In: Conference on Human Language Technology and Empirical Methods in Natural Language Processing, pp. 347–354. ACL, Stroudsburg (2005)
4. Baccianella, S., Esuli, A., Sebastiani, F.: SentiWordNet 3.0: an enhanced lexical resource for sentiment analysis and opinion mining. In: International Conference on Language Resources and Evaluation, pp. 2200–2204. ELRA, Paris (2010)
5. Lu, Y., Castellanos, M., Dayal, U., Zhai, C.: Automatic construction of a context-aware sentiment lexicon: an optimization approach. In: 20th International Conference on World Wide Web, pp. 347–356. ACM, New York (2011)
6. Qiu, G., Liu, B., Bu, J., Chen, C.: Expanding domain sentiment lexicon through double propagation. In: 21st International Joint Conference on Artificial Intelligence, pp. 1199–1204. Morgan Kaufmann, San Francisco (2009)
7. Kanayama, H., Nasukawa, T.: Fully automatic lexicon expansion for domain-oriented sentiment analysis. In: Conference on Empirical Methods in Natural Language Processing, pp. 355–363. ACL, Stroudsburg (2006)
8. Turney, P., Littman, M.L.: Unsupervised learning of semantic orientation from a hundred-billion-word corpus. Technical report (2002)
9. Zhang, L., Ghosh, R., Dekhil, M., Hsu, M., Liu, B.: Combining lexicon-based and learning-based methods for twitter sentiment analysis. Technical report (2011)
10. Gindl, S., Weichselbraun, A., Scharl, A.: Cross-domain contextualisation of sentiment lexicons. In: 19th European Conference on Artificial Intelligence. WebLyzard, Vienna (2010)
11. Weichselbraun, A., Gindl, S., Scharl, A.: Extracting and grounding context-aware sentiment lexicons. IEEE Intell. Syst. **28**, 39–46 (2013)
12. Ding, X., Liu, B., Yu, P.S.: A holistic lexicon-based approach to opinion mining. In: International Conference on Web Search and Data Mining, pp. 231–240. ACM, New York (2008)
13. Agarwal, B., Poria, S., Mittal, N., Gelbukh, A., Hussain, A.: Concept-level sentiment analysis with dependency-based semantic parsing: a novel approach. Cogn. Comput. **7**, 487–499 (2015)
14. Kiritchenko, S., Zhu, X., Mohammad, S.M.: Sentiment analysis of short informal texts. J. Artif. Intell. Res. **50**, 723–762 (2014)

15. Kaji, N., Kitsuregawa, M.: Building lexicon for sentiment analysis from massive collection of HTML documents. In: Joint Conference on Empirical Methods in Natural Language Processing and Computational Natural Language Learning, pp. 1075–1083. ACL, Stroudsburg (2007)

16. Wang, S., Manning, C.D.: Baselines and bigrams: simple, good sentiment and topic classification. In: 50th Annual Meeting of the Association for Computational Linguistics: Short Papers, pp. 90–94. ACL, Stroudsburg (2012)

17. De Marneffe, M.C., Manning, C.D.: Stanford typed dependencies manual. Technical report (2008)

18. Cambria, E., White, B.: Jumping NLP curves: a review of natural language processing research. IEEE Comput. Intell. Mag. **9**, 48–57 (2014)

19. Poria, S., Agarwal, B., Gelbukh, A., Hussain, A., Howard, N.: Dependency-based semantic parsing for concept-level text analysis. In: Gelbukh, A. (ed.) CICLing 2014. LNCS, vol. 8403, pp. 113–127. Springer, Heidelberg (2014). doi:10.1007/978-3-642-54906-9_10

20. Pang, B., Lee, L.: Seeing stars: exploiting class relationships for sentiment categorization with respect to rating scales. In: 43rd Annual Meeting on Association for Computational Linguistics, pp. 115–124. ACL, Stroudsburg (2005)

21. Pang, B., Lee, L., Vaithyanathan, S.: Thumbs up?: sentiment classification using machine learning techniques. In: ACL 2002 Conference on Empirical Methods in Natural Language Processing, pp. 79–86. ACL, Stroudsburg (2002)

22. Hu, M., Liu, B.: Mining and summarizing customer reviews. In: 10th ACM SIGKDD International Conference on Knowledge Discovery and Data Mining, pp. 168–177. ACM, New York (2004)

23. Nakagawa, T., Inui, K. and Kurohashi, S.: Dependency tree-based sentiment classification using CRFs with hidden variables. In: Annual Conference of the North American Chapter of the Association for Computational Linguistics, pp. 786–794. ACL, Stroudsburg (2010)

24. Arora, S., Mayfield, E., Penstein-Rosé, C., Nyberg, E.: Sentiment classification using automatically extracted subgraph features. In: NAACL HLT 2010 Workshop on Computational Approaches to Analysis and Generation of Emotion in Text, pp. 131–139. ACL, Stroudsburg (2010)

Twitter User Classification with Posting Locations

Naoto Takeda[1]($^{(\boxtimes)}$) and Yohei Seki[2]($^{(\boxtimes)}$)

[1] Graduate School of Library, Information and Media Studies,
University of Tsukuba, Tsukuba-shi, Ibaraki 305-8550, Japan
s1621623@u.tsukuba.ac.jp
[2] Faculty of Library, Information and Media Science,
University of Tsukuba, Tsukuba-shi, Ibaraki 305-8550, Japan
yohei@slis.tsukuba.ac.jp

Abstract. Twitter contains a large number of postings related to the reputation of products and services. Analyzing these data can provide useful marketing information. Inferring the user class would make it possible to extract opinions related to each class. In this paper, we propose a method that treats each user's posting location for a tweet as a feature in the analysis of user classes. The proposed method creates clusters of geotags (obtained from Twitter tags) to identify the locations most often visited by the target user, which are then used as features. As an example, we conducted experiments to classify targets based on three classes: "student," "working member of society," and "housewife." We obtained an average F-measure of 0.779, which represents an improvement on baseline results.

Keywords: Inferring occupation · Geolocation · Twitter

1 Introduction

Twitter[1] is a popular microblogging service that enables its users to read and write short messages of up to 140 characters. It is now a mainstream social networking service and is becoming a significant element of social infrastructure. Because of its ability to reflect the user's thoughts and actions in real time, Twitter has attracted much research interest in recent years. For this reason, identifying user attributes such as gender, age, and occupation could enable analysts to answer questions such as "What brands are popular among young female users?" or "Which cars do working members of society prefer?" using attribute-based trend analysis. Extracting opinions through Twitter would be less expensive than carrying out traditional questionnaire-based surveys and would permit real-time assessment.

However, attributes such as gender, age, and occupation are not usually disclosed on Twitter. From previous research, only 24.4 % of users disclose their

---

[1] https://twitter.com/.

© Springer International Publishing AG 2016
A. Morishima et al. (Eds.): ICADL 2016, LNCS 10075, pp. 297–310, 2016.
DOI: 10.1007/978-3-319-49304-6_35

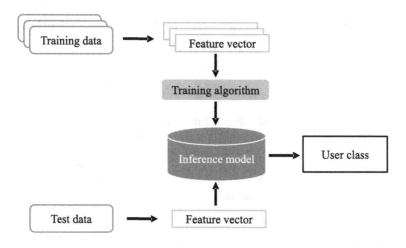

Fig. 1. Process of inferring the user class

occupation in their profiles [7]. For this reason, it is difficult to extract opinions or relate them to the user class as traditional surveys can do. Therefore, some research projects are focusing on approaches to this problem of inferring user classes from user profiles [2,12,13].

In recent years, new services such as Google Now[2] and WebPlaces[3] have offered information based on location data. Research projects and approaches are also beginning to use location information (explained in more detail in Sect. 2.2). In particular, it has been shown that combining location information with the content and time of a posting can reveal new insights, enabling the creation of inference models more accurate than existing methods [4]. In this paper, using location information from users, we infer the user class by a method that focuses on differences between posting locations.

Twitter postings reveal user features such as specific gender-related terms and various posting locations related to the user's occupation. In this study, we analyzed the classes of Twitter users by selecting features and designing an inference model based on machine learning. In one example, inferring the "housewife" class would offer an opportunity to collect housewives' opinions about childcare support. Figure 1 provides an outline of the proposed method. In this research, we used the following three features to infer user class:

- proportion of the postings for each hour of the day at each location,
- characteristic terms for each class in tweets, and
- proportion of the postings for each hour of the day.

These features are described in detail in Sect. 3.

---

[2] https://www.google.com/intl/ja/landing/now/.
[3] http://www.webplaces.com/.

2   Related Work

2.1   Research on Inferring the Classes of Twitter Users

In this research, a feature vector that includes characteristic terms for each class has been used as an indicator of identity. Cheng et al. [2] extracted terms characteristic of each region and inferred the user's place of residence with 51.0 % accuracy. Rao et al. [13] inferred the user's gender, age, political outlook, and regional origin using the number of followers, the tweet's contents, and the retweet frequency. Preoţiuc-Pietro et al. [12] proposed a method for occupation inference that used general user information, statistics about the tweets (for example, number of followers or average number of tweets/day), and the topics of tweets. The nine target occupations were decided using the Standard Occupational Classification[4]. An accuracy evaluation was carried out, resulting in an average accuracy of 52.7 %.

2.2   Research on Tweet Posting Times and Locations

In our research, we focus on how locations visited by the user each day of the week and each hour of the day lead to differences in target classes. For instance, users belonging to the "housewife" class are likely to tweet during the daytime on weekdays near their place of residence, whereas "students" and "working members of society" rarely do this. By using the proportion of postings per hour and per day of the week as features, it is possible to make highly accurate inferences about the user's class. Gao et al. [4] used time patterns to show that higher accuracy could be achieved by combining the posting time and day of the week with the location, when compared with a Markov-process method that used only location information. Ye et al. [15] analyzed posting times and tweet content, showing that different topics (for example, "university" or "parties") were more likely to be mentioned in particular time slots and on particular days of the week.

3   Method

3.1   The Number of Postings per Hour for Each Location

First, by clustering geotags attached to tweets, we can extract the locations frequently visited by a user. The clustering method used in this research is a density-based spatial clustering algorithm with noise (DBSCAN), as proposed by Ester et al. [3]. Because DBSCAN is a clustering method based on the density of data sets, it enables researchers to obtain high-density clusters. DBSCAN has two parameters, namely *MinPts* (a threshold for the quantity of data belonging to a cluster) and *Eps* (a threshold for distances between data points). In the clustering procedure, a cluster is considered to be a set of points containing at

---

[4] http://www.bls.gov/soc/.

Table 1. Example of a location-information API response

Name	Category	...	Score
Tokyo midtown	Shopping center, mall, commercial complexes	...	87.910
Galleria	Shopping center, mall, commercial complexes	...	87.366
Presse premium Tokyo midtown	Other supermarkets	...	87.015

least $MinPts$ data points within a radius of Eps. Data not belonging to any cluster are considered as noise.

We used the following algorithm, which enables the application of DBSCAN to Twitter geotags and extracts the locations often visited by users.

1. Collect tweets containing geotags posted by a target user.
2. Compute the geographical distances between data points within geotag sets and perform clustering using DBSCAN.
3. From the extracted clusters, detect those with posting dates spread over 7 days or more and consider them "often visited places".

The parameter values used for DBSCAN were $MinPts = 5$ and $Eps = 100$ m.

Next, we attached labels to the clusters. We used the Yahoo! Open Local Platform location-information application-programmer-interface (API)[5] provided by Yahoo! Japan. The location-information API takes latitude and longitude as required parameters and returns the names of main landmarks and locations in the area. Several major spots may appear in the response field with scores that take into consideration the level of importance and scope of influence defined for each type of location. For instance, an input latitude = 35.66521320007564 and longitude = 139.7300114513391 (Akasaka 9, Minato-ku, Tokyo) could return the responses shown in Table 1.

Here, we use "score" and "category" within the responses as location labels. "Score" indicates the probability of it being the right location. "Category" represents a category associated with the location, such as "university or graduate school," or "shopping center or mall, commercial complexes." We assign location labels using the location-information API as follows:

1. Input the center of gravity of the extracted cluster via the API.
2. Consider responses for which the response field "score" is at least 70, with the "category" of the spot having the highest score becoming the location label for the cluster.
3. If the maximum value of the response field "score" is less than 70, the location label for that cluster is set to "none."
4. For the clusters tagged as "none," select the cluster with the largest number of points, and tag it as "around the place of residence."

---

[5] http://developer.yahoo.co.jp/webapi/map/openlocalplatform/v1/placeinfo.html.

However, if there are a large number of labels involved, some may best be treated as noise. Therefore, in Sect. 4.3, we consider in more detail the location labels to be used. In addition, because often-visited places may vary according to the time and day of the week, we compute the proportion of postings for each hour of each day of the week to use as a feature.

3.2 Terms Characterizing Specific Classes that Appear in Tweets

We also consider as features the characteristic terms that appear in tweets from user groups that pertain to the target class. Characteristic terms used as features are selected based on mutual information [8], which expresses the mutual dependency between two random variables. The mutual information $I_{(N)}$ between a class and a term is computed using Eq. (1). This method is often used by researchers for text classification [9,11]. Eq. (1) is applied to all the target classes and terms appearing in the training data.

$$I_{(N)} = \frac{N_{11}}{N} \log 2 \frac{NN_{11}}{N_{1.}N_{.1}} + \frac{N_{01}}{N} \log 2 \frac{NN_{01}}{N_{0.}N_{.1}} + \frac{N_{10}}{N} \log 2 \frac{NN_{10}}{N_{1.}N_{.0}} + \frac{N_{00}}{N} \log 2 \frac{NN_{00}}{N_{0.}N_{.0}} \quad (1)$$

Here, N_{11} represents the number of Twitter data items that pertain to the class and contain the term among the totality of items in the training data. N_{10} is the number of Twitter data items that do not pertain to the class but do contain the term in the training data. N_{01} represents the number of Twitter data items that pertain to the class but do not contain the term in the training data. Finally, N_{00} is the number of Twitter data items that do not pertain to the class and do not contain the term in the training data. Therefore, $N_{.1}$ equals $N_{01} + N_{11}$. In Eq. (1), a large value indicates an output of terms biased toward the class. Terms are considered characteristic features of classes when they are ranked in the top 2,000 in terms of computed mutual information. We use a term's relative frequency within the target user's entire set of tweets as the feature's value. If the same term appears for more than one class, the terms chosen as features are those pertaining to the class with the higher score.

3.3 The Proportion of Tweets per Hour

Finally, we use the time of posting as a feature. We extract the posting time of all of the target user's tweets and compute the number of tweets posted for every hour and every day of the week. However, even in the case of users from the same class, the number of postings can vary considerably from user to user. For this reason, we consider as a feature the proportion of postings rather than the actual number of postings per hour.

4 Classes for Inference and Feature Selection

4.1 Selecting Classes for Inference

In selecting classes for inference, we manually labeled the occupations for 600 accounts selected randomly from the data obtained by Twitter crawling. In cases where it was difficult to determine a user's occupation from the user profile, we referred to past tweets before choosing labels. The "student" class was identified as representing users who go to school in the daytime on weekdays. The "working member of society" class involved full-time employees who travel to companies in the daytime on weekdays. The "housewife" class comprised married and female users. The "company/group" class represented groups who used their accounts for advertising. For accounts that only retweet postings or post about specific hobbies, we considered the occupation "unknown." In addition, because relatively few accounts were labeled "no occupation" or "part-time worker," we classified them as "others," together with those considered as "unknown." In cases where the user might belong to multiple classes, we prioritized "working member of society", "housewife", "student", and other classes in that order (to best suit marketing applications). In this experiment, no users belonged to multiple classes.

These results are shown in Table 2. Based on this table, as an example of inferring user classes from posting locations, we analyzed the following three classes, "student," "working member of society," and "housewife" (close to 80 % of accounts). Because accounts owned by companies or groups rarely contained tweets with geotags and did not represent individual users, these were eliminated from the target classes.

Table 2. Proportions of manually labeled "occupations"

Class	Proportion
Student	**0.502**
Working member of society	**0.290**
Company/group	0.108
Housewife	**0.032**
Twitter bot	0.017
Others	0.051

4.2 Selecting Location Labels

To obtain the number of postings per location, we identified location labels. For the 300 accounts that posted at least 200 geotags, we clustered the geotags using the method described in Sect. 3.1 and input the center of gravity of each cluster into the location-information API. Table 3 shows the top 15 location categories obtained.

In Table 3, because "None" indicates that no location has been identified, this cannot be used as a feature. Instead, the cluster with the largest number of postings classified as "none" was reassigned the location label "around the

Table 3. Location categories obtained from the location-information API

Category	Proportion
None	0.331
Other supermarkets	0.046
Shopping centers, malls, commercial complexes	0.044
Hotels	0.028
Bookstores	0.025
McDonald's	0.023
Drugstores	0.022
Other casual restaurants	0.020
Stations (JR local lines)	0.019
Stations (other lines)	0.019
Universities and graduate schools	0.015
Elementary schools	0.015
Family Mart	0.017
Lawson	0.014
Seven-Eleven	0.013

place of residence," and this was used as a feature. The location label "elementary schools" and those involving convenience stores, such as "Family Mart," "Lawson," and "Seven-Eleven," were eliminated because there are branches all over the country, which could lead to an incorrect analysis of locations near the clusters adopted. Another observation is that "station" may refer to "subway station," "Japan Railway (JR) station," or "other railway-company station." All of these categories were grouped together under the "stations" label. In the same way, "McDonald's" and "other casual restaurants" were merged. Finally, the categories "high school" and "junior high school" were merged with "universities and graduate schools" under a general "school" label. To summarize the above procedure, we adopted nine location labels, namely "around the place of residence," "other supermarkets," "shopping centers, malls, commercial complexes," "hotels," "bookstores," "drugstores," "other casual restaurants," "stations," and "schools."

4.3   The Selection of Characteristic Terms

We carried out an experiment to select the features of terms to characterize a class (as explained in Sect. 3.2). To select the characteristic terms, we collected 100 Twitter users for each class. To determine the user's class, we checked the user profile, where "20-year-old student", for example, would identify the "student" class. This group comprised 300 users whose tweets were then used as training data. We performed a morphological analysis of the training data tweets, using MeCab [6]. Japanese is an agglutinative language that should be analyzed using a word segmentation tool. MeCab is an open-source morphological analysis tool for segmenting words. We also computed the mutual information per class for all of the terms that appeared in the training data. The top 2,000 terms for each class (6,000 terms in total) were used to make a feature vector. Table 4 presents examples of the characteristic terms for each class.

Table 4. Examples of the characteristic terms associated with classes

Student	Working member of society	Housewife
Post	News	Good morning
NAVER[a]	"Konkatsu"[b]	Son
Curation	Net	Happiness
Pokemon	Activity	Husband
Japanese "sake"	Working member of society	My family

[a] http://matome.naver.jp/
[b] Search for a marriage partner

5   User Class Inference Using the Posting Location

5.1   Objective

To investigate the validity of inferring three classes ("student," "working member of society," and "housewife") from the posting location, we compared them against a baseline method. The proposed method used a combined vector that contained the proportion of postings for each hour and the location as features, together with a baseline feature vector. The number of dimensions of the vector in the proposed method was 24 (per hour) × 7 (per day) × 9 (the number of the location categories) = 1,512 dimensions. The baseline comprised a combined vector containing terms that characterize each class, and a vector containing the proportion of postings for each hour. The number of dimensions of the vector in the baseline was 24 (per hour) × 7 (per day) = 168 dimensions. The difference between the proposed method and the baseline is therefore only the addition of location information. In previous research [10,14], characteristic terms that infer gender or age have been used as features of the baseline. In contrast, we conducted additional research to infer the user occupation. The day of the week and time of the posting are important data for inferring user occupation because posting time and occupation are closely related. Therefore, the features of the day of the week and time of the posting were added to the baseline.

Based on the results of these experiments, we investigated the locations and times biased toward specific classes and considered them as new features to improve accuracy.

5.2   Data and Methods

The experimental data involved all tweets in Japanese posted during a 1-year period (from July 22, 2014 through July 21, 2015) from users with a Japanese geotag who had posted at least 200 tweets (as well as their own tweets). Twitter streaming APIs[6] were used for data collection. Users with the terms "student," "working member of society," and "housewife" in their profiles were extracted, and 200 users for each class (600 users in total) were selected as sources of experimental data. We checked that the accounts used for this data did not overlap with those used for the analysis in Sect. 4.3. Their classes were manually confirmed. Users without clusters of frequently visited places and those involving 50 clusters or more were removed as representing noise.

We used the accuracy, precision, recall, and F-measure of each class in the evaluation. The assessment was based on a tenfold cross-validation. Support-vector-machine (SVM) and random-forest models were used for classification because they had been used in previous research [1,16] as high-performance classifiers. In this experiment, we used a multilabel classification function for both classifiers. LIBSVM[7] and scikit-learn[8] were used in our implementation. LIBSVM and scikit-learn are open source machine learning libraries. Because the results of the random-forest model can vary because of the random sampling of initial values, a tenfold cross-validation was carried out, and the average value was used in the evaluation.

5.3   Results

Experimental results for the classifiers are shown in Tables 5 and 6. An improvement was found in the precision, recall, F-measure, and accuracy of each class using the SVM model. In comparing the classifiers, the SVM model obtained higher inference accuracy than the random-forest model.

5.4   Discussion

Based on the results obtained, and analyzing the cases of incorrect class inference, examples were found where the location used for inference was incorrect. Particularly in cases where the registered location was not near the center of gravity of the adopted cluster, the location inference could fail. For instance, if there is a school nearby, the location "school" may be incorrectly assigned to tweets that happened to be posted outside a school. Short phrases such as "good morning" and "good night" were often found in postings made by incorrectly classified users. There were many tweets that used the Swarm[9] check-in function. Such tweets and comments contain only information related to the current location or place, such as "I'm in Shinjuku Station in Shinjuku-ku, Tokyo." Users

---

[6] https://dev.twitter.com/streaming/overview.
[7] https://www.csie.ntu.edu.tw/~cjlin/libsvm/.
[8] http://scikit-learn.org/stable/.
[9] https://www.swarmapp.com/.

Table 5. Inference accuracy based on the SVM model

Method	Class	Precision	Recall	F-measure	F-measure average	Accuracy
Proposed method	Student	**0.800**	**0.776**	**0.784**	**0.768**	**0.772**
	Working member of society	**0.751**	**0.700**	**0.718**		
	Housewife	**0.767**	**0.856**	**0.801**		
Baseline	Student	0.778	0.745	0.759	0.750	0.750
	Working member of society	0.720	0.688	0.701		
	Housewife	0.762	0.832	0.791		

Table 6. Inference accuracy based on the random-forest model

Method	Class	Precision	Recall	F-measure	F-measure average	Accuracy
Proposed Method	Student	0.721	0.810	0.758	**0.728**	**0.732**
	Working member of society	**0.681**	0.667	**0.665**		
	Housewife	0.811	**0.727**	**0.760**		
Baseline	Student	0.727	0.815	0.763	0.726	0.730
	Working member of society	0.669	0.675	0.664		
	Housewife	0.814	0.708	0.751		

with a large number of such tweets are not well suited to inference methods involving vectors containing characteristic terms as features, and this may have reduced the accuracy.

Considering separately the results for the three classes, in the case of "student," improvement was caused by postings within clusters with the location label "school," which did not appear in other classes. Conversely, for the class "housewife," the proposed method showed a high F-measure. This can be explained by the strong relation between the posting location, posting time, and the terms posted by those with the "housewife" class in comparison with the

Table 7. Correct classes and classes inferred using the proposed method

Correct classes / Class inferred	Student	Working member of society	Housewife
Student	160	35	11
Working member of society	30	149	35
Housewife	10	16	154

Table 8. Posting times and locations exhibiting a tendency toward certain classes, according to mutual information

Student	Working member of society	Housewife
Monday 2 pm, school	Thursday 11 pm, around place of residence	Tuesday 5 pm, around place of residence
Wednesday 3 pm, school	Tuesday 10 pm, around place of residence	Wednesday 11 am, around place of residence
Tuesday 6 am, around place of residence	Monday 11 pm, around place of residence	Monday 4 pm, around place of residence
Wednesday 7 am, around place of residence	Sunday 1 am, around place of residence	Thursday 3 pm, around place of residence
Thursday 12 pm, school	Wednesday 10 pm, around place of residence	Wednesday 10 am, around place of residence

other classes. Another observation is that the results for "working member of society" were relatively inaccurate for both the baseline and proposed methods. Table 7 shows the numbers of correct classes and the numbers of classes inferred by the proposed method based on the SVM model. The results indicate that the class "working member of society" was susceptible to incorrect classification as either "student" or "housewife." We considered that, because "working member of society" covers a wide range of ages, it is difficult to find common features when inferring terms and visited places.

We carried out another experiment to investigate location labels with posting times for those cases where people in a certain class visited frequently. The data for the investigation involved 100 different users from those used in previous experiments. Table 8 shows the five highest mutual-information values relating to each class and posting time/location.

Within the class "student," it was found that the label "school," which does not appear in other classes, occupies a high rank. In the "working member of society" case, all location labels were "around place of residence." Regarding posting times, it was found that a large number of postings occurred at night. One possible explanation is that working members of society probably tweet after they have come home from work. In the case of "housewife," all of the location labels were "around place of residence," as was the case with "working members of society." However, one peculiarity was that these tweets were posted on weekday afternoons (after 12:00 noon), a pattern that was not observed for the other classes.

Based on these observations, inferences were made by considering a vector formed by the number of postings in the 100 cases where posting locations and

Table 9. Classification accuracy after adding features based on posting times and locations that exhibit a tendency toward certain classes

Method	Class	Precision	Recall	F-measure	F-measure average	Accuracy
Proposed method (adding features)	Student	**0.800**	**0.798**	**0.792**	**0.779**	**0.782**
	Working member of society	**0.760**	**0.723**	**0.733**		
	Housewife	**0.783**	**0.852**	**0.812**		
Baseline	Student	0.778	0.745	0.759	0.750	0.750
	Working member of society	0.720	0.688	0.701		
	Housewife	0.762	0.832	0.791		

times were most affected by each class. This vector was then merged with the existing vector for the proposed method. The baseline for comparison used a combined vector comprising a vector containing characteristic terms for each class as features and a vector formed by the relative number of posting in each hourly slot. This is the same as the baseline described in Sect. 5.3. Classification was carried out using LIBSVM. The results of the additional experiments are shown in Table 9. By adding the vector whose features involve posting times and locations that are biased toward each class, it was possible to improve the precision, recall, F-measure, and accuracy.

6   Conclusions

In this paper, experiments were conducted using actual data, and the validity of the proposed method (using posting locations) was verified. An improvement was found in the precision, recall, F-measure, and accuracy for each class. However, for the "working member of society" group, the analysis revealed frequent misclassification errors, resulting in a relatively low F-measure. We consider that this was caused by the large variation found within the "working member of society" class in terms of age, making it difficult to find common characteristics for term usage and places visited.

The discussion also included ways to improve the accuracy of location inference. In future work, we plan to identify the posting location from content without geotags because tweets with geotags are generally rare [2,5]. Specifically, by using location labels as correct-answer data, we can select characteristic terms related to specific places as features for inferring the posting location. It will then be possible to apply the proposed method to users who do not post tweets with geotags. Finally, we plan to improve the assessment accuracy by considering the distances between clusters.

Acknowledgment. This work was partially supported by a JSPS Grant-in-Aid for Scientific Research (B) (#16H02913).

References

1. Brdar, S., Ćulibrk, D., Crnojević, V.: Demographic attributes prediction on the real-world mobile data. In: Proceedings of the Mobile Data Challenge by Nokia Workshop in conjunction with International Conference on Pervasive Computing, Newcastle, UK, June 2012
2. Cheng, Z., Caverlee, J., Lee, K.: You are where you tweet: a content-based approach to geo-locating twitter users. In: Proceedings of the 19th ACM International Conference on Information and Knowledge Management (CIKM2010), Toronto, ON, Canada, pp. 759–768, October 2010
3. Ester, M., Kriegel, H.P., Sander, J., Xu, X.: A density-based algorithm for discovering clusters in large spatial databases with noise. In: Proceedings of the 2nd International Conference on Knowledge Discovery and Data Mining (KDD 1996), Portland, OR, USA pp. 226–231, August 1996
4. Gao, H., Tang, J., Liu, H.: Mobile location prediction in a spatio-temporal context. In: Proceedings of the Mobile Data Challenge by Nokia Workshop in conjunction with International Conference on Pervasive Computing, Newcastle, UK, June 2012
5. Kinsella, S., Murdock, V., O'Hare, N.: "I'm eating a sandwich in glasgow": modeling locations with tweets. In: Proceedings of the 3rd International Workshop on Search and Mining User-generated Contents (SMUC 2011), Glasgow, UK, pp. 61–68, October 2011
6. Kudo, T., Yamamoto, K., Matsumoto, Y.: Applying conditional random fields to Japanese morphological analysis. In: Proceedings of the Conference on Empirical Methods in Natural Language Processing (EMNLP 2004), Barcelona, Spain, pp. 230–237, April 2004
7. Lee, J., Ahn, J., Oh, J.S., Ryu, H.: Mysterious influential users in political communication on Twitter: user's occupation information and its impact on retweetability. In: Proceedings of the iConference 2015, Newport Beach, CA, USA, March 2015
8. Manning, C.D., Raghavan, P., Schuetze, H.: Introduction to Information Retrieval, pp. 272–275. Cambridge University Press, Cambridge (2008). Chap. 13.5.1
9. Narayanan, V., Arora, I., Bhatia, A.: Fast and accurate sentiment classification using an enhanced naive Bayes model. In: Yin, H., Tang, K., Gao, Y., Klawonn, F., Lee, M., Weise, T., Li, B., Yao, X. (eds.) IDEAL 2013. LNCS, vol. 8206, pp. 194–201. Springer, Heidelberg (2013). doi:10.1007/978-3-642-41278-3_24
10. Otterbacher, J.: Inferring gender of movie reviewers: exploiting writing style, content and metadata. In: Proceedings of the 19th ACM International Conference on Information and Knowledge Management (CIKM 2010), Toronto, Canada, pp. 369–378, October 2010
11. Peng, H., Long, F., Ding, C.: Feature selection based on mutual information: criteria of max-dependency, max-relevance, and min-redundancy. IEEE Trans. Pattern Anal. Mach. Intell. **27**(8), 1226–1238 (2005)
12. Preoţiuc-Pietro, D., Lampos, V., Aletras, N.: An analysis of the user occupational class through twitter content. In: Proceedings of the 53rd Annual Meeting of the Association for Computational Linguistics (ACL 2015), Beijing, China, pp. 1754–1764, July 2015

13. Rao, D., Yarowsky, D., Shreevats, A., Gupta, M.: Classifying latent user attributes in twitter. In: Proceedings of the 2nd International Workshop on Search and Mining User-Generated Contents (SMUC 2010), Toronto, ON, Canada, pp. 37–44, October 2010
14. Schler, J., Koppel, M., Argamon, S., Pennebaker, J.: Effects of age and gender on blogging. In: Proceedings of the AAAI Spring Symposium Computational Approaches to Analyzing Weblogs, Menlo Park, CA, USA, pp. 191–197, March 2006
15. Ye, M., Janowicz, K., Mülligann, C., Lee, W.C.: What you are is when you are: the temporal dimension of feature types in location-based social networks. In: Proceedings of the 19th ACM SIGSPATIAL International Conference on Advances in Geographic Information Systems, Chicago, IL, USA, pp. 102–111, November 2011
16. Zamal, F.A., Liu, W., Ruths, D.: Homophily and latent attribute inference: inferring latent attributes of twitter users from neighbors. In: Proceedings of the Sixth International AAAI Conference on Weblogs and Social Media (ICWSM 2012), Palo Alto, CA, USA, pp. 387–390, June 2012

Temporal Analysis of Comparative Opinion Mining

Kasturi Dewi Varathan[1]([⊠]), Anastasia Giachanou[2], and Fabio Crestani[2]

[1] Department of Information System,
Faculty of Computer Science and Information Technology,
University of Malaya, Kuala Lumpur, Malaysia
kasturi@um.edu.my
[2] Faculty of Informatics, Università Della Svizzera Italiana (USI),
Lugano, Switzerland
{anastasia.giachanou,fabio.crestani}@usi.ch

Abstract. Social media have become a popular platform for people to share their opinions and emotions. Analyzing opinions that are posted on the web is very important since they influence future decisions of organizations and people. Comparative opinion mining is a subfield of opinion mining that deals with identifying and extracting information that is expressed in a comparative form. Due to the fact that there is a huge amount of opinions posted online everyday, analyzing comparative opinions from a temporal perspective is an important application that needs to be explored. This study introduces the idea of integrating temporal elements in comparative opinion mining. Different type of results can be obtained from the temporal analysis, including trend analysis, competitive analysis as well as burst detection. In our study we show that temporal analysis of comparative opinion mining provides more current and relevant information to users compared to standard opinion mining.

Keywords: Temporal analysis · Comparative opinion mining

1 Introduction

Nowadays people spend a significant amount of time to share their opinion on web and on social media about various products or entities. The opinions and emotions that are posted on social media influence decisions of other people. In the past, the main source of information was formal media such as newspapers, yearly reports, surveys and this information was used to monitor marketing, sales, performance, quality, etc. However, nowadays people are influenced by reviews and opinions that are publicly available and are based on the experience of other people. Also, business organizations frequently rely on real time customers' reviews in making strategic decisions. Opinion mining is very useful in extracting crucial information and plays a significant role in determining the opinion of the public.

© Springer International Publishing AG 2016
A. Morishima et al. (Eds.): ICADL 2016, LNCS 10075, pp. 311–322, 2016.
DOI: 10.1007/978-3-319-49304-6_36

Analyzing public opinion is very important for various applications. However, the huge amount of data posted everyday makes the extraction of information very difficult. Many digital libraries have been created to deal with this unprecedented growth of data and this eventually has led to the need of better retrieval systems. Analytical presentation of digital content has become a necessary element nowadays. Many works have tried to provide effective analytical views of the content. However, analytical presentation of opinions or data or documents alone is insufficient because this only shows how much people discuss and how they feel about certain products or services. This information may lead to incorrect judgments because opinion holders probably do not have any experience on other products or services. On the other hand, a *comparative opinion* is provided by opinion holders who have experience about more than one product or service and therefore they are more crucial for companies who can use this information to improve their products. For example, the sentence *the speed of BMW cars is much higher than that of Mercedes* is comparative and provides more precise information compared to the general opinion sentence *BMW cars are fast*.

Researchers have started exploring comparative opinion mining long time ago. The first widely known paper on comparative opinion mining was presented by Jindal and Liu [13]. We have gone through almost a decade of research on comparative opinion mining and digital libraries. In these 10 years, to the best of our knowledge, comparative opinion mining has not been studied from the perspective of temporal analysis. Temporal element is an important aspect in digital library design [1] and facilitates the understanding of longitudinal comparative data. However, most of the past research considered temporal aspects of opinion and not of comparative opinion specifically. Examples include fields raging from tweets sentiment analysis [24] to pattern discovery [6,15].

We should note that our aim is not to propose a new technique for mining comparative opinions, but to explore comparative opinion mining from a temporal perspective. This paper presents our first attempt on temporal comparative opinion mining that is based on our past experience with temporal analysis [16] and comparative opinion mining [32]. In this paper, we explore how time can be utilized by customers as well as business organizations in making intelligent decisions. Although our idea is relatively simple, to the best of our knowledge, this is the first research which studies comparative opinion mining from a temporal perspective.

The rest of the paper is organized as follows. Section 2 describes previous work on comparative opinion mining. Section 3 presents a conceptual model to enable readers to understand the temporal analysis pertaining to comparative opinion mining. The following section presents the results obtained from this temporal analysis and how it can benefit customers as well as business organizations. Section 5 presents the comparison between opinion and comparative opinion using temporal analysis. Finally, Sect. 6 summarizes the study and suggests directions of future work.

2   Related Work

Many people spend significant amount of time to share their opinions on the web. Brightlocals local online review survey shows that around 88 % of people look up for online opinions with the aim to take a better decision. However, going through all these opinions in making decision is a tedious task [25]. A more focused approach is needed in handling this information.

Jindal and Liu are the first who focused on comparative opinion mining [13]. Much research has been conducted on comparing opinions from reviews, blogs, forums, news, etc. [3,11,34]. There are also many websites for comparisons of products or services such as Cheapoair, Expedia, Booking.com, etc. All these sites do not take reviews into consideration. On the other hand, sites such as Tripadvisor, Amazon.com utilize reviews for recommendations but they do not consider comparative opinions at all. Comparative opinion mining is not about comparing opinions of people [2] but about showing the relation between entities and the preference of the opinion holder on the entities. On the contrary, opinion statements merely give an idea of which products or services are the ones that users most talked about [2].

Comparative opinion gives more information to users than just an opinionated text [20]. In comparative opinions more precise information is presented on products or services that are comparable. In order to write such a review, the opinion holder generally has experience or knowledge of the compared products [9]. A good decision can only be made by looking at important options available and how these options are compared. Although a review contains approximately 10 % of comparative opinion [17], this percentage gives a significant impact to the stakeholders.

Past research on comparative opinion mining mostly focused sentence detection, entity detection, relation detection and feature detection. As for sentence detection, research were focused on on how comparative opinion sentences can be effectively identified and retrieved [13,34]. Entity detection in comparative opinions were focused on identifying the entities which consist of product, services, brands or models from the comparative opinionated text [21,29,35]. Relation detection emphasizes on retrieving the relationship that could exist between entities so that comparisons could be performed between the entities [11,19]. As for feature detection, research were narrowed to identifying the attributes that describes the entity such as size, price, capacity, etc [27].

Temporal perspective has been explored on digital photo collections [8], digital archives [28], network analysis [30] and even real time events [26]. On the other hand, the effect of temporal analysis of comparative opinion mining has not been explored yet, although there is some significant research on plain opinionated text [3,4]. Temporal analysis is considered by Alves et al. based on time series on user generated data in twitter [3]. Temporal analysis is also used for prediction purposes by Tu et al. [31]. This kind of analysis is also important in relation to comparative opinion mining as it reveals a lot of information from the perspective of time that is very useful to business organizations or customers or general audience. From the business organization point of view, it reveals information on the analysis of comparative opinion reviews on their own products compared to those of the competitors.

3   Temporal Analysis on Comparative Opinion Mining

As already mentioned, our aim is to study comparative opinion mining from a temporal perspective. To this end, we focus on a direct approach in performing the analysis. Figure 1 shows the detailed design of our methodology.

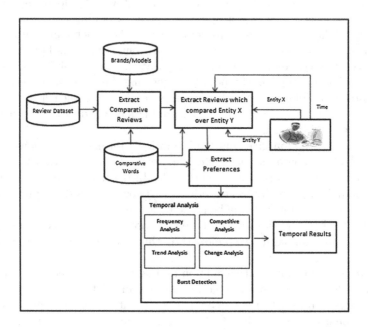

Fig. 1. Baseline methodology

The first step is to extract comparative reviews from a dataset. This retrieval is performed with the use of a brand/model database and a set of comparative words provided by Jindal and Liu [14]. The brand/model database is needed since many reviews do not contain explicit brand information. There is a common practice in most of the reviews in which reviewers prefer to write their reviews based on model name or number rather than brand names. To this end, we retrieve all the models names or numbers associated with entity used in the dataset from Wikipedia. Once all the reviews are retrieved, the user will then input the entities in which they wish to compare together with the time information. The time information could be a range or a specific data that consist of date or timespan information. All reviews which contains the comparative sentences within the specified time will then be extracted. The preferences of each of the entities selected are retrieved. We adopt the method proposed by Gu and

Yoo [10] for classifying the preference of one entity to another with the use of the comparative words provided by Jindal and Liu [14]. The temporal analysis process begins once all the preferences are classified accordingly.

There are many different types of analysis that could be made within the domain of temporal analysis since it covers a wide spectrum. In this research, we focus on frequency analysis, trend analysis, competitive analysis and burst detection. Temporal results are obtained based on the temporal analysis performed on the comparative reviews.

4   Results and Discussions

For our experiments we use the dataset built by Branavan et al. [5] that contains camera reviews. This is a publicly available dataset that contains 12,586 camera reviews extracted from Epinions.com[1]. The comparative opinion statements from the reviews are extracted based on a set of comparative keywords [14] such as better, prefer, superior, etc. The extracted comparative statements are cross-referred with Kessler and Kuhn [18] who retrieved 11,232 sentences and obtained 1,707 annotated comparative sentences from the same dataset. A precision of 78.6 % is obtained in which our comparative sentences matches Kessler and Kuhn's annotations.

To present our methodology more formally, we introduce some notation. Let t denote the time, then $t_i, t_{i+1}, t_{i+2}, \ldots, t_{i+N}$ are temporal expressions which could refer to years, months, days, hours, etc., depending on the users preference. In the following experiments, we have considered the value of t as years and concentrated on comparing only two entities. We used different camera brands as entities, but this research could also be extended to other domains.

4.1   Frequency Analysis

Frequency analysis is based on the rate on which a specific entity is compared with other entities. This rate gives an idea on how many times this entity is compared in the reviews within a period of time. As in our study we use year as a time unit, this reveals the number of times in a year that this entity is compared with other entities. From this information, we can derive how popular this entity is. This ratio can be calculated as follows:

$$Freq(x, N) = \frac{\sum_{t_i}^{N} \frac{|OpR_x|}{|R_x|}}{N}$$

where $|OpR_x|$ is the number of comparative opinion sentences of the entity x, $|R_x|$ is the number of reviews of the entity x and N is the number of years in the analysis.

Knowing the co-existence of brands in comparative sentences is also equally important in order to measure the ratio on which these brands are compared

---

[1] See: http://www.epinions.com/.

within a stipulated time. This will reveal the *competition* between the two compared brands. This ratio can be calculated as follows:

$$Freq(x, y, N) = \frac{\sum_{t_i}^{N} \frac{|OpR_x| \cap |OpR_y|}{|R_x|}}{N}$$

where $|OpR_x|$ and $|OpR_y|$ is the number of comparative opinion sentences of the entity x and y respectively, and $|R_x|$ the number of reviews of the entity x.

The following formula shows how temporal elements could be useful in finding the preference of an entity versus another entity for a specific duration of time. This kind of temporal presentation reveals the trend between these two entities from the perspective of the reviewers and is calculated as follows:

$$Pref(x, y, N) = \sum_{t_i}^{N} \frac{Pref(x, y)}{N}$$

where $Pref(x, y)$ is the preference of the entity x compared to entity y and is calculated as follows:

$$Pref(x, y) = \frac{|Pos_{x,y}|}{|OpR_{x,y}|}$$

where $|Pos_{x,y}|$ is the number of positives reviews of x over y and $|OpR_{x,y}|$ is the number of the common comparative opinion sentences of the entities x and y.

4.2   Trend Analysis

Trend analysis is important for knowing the preference of brands from a temporal perspective. Research on identifying trend in digital libraries started many years ago. Temporal analysis of opinions is useful to identify the most popular entities. There is much research focused on trend analysis using mere opinions. Mehmood et al. [23] focused on trend analysis using social media content and analyzed how people think, assess, discuss and present different issues. However, they did not explore how the different issues are preferred compared to another. Zhou et al. [36] focused on trend of sentiment analysis for social events but they did not take into consideration the trend analysis of comparative opinions on events. To the best of our knowledge, past research on trend analysis did not reveal the preference of one entity compared to another on comparative opinions and failed to incorporate temporal perspective. The main focus was on comparing documents or data rather than dealing directly with comparative documents and comparative data that already existed in libraries. These kind of documents and data are very valuable as they provide more precise information compared to non-comparative.

Figures 2a and b show the trend of preference of *Nikon* over *Canon* and *Sony* over *Canon*. Both figures show that *Canon* is always preferred compared to *Nikon* and *Sony* except on the year 2001 and 2005. In 2001, *Sony's* preference was on par with *Canon* (i.e. 50% each). Meanwhile in 2005, *Nikon* surprisingly

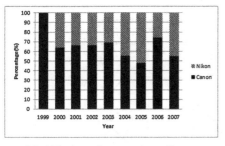
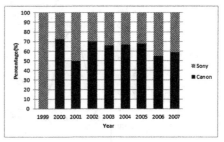

(a) *Nikon* preference over *Canon*   (b) *Sony* preference over *Canon*

Fig. 2. Trend analysis

overtook *Canon*. As there is no comparative review made for *Sony* preference over *Canon* on 1999 in the dataset, the respective column is left empty (Fig. 2b). The figure also shows that *Sony* and *Nikon* are steadily compared with *Canon* from 2000 until 2007. This trend analysis helps users to decide among the options available and business organizations such as *Canon* in knowing their rivals from the users' comparative perspective. This helps in detecting their strengths as well as their weaknesses. It also shows the sustainability of an entity and its reputation.

4.3 Competitive Analysis

Competitive analysis is very important for companies as it can reveal useful information about their popularity across customers in relation to their competitors. In other words, a company can use competitive analysis to see the proportion of positive compared to negative comparative reviews they received. This is important for their marketing and strategic management decision making process. Past research on competitive analysis focused on opinions and not on comparative opinions. This is evident from several research that used user generated data in mining competitive analysis [7,12].

This section explores the use of temporal elements in competitive analysis of an entity based on comparative opinions. We have chosen *Canon* since it is the most popular camera brand in the dataset. This analysis exhibits information given by the opinion holder referring to preferences of *Canon* over other brands (Fig. 3). On the other hand, the preference of other brands compared to *Canon* is also analyzed and since this shows a negative effect on *Canon*, we classified these comparative reviews as negative.

We use the same graphical representation that was used by Alves et al. [3] for sentiment analysis of tweets. The positive side indicates the preference of *Canon* versus other brands and vice versa. From this analysis, we observe that there is a inverse effect on the preference of *Canon*. When *Canon* became the preferred brand, the opinion holders also preferred other brands over *Canon*. This is evident in 2000. Meanwhile there is a significant drop in year 2001 which shows

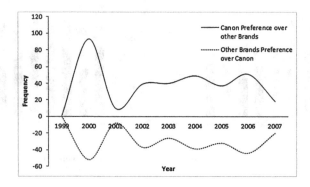

Fig. 3. Competitive analysis: *Canon* preference over other brands and viceversa

that preference of *Canon* over other brands did not receive much comparative opinions among opinion holders. The overall competitive analysis reveals that a great competition exists between *Canon* and other brands and no monopolization effect was found.

4.4   Burst Detection

Burst detection can be useful when tracking emerging topics or entities on large volumes of documents streams including scientific literatures, archives, etc. Besides these document sources, a burst can be triggered and detected widely in social media which contain real time data. The accessibility and availability of real time data has contributed mainly for the burst. Burst can be identified when there is a sudden change in the data stream. Bursts in opinions can influence users and may affect the decision of a future purchaser or service seeker.

Bursts can also be caused by spammers; a study by Wang et al. [33] indicated that spammers are creating fake reviews to mislead the consumers. This is because they understood that burst can influence and decide the future of a product or service in terms of whether this product or service is going to grow or loose. Research by Maynard et al. [22] focused on detecting burst by visualizing opinion dynamics based on time. Meanwhile research by Bjorkelund and Burnett [4] managed to detect burst from hotel reviews that were provided by the travelers. All this research is only concentrating on opinionated text and not specifically on comparative opinions or comparative data, thus the results obtained only show the sudden increase or decrease in the popularity of an object rather than preference.

Temporal analysis on burst detection of comparative opinion show that it can be explicitly seen as happening in the preference of *Canon* over *Pentax* (see Fig. 4). The preference of *Canon* over *Pentax* raised steadily from 2001 until 2006. This shows that between these two brands, the preference of *Canon* overtook the preference of *Pentax* as years passed by.

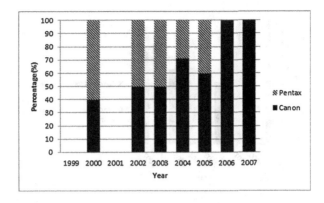

Fig. 4. Burst detection: *Canon* preference over *Pentax*

5   Comparison Between Temporal Analysis of Opinion and Comparative Opinion Mining

This section shows the comparison of temporal analytical presentation of opinion and comparative opinion mining. This comparison is essential to further strengthening the effect and usefulness of temporal analysis on comparative opinion mining.

We compare *Canon* to *Pentax* with respect to opinions and comparative opinions. Figure 5 shows that there is a exponential growth over time in preference of *Canon* over *Pentax*. On the other hand, the opinion of *Canon* versus *Pentax* shows that *Canon* obtained a very high score compared to *Pentax*. This finding clearly shows that opinion analysis alone does not reveal the preference of one brand over another based on time. Besides that, it also indicates that the most talked about brand is not necessarily the preferred brand. The opinion holder may have shared their negative opinion on this brand and this influences the ratio. This kind of information is very useful for business organizations and for people when they want to take decisions.

The comparison between *Canon* and *Pentax* shows that temporal analysis of comparative mining managed to give precise information. This can help many business organizations to detect the strengths and weaknesses of their own brand or their competitors within a given time. They can also make use of the growth or loss effect on their brand compared to others. If there is a growth or loss in all the other brands, this could be based on external factors that they need to look at. For example, if there is a drop in preference of all the camera brands, it could be due to the growth of mobile phones that include a camera. People might be prone to buying phones with better camera features rather than buying a camera. The comparison also shows that fluctuation between preference can be easily viewed and identified with temporal elements in comparative opinion mining. On the other hand, it can be hard to notice it by analyzing plain opinions.

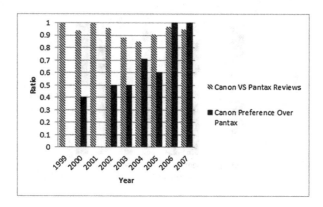

Fig. 5. Comparison of reviews and comparative reviews: *Canon* and *Pentax*

6 Conclusions

In this paper, we explored comparative opinion mining from a temporal perspective. We believe that the temporal aspect can be useful for many business organizations as well as individuals in taking decisions. An important finding of our study is the usefulness of temporal analytical presentation of comparative opinion mining. Business organizations will be able to evaluate their products compared to their rivals from users' perspective. Online consumers also can benefit from this information in making purchase decisions.

In the context of digital libraries opinion mining and in particular comparative opinion mining can be useful in the analysis of libraries customers' reviews and opinions with the aim to draw some temporal analysis of possible improvements in services offered. Temporal analysis of comparative opinions can also be useful to identify customers' emerging or fading interests to direct the acquisition policies of digital libraries. These are just a few of the possible applications of this type of analysis.

Finally, we believe that this study devises a path for new researchers to venture into temporal analysis of digital libraries. Temporal analysis of comparative opinion mining can be extended to comparative document mining, comparative literature mining or even comparative archive mining. In future, we plan to explore features of these entities from a temporal perspective. since this can help for a better understanding of the reasons of change in opinions or the instability of such opinions. Also, we plan to explore sarcasm, irony and spam in opinions and in comparative opinions.

Acknowledgments. This research was partially funded by Swiss Secretariat of Education, Research and Innovation (SERI).

References

1. Adams, A., Blandford, A.: Digital libraries' support for the user's information journey. In: Proceedings of the JCDL2005, pp. 160–169. ACM (2005)
2. Aggarwal, C.C., Zhai, C. (eds.): Mining Text Data. Springer, Heidelberg (2012)
3. Alves, A.L.F., Baptista, C.S., Firmino, A.A., Oliveira, M.G., Figueirêdo, H.F.: Temporal analysis of sentiment in tweets: a case study with FIFA confederations cup in Brazil. In: Decker, H., Lhotská, L., Link, S., Spies, M., Wagner, R.R. (eds.) DEXA 2014. LNCS, vol. 8644, pp. 81–88. Springer, Heidelberg (2014). doi:10.1007/978-3-319-10073-9_7
4. Bjørkelund, E., Burnett, T.H.: Temporal Opinion Mining. Master's thesis, Norwegian University of Science and Technology, Trondheim, Norway (2012)
5. Branavan, S., Chen, H., Eisenstein, J., Barzilay, R.: Learning document-level semantic properties from free-text annotations. J. Artif. Intell. Res. **34**, 569–603 (2009)
6. Cheng, Z., Caverlee, J., Lee, K., Sui, D.Z.: Exploring millions of footprints in location sharing services. In: Proceedings of the ICWSM 2011, vol. 2011, pp. 81–88. AAAI Press (2011)
7. DiGrazia, J., McKelvey, K., Bollen, J., Rojas, F.: More tweets, more votes: social media as a quantitative indicator of political behavior. PLoS ONE **8**(11), e79449 (2013)
8. Figueirêdo, H.F., Lacerda, Y.A., Paiva, A.C., Casanova, M.A., de Souza Baptista, C.: PhotoGeo: a photo digital library with spatial-temporal support and self-annotation. Multimed. Tools Appl. **59**(1), 279–305 (2012)
9. Fujimoto, K.: Investigation of potency-magnitude relations of eWOM messages with a focus on intensified comparative expressions. In: Proceedings of the ICCI*CC 2012, pp. 163–173. IEEE (2012)
10. Gu, Y.H., Yoo, S.J.: Searching a best product based on mining comparison sentences. In: Proceedings of the SCIS & ISIS 2010, vol. 2010, pp. 929–933. Japan Society for Fuzzy Theory and Intelligent Informatics (2010)
11. He, S., Yuan, F., Wang, Y.: Extracting the comparative relations for mobile reviews. In: Proceedings of the CECNet 2012, pp. 3247–3250. IEEE (2012)
12. He, W., Zha, S., Li, L.: Social media competitive analysis and text mining: a case study in the pizza industry. Int. J. Inf. Manage. **33**(3), 464–472 (2013)
13. Jindal, N., Liu, B.: Identifying comparative sentences in text documents. In: Proceedings of the SIGIR 2006, pp. 244–251. ACM (2006)
14. Jindal, N., Liu, B.: Mining comparative sentences and relations. In: Proceedings of the AAAI 2006. pp. 1331–1336. AAAI Press (2006)
15. Jurgens, D., Lu, T.C.: Temporal motifs reveal the dynamics of editor interactions in wikipedia. In: Proceedings of the ICWSM 2012, pp. 162–169. AAAI Press (2012)
16. Keikha, M., Gerani, S., Crestani, F.: Time-based relevance models. In: Proceedings of the SIGIR 2011, pp. 1087–1088. ACM (2011)
17. Kessler, W., Kuhn, J.: Detection of product comparisons-how far does an out-of-the-box semantic role labeling system take you? In: Proceedings of the EMNLP 2013, pp. 1892–1897. ACL (2013)
18. Kessler, W., Kuhn, J.: A corpus of comparisons in product reviews. In: Proceedings of the LREC 2014, pp. 2242–2248. European Language Resources Association (ELRA) (2014)

19. Kurashima, T., Bessho, K., Toda, H., Uchiyama, T., Kataoka, R.: Ranking entities using comparative relations. In: Bhowmick, S.S., Küng, J., Wagner, R. (eds.) DEXA 2008. LNCS, vol. 5181, pp. 124–133. Springer, Heidelberg (2008). doi:10.1007/978-3-540-85654-2_15

20. Liu, B.: Sentiment analysis and opinion mining. Synth. Lect. Hum. Lang. Technol. 5(1), 1–167 (2012)

21. Liu, C., Xu, R., Liu, J., Qu, P., Wang, H., Zou, C.: Comparative opinion sentences identification and elements extraction. In: Proceedings of the ICMLC 2013, vol. 4, pp. 1886–1891. IEEE (2013)

22. Maynard, D., Gossen, G., Funk, A., Fisichella, M.: Should i care about your opinion? Detection of opinion interestingness and dynamics in social media. Future Internet 6(3), 457–481 (2014)

23. Mehmood, A., Palli, A.S., Khan, M.: A study of sentiment and trend analysis techniques for social media content. Int. J. Modern Educ. Comput. Sci. (IJMECS) 6(12), 47 (2014)

24. O'Connor, B., Balasubramanyan, R., Routledge, B.R., Smith, N.A.: From tweets to polls: linking text sentiment to public opinion time series. In: Proceedings of the ICWSM 2010, no. 122–129. AAAI Press (2010)

25. Romero, D.M., Galuba, W., Asur, S., Huberman, B.A.: Influence and passivity in social media. In: Gunopulos, D., Hofmann, T., Malerba, D., Vazirgiannis, M. (eds.) ECML PKDD 2011. LNCS (LNAI), vol. 6913, pp. 18–33. Springer, Heidelberg (2011). doi:10.1007/978-3-642-23808-6_2

26. Sakaki, T., Okazaki, M., Matsuo, Y.: Tweet analysis for real-time event detection and earthquake reporting system development. IEEE Trans. Knowl. Data Eng. 25(4), 919–931 (2013)

27. Sun, J., Long, C., Zhu, X., Huang, M.: Mining reviews for product comparison and recommendation. Polibits 39, 33–40 (2009)

28. Tivy, A., Howell, S.E., Alt, B., McCourt, S., Chagnon, R., Crocker, G., Carrieres, T., Yackel, J.J.: Trends and variability in summer sea ice cover in the Canadian arctic based on the Canadian ice service digital archive, 1960–2008 and 1968–2008. J. Geophys. Res. Oceans 116(C3) (2011). doi:10.1029/2009JC005855

29. Tkachenko, M., Lauw, H.W.: Generative modeling of entity comparisons in text. In: Proceedings of the CIKM 2014, pp. 859–868. ACM (2014)

30. Tremayne, M.: Anatomy of protest in the digital era: a network analysis of twitter and occupy wall street. Soc. Mov. Stud. 13(1), 110–126 (2014)

31. Tu, W., Cheung, D., Mamoulis, N.: Time-sensitive opinion mining for prediction. In: Proceedings of the AAAI 2015. AAAI Press (2015)

32. Varathan, K.D., Giachanou, A., Crestani, F.: Comparative opinion mining: a review. J. Assoc. Inf. Sci. Technol. (2016, in press)

33. Wang, G., Xie, S., Liu, B., Yu, P.S.: Identify online store review spammers via social review graph. ACM Trans. Intell. Syst. Technol. 3(4), 61:1–61:21 (2012)

34. Wang, W., Zhao, T., Xin, G., Xu, Y.: Exploiting machine learning for comparative sentences extraction. Int. J. Hybrid Inf. Technol. 8(3), 347–354 (2015)

35. Xu, K., Liao, S.S., Li, J., Song, Y.: Mining comparative opinions from customer reviews for competitive intelligence. Decis. Support Syst. 50(4), 743–754 (2011)

36. Zhou, X., Tao, X., Yong, J., Yang, Z.: Sentiment analysis on tweets for social events. In: Proceedings of the CSCWD 2013, pp. 557–562. IEEE (2013)

Social Media

Social Q&A Question-and-Comments Interactions and Outcomes: A Social Sequence Analysis

Sei-Ching Joanna Sin[✉], Chei Sian Lee, and Yin-Leng Theng

Wee Kim Wee School of Communication and Information,
Nanyang Technological University, Singapore, Singapore
{joanna.sin,leecs,tyltheng}@ntu.edu.sg

Abstract. Scholars and developers have long recognized that the collections of user-generated content at social questions and answers (SQA) sites can benefit open knowledge sharing and resolve individual information needs. This has prompted strong interest in improving the quality of SQA postings, and the creation, curation, and use of these collections. While interactivity is a key feature of SQA, few studies have investigated the interaction sequence between the OP (original poster) and commenters. Drawing from Robert Taylor's question-negotiation perspective, we posit that interaction patterns may affect SQA outcomes. Social sequence analysis (SSA) and the R package TraMineR were used to analyze the commenting sequences of Stack Overflow postings (8,132 questions and 16,598 comments). The relationships between commenting sequence structure and outcome metrics (e.g., question score, view count) were then tested with logistic regressions. Implications of the results for SQA research, SQA site design, and digital literacy training are discussed.

Keywords: Social Q&A · Question negotiation · Commenting behavior · Social sequence analysis

1 Introduction

The popularity of social questions and answers (SQA) sites, such as Answers.com, Quora, Stack Exchange, and Yahoo! Answers, has helped amass large collections of user-generated content. Some platforms such as Stack Exchange not only allow users to post and rate questions and answers, but users can also comment on and edit questions posted by others. They can also tag, flag, or vote to close (or reopen) a question. These give users the ability to both collectively create and curate collections [1].

These user-generated collections have a strong potential to facilitate public knowledge sharing and to meet individual information needs. To help realize these potentials, many scholars and developers have explored ways to increase the quality of SQA postings and to effectively create, curate, retrieve, and use this user-generated content [2, 3]. Such investigations have included research on predictors of answer quality, classification of questions, and motivation and behavior of users, for example. However, while interactivity and collaboration among users are key characteristics of SQA, few studies have comprehensively investigated the flow of the interaction itself [4].

© Springer International Publishing AG 2016
A. Morishima et al. (Eds.): ICADL 2016, LNCS 10075, pp. 325–338, 2016.
DOI: 10.1007/978-3-319-49304-6_37

Compared to SQA answers, comments (which tend to be short remarks) have received less attention. Efforts to address these research gaps are nascent. Currently, little is known regarding how an entire questioner-commenter conversation thread tends to unfold over time. For example, does the original poster (OP) of the question usually post additional messages in response to others' comments? Would different interaction patterns make a difference? The dearth of such investigations hinders a thorough understanding of user behavior and the potential antecedents to receiving quality answers.

To contribute toward understanding user interaction patterns and outcomes, this study drew inspiration from Robert Taylor's question-negotiation perspective [5]. Librarians often conduct reference interviews to guide users to better identify and express their actual need. We posit that the interactions between the OP and commenters in SQA can be viewed as a question-negotiation process. Due to the asynchronicity and open nature of SQA, we hypothesize that the SQA negotiation pattern can be more diverse than that of traditional reference interactions. Empirical analysis is thus needed to investigate the questioner-commenter interaction sequences as well as test whether these sequences make a difference in the answer outcomes. Specifically, this study addresses the following research questions:

- RQ1: What are the properties of the questioner-commenter interaction sequence as a whole (e.g., length, whole-sequence pattern, representative sequence)?
- RQ2: Do these sequence patterns contribute to different outcomes (e.g., question scores, number of answers)?

To investigate these questions, we applied social sequence analysis (SSA), which is a set of techniques for researchers to "study, measure, classify and visualize sequences of social phenomena" (p. 21) [6]. SSA is gaining attention but is rarely used in SQA research. Currently, the dearth of research on the entire SQA interaction sequence may be partly attributed to methodological issues. Studying an entire sequence of temporal data requires extra effort, particularly in operationalizing and quantifying the properties of the whole-sequence pattern. These efforts are important for developing valid and parsimonious measures. SSA can help bridge this methodological problem.

To the best of our knowledge, this is the first study that analyzed the SQA question-comment sequence as a whole using SSA. This study's contributions are threefold. First, on a conceptual level, we theorized the SQA question-comment sequence as a question-negotiation process. In addition, by focusing on the entire interaction sequence, we proposed a novel line of research on predictors of answer quality. Second, on the method level, the study tested the use of SSA, which will broaden the repertoire of SQA research methods. Third, from an empirical standpoint, the findings will provide insights in whether certain interaction patterns contribute to better outcomes. These findings can inform digital literacy training to guide SQA users on effective ways to interact. Site developers may also draw from this line of interaction-pattern research to develop features that help users enact certain effective interaction patterns.

2 Literature Review

2.1 Predictors of Answer Quality

Attesting to the significance of SQA, there are many streams of research on this topic. One central stream of research investigates the predictors of answer quality. The more frequently investigated predictors can be broadly grouped into the following categories: (1) message-related predictors, which can be subdivided into (1a) the nature of the question (e.g., domain, topic, type of questions) [e.g., 7, 8], and (1b) the presentation of the question (e.g., linguistic features such as readability, sentiment) [e.g., 8–10]; (2) user-related predictors (e.g., user expertise, reputation, prior efforts, tie strengths) [e.g., 9–12]; and (3) platform- and community-related predictors (e.g., design features of the site, nature and size of the community, community norms) [e.g., 2, 8].

For the message-related predictors of answer quality, the unit of observation tends to be on the individual posting. Receiving little investigation is the nature of the entire conversation thread (i.e., the whole sequence of back-and-forth conversations among posters) [4]. From a gestalt perspective, the sum is more than its parts. Beyond studying individual components (the individual posting), investigating the entire sequence may provide additional insights into SQA user behaviors and answer outcomes.

2.2 SQA Interaction Patterns

Research that help to address the gap on interaction sequence is nascent. While the few extant studies differ from the current paper in that they either do not cover the entire sequence or are focused on a different aspect of the pattern, and SSA is not used, they are invaluable in demonstrating the contribution of examining SQA interactions.

In a study of the SQA site Answerbag, Gazan investigated *microcollaborations*, which is defined as "brief, informal expressions of mutual interest and mutual effort toward seeking information on a given topic" (p. 693) [13]. Pertinent to interaction patterns is the analysis of the "locations of microcollaborations" (p. 698), which focus on location pairs. Among 122 pairs, "answer-comment" was the most frequently found pattern. This is followed by "comment-subsequent comment" and "link-new question" [13]. While the study did not use SSA, this location-pair analysis was akin to the study of substrings—specifically, *two-gram*—in SSA.

A focus on pairs of users is also prominent in Liu and Jansen's study of 1,003 questions and 4,901 corresponding replies from Sina Weibo [4]. The study explored the frequency of interaction between unique questioner and answerer pairs, and 2,206 instances were found. A plurality of these pairs interacted only once [4].

The two studies above focused on the frequency of interaction and had pairs of users as a unit. Savolainen [14] presents a fresh angle of research that examines the substance of the interaction, specifically, the argument patterns. The study went beyond pairs of interaction to include multiple steps. The *mixed* pattern, for example, comprises an initial claim, counterclaim(s) and/or rebuttal(s), and support. Among the sample of 100 Yahoo! Answers threads (1,020 messages) that discuss global warming, failed opening was found most frequently, followed by oppositional, nonoppositional, and mixed patterns

[14]. While our paper focused on structural properties of the conversation sequence (and not the substance of the conversation), the two studies share an underlying view. The view is that the back-and-forth exchanges among SQA users can affect how the thread and the topic are perceived. For example, the findings suggest that oppositional and mixed patterns are advantageous for other readers when evaluating the credibility of the answers [14]. In the present study, we similarly posit that the conversations among posters can be impactful on the answer outcomes. Our proposition is inspired by Taylor's question-negotiation process, which is discussed below.

2.3   Taylor's Question-Negotiation Process

Taylor's formulation of question-negotiation process was developed in the early years of computerized retrieval systems and is still influential in the training of reference librarians. Taylor conceptualized information seeking among human sources as a nego-tiation process in which "one person tries to describe for another person not something he knows, but rather something he does not know" (p. 180) [5]. Taylor observed that when an individual first articulates his/her information need, the initial question does not always neatly reflect the individual's actual unexpressed need (i.e., the visceral need). Extra efforts are required to uncover the visceral need through a negotiation process. Librarians are thus trained to conduct reference interviews, in order to guide the inquirer to better express his/her information need [5].

We propose that the conversation between questioner and commenters can be conceptualized as a question-negotiation process. It has been observed that in SQA, the OP does not always ask a question clearly or provide sufficient information [15]. Commenters may ask the questioner for clarifications or suggest ways to improve the questions. These comments may improve the quality of the question and thus enhance the likelihood of the question being rated positively by other users and achieving a high Question Score, as well as getting quality answers. On the other hand, commenters have been observed to express disapproval (e.g., chastising OPs for cross-posting) or some-times even challenge the value of a particular question. Depending on if and how the OP responds, some interactions may negatively affect the answer outcomes. The SQA interaction is a relatively open process, potentially involving users of varying skills and worldviews. Such interactions on SQA are likely to be more diverse than the one-to-one interaction between a library user and a trained librarian. This diversity renders the interactions among SQA users less predictable and fascinating to study.

3   Research Method

3.1   Data Collection Method

A nonreactive data collection method was used in this study to analyze the raw posting data made available by the Stack Exchange Network (SE). The nonreactive method had the advantages of avoiding naturalistic generalization issues, which may be caused by artificial experimental settings. Social desirability issues, for which respondents may alter their behavior or give inaccurate responses when they know they are being studied, are also avoided.

3.2 Sampling Design

This study focused on Stack Overflow (SO), an SQA for programmers. It is the largest among the 156 SQA communities under SE. The design of SO and other SE sites affords specific SQA analyses. This is because the site allows users to post comments to a question or to a specific answer, and to rate the question and answers separately. This allows fine-grained analysis, particularly for studies such as the current one that seek to analyze questioner-commenter interactions in detail. SO was also chosen for its prominence. It hosted 12 million questions, has 5.8 million users, and has received 5.7 billion page views [16].

The current analysis used the official March 2016 raw data in XML format, which was made available by SE under the CC BY-SA 3.0 license [17]. For this exploratory study, we selected a small section of the SO site. All the questions asked on February 1, 2016 and all the comments related to these questions were selected. We chose February 1st so that the sample will include at least one month's worth of comments (the cut-off date for this dataset is March 6, 2016). This sample frame yielded a total of 24,730 postings. This number included 8,132 questions posted on SO on February 1, 2016 and 16,598 comments in response to those questions.

3.3 Data Analysis Method

SSA. The study applied social sequences analysis (SSA), also called sequential analysis or sequence analysis. SSA is often used to study "empirically observed, temporally ordered regularities" (p. 22) [6]. However, it is versatile and is also used for studying other orders, such as spatial order, preference order, and cognitive schema. SSA techniques allow researchers to "treat the whole sequences as units of study" (p. 3) [6]. SSA is in part inspired by research in biology, such as on DNA sequences. It has been applied in areas such as sociology, psychology, life-course research, and time-use studies. Thongtanunam and colleagues applied SSA in their research on finding expertise in Stack Exchange. The study focused on SQA users, specifically, their badge achievement history [18]. The SQA postings and the interaction sequence − the topic of the current study − were not examined.

Overall, application of SSA in SQA research has been rare. We postulated that SSA can complement popular sequence analysis methods such as high-order or hidden Markov chains, especially in cases such as SQA posting sequences. This is because the number of states (e.g., unique users in each sequence, 17 for this sample set) and the length of the posting sequences can be high (e.g., 55 for this sample set), which could render analyzing the entire sequence with high-order or hidden Markov chains difficult. Given SSA's focus on the temporal dimension and its ability to analyze long interaction sequences, it is a promising method for studying SQA postings.

Data preparation. The raw data required several stages of preparation, so the final dataset was arranged as a question-comment sequence that is suitable for subsequent SSA. The steps are as follows.

(1) The posts.xml and comments.xml data were linked using the *Id* and *PostId* fields.
(2) The sequence within each thread was ordered using the timestamp of the postings.
(3) The *UserId* indicated whether the postings within a thread were from the same or different users. We derived a schema to transform *UserId* to an abstract form that reflected the user's structural position in the sequence. The following procedures were used, with the result that each unique poster within a particular thread was assigned a unique code. The code assigned was based on the position where the unique poster *first* appeared in a thread.

The steps were: (3a) The OP, who initiates the question, always appears first in each thread. Therefore, OP in this study is always designated as *A* (shown in burgundy in Figs. 1 and 2). (3b) Other unique users were assigned a unique code from *B* onwards. For example, a unique poster who first showed up in the 2nd position in the thread (which is the first comment) will be designated as *B*. The unique poster who joined the conversation thread in the 3rd position is *C,* and so forth. To give a hypothetical example, assume that thread 1 is: John-Emma-John-Max-Emma and thread 2 is Emma-Beth-John-Emma-Max-Beth-Aiden. The transformed sequence for thread 1 is: A-B-A-D-B. Thread 2 would become: A-B-C-A-E-B-G. It can be seen here that the codes reflect structural positions within a specific thread. The name/ID of the person is not reflected in the transformed sequences (e.g., Emma is coded as *B* in thread 1, but as *A* in thread 2). This is different from social network analysis, in which the name/ID of the poster is often used.

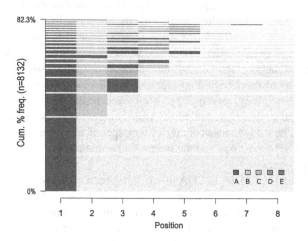

Fig. 1. Top-20 whole-sequence patterns

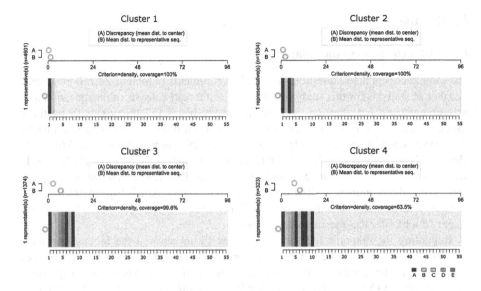

Fig. 2. Representative sequences of the four clusters

(4) The transformed sequences were then loaded into TraMineR for further analysis.

Analysis: RQ1. SSA was used to measure the most frequently occurring whole-sequence pattern (WSP) for the entire dataset. Clustering was then used to identify the core and distinctive sequence patterns. This is done by first computing dissimilarity measures, followed by a hierarchical cluster analysis using the *Cluster* package with the Ward method that seeks to minimize residual variance [19]. The characteristics of these distinctive clusters, specifically their representative sequences, were then presented to examine how SQA questioners and commenters tend to interact.

Analysis: RQ2. RQ2 investigated the relationships between sequence patterns (i.e., cluster membership from RQ1) and four outcomes (Question Score, View Count, Answer Count, Accepted Answer). Accepted Answer is a dichotomous variable (*yes* or *no*), capturing whether the OP has picked one answer as the accepted answer. The other three outcome variables were continuous. Data diagnostics indicated that the distributions of the continuous outcome variables were non-normal. They were, therefore, dichotomized to indicate either *low* or *high* levels using the sample mean as the cutoff point. Logistic regressions were then conducted for all four analyses in RQ2.

Software. The sample data were parsed, linked, and analyzed with R [20]. SSA was conducted with the TraMineR package [21] and supplemented by the WeightedCluster package [22]. The Cluster package [19] was used for hierarchical clustering analysis. Logistic regressions were conducted using the glm function.

4   Results

4.1   Characteristics of the Sample

The sample covers 8,132 questions and 16,598 comments (a total of 24,730 postings). The unit of analysis for this study is a thread. Each thread consists of one question and all comments to that question. In total, the study has 8,132 threads, with postings contributed by 11,437 unique users. On average, each thread involves approximately two posters (including the OP) ($M = 1.98$, $SD = 1.19$, Median (Mdn) = 2, Min. = 1, Max. = 17). On average, each question received 2.04 comments ($SD = 2.92$, $Mdn = 1$, Min. = 0, Max. = 54). Frequency counts show that slightly fewer than half of the questions received no comment at all ($n = 3953$, 48.6 %). Among the 4,729 questions (58.2 %) that did receive comments, on average, the first comment appeared 23,135.64 s (approximately 6.4 h) after the question was posted.

Regarding the outcome measures, the View Count showed the highest variation ($M = 41.23$, $SD = 78.35$, $Mdn = 34$, Min. = 2, Max. = 4,892). The Question Score, which reflects the number of up votes minus the number of down votes a question received from SQA users, also showed a wide range ($M = 0.42$, $SD = 2.20$, $Mdn = 0$, Min. = 11, Max. = 114). Nevertheless, its variation is not as marked as that of the View Count. The Answer Count is relatively low; on average there were 1.08 answers per question ($SD = 0.99$, $Mdn = 1$, Min. = 0, Max. = 7). Only 38.5 % ($n = 3,131$) of the threads have an accepted answer.

4.2   RQ1: Properties of the Interaction Sequence

Sequence length. The sequence length in the sample varies quite notably. The shortest sequence has a length of one (A); that is, the thread contains only the question. There is no comment. The longest sequence length is 55 with the following pattern: A-B-A-D-E-F-A-H-A-J-K-L-D-A-K-A-J-K-A-A-J-L-A-A-B-L-AA-A-A-L-A-AA-L-AH-AI-L-AH-A-A-AA-A-L-A-AA-A-AA-AU-AV-AH-AX-A-E-BA-A-BC. This sequence involves 17 unique posters. The OP (coded as A) showed up 20 times in this thread. For the entire sample ($N = 8,132$), the average sequence length is 3.04 ($SD = 2.92$).

Top whole-sequence patterns (WSPs). Figure 1 shows the top 20 most frequently occurring WSPs. In the figure, alphabets A to E represent unique users. The x-axis (Position) indicates the location of a particular SQA posting in the entire interaction sequence, where 1 is the first posting (i.e., the question). The y-axis shows the percentage cumulative frequency of pattern occurrence. These top-20 WSPs account for 82.3 % of the sample. The lowest row in the figure shows the most-frequent pattern, which is A (i.e., question only). The second most-frequent pattern is A-B (a question and a comment from different users), followed by A-B-A (in which the OP came back to respond to another user's comment), A-B-C (three users, each contributing once), and A-B-A-B (a back-and-forth conversation pattern between the OP and a commenter).

Distinctive WSPs. The discussion, thus far, has presented the properties of the entire sample set. The next steps involved identifying distinctive WSPs among the 8,132 threads. This was conducted by first calculating the distance/dissimilarity matrix (the distance between all pairs of sequences) in TraMineR. The optimal matching (OM) matrix was computed and then used for hierarchical cluster analysis with the Ward method. A 4-cluster solution was selected with the aid of cluster quality measures (e.g., Point Biserial Correlation and the CH index), which were used for comparing the quality of the clustering solutions based on different number of clusters. These measures were calculated with the WeightedCluster package [22].

The representative sequence (RS) for the four clusters was identified using TraMineR. RS serves as a summary of a set of categorical sequences, which is otherwise hard to identify. Using the dissimilarity matrix and a search algorithm based on a criterion, such as neighborhood density, TraMineR is able to extract the key features of a sequence set [21]. Figure 2 shows the resultant RSs.

Figure 2 shows the RS of each cluster. Alphabets A to E represent unique users in the sequence, with A indicating the OP. Similar to Fig. 1, the x-axis in Fig. 2 reflects the position of a posting in the entire sequence. For example, for Cluster 1, Position 1 is occupied by A. This is interpreted as the first posting in the sequence (the question) was posted by user A (the OP). Position 2 of Cluster 1 is occupied by B. This is interpreted as the second posting in the sequence was posted by a different user (user B).

C1 covers 4,601 sequences (56.6 % of the sample), which is the largest among the four clusters. The RS of C1 has the shortest sequence length (two steps only). The A-B pattern indicates a question and a comment posted by two users. C2 has 1,834 sequences (22.6 %). This RS is slightly longer (four steps), showing an A-B-A-D sequence. This reflects slightly more user participation. There were three different posters, and the OP came back to post a comment. C3 includes 1,374 sequences (16.9 %). Its RS shows an A-B-C-D-E-A-C-A pattern. The sequence is notably longer (eight steps). In the beginning part of the RS, there is a consecutive sequence of postings by different users (A-B-C-D-E), hinting at some diversity. This is followed by a second part (A-C-A) in which the OP (A) began to engage in commenting, and another poster (C) also commented again. C4 covers 323 sequences (4.0 %), the smallest among the four clusters. Its RS pattern is A-B-C-D-A-B-A-A-B-A. This is the longest among the four clusters (10 steps). The OP showed relatively high engagement. However, there were fewer unique posters involved (four posters) than in C3 (five posters). A notable part of the sequence (the second part: A-B-A-A-B-A) indicates rather active interactions between two users (OP and commenter B).

Overall, C1 represents a minimal interaction sequence. C2 represents a short interaction sequence in which the OP shows some level of engagement as shown by his/her replying to a comment once. C3 shows a rather lively interaction sequence. The pattern involves several posters. The OP is relatively active in replying to others' comments, but not to the point of dominating the interaction. C4 shows notable interactions in terms of number of postings. At the same time, the pattern is not as diverse as C3. The OP in C4 participates actively; half of the postings in the sequence is from the OP.

4.3   RQ2: Relationship Between Sequence Patterns and Outcomes

With the four distinctive sequence patterns identified through the analysis in RQ1, we tested whether the different patterns would see different outcomes. Four logistic regressions were conducted, one for each outcome variable (Question Score, View Count, Answer Count, Accepted Answer). As discussed in Sect. 3.3, after data processing, all four outcome variables are dichotomous (*low* or *high* for the first three outcomes; *no* or *yes* for Accepted Answer). The independent variable is Cluster Membership. This is based on the hierarchical cluster analysis identified in RQ1, where each sequence was classed into one of the four clusters. In the logistic regression analysis, the reference group is Cluster 1 (hereafter, *Cluster* will be denoted as *C*). The odds ratio (*OR*) serves as an effect size measure. An *OR* larger than 1 indicates a higher likelihood of a better outcome (in the *high/yes* outcome category) than in the reference group (C1).

Statistically significant differences by cluster membership are found for all four outcomes. Table 1 summarizes the results. Specifically, for Question Score, C4 is significantly different from the reference group (C1). The *OR* is 1.59, indicating that threads in C4 have 1.59 times higher odds than C1 to be in the *high* Question Score category. C2 and C3 show no statistically significant differences from C1. For View Count, C2, C3, and C4 are all significantly different from C1. Their *OR*s are especially notable ($OR_{C2} = 1.88$, $OR_{C3} = 2.97$, $OR_{C4} = 8.11$), indicating higher odds of having higher view counts than C1. The *OR* for C4 is particularly high. Results for Answer Count are similar to that of View Count. All three clusters are significant. The main difference is that the *OR*s for Answer Count ($OR_{C2} = 1.44$, $OR_{C3} = 1.45$, $OR_{C4} = 1.72$) are not as high as those for View Count. Here, the *OR*s for C2 and C3 are quite similar. For Accepted Answer, only one significant result was found. C3 has slightly higher odds (1.13 times higher) than C1 to be in the *yes* (has accepted answer) category.

Table 1. Logisitic regression results: cluster sequence patterns and outcomes ($N = 8{,}132$)

Cluster	Question score			View count		
	z	OR	p	z	OR	p
C2	1.43	1.09	0.152	10.72	1.88	0.000[***]
C3	1.80	1.13	0.072	17.08	2.97	0.000[***]
C4	3.92	1.59	0.000[***]	16.05	8.11	0.000[***]
Cluster	Answer count			Accepted answer		
	z	OR	p	z	OR	p
C2	5.79	1.44	0.000[***]	1.40	1.08	0.162
C3	5.37	1.45	0.000[***]	1.97	1.13	0.049[*]
C4	4.38	1.72	0.000[***]	1.80	1.23	0.072

Note: Reference group: Cluster 1. * $p < .05$; ** $p < .01$; *** $p < .001$

5 Discussion

The study investigated the sequence and outcomes of SQA questioner-commenters interaction using SSA. To the best of our knowledge, this is one of the first studies of its kind on this topic. The results showed several distinctive WSP patterns, suggesting that from a methodological standpoint, SSA can be a useful analytic tool for SQA inter-action sequence research. The current analysis found that the most frequent WSP was A (a question without any comment). The sample means for the number of comments and the number of posters per thread were relatively low (Sect. 4.1). This is in line with prior studies that found a notable portion of SQA questions did not receive much atten-tion [4]. At the same time, the current study also shows the other side of the spectrum, in which long sequence and complex interaction patterns were exhibited.

When examining the top WSPs (Fig. 1), the structural positions of the OP is worth discussing. By design, OPs would always appear in the first position. Beyond that, Fig. 1 shows that in many of the top 20 sequences, the OPs re-appear in subsequent positions (often multiple times). This reflects relatively active engagement by these OPs in responding to the comments of others. The RSs of three of the four clusters (Fig. 2) also reveal a back-and-forth pattern involving the OP (C2: A-B-A; C3: A-C-A; C4: A-B-A, which happened twice). Given these findings, we propose that future studies investigate the OPs positional pattern in more depth. SSA techniques, such as on substrings (partial sequences), position reports, and transition matrices, can be applied to focus on the participation and turn-taking behavior of the OPs. If and how these OP posting patterns contribute to the answer outcomes can then be tested.

The logistic regression analyses on RQ2 found statistically significant differences in outcome measures by cluster membership (which represents the four distinctive WSP clusters discovered in RQ1). The overall implication from RQ2 is that more complex patterns (e.g., C3 and C4) tend to have higher likelihoods of receiving better outcomes (e.g., receiving favorable ratings on the quality of the question, as reflected by a high Question Score; receiving more answers) than short interaction sequences (C1).

In terms of research implication, the above finding is in line with Taylor's question-negotiation perspective, suggesting that nuanced negotiation can contribute to better information seeking outcomes. Further analysis of SQA interactions using the question-negotiation perspective is thus promising. There are also two practical implications. Digital literacy training may encourage users to post and respond to comments (which are usually relatively short and may not take too much of the users' time). SQA devel-opers may also design their site in a way that facilitates the posting and viewing of the comments. This is a strength of SO and SE, in which the comments on the questions and on the answers are in separate sections. Comments on the questions are displayed immediately below the questions, which can help users to view the comments in context. Other sites do not always provide such features. Users will have to circumvent the site design [13] by putting their comments in the answers section, where they may be less visible to readers. This may subsequently reduce the impact of those comments.

When examining the results in more depth, based on the number of significant differences and the *ORs* in RQ2, out of the four outcome measures, View Count varied with WSP cluster patterns the most. This is followed by Answer Count, Question Score, and finally Accepted Answer. The finding that Accepted Answer saw the least variations with WSP cluster patterns is particularly interesting. Accepted Answer is used quite frequently as a measure of answer quality in SQA studies. Here, C3 was found to be significant (but not C4, which was significant in all other outcomes and had high ORs). A key difference between C3 and C4 is that while C4 had the longest sequence and frequent participation from the OP, C3 had the highest number of unique posters.

We posit that while OP's active engagement can contribute to better outcomes, having more unique posters may bring a different nature of positive contribution to the answer outcomes. This may involve a mechanism similar to the strength of weak ties. Higher numbers of unique posters could bring in more diverse perspectives and recommendations, thus contributing to a better likelihood of receiving an acceptable answer. Future studies may test this tentative hypothesis further. Whether users are more keen in responding to active questions (e.g., those with more comments and interactions), thus establishing a positive feedback loop; and whether OPs with high level of participation (e.g., C4) tend to be more reluctant in accepting answers are also questions that would benefit from further examination. Answers to these questions would deepen our understanding of the SQA question-negotiation process. They will help provide the basis for conceptualizing and expanding Taylor's question-negotiation perspective for studying SQA, in which question-negotiations are no longer guided by an information professional, but by multiple users with diverse skills, experience, and motivations.

Several areas of future research can be identified. The current study has the limitation of focusing on a sample set within one SQA community under SE. Thus, the results may not be generalizable to other SQA communities or sites due to different community norms and site designs. Comparative studies involving multiple communities and sites would help test whether the results of this study are also observed in other sites. In terms of research focus, the current study investigated only structural (positional) properties of the conversation sequence and only analyzed whole-sequence patterns. The narrow scope of this study is due to the dearth of detailed research on these two areas. Given that the current study has found significant differences in structural positions, which indicate that research in this new area can yield insights, we propose an additional layer of research. We propose to draw from prior studies on the semantics, arguments, and sentiments of SQA postings [e.g., 9, 14, 23, 24], and combine these analyses with SSA. That is, future research can trace how the style, substance, and mood of the conversation sequence unfolds over time. Analysis can then be conducted to test whether answer outcomes vary with the aforesaid conversation patterns.

6   Conclusion

The current study applied social sequence analysis to examine the question-comment sequence in 8,132 Stack Overflow threads. Notable variations in sequence length and whole-sequence patterns were found. Four clusters of distinctive patterns were identified, and the logistic regression results indicate that more complex and diverse sequences tend to have better answer outcomes. We posit that the behavior of the OP and the properties of unique posters are interesting areas for further research. We also propose leveraging social sequence analysis to investigate additional properties of the interaction sequence (e.g., textual, argumentation, and affective properties), as well as expanding Taylor's question-negotiation perspective for SQA interaction research. This new line of research will be of use to studies of user behavior and the question-negotiation process, digital literacy training, SQA site design, and SQA research methods. It will contribute to a deeper understanding of users' interactions on SQA, and help inform the development and provision of SQA applications and training. Ultimately, concrete efforts in these areas will bring us closer to quality SQA questions and answers, as well as effective open knowledge sharing.

Acknowledgements. This work was supported by the Nanyang Technological University Academic Research Fund (RG58/14) of Nanyang Technological University.

References

1. Ahn, J., Butler, B.S., Weng, C., Webster, S.: Learning to be a better q'er in social Q&A sites: social norms and information artifacts. Proc. Am. Soc. Inf. Sci. Technol. **50**, 1–10 (2013)
2. Shah, C., Oh, S., Oh, J.S.: Research agenda for social Q&A. Libr. Inf. Sci. Res. **31**, 205–209 (2009)
3. Gazan, R.: Social Q&A. J. Am. Soc. Inf. Sci. Technol. **62**, 2301–2312 (2011)
4. Liu, Z., Jansen, B.J.: Question and answering made interactive: an exploration of interactions in social Q&A. In: 2013 International Conference on Social Intelligence and Technology, pp. 1–10 (2013)
5. Taylor, R.S.: Question-negotiation and information seeking in libraries. Coll. Res. Libr. **29**, 178–194 (1968)
6. Cornwell, B.: Social sequence analysis: methods and applications. Cambridge University Press, New York (2015)
7. Chua, A.Y.K., Banerjee, S.: Where to ask and how to ask? The case of community question answering sites. In: Science and Information Conference (SAI) 2014, pp. 888–895 (2014)
8. Harper, F.M., Raban, D., Rafaeli, S., Konstan, J.A.: Predictors of answer quality in online Q&A sites. In: Proceedings of the SIGCHI Conference on Human Factors in Computing Systems, pp. 865–874. ACM, Florence, Italy (2008)
9. Agichtein, E., Castillo, C., Donato, D., Gionis, A., Mishne, G.: Finding high-quality content in social media. In: Proceedings of the 2008 International Conference on Web Search and Data Mining, pp. 183–194. ACM, Palo Alto, California, USA (2008)
10. Baltadzhieva, A., Chrupa, G.: Question quality in community question answering forums: a survey. SIGKDD Explor. Newsl. **17**, 8–13 (2015)
11. Saha, R.K., Saha, A.K., Perry, D.E.: Toward understanding the causes of unanswered questions in software information sites: a case study of Stack Overflow. In: Proceedings of the 2013 9th Joint Meeting on Foundations of Software Engineering, pp. 663–666. ACM, Saint Petersburg, Russia (2013)
12. Jeon, J., Croft, W.B., Lee, J.H., Park, S.: A framework to predict the quality of answers with non-textual features. In: Proceedings of the 29th Annual International ACM SIGIR Conference on Research and Development in Information Retrieval, pp. 228–235. ACM, Seattle, Washington, USA (2006)
13. Gazan, R.: Microcollaborations in a social Q&A community. Inf. Process. Manage. **46**, 693–702 (2010)

14. Savolainen, R.: The structure of argument patterns on a social Q&A site. J. Am. Soc. Inf. Sci. Technol. **63**, 2536–2548 (2012)
15. Nam, K.K., Ackerman, M.S., Adamic, L.A.: Questions in, knowledge in?: a study of Naver's question answering community. In: Proceedings of the SIGCHI Conference on Human Factors in Computing Systems, pp. 779–788. ACM, Boston, MA, USA (2009)
16. Stack Exchange: About (2016). http://stackexchange.com/about
17. Stack Exchange: Data dump (2016). https://archive.org/details/stackexchange
18. Thongtanunam, P., Kula, R.G., Cruz, A.E.C., Yoshida, N., Ichikawa, K., Iida, H.: Mining history of gamification towards finding expertise in question and answering communities: experience and practice with Stack Exchange. Rev. Socionetwork Strat. **7**, 115–130 (2013)
19. Maechler, M., Rousseeuw, P., Struyf, A., Hubert, M., Hornik, K.: Cluster: cluster analysis basics and extensions (2016)
20. R Core Team: R: A language and environment for statistical computing (2016). https://www.R-project.org/
21. Gabadinho, A., Ritschard, G., Müller, N.S., Studer, M.: Analyzing and visualizing state sequences in R with TraMineR. J Stat. Softw. **40**, 1–37 (2011)
22. Studer, M.: WeightedCluster library manual: a practical guide to creating typologies of trajectories in the social sciences with R. LIVES Working Papers, vol. 24 (2013)
23. Novielli, N., Calefato, F., Lanubile, F.: Towards discovering the role of emotions in Stack Overflow. In: Proceedings of the 6th International Workshop on Social Software Engineering, pp. 33–36. ACM, Hong Kong, China (2014)
24. Blooma, M.J., Kurian, J.C., Chua, A.Y.K., Goh, D.H.L., Lien, N.H.: Social question answering: analyzing knowledge, cognitive processes and social dimensions of micro-collaborations. Comput. Educ. **69**, 109–120 (2013)

Why Do People View Photographs on Instagram?

Chei Sian Lee$^{(\boxtimes)}$ and Sei-Ching Joanna Sin

Wee Kim Wee School of Communication and Information,
Nanyang Technological University, Singapore, Singapore
{leecs, joanna.sin}@ntu.edu.sg

Abstract. Drawing from the uses and gratifications framework, the aim of the present study is to examine the needs driving users to view photographs on Instagram, a popular photo-sharing social networking service. Data (N = 115) were collected from an online survey. A principal component factor analysis indicated that there were four cluster of needs. Specifically, we found that users were driven by diversion needs, surveillance needs, personal relationship needs, and voyeuristic needs. Further data analysis revealed and found that age, number of followers and number of followings on Instagram are related to the gratifications users seek on Instagram. Specifically, we found that older respondents were more likely to seek gratifications to meet personal relationship and surveillance needs. We also found that users with more followers viewed photos to seek for diversion and voyeurism needs. Implications of our work are also discussed.

Keywords: Photo-viewing · Photo social network services · Motivations · Gratifications

1 Introduction

Viewing photographs in social media has become a routine activity for many social media users as millions of photographs were posted on social media sites each day [1]. In fact, individuals are more likely to share photographs than text, audio or video in everyday information sharing in social media [2]. Specifically, over 300 million photographs uploaded per day on Facebook [3]. In addition, the use of photo-sharing social networking services (PSNS) such as Instagram, Flickr, and Pinterest is on the rise. These PSNS offer easy sharing and viewing of photographs directly from mobile phones which enable content sharers and seekers to interact through images.

In a separate but related stream of research, it has been found that visual communication through images and photographs can capture attention which enables more effective communication than pure textual communication [4]. Indeed, the ability of visual stimuli to communicate and influence is undeniable. Specifically, the visual elements in these images and photographs are powerful and can even affect viewers emotionally and cognitively [5]. Hence, it is not surprising that many people are dependent on photo consumptions to meet their needs. This explain why the use of PSNS has been integrated into the daily social networking activities of many social media users.

© Springer International Publishing AG 2016
A. Morishima et al. (Eds.): ICADL 2016, LNCS 10075, pp. 339–350, 2016.
DOI: 10.1007/978-3-319-49304-6_38

Different people may use SNS differently as they are seeking for different gratifications. Indeed, age is a strong determinant of the frequency and quality of an individual's social media usage [6]. It was also reported that females tend to rely on SNS for community support than males [7]. Hence, individual with different needs are likely to look for different gratifications in PSNS. Further, while there is an expanding body of research related to SNS, most of the studies focus on widely adopted and general SNS such as Facebook and Twitter [e.g. 8], studies on PSNS are more limited in comparison. Since photographs can connect with people at the emotional level and invoke stronger reaction than textual content results obtained from these SNS may not be directly applicable to PSNS. Further, research on SNS tends to target university students or teenagers [e.g. 9]. Research on the social and psychological needs driving adult users to view content (i.e. view photos) on PSNS are still not well understood in the literature.

To fill this research gap, this exploratory study examines the needs driving social media users to view photographs on PSNS. The PSNS chosen is Instagram, which is currently one of the most popular and important PSNS platform [10]. The objectives of the present study are two-fold. First, this study draws from the uses and gratifications theory (U&G) to investigate the needs driving users to seek content (i.e. view photos) on Instagram. Second, this study aims to examine the relationship between the demographic profiles of Instagram users and the needs gratified from viewing photos. This theory is appropriate in the current study because it has been widely used in the literature to explain the social and psychological needs that motivate individuals to select particular media channels [11]. In sum, the present study aims to investigate the following research questions: (1) *What are the needs users seek to gratify from viewing photographs on Instagram?* (2) *What are the associations between gratifications sought from viewing photographs and the demographic profiles of Instagram users?*

2 Literature Review

2.1 Overview of Instagram

Instagram was launched in October 2010 and reached 400 million users in September 2015 [12]. Instagram is a free photo and video-sharing SNS that can be easily accessed on smartphones of different operating systems as well as desktop computers. Users can take photographs within the application or share existing photographs stored in their cameras. Instagram exhibits especially high levels of user engagement, meaning a majority of its users check the site on a daily basis. According to a recent Pew Research Center study, 59 % of Instagram users visit the site at least once a day, with 35 % visiting multiple times per day, while 38 % of Twitter users are visiting daily with 25 % visiting multiple times per day [13]. Finally, Instagram is currently ranked the most popular PSNS [14]. Instagram operates like a digital library of visual resources where content creators curate content that is meticulously created allowing content consumers to seek and browse visual content about events and people.

2.2 Uses and Gratifications Theory

Originally developed from mass communications research as a paradigm to study consumer motivations for media usage and access, uses and gratifications focuses on why consumers turn to the media to satisfy their social and psychological needs. It attempts to explain what social and psychological needs motivate audiences to select particular media channels and content [11]. Four main needs were outlined in the literature and there were *diversion, personal relationships, personal identity* and *surveillance needs* [15]. First, *diversion needs* involve a need to escape or a need for emotional release. Second, *personal relationship needs* are motives to connect to others. Third, *personal identity needs* include use of the media or channel to help people form, adjust and understand their own identity. Finally, *surveillance needs* inspire use of the media for information and understanding of the audience's environment. Hence, in this study, our aim is to uncover the needs associated with photographs viewing on Instagram through the lens of uses and gratifications.

It should be noted that the U&G perspective has been widely applied to investigate audience's gratifications in a variety of media channels including mobile gaming applications [e.g. 16], and specific informational content such as news content [e.g. 17]. From a U&G perspective, selecting a media channel is an actively involved procedure in which audiences evaluate the potential benefits of media usage. This means that audiences undoubtedly play an active role in seeking information from the platform to meet their needs. Research has classified the gratifications users seek based on the orientations of media usage to meet their needs [18, 19]. Specifically, researchers typically categorize the gratifications along two dimensions - content gratifications and process gratifications [e.g. 20]. Specifically, it was found that people use media either for the content/information carried by a medium (i.e. content gratifications) or enjoyment of the actual usage process (i.e. process gratifications). A third dimension – social gratifications has been proposed subsequently since it was reported that Internet and social media users derive satisfaction provided by the social connections afforded by the online environment [21]. In other words, social gratifications are concerned with the enjoyment of forging social ties. In aligning the needs of users with the three gratifications dimensions, past research has suggested that content gratifications are related to gratifications derived from content consumption hosted on the platform to meet surveillance and personal relationship needs [22]. Process gratifications focus on the experience when using the social media platform. Specifically, process gratifications are related to the gratifications derived in the form of enjoyment and fun users gained from participation hence meeting diversion needs. In particular, process gratifications are also known as ritualized gratifications which are related to habitual use of media for consuming time and diversion, contributing to a high level of attachment and affinity with the medium (e.g. entertainment, enjoyment, escapism) [19, 23]. As for the social gratifications dimensions, recent social media research has indicated that people have social needs which may manifest in the form of personal relationships and personal identity needs and will seek to gratify these needs to connect with others on social media platforms [24]. Indeed, past research has provided evidence that social media have transformed people's media behavior from a personal activity to an interpersonal one, which help people to attain social gratifications [21, 25].

In sum, it has been proposed from the U&G perspective that the gratifications sought are related to process, content and social gratifications and the needs driving PSNS users to search for these gratifications are diversion, personal relationship, personal identity and surveillance needs.

2.3 Gratifications Derived from Viewing Photos on Instagram

Digitalization has changed how we share and view photographs. Social media, in particular PSNS, allow users to document their daily lives with photographs [26]. Thus, everyday moments can be immortalized in photographs and allowing viewers to peek into the everyday lives of ordinary people by viewing the photographs shared on PSNS. Specifically, viewing photographs in Instagram may become a daily habit to gratify diversion needs (e.g. to pass the time, to de-stress, to enjoy). On Instagram and other PSNS, people can even scroll through a user's profile and view all of the photos that a particular user has uploaded. Such behavior has given rise to the term "mediated voyeurism" which was coined by Calvert [27]. According to Calvert [27], mediated voyeurism refers to the use of mass media and Internet to enable the consumption of images and information about others' apparently real and unguarded lives. In essence, mediated voyeurism is a form of online content viewing behavior to meet surveillance needs due to a desire to learn about other people [28]. In addition, prior research has indicated that motivations for engaging in mediated voyeurism include finding other people to relate to and trying to gain knowledge about others [27]. Here, we would like to propose that needs for surveillance should be differentiated from voyeuristic needs when it comes to photograph viewing on Instagram. We are of the viewpoint that Instagram has the potential to be a venue for voyeurism as photograph viewings are means to find out and learn about other users. More specifically, we propose that in addition to surveillance needs proposed in the literature, the needs for voyeurism could be an important angle in understanding the gratifications people derived from viewing photographs on Instagram.

Research on social media use has established that individuals derive social gratifications from the use of social media [16, 25]. Social gratifications are particularly important for SNS as these platforms allow individuals to gratify their social needs [29]. In particular, it was reported that individuals use Facebook to satisfy the needs for social connections [30]. Likewise, we deem that social gratifications are also important for Instagram users. Specifically, Reagans and McEvily [31] elaborated that individuals who have a strong emotional attachment with other members of the network are more likely to seek gratifications for relationship maintenance. Here, we argue that the motivations to view photographs in Instagram stemmed from the desire to maintain relationships with Instagram users.

Social needs also revolve gaining a sense of belonging. Burke et al. [32] examined photograph contribution on Facebook and found that the photograph posting would lead to interactions with the online community and ultimately creating a sense of belonging for the participants. This means that continued participation and content contribution from members are crucial for gathering support in online communities. Specifically, we deem that photographs can connect with people at the emotional level.

Collectively, viewing photos on Instagram has the potential to gratify different cluster of needs which may include diversion, surveillance, voyeuristic and social needs.

3 Methodology

3.1 Sample

A self-administered online questionnaire was developed to collect data. The focus of the study is on adult Instagram users. Snowball sampling was used to recruit respondents as members of the Instagram population were difficult to locate at the point of data collection [33]. A total of 129 survey responses were collected with 115 usable ones. Our sample consisted of seventy-six (66 %) females and thirty-nine (34 %) males. Eighty-two respondents (71 %) were between 21 to 30 years old and thirty-three respondents (29 %) were between 31 to 50 years old. Forty-seven respondents (71 %) reported that they had less than 50 followers while twenty-nine respondents (25 %) reported that they had more than 150 followers. In terms of the size of followings, forty-three respondents (37 %) had less than 50 followings and twenty respondents (16 %) indicated that they had more than 200 followings.

3.2 Measures

Photographs viewing is operationalized by asking the users to indicate the frequency to which they use Instagram to view photos as well as their intention to continue to view photos on Instagram. The measurements assessing gratifications were drawn from previous U&G studies [16, 25]. Content, process and social gratifications were incorporated into the survey instrument to enable us to uncover the needs associated with photographs viewings on Instagram. Questions associated with content gratifications include "*I view photographs on Instagram to gain knowledge*" and "*I view photographs on Instagram to stimulate my thinking*" while questions associated with process gratification include "*I view photographs on Instagram to pass time*" and "*I view photographs on Instagram to relieve stress*". Questions related to social gratifications include "*I view photographs on Instagram because I can make new friends by simply commenting/liking a photo*" and "*I view photograms to see how my family/friends are doing*". All in all, a total of 24 questions were developed to assess the different gratification dimensions and they were measured using a 5-point Likert scale with a range of 1 (Strongly disagree) to 5 (Strongly agree).

3.3 Analyses and Results

The entire set of 24 items from the content, process and social gratifications was analyzed by a principal component factor analysis using Varimax rotation. Four items were dropped due to low factor loadings and three items were dropped due to high cross factor loadings. The remaining 17 items fell into four factors. The results from the Factor Analysis are shown in Table 1.

Table 1. Factor analysis for perceived gratifications (N = 115)

	Factors			
	1	2	3	4
Diversion needs				
Relieve stress	.779	.245	.103	.147
Pass time	.756	−.306	.068	.059
Escape from routine	.666	.229	.224	.214
Therapeutic	.661	.467	.180	.189
Feel relaxed	.604	.292	.070	.371
Surveillance needs				
Stimulate thinking process	.313	.800	.245	.085
Gain knowledge	.134	.789	.167	.138
Start discussion	.050	.719	.362	.166
Personal relationship needs				
Make new friends	.145	.208	.751	−.051
Check out people's self-expression	.184	.327	.622	.438
Participate in events	−.144	.478	.615	−.064
Read people's comments	.426	−.118	.598	.456
Motivate sharing	.368	.411	.562	.150
Read captions	.422	.283	.526	.340
Voyeuristic needs				
Find out more people	.211	.295	.239	.753
Find out how others are doing	.177	−.119	−.128	.722
Check out how people express their creativity	.151	.363	.234	.692
Variance explained	42.43	12.36	6.95	6.00
Eigenvalue	7.21	2.10	1.18	1.02

The first factor termed "*Diversion needs*" describes gratifications related to the usage process (e.g. relieve stress, relaxing, therapeutic etc.) of viewing photos on Instagram. This factor relates to process-oriented gratifications where the focus is on experiences of the users during the viewing process. It should be noted that this factor accounts for more than 42 % of variance. This suggests that viewing photographs on Instagram is, indeed, an effective online channel for social media users to escape from their routines. The second factor termed "*Surveillance needs*" describes content-oriented gratifications characterized by the need to gain new information and insights from the content (photographs) on Instagram. This factor indicates that viewing photographs on Instagram can help users to acquire news and new information. The third factor termed "*Personal relationship needs*" is characterized by the need to stay connected with other contacts on Instagram. Here, the motives to view photographs stem from the social utility and companionship derived from the social networks on Instagram. Finally, the fourth factor was termed "*Voyeuristic needs*", which is characterized by the need to finding out what other users on Instagram are doing. While factor 2 relates more to information provided by the photographs, factor 4 is more focused on the user who shared the photographs. Specifically, factor 4 highlighted users' persistence to keep track and been informed of other users on Instagram. Ultimately, viewing photographs on Instagram helped to satisfy their needs to find out what other users are doing.

A correlational analysis was conducted to explore if there were any relationships between the gratifications sought among our respondents. From Table 2, the results indicate that older respondents were more likely to seek gratifications to meet personal relationship and surveillance needs. We also found that users with more followers viewed photos to seek for diversion and voyeuristic needs. Interestingly, individuals with large number of followings were motivated by different cluster of needs including needs for personal relationship, surveillance, diversion and voyeurism. There were no statistically differences in the gratifications sought between men and women.

Table 2. Correlation analysis (N = 115)

Profiles of Instagram Users	Social-oriented gratifications to meet *personal relationship* needs	Content-oriented gratifications to meet *surveillance* needs	Process-oriented Gratifications to meet *diversion* needs	Content-oriented gratifications to meet *voyeuristic* needs
Gender	.049	−.031	.091	.120
Age	.265**	.186*	−.100	.063
No. of followers	.066	.160	.198*	.237*
No. of followings	.202*	.273**	.352**	.263**

Note: ** Correlation is significant at the 0.01 level (2-tailed)
* Correlation is significant at the 0.05 level (2-tailed)

It should be noted that in addition to asking respondents to indicate the gratifications they sought from using Instagram which were their positive experiences, respondents were also asked to describe any negative experiences they had with using Instagram. This would allow the researchers to draw a more accurate conclusion of the respondents' perception and use of Instagram. Some of the common negative experiences mentioned by the respondents included "loss of privacy", "online stalking", and "online criticism".

4   Discussion

Using Instagram as our research context, we set out to investigate the gratification factors driving users to view photographs from the U&G perspective. Our results reveal that there are four distinct cluster of needs associated with viewing photographs on Instagram. Specifically, we found that users were driven to view photographs on Instagram to gratify diversion, surveillance, personal relationship, and voyeuristic needs. Our second objective is to examine individual profiles in terms of gender, age, the number of followers and the number of followings on gratifications sought on Instagram.

We found that the profiles of individual influenced the gratifications sought. First, social gratifications to meet personal relationship needs and content gratifications to meet surveillance needs were sought by older respondents and respondents with larger numbers of followings. It should be noted that Jang et al. [34] compared teenager and adult users in Instagram and concluded that the two groups of users used Instagram differently. They found that teenage users posted "selfies" and engaged in self-representation activities to develop and maintain social connection with friends highlighting a strong need for personal identity. Our results shed light that viewing photographs on Instagram and other PSNS allow adult users to keep in touch with people they know in real life (i.e. friends, relatives). Since photographs posted on Instagram typically reveal detailed information about the user such as hobbies, social activities and social circles, one can make use of Instagram to keep tab on their social networks or even to check on someone they just met socially. This is related to the notion of "social searching" proposed by Lampe and colleagues [35] to describe the use of SNS to find information about somebody specific with whom the user already has an offline connection. Instagram is becoming a popular tool for individuals to search for friends and to maintain relationships. Besides meeting the personal relationship needs, the content from the photos viewed are also valuable to provide more contextual information about the social network environment (i.e. events, activities, latest happenings) hence meeting surveillance needs and creating a sense of belonging.

Next, process gratifications to meet diversion needs and content gratifications to meet voyeuristic needs were associated with larger number of followers and followings. Indeed to many users, Instagram is a photo editing app allowing them to meticulously create and curate images so that they are able to showcase their best photographs to their followers. This is because Instagram enables the editing of photographs through the use of photographic filters and Polaroid-style formatting. It is a distinctive feature made intentionally to make photos to appear nostalgic. Hence, the filters offered have the ability to transform Instagram photos images into abstraction. This allows viewers of the photographs to escape to whatever feelings, memories and experiences the images evoked and as such gratifying their diversion needs [34].

In terms of viewing photographs to meet voyeuristic needs, we draw from Blazer's work [28] to explain our findings. According to Blazer [28], people who have voyeuristic needs are those that "seek simulation by visual means (p. 379)" and these needs stem from our natural curiosities. Interestingly, it appears that many people in our society have voyeuristic tendencies. This explains the proliferation of reality-based television programs [36]. Web 2.0 platforms in particular PSNS allow users to share their photographs, document and share their daily lives with their connections. Indeed, many contributors on PSNS share photographs of their meals, places they visit, purchases, and clothes (also known as "outfits of the days"). Hence, Instagram is a platform to allow viewers to peek into the personal lives of other users to satisfy their curiosities and gratify their voyeuristic needs. However, such "mediated voyeurism" sometimes carries a negative connotation, and maybe considered a negative pervasive behavior. Indeed, around 85 % and 64 % of our respondents reported that loss of privacy and online stalking as negative experiences they had with Instagram. People therefore, should raise their awareness because they may unknowingly disclose private and personal information through the photos shared on PSNS. In addition, prior research also warns that people who are more likely to be curious about others will either engage in social comparison [37] or seek for social identity to satisfy their voyeuristic needs [36]. Our results indicate that voyeuristic needs are likely to be prevalent among Instagram users.

5 Implications and Limitations

The aim of this research is to explore the underlying needs driving users to view photographs on Instagram. The present study contributes to theory in several ways. First, to our knowledge, this is one of the first studies that draw from diverse literature (e.g. communication, information science, information retrieval) to investigate the needs adult users are seeking when they view photographs on Instagram. Hence, our conceptualization and research model provides a theoretical foundation that can be used to conduct further investigations on the use of Instagram in other contexts where adults are the main group of users (e.g. workplace). Second it should be noted that while diversion, surveillance and personal relationship needs were drawn from past U&G studies, the need for voyeurism however is derived from recent observation within the social media literature. Specifically, like many other social media sites such as Facebook and YouTube, Instagram also embraces the notion of "share your life" as indicated on the Instagram website [38]. This notion may have given rise to the needs to view and peek into the everyday lives of other people (both celebrities and ordinary people) through content viewing on these platforms. In particular, the present study highlighted that in addition to surveillance and personal relationship needs which stem from content and social gratifications respectively, users also have needs to find out about other people which we referred to as voyeuristic needs in this study. Interestingly, we found that such needs are distinctively different from other existing cluster of needs reported in the literature. Future research using U&G to examine social media use should consider incorporating this new cluster of need.

This study also has practical implications. First, our findings on the effects of age, number of followers/followings and gratifications sought have major implications on the use of Instagram especially for commerce purposes. For instance, businesses and organizations need to determine the needs of their followers and develop campaigns with appropriate orientation (i.e. content, process, social). Second this study shed lights on the cluster of needs driving users to view photographs on Instagram and provides insights on how to harness the collaborative spirit between contributors and consumers of visual content. Our findings will also guide designers and developers to incorporate features that help to gratify the needs of users on PSNS. Third, our results suggest that Instagram operates likes a digital museum and is a virtual space for curated virtual content that is carefully created by the content sharers. Specifically, this study shows that photographs might act as a resource for information seekers to learn about social events as well as to find out personal and detailed information about other users on the network. This has implications on big data research on image and visual analytics as this stream of work is still at an early stage. The findings in this study will hopefully help to pave the road ahead for exploring the idea of big data research focusing on processing and interpretation big and networked image data sets from social media platforms.

There are some limitations in the present study. First, we investigated the usage of one photo-sharing social networking site, which may limit the generalizability of our findings. Indeed, different PSNS platforms have distinct features, which may be used to satisfy different users' gratifications [39]. Second, we acknowledge the limitation of the snowball sampling used in the current study and understand that snowball samples should not be considered to be representation of the population being studied. However, it should be noted that snowball sampling has been used in recent social media studies [33]. Finally, the profile of our respondents were adults who were based in Singapore. This could limit the generalizability of our findings as outcomes could differ with respondents from other cultures or countries. Nonetheless, despite these shortcomings, the present study contributes to a better understanding of the needs of adult users associated with photographs viewing behavior on Instagram.

Acknowledgements. The authors would like to thank Nur Alifah Binte Abu Bakar and Raudhah Binti Muhammad Dahri for providing research assistance.

References

1. Bakhshi, S., Shamma, D.A., Gilbert, E.: Faces engage us: photos with faces attract more likes and comments on Instagram. In: Proceedings of the 32nd Annual ACM Conference on Human Factors in Computing Systems, pp. 965–974. ACM, Toronto, Ontario, Canada (2014)
2. Goh, D.H.-L., Ang, Rebecca, P., Chua, Alton, Y.,K., Lee, C.S.: Why We Share: A Study of Motivations for Mobile Media Sharing. In: Liu, J., Wu, J., Yao, Y., Nishida, T. (eds.) AMT 2009. LNCS, vol. 5820, pp. 195–206. Springer, Heidelberg (2009). doi:10.1007/978-3-642-04875-3_23
3. Houghton, D., Joinson, A., Caldwell, N., Marder, B.: Tagger's delight? Disclosure and liking in Facebook: the effects of sharing photographs amongst multiple known social circles (2013)
4. Martin, J., Martin, R.: History through the lens: every picture tells a story. Seeing is believing? approaches to visual research, pp. 9–22
5. Rosen, C.: The image culture. New Atlantis **10**, 27–46 (2005)
6. Pittman, M., Reich, B.: Social media and loneliness: why an Instagram picture may be worth more than a thousand Twitter words. Comput. Hum. Behav. **62**, 155–167 (2016)
7. Lee, C.S.: Exploring emotional expressions on youtube through the lens of media system dependency theory. New Media Soc. **14**, 457–475 (2012)
8. Urista, M.A., Dong, Q., Day, K.D.: Explaining why young adults use myspace and Facebook through uses and gratifications theory. Hum. Commun. **12**, 215–229 (2009)
9. Ellison, N.B., Steinfield, C., Lampe, C.: The benefits of Facebook "friends": social capital and college students' use of online social network sites. J. Comput. Mediat. Commun. **12**, 1143–1168 (2007)
10. Milanovic, R.: The world's 21 most important social media sites and apps in 2015. http://www.socialmediatoday.com/social-networks/2015-04-13/worlds-21-most-important-social-media-sites-and-apps-2015

11. Ruggiero, T.E.: Uses and gratifications theory in the 21st century. Mass Commun. Soc. **3**, 3–37 (2000)
12. Kharpal, A.: Facebook's Instagramhits 400 m users, beats Twitter. In: CNBC (2015). http://www.cnbc.com/2015/09/23/instagram-hits-400-million-users-beating-twitter.html
13. Duggan, M.: Mobile messaging and social media – 2015, Pew Research Center (2015). http://www.pewinternet.org/2015/08/19/mobile-messaging-and-social-media-2015/
14. eBizMBA: top 15 most popular photo sharing sites (2016). http://www.ebizmba.com/articles/photo-sharing-sites
15. McQuail, D., Blumler, J.G., Brown, J.R.: The television audience: a revised perspective. In: McQuail, D. (ed.) Sociology of mass communcation, pp. 135–165. Penguin, Harmondsworth (1972)
16. Lee, C.S., Goh, D.H.L., Chua, A.Y.K., Ang, R.P.: Indagator: investigating perceived gratifications of an application that blends mobile content sharing with gameplay. J. Am. Soc. Inf. Sci. Technol. **61**, 1244–1257 (2010)
17. Ma, L., Lee, C.S., Goh, D.H.-L.: That's news to me: the influence of perceived gratifications and personal experience on news sharing in social media. In: Proceedings of the 11th Annual International ACM/IEEE Joint Conference on Digital Libraries, pp. 141–144. ACM, Ottawa, Ontario, Canada (2011)
18. Hanson, G., Haridakis, P.: Youtube users watching and sharing the news: a uses and gratifications approach. J. Electron. Publishing **11**, 6 (2008)
19. Rubin, A.M.: Ritualized and instrumental television viewing. J. Commun. **34**, 67–77 (1984)
20. Stafford, T.F., Stafford, M.R., Schkade, L.L.: Determining uses and gratifications for the Internet. Decis. Sci. **35**, 259–288 (2004)
21. Lee, C.S., Ma, L.: News sharing in social media: the effect of gratifications and prior experience. Comput. Hum. Behav. **28**, 331–339 (2012)
22. Lin, C., Salwen, M.B., Abdulla, R.A.: Uses and gratifications of online and offline news: new wine in an old bottle. In: Salwen, M.B., Garrison, B., Driscoll, P.D. (eds.) Online News and the Public, pp. 221–236. Lawrence Erlbaum, Mahwah (2005)
23. Rafaeli, S., Ariel, Y.: Online motivational factors: incentives for participation and contribution in Wikipedia. In: Barak, A. (ed.) Psychological Aspects of Cyberspace: Theory, Research, Applications, pp. 243–267. Cambridge University Press, Cambridge (2008)
24. Chen, G.M.: Tweet this: A uses and gratifications perspective on how active Twitter use gratifies a need to connect with others. Comput. Hum. Behav. **27**, 755–762 (2011)
25. Park, N., Kee, K.F., Valenzuela, S.: Being immersed in social networking environment: Facebook groups, uses and gratifications, and social outcomes. CyberPsychol. Behav. **12**, 729–733 (2009)
26. Murray, S.: Digital images, photo-sharing, and our shifting notions of everyday aesthetics. J. Vis. Cult. **7**, 147–163 (2008)
27. Calvert, C.: Voyeur Nation: Media, Privacy, and Peering in Modern Culture. Westview Press, Boulder (2000)
28. Blazer, S.M.: Rear window ethics: domestic privacy versus public responsibility in the evolution of voyeurism. Midwest Q. **47**, 379 (2006)
29. Boyd, D.M., Ellison, N.B.: Social network sites: definition, history, and scholarship. J. Comput. Mediat. Commun. **13**, 210–230 (2007)
30. Quan-Haase, A., Young, A.L.: Uses and gratifications of social media: a comparison of Facebook and instant messaging. B. Sci. Technol. Soc. **30**, 350–361 (2010)
31. Reagans, R., McEvily, B.: Network structure and knowledge transfer: the effects of cohesion and range. Admin. Sci. Q. **48**, 240–267 (2003)

32. Burke, M., Marlow, C., Lento, T.: Feed me: motivating newcomer contribution in social network sites. In: Proceedings of the SIGCHI Conference on Human Factors in Computing Systems, pp. 945–954. ACM, Boston, MA, USA (2009)

33. Fabiola, B., Ignasi, B.: Social research 2.0: virtual snowball sampling method using Facebook. Internet Res. **22**, 57–74 (2012)

34. Jang, J.Y., Han, K., Shih, P.C., Lee, D.: Generation like: comparative characteristics in Instagram. In: Proceedings of the 33rd Annual ACM Conference on Human Factors in Computing Systems, pp. 4039–4042. ACM, Seoul, Republic of Korea (2015)

35. Lampe, C., Ellison, N., Steinfield, C.: A Face(book) in the crowd: Social searching vs. Social browsing. In: Proceedings of the 2006 20th Anniversary Conference on Computer Supported Cooperative Work, pp. 167–170. ACM, Banff, Alberta, Canada (2006)

36. Papacharissi, Z., Mendelson, A.L.: An exploratory study of reality appeal: uses and gratifications of reality TV shows. J. Broadcast. Electron. Media **51**, 355–370 (2007)

37. Gibbons, F.X., Buunk, B.P.: Individual differences in social comparison: development of a scale of social comparison orientation. J. Pers. Soc. Psychol. **76**, 129 (1999)

38. Instagram, FAQ (2016). https://www.instagram.com/about/faq/

39. Hargittai, E.: Whose space? Differences among users and non-users of social network sites. J. Comput. Mediat. Commun. **13**, 276–297 (2007)

Sharing Brings Happiness?: Effects of Sharing in Social Media Among Adult Users

Winston Jin Song Teo[(⊠)] and Chei Sian Lee

Wee Kim Wee School of Communication and Information, Nanyang
Technological University, Singapore, Singapore
wteo005@e.ntu.edu.sg, leecs@ntu.edu.sg

Abstract. Given that sharing is a fundamental activity among social media users, this study explores the associations between sharing activities in social media and their psychological social well-being in two age groups – young and mature adults. We focus on two dimensions of social and psychological well-being which are life satisfaction and loneliness. We examine four social media platforms which are social networking sites, microblogging services, video-sharing sites and photo- sharing sites. The study comprised of 171 adult social media users in Singapore. Data analyses revealed that young adults who participated in more sharing activities in social networking sites reported higher life satisfaction and lower loneliness. Mature adults who participated more in sharing activities on social networking sites reported lower life satisfaction and higher loneliness. Implications and future research directions are discussed.

Keywords: Sharing · Social media · Loneliness · Life satisfaction · Social and psychological well-being

1 Introduction

The popularity of social media platforms such as social networking sites (e.g. Facebook), microblogs (e.g. Twitter), videos and photos sharing sites (e.g. Youtube and Instagram) contribute to a large and ever-growing online collection of user- generated digital content. Indeed, social media users serve important roles as both content creators and consumers as part of their daily social activities. Indeed, they routinely contribute and consume content of varies formats (e.g. photos, videos, tags, profile) in different social media platforms. Given the increasingly prominent role of social media in people's daily lives, an understanding of content sharing behavior in social media and their relations on individuals' well-being is important.

There has been a proliferation of social media platforms with varying niches and target markets [1]. While Facebook remain the largest and most popular social computing application currently, photo-sharing (e.g. Instagram) and microblogging platforms (e.g. Twitter) are their closest competitors worldwide. YouTube, the world's leading online video-sharing platform, boasts a reach of 1 billion active users monthly [2]. Twitter and Sina Weibo currently have 232 million and 54 million active users respectively [3, 4]. Instagram, a relatively young social media platform with a niche in a photo sharing has an active user base of 300 million [5].

© Springer International Publishing AG 2016
A. Morishima et al. (Eds.): ICADL 2016, LNCS 10075, pp. 351–365, 2016.
DOI: 10.1007/978-3-319-49304-6_39

Among the various activities users can participate in social media, content sharing is the most fundamental and significant activity in the social media environment. The content shared can be in different forms (i.e. rating, videos, comments, photos, and links). Social media users routinely and incessantly disseminate content across platforms by simply clicking a "share" button. For example, a YouTube video can be shared on another person's Facebook. While each social medium has its distinctive functions and purposes, sharing is one of the primary activities across various social media platforms. Sharing in social media is typically initiated by a user who generates the content and then disseminates the content to his/her social network on the selected platform [6, 7]. Hence, in this study we adopt a holistic view of content sharing in social media by examining a spectrum of sharing activities which include status updates, editing profile, sharing photos/videos, and sharing content from another source (e.g. sharing news stories in social media) [8].

This increase use and reliance of social media by users to share content to express individuality, share snippets of their lives, verbalize and share their thoughts and beliefs to the masses, or even to keep track on their friends' life, suggests that social media can affect one's social and psychological well-being. Indeed, the use of social media and its effects on well-being is a growing body of research. [9] suggested that social media use enables the development and maintenance of social connectedness in an online environment, which in turn leads to greater satisfaction in life. Likewise, other studies have shown that social media play important roles in the development of one's social capital and social capital is typically described as a construct to measure the benefits one receives from one's relationships with other people [10]. Specifically, YouTube was found to be a viable platform to support emotional exchanges [11] which has potential positive influences on one's well-being. However, other scholars have presented conflicted claims of the relationship between social media use and well- being [12, 13]. It also appears that age may play significant influences on the relationship between individuals' well-beings and their sharing activities in social media but there was no conclusive evidence on adult users as most past research studied teenagers and not adults. Further, we observed that many of these past studies did not differentiate between different social activities in social media (e.g. sharing, viewing) or they focused on the sharing of a particular type of content (e.g. tags, photos) or they examined one particular platform (e.g. Facebook). In sum, the associations between sharing in widely used social media platforms and the social and psychological well-being of the users are not well understood.

With the pervasive use of social media, an in-depth and holistic look into social media sharing activities on widely available social platforms and their relationships to adults' well-being is a necessary endeavor. In particular, we focus on two important dimensions of social and psychological well-being and they are life satisfaction and loneliness. Further, the present study attempts to investigate the effects of sharing in four types of widely used social media platforms on life satisfaction and loneliness. The four chosen platforms are social networking sites (SNS), microblogging services (MB), video-sharing sites (VS) and photo-sharing sites (PS).

2 Literature Review

2.1 Social Media

Social media are technologies that facilitate social interaction, make possible collaboration, and enable deliberation across stakeholders [14]. These technologies include blogs, wikis, media (audio, photo, video, text) sharing tools, networking platforms and virtual worlds. To enables us to explore social media as a multi- dimensional construct to reduce potential confounds, and narrow down specific association between psychosocial constructs and social media use, this study will focus on four most popular social media categories to date: social networking sites (SNS), microblogging services (MB), video-sharing sites (VS) and photo-sharing sites (PS).

SNS such as Facebook, Linkedin, and Renren allow users to represent themselves through profiles, articulate their social networks, and accumulate or maintain new ties with others [1]. These web-based services may be oriented towards social or professional contexts, and allow their users to communicate with their list of connections privately or publicly through texts or multimedia content. MB, unlike SNS, typically only allows it users to publish smaller elements of content (e.g. short sentences, individual images, links) to its list of connections or followers. VS and PS sites such as Youtube or Instagram are niche social media platforms that lets it users upload and share pictures or video clips only to their followers [15].

2.2 Sharing in Social Media

Sharing is fundamental to the development of all human relationships. Research has shown that tradition notion of sharing (e.g. a book, smile, good news) in all its forms is a truly powerful way to bring happiness to the sharers [16]. However, sharing in social media challenges the tradition notion of sharing. Specifically, sharing in social media refers to any form of user-generated content initiated by the user and may be disseminated to a mass audience. It includes, (i) status updates/editing profile, (ii) sharing photos/videos, and (iii) sharing content from another source (e.g. from another user or a third party side) [7]. Unlike traditional sharing, sharing in social media is a voluntary and social activity which may lead to the creation of resources (e.g. social capital) that will benefit both content consumers and sharers through the act of sharing [17]. Further, the range of sharing in social media is not limited to a close knitted group of people but rather the shared content can be shared with unlimited number users across multiple platforms outside the control or intent of the original sharer [18]. Therefore, sharing in social media is distinctive because sharers are not able to know or recognize the consumers who will benefit from the content they shared.

2.3 Effects of Sharing in Social Media

Since the onset of online social networking, much research has been produced in the realm of social media effects on users, specifically, user habits and behaviors when using social media and how such platforms may enhance users' social and psychological well-being or reinforce undesirable behaviors [6, 10]. In particular, the diverse usage or activities users partake in while engaging in different types of social media platforms might have resulted in different outcomes. Put simply, individual's social and psychological well-being may have potential influences on the sharing behaviors and these influences maybe bi-directional.

The concept of well-being has been reviewed and debated in theory [19, 20] as well as in measurement and empirical research [20, 21]. It belongs to a growing body of research in the direction of what [22] terms as 'Positive Psychology' [23]. Life satisfaction is considered by [24] to be a component of social and psychological well-being. In the realm of social networking, life satisfaction is a facet of what [25] posits as social capital. Social capital are avenues available to individuals through social interactions [26, 27] and it serves to improve a person's well-being and quality of life [28]. It is also linked to one's social ties and interpersonal communications that are related to life satisfaction and happiness [28, 29]. [11] found that the use of SNS (i.e. Facebook) help in improving the social capital of students and ultimately enhancing life satisfaction. Likewise, [12] found a significant positive correlation between individuals' well-being and the frequency they edited their Facebook pages. However, it is not clear if similar outcomes will be found on other social media platforms. Our first focus in this study is then to examine the relationship between sharing in social media and life satisfaction.

Loneliness is another important indicator of a person's social and psychological well-being. Specifically, loneliness is a psychological state resulting from a discrepancy between one's desired and actual social network [30]. People feel lonely when they perceive their social networks or relationships to be significantly deficient in either quality or quantity. Similar to other human experiences, feelings of loneliness can be managed but may never be completely prevented [31]. Several studies have found evidence that loneliness relate to lower well-being. Specifically, trajectory studies in adulthood have demonstrated that frequent and long-term experiences of loneliness have been linked to a host of negative health outcomes, including the risk of earlier death [32]. The relationship between loneliness and Internet usage has been examined in the literature. It was reported that respondents who spent more time on the Internet reported greater feelings of loneliness than people who did not use the Internet as often [13, 33, 34]. Research on lonely people's use of SNS has found that they tend to be shy [35] and anxious about face-to-face interactions [36], thus they use Facebook to past time and alleviate lonely feelings [37]. This finding – given the positive relationship between the lack of social skills and loneliness – indicates that lonely people may spend more time on social media than less lonely people. However, pertaining to the social skills deficit explanation of loneliness, lonely people tend to engage in social activities to a lesser extent [38]. In their study on Internet use and predictors, [39] found that those who had rewarding interpersonal interaction and were less anxious with face-to-face communication used the internet for other purposes rather than for interpersonal utility. They interpreted this finding to indicate a possibility that those who had less rewarding interpersonal communication and were anxious with face-to-face communication used the Internet for interpersonal utility as a functional alternative and stated that future research should look into more in-depth analysis of this aspect of Internet communication [39].

Although it may be true that lonely people rely on social media to feel connected and increase sociability and that such platforms allow them a safe space as opposed to face-to-face socializing, the behavior they exhibit when using social media may vary in comparison to less lonely people. For instance, [6] found that a higher level of loneliness was inversely related to communicating activities such as commenting and writing on other users' walls in SNS. In light of the mixed findings regarding the association between loneliness and sharing in social media, this study therefore seeks to better understand the association between social media and well-being.

2.4 Age

Previous studies on adoption of modern communication technologies such as Internet, electronic discussion forum, online services have found that age has an effect on users [40]. [41] state that older people often have distinct attitudes and expectations towards technologies, making it sometimes difficult for them to see the possible benefits. However, other studies indicated that some elders are receptive towards more advanced communication technologies that help to strengthen social relationships and establish new lines of communication with like-minded people [42]. Taken together, it is likely that age may have potential effects on the relationships between person's social psychological well-being (i.e. life satisfaction and loneliness) and their sharing activities in SNS, MB, VS and PS. Thus, we put forward the following specific research questions:

RQ1a: How will age affect the relationship between life satisfaction and content sharing in SNS?

RQ1b: How will age affect the relationship between loneliness and content sharing in SNS?

RQ2a: How will age affect the relationship between life satisfaction and content sharing in MB?

RQ2b: How will age affect the relationship between loneliness and content sharing in MB?

RQ3a: How will age affect the relationship between life satisfaction and content sharing in VS?

RQ3b: How will age affect the relationship between loneliness and content sharing in VS?

RQ4a: How will age affect the relationship between life satisfaction and content sharing in PS?

RQ4b: How will age affect the relationship between loneliness and content sharing in PS?

2.5 The Singapore Context

As an economically and technologically advanced city-state, Singapore enjoys almost universal Internet access, with more than 88 % of resident households having access to at least one computer at home and an Internet connection [43]. Unsurprisingly, Singaporeans are also one of the most active social media consumers in the world, with more than 90 % of Internet users possessing at least one social media account, ahead of the global average of almost 70 % [44, 45]. Other social media platforms such as Twitter and Youtube are also popular. More than 6 in 10 Singaporean Internet users possess a Youtube account [45] and 15 % of the population in Singapore uses Twitter regularly [46]. While digital natives – adolescents and young adults aged 15 to 24 – form the largest user base of such social media platforms, user growth from age group 35–44 were also observed [47, 48]. Previous scholarly and industry research has revealed that the popularity of these online spaces have led to an increase in social media sharing behaviors such as voicing of political opinions or interacting with related content while watching television [49, 50].

Global surveys on overall happiness in the last decade have also indicated an improvement in social well-being among Singaporeans in the last decade [51, 52]. As of 2016, Singapore was ranked the 22nd happiest country in the world and the happiest in Asia Pacific [53]. Specifically, research has reported that having strong and supportive interpersonal relationships, particularly among spouses and family members, deeply influence Singaporeans' overall perception of happiness or life satisfaction among older adults [54–57]. In accordance with this view, [58] found that perceived loneliness, rather than living alone, contributed to a higher score of Geriatric Depression Scale (GDS) among community-dwelling older adults. Regular social interaction thus appears to mitigate feelings of loneliness for older adults and is documented as one of the main reasons for life satisfaction [59]. This implies that age has potential influences on Singaporeans' well-being.

While previous studies have suggested that active use of social media – in contrast to passive consumption – may help to alleviate feelings of loneliness and indirectly influence tertiary students' social psychological well-being positively [11, 12, 37, 60], little is known about the relationship between social media sharing and well-being among adults in Singapore. This study thus attempts to fill in this knowledge gap and add an Asian perspective from a predominantly Western demographic in this area of research. Furthermore, as discussed earlier, Singapore is a particularly unique spot to investigate the social consequences of social media technologies due its high social media penetration and purported increase in overall happiness over recent years.

3 Methodology

3.1 Procedure and Sample

A self-administered questionnaire was used to collect data from respondents. The survey was hosted on Qualtrics, a web survey software to which the authors had a university-wide subscription account, and was fielded in March 2015. Surveys were first distributed to students at a comprehensive university in Singapore through email invitations or personal messages through the university's various social media channels (e.g. College of Engineering Facebook page). All invitations included a short description of the study, information about confidentiality and a link to the survey.

Out of the 188 questionnaires that were taken and distributed by students; 171 completely filled surveys were returned, yielding a 91 % response rate. Questionnaire distribution was voluntarily undertaken by participants without any compensation or extra class credit.

The first part of the study required participants to complete a section on demographical information as well as their usage of social media to determine their eligibility for the study. The survey was terminated if participants were found to be ineligible for the study (i.e. below 21 years old, are not Singaporeans or Singapore Permanent Residents, and/or did not use social media). Questions on loneliness and life satisfaction were asked prior to questions on social media use to avoid priming the participants.

The final sample consisted of 86 males (50.3 %) and 85 females (49.7 %.). Respondents ranged in age from 21 to 55 years old (M = 31, SD = 7.25). The average number of social media contacts was in the range of 64 to 279 'friends' or 'followers', and the average amount of time each participant spent on social media was in the range between 22 to 30 min. The demographic profiles of the participants are summarized in Table 1.

Table 1. Sample demographics (N = 171).

Demographic variables		N	(%)
Gender	Men	86	50.3
	Woman	85	49.7
Age	21–25	53	31
	26–30	37	21.6
	31–35	20	11.7
	36–40	44	25.7
	>40	17	9.9

3.2 Measures

Social media usage was assessed by measuring the frequency which one uses SNS, MB, VS, PS to share content. The 3-item self-report is drawn from the classification of social network activities by [7]. Items such as 'In general, how often do you update your status or profile on SNS?" and "In general, how often do you share content uploaded from another user or source on MB ('Retweet')?" were rated on a 5-point scale (1 = 'Very Infrequent', 5 = 'Very Frequent'). Items are scored such that higher scores indicate high level of participation in that activity. The study showed acceptable reliability for values (α = .86).

Life satisfaction [61] is a 5-item self-reported scale. Participants indicated their agreement with statements such as "I am satisfied with life" and "The conditions of my life are excellent" on a 7-point Likert scale ranging from 1 = strongly disagree to 7 = strongly agree. The minimum and maximum scores range from 5 to 35, with scores below 9 indicating extreme dissatisfaction and scores above 30 indicating extreme satisfaction. Results from previous studies have supported its high internal consistency (Cronbach's α = .89) [62]. The scale showed excellent reliability (α = .98) in the current study.

UCLA Loneliness Scale (Version 3) [63] was used to determine individuals' perceived loneliness levels as it has demonstrated high levels of internal consistency of alpha .89 to .96 in several studies [64, 65]. In this 20-item scale, participants were asked to rate how frequent their feelings coincide with statements such as "How often do you feel that you lack companionship?" on a 5-point Likert-type scale (1 = Never to 5 = Always). Higher overall scores on this measure indicate higher levels of loneliness. Scores above 70 suggest severe loneliness. The scale showed excellent reliability (α = .98) in the current study.

To shed light on the sharing behaviors of adult users, the focus of this study is restricted to adults who are twenty-one years and above as non-adult users may introduce potential confounds. Specifically, it has been widely reported that teenagers use social media differently from adults [66]. To examine the effects of age, the sample was split into 2 separate age groups– young adults (i.e. 21 to 35 years old) and mature adults (i.e. more than 36 years old). Young adults have been identified as 35 years or younger as delineated by the National Youth Council of Singapore in Singapore where the present study was conducted.

4 Results

Normality was first assessed by inspecting histograms. It was revealed that the constructs (e.g. life satisfaction) were not normally distributed. This may due to the nature of questions in these measures (e.g. items on loneliness, self-esteem and contentment). As such, non-parametric tests such as Mann-Whitney U test and Spearman's rank-order correlation were used in this study.

An independent sample Mann-Whitney U test revealed that there were no significant gender differences between all variables. Social networking was the only social media category in which all the respondents participated. 56.1 % of the sample participated in photo-sharing applications while only 36.2 % and 28.7 % of them participated in microblogging and video-sharing applications respectively. The mean global life satisfaction score was 22.7 (SD = 9.1), with only 48.5 % of the participants scoring more than 25 points, indicating that less than the majority were satisfied or extremely satisfied with their current lives. In terms of loneliness, less than a quarter of respondents experienced a low or average level of loneliness, with a mean score of 53.1 (SD = 18.4).

A series of Spearman correlation analyses was performed to address the relationships between sharing in social media and life satisfaction/loneliness for both groups (young adults and mature adults). Table 2 displays the results of these analyses. As expected, for young adults, there was a significantly positive correlation between sharing in SNS, MB and VS and life satisfaction. However, for mature adults, there was a significantly negative correlation between sharing in SNS and life satisfaction. No significant correlations were found for sharing in PS and life satisfaction for both young and mature adults.

Table 2. Sharing in social media and life satisfaction

		Life satisfaction (Young Adults)	Life satisfaction (Mature Adults)
Social media	Sharing in SNS	.423**	−.490**
	Sharing in MB	.272*	0.227
	Sharing in VS	.326*	−0.399
	Sharing in PS	0.21	−0.463

Note: a. Young adults (21–35 yrs, $n = 110$), Mature adults
   (> 35 yrs, $n = 61$)
   b. SNS - Social Networking Sites, MB – Microblogging
   Services, VB –Video Sharing Sites, PS –Photo Sharing
   Sites.
   c. * $p < .05$, ** $p < .01$ (2-tailed)

Table 3 shows the relationship between sharing in social media and loneliness. There was a significantly negative association between loneliness and sharing in SNS for young adults. Among the mature adults, we found that there was significant positive association between loneliness and sharing in SNS and PS. No significant correlations were found for sharing in MB and VS and life satisfaction for both young and mature adults.

Table 3. Sharing in social media and loneliness

		Loneliness (Young Adults)	Loneliness (Mature Adults)
Social media	Sharing in SNS	−.449**	.556**
	Sharing in MB	−0.248	0.294
	Sharing in VS	−0.268	0.655
	Sharing in PS	−0.14	.544*

Note: a. Young adults (21–35 yrs, $n = 110$), Mature adults
   (> 35 yrs, $n = 61$)
   b. SNS - Social Networking Sites, MB – Microblogging
   Services, VB –Video Sharing Sites, PS –Photo Sharing
   Sites.
   c. * $p < .05$, ** $p < .01$ (2-tailed)

5   Discussion

The primary purpose of this study is to examine the associations between social and psychological well-being and sharing in social media in both young and mature adults. Specifically, we focus on two important dimensions of social psychological well-being which are life satisfaction and loneliness. In terms of social media platforms, we focus on four types of widely popular and accessible social media platforms which include social network services, microblogging, video sharing sites and photo sharing sites. Our results suggest that there are significant differences on the effects of sharing in social media and social psychological well-being between young and mature adults.

Specifically, we found positive correlations between sharing in social media and life satisfaction among young adults but negative correlations for mature adults. In the case of loneliness, our results indicate that sharing in social media was positively associated with loneliness among the mature adults but we found inverse associations for young adults.

For young adults, there were significant positive correlations between life satisfaction and sharing in most platforms (i.e. SNS, MB and VS). In the case of loneliness, our results showed that sharing in SNS was negatively associated with loneliness for young adults. Collectively, our results suggest that sharing in social media has positive association with psychological social well-being for this group. Young adults, especially those who are in the early 20 s, are in the midst of exploring and finding their own identities, and hence their sharing activities in social media reflect their developmental goals. To further explain this finding, we draw from [67] 's research on self-presentation, which states that individuals are constantly trying to influence the impression others develop of them as a way of ultimately influencing others' attitudes and behaviors [68]. In our case, young adults share content on social media, in particular SNS, MB and VS mainly so that they can socially identify who they are and manage how others perceive them. As discussed earlier, sharing in social media refers to user generated content that is communicated to a wide circle of contacts (in contrast to targeted, one-on-one communication). The type and number of sharing activities vary across platforms and includes "status updates" on SNS, "re-tweeting" content on MB and uploading a publicly listed video on VS. The results suggest that social media are empowerment tools to these young adults as they are able to take advantage of the affordances of these platforms to selectively self-present themselves in favorable light to their online social networks [12].

Unexpectedly, in the case of mature adults, we found that sharing in social media have detrimental associations with their social psychological well-beings. Specifically, we found significant positive associations between loneliness and sharing in SNS and PS. Likewise, significant negative association was found between sharing in SNS and life satisfaction. We further observed that the online social network size among the mature adults and found that they generally had smaller online social network than young adults. Specifically, we found that young adults had significantly more "friends" or social connections in SNS and PS platforms. As such, we explain that the mature adults are not able to fully capitalize on their social networks to enhance their social and psychological well-beings since they have fewer connections or "friends" in social media. Our finding here on mature adults is consistent with past findings which suggests that people use Facebook to past time and alleviate lonely feelings [37]. In other words, it is plausible that lonely mature adults may spend more time sharing in SNS and PS than less lonely mature adults. This is an important finding for mature adults as past research has indicated that prolonged use of social media may lead to symptoms of depression [69]. Future works to better understand the emotional and social needs of mature adults to limit the detrimental consequences on their social psychological well-beings are needed.

The results presented in this study have both academic and practical implications. From an academic perspective, this study is a preliminary step towards understanding how content sharing in social media can have varying consequences for social and psychological well-being among adults. Consistent with an earlier argument by [8] that the type of activities users engages in SNS better predicts psychological consequences of SNS use, than do generic measures such as time spent [13] or Facebook intensity [11], our results indicated a significant negative correlation between sharing on SNS and loneliness, and a positive correlation between sharing on most social media platforms and life satisfaction for young adults. Thus, the present findings contribute to reconciling the mixed findings on mediated communication and psychological effects [6, 39] by investigating different age groups. Further, the current study contributed to the literature by adopting a multi-dimension perspective of sharing in social media across different platforms [13, 70].

From a practical standpoint, the negative correlations between social media sharing and psychosocial well-being among older adults suggest that this demographic of users in Singapore may not be using social media as effectively as their younger counterparts and may require further assistance. As suggested earlier, lonely mature adults may have fewer pre-existing ties on these online platforms and thus are not able to fully leverage on these networks. Further, our results have implications on social media literacy and policy-makers may consider our research implications to craft better programs for public education and create policies to help certain groups (especially older age groups) that may suffer from negative effects of social media sharing. In addition, findings from our study may serve as a reference to social media service providers when developing or enhancing their software to be mindful of user online information behaviors and the possible effects on their users. Specifically, the success of any social media platforms depends on user contributions to provide value to their products, and as a result, designers of such systems build features targeted at increasing the amount of content a given user contributes. Ultimately, understanding the effects of sharing in social media on the social and psychological social well-being of social media users is important in designing and developing of social media platforms.

6 Limitations and Future Directions

This study does have some limitations that should be considered. The first limitation lies in the sampling method. As the respondents were recruited through convenience and snowball sampling, the sample in our study may be homogenous and may not accurately represent the general population in Singapore. Another limitation is that the current study was based on a cross-sectional design; hence causal inferences regarding the relationship among variables cannot be directly determined. Future research may include collecting multiple stages of data in order to test longitudinal models with cross- lagged effects, which would corroborate the causal direction of the relationships between psychosocial variables and social media measures. It is worthy to note that in regards to the young adults sample, the findings of this study is consistent with previous experiments that reported a positive relationship between active Facebook use and life satisfaction [12, 60]. In future, more objective measurements of sharing in social media, like the collection of secondary data from these sites could be used in conjunction with the existing scales to provide more detailed information on the relationship between social media use and social and psychosocial well-being.

References

1. Boyd, D.M., Ellison, N.B.: Social network sites: Definition, history, and scholarship. J. Comput. Mediat. Commun. **13**, 210–230 (2008)
2. Youtube: Youtube Press room (2005). https://www.youtube.com/yt/press/index.html. Accessed 2 April 2016
3. U.S. Securities and Exchange Commission: Amendment No. 1 To Form S-1 Registration Statement Under the Securities Act of 1933 (2013). https://www.sec.gov/Archives/edgar/data/1418091/000119312513400028/d564001ds1a.htm. Accessed 2 April 2016
4. TechWeb: Sina Weibo valuation of 60 billion dollars in advertising revenue broke the single-season $30 million (2013). http://www.techweb.com.cn/internet/2013-08-13/1316353.shtml. Accessed 2 April 2016
5. Instagram: Press (2016). http://instagram.com/press/. Accessed 2 April 2016
6. Jin, B.: How lonely people use and perceive Facebook. Comput. Hum. Behav. **29**, 2463–2470 (2013)
7. Burke, M., Kraut, R., Marlow, C.: Social capital on Facebook: differentiating uses and users. In: Proceedings of the SIGCHI Conference on Human Factors in Computing Systems, pp. 571–580. ACM, Vancouver (2011)
8. Lee, C.S., Ma, L.: News sharing in social media: the effect of gratifications and prior experience. Comput. Hum. Behav. **28**, 331–339 (2012)
9. Grieve, R., Indian, M., Witteveen, K., Anne Tolan, G., Marrington, J.: Face-to-face or Facebook: can social connectedness be derived online? Comput. Hum. Behav. **29**, 604–609 (2013)
10. Steinfield, C., Ellison, N., Lampe, C.: Social capital, self-esteem, and use of online social network sites: a longitudinal analysis. J. Appl. Dev. Psychol. **29**, 434–445 (2008)
11. Lee, C.S.: Exploring emotional expressions on YouTube through the lens of media system dependency theory. New Media Soc. **14**, 457–475 (2012)
12. Gonzales, A.L., Hancock, J.T: Mirror, mirror on my Facebook wall: effects of exposure to Facebook on self-esteem. Cyberpsychol. Behav. Soc. Netw. **14**, 79–83 (2011)
13. Kalpidou, M., Costin, D., Morris, J.: The relationship between Facebook and the well-being of undergraduate college students. Cyberpsychol. Behav. Soc. Netw. **14**, 183–189 (2011)
14. Bryer, T.A., Zavattaro, S.: Social media and public administration: theoretical dimensions and introduction to symposium. Adm. Theory Praxis. **33**, 325–340 (2011)
15. Lee, C.S., Abu Bakar, N.A.B., Muhammad Dahri, R.B., Sin, S.-C.J.: Instagram this! sharing photos on instagram. In: Allen, Robert, B., Hunter, J., Zeng, Marcia, L. (eds.) ICADL 2015. LNCS, vol. 9469, pp. 132–141. Springer, Heidelberg (2015). doi:10.1007/978-3-319-27974-9_13
16. Lambert, N., Gwinn, A., Baumeister, R., Strachman, A., Washburn, I., Gable, S., Fincham, F.: A boost of positive affect: the perks of sharing positive experiences. J. Soc. Pers. **30**, 24–43 (2012)
17. John, N.A.: Sharing and Web 2.0: The emergence of a keyword. New Media Soc. 3, 1–16 (2012)
18. Wittel, A.: Qualities of sharing and their transformations in the digital age. Int. Rev. Inf. Ethics. **16**, 3–8 (2011)
19. Angner, E.: Subjective well-being. J. Socio-Econ. **39**(3), 361–368 (2010)
20. Diener, E.: Subjective well-being. In: Lopez, S.J., Snyder, C.R. (eds.) The Oxford Handbook of Positive Psychology, pp. 63–73. Oxford University Press, New York (2009)
21. Kahneman, D., Krueger, A.B.: Developments in the measurement of subjective well-being. J. Econ. Perspect. **20**, 3–24 (2006)

22. Seligman, M., Csikszentmihalyi, M.: Positive psychology: an introduction. Am. Psychol. **55**, 5–14 (2000)
23. Pavot, W., Diener, E.: The Satisfaction With Life Scale and the emerging construct of life satisfaction. J. Pos. Psychol. **3**, 137–152 (2008)
24. Pavot, W., Diener, E.: Review of the satisfaction with life scale. Psychol. Assessment. **5**, 164–172 (1993)
25. Putnam, R.D., Goss, K.A.: Introduction. In: Putnam, R.D. (ed.) Democracies in flux: the evolution of social capital in contemporary society, pp. 3–19. Oxford University Press, New York, N.Y. (2002)
26. Lin, N.: A network theory of social capital. In: Castiglione, D., van Deth, J.W, Wolleb, G. (eds.) The Handbook of Social Capital, pp. 69–92. Oxford University Press, New York (2008)
27. Putnam, R. D.: Bowling together (2004). http://www.oecdobserver.org/news/fullstory.php/aid/1215/Bowling_together.html. Accessed 10 Feb 2014
28. Valenzuela, S., Park, N., Kee, K.: Is there social capital in a social network site?: Facebook use and college students' life satisfaction, trust, and participation. J. Comput. Mediat. Comm. **14**, 875–901 (2009)
29. Pavot, W., Diener, E., Colvin, C., Sandvik, E.: Further validation of the satisfaction with life scale: evidence for the cross-method convergence of well-being measures. J. Pers. Asses. **57**, 149–161 (1991)
30. Peplau, L.A., Perlman, D.: Perspectives on loneliness. In: Peplau, L.A., Perlman, D. (eds.) Loneliness: A Sourcebook of Current Theory, Research and Therapy, pp. 1–18. Wiley Interscience (1982)
31. Rokach, A., Brock, H.: Coping with loneliness. J. Psychol. **132**, 107–127 (1998)
32. Patterson, A., Veenstra, G.: Loneliness and risk of mortality: a longitudinal investigation in Alameda County, California. Soc. Sci. Med. **71**, 181–186 (2010)
33. Caplan, S.E.: Problematic Internet use and psychosocial well-being: Development of a theory-based cognitive–behavioral measurement instrument. Comput. Hum. Behav. 18, 553– 575 (2002)
34. Kraut, R., Patterson, M., Lundmark, V.: Internet paradox: a social technology that reduces social involvement and psychological well-being? Am. Psychol. **53**, 1017–1031 (1998)
35. Cheek, J.M., Busch, C.M.: Influence of shyness on loneliness in a new situation. Pers. Soc. Psychol. B. **7**, 573–577 (1981)
36. Segrin, C., Kinney, T.: Social skills deficits among the socially anxious: rejection from others and loneliness. Motiv. Emotion. **19**, 1–24 (1995)
37. Sheldon, P.: The relationship between unwillingness-to-communicate and students' facebook use. J. Media Psychol. **20**, 67–75 (2008)
38. Russell, D., Peplau, L., Cutrona, C.: The revised UCLA Loneliness Scale: Concurrent and discriminant validity evidence. J. Pers. Soc. Psychol. **39**, 472–480 (1980)
39. Papacharissi, Z., Rubin, A.: Predictors of internet use. J. Broadcast. Electron. Media. **44**, 175–196 (2000)
40. Lee, C.S., Goh, D.H.-L., Chua, A.Y.K., Ang, R.P.: Indagator: investigating perceived gratifications of an application that blends mobile content sharing with gameplay. J. Am. Soc. Inf. Sci. Tec. **61**, 1244–1257 (2010)
41. Gregor, P., Newell, A.F., Zajicek, M.: Designing for dynamic diversity: Interfaces for older people. In: Proceedings of the Fifth International ACM Conference on Assistive Technologies, pp. 151–156. ACM, Edinburgh (2002)
42. Mcmellon, C., Schiffman, L.: Cybersenior empowerment: how some older individuals are taking control of their lives. J. Appl. Gerontol. **21**, 157–175 (2002)

43. Info-communications Development Authority of Singapore: Annual survey on Infocomm Usage in Households and by Individuals for 2014 (2015). https://www.ida.gov.sg/~/media/Files/Infocomm%20Landscape/Facts%20and%20Figures/SurveyReport/2014/2014%20HH%20public%20report%20final.pdf. Accessed 2 April 2016
44. Digital Influence Lab.: Digital Marketing Statistics in Singapore – 2015 (2015). http://digitalinfluencelab.com/singapore-digital-marketing-stats/. Accessed 2 April 2016
45. Wong, A.: Facebook, WhatsApp top ranked in Singapore (2014). http://www.todayonline.com/tech/facebook-whatsapp-top-ranked-singapore. Accessed 7 May 2016
46. Statista: Penetration of leading social networks in Singapore as of 4th quarter 2015 (2015). http://www.statista.com/statistics/284466/singapore-social-network-penetration/. Accessed 2 April 2016
47. Singapore Business Review: 5 important statistics about Facebook users in Singapore (2012). http://sbr.com.sg/leisure-entertainment/news/5-important-statistics-about-facebook-users-in-singapore. Accessed 7 May 2016
48. Info-communications Development Authority of Singapore: Publication of Infocomm Technology Roadmap 2012 (2012). https://www.ida.gov.sg/~/media/Files/Infocomm%20Landscape/Technology/TechnologyRoadmap/SocialMedia.pdf. Accessed 2 April 2016
49. Matuszak, G., Elms, D., Wissmann, P.: The rise of the digital multitasker (2013). https://www.kpmg.com/ES/es/ActualidadyNovedades/ArticulosyPublicaciones/Documents/Digital-Debate-2013.pdf. Accessed 5 May 2016
50. Skoric, M.M., Poor, N.D., Liao, Y., Tang, S.W.H.: Online organization of an offline protest. In: Proceedings of the 44th Hawaii International Conference on System Sciences, pp. 1–8. IEEE, Kauai (2011)
51. Helliwell, J., Layard, R., Sachs, J.: World Happiness Report (2012). http://worldhappiness.report/wp-content/uploads/sites/2/2012/04/World_Happiness_Report_2012.pdf. Accessed 2 April 2016
52. Helliwell, J., Layard, R., Sachs, J.: World Happiness Report 2013 (2013). http://worldhappiness.report/wp-content/uploads/sites/2/2013/09/WorldHappinessReport2013_online.pdf. Accessed 2 April 2016
53. Helliwell, J., Layard, R., Sachs, J.: World Happiness Report 2016 Volume 1 (2016). http://worldhappiness.report/wp-content/uploads/sites/2/2016/03/HR-V1_web.pdf. Accessed 2 April 2016
54. Housing & Development Board: Public housing in Singapore: Well-being of communities, families and the elderly. HDB Sample Household Survey 2008, Housing and Development Board (2010)
55. Tambyah, S.K., Tan, S.J., Kau, A.K.: The quality of life in Singapore. In: SOCI 92, pp. 337–376 (2009)
56. Veenhoven, R.: Happiness: also known as "life satisfaction" and "subjective well-being". In: Kenneth, K.C., Michalos, A.C., Sirgy, J. (eds.) Handbook of Social Indicators and Quality of Life Research, pp. 63–77. Springer, New York (2011)
57. Veenhoven, R.: Cross-national differences in happiness: cultural measurement bias or effect of culture? IJW. 2, 333–353 (2012)
58. Lim, L.L., Kua, E.H.: Living alone, loneliness, and psychological well-being of older persons in Singapore. Curr Gerontol Geriatr Res. 2011 (2011)
59. Kua, E.: Some old-age truths about happiness (2012). http://newshub.nus.edu.sg/news/1209/PDF/TRUTHS-tdy-12sep-p10&p12.pdf. Accessed 2 May 2016
60. Gentile, B., Twenge, J. M., Freeman, E. C., Campbell, W. K.: The effect of social networking websites on positive self-views: an experimental investigation. Comput. Hum. Behav. 28, 1929–1933 (2012)

61. Diener, E., Emmons, R. A., Larsen, R. J., Griffin, S.: The Satisfaction with Life scale. J. Pers. Assess. **49**, 71–75 (1985)
62. Valkenburg, P., Peter, J., Schouten, A.: Friend networking sites and their relationship to adolescents' well-being and social self-Esteem. Cyberpsychol. Behav. **9**, 584–590 (2006)
63. Russell, D.: UCLA loneliness scale (version 3): reliability, validity, and factor structure. J. Pers. Asses. **66**, 20–40 (1996)
64. Bozoglan, B., Demirer, V., Sahin, I.: Loneliness, self-esteem, and life satisfaction as predictors of Internet addiction: a cross-sectional study among Turkish university students. Scand. J. Psychol. **54**, 313–319 (2013)
65. Demir, A.: Reliability and validity of the UCLA Loneliness Scale. Turkish J. Psychol. **7**, 14–18 (1989)
66. Jang, J.Y., Han, K., Shin, P.C., Lee, D.: Generation like: comparative characteristics in instagram. In: Proceedings of the 33rd Annual ACM Conference on Human Factors in Computing Systems, pp. 4039–4042. ACM, New York (2015)
67. Goffman, E.: The Presentation of Self in Everyday Life. Penguin, London (1982)
68. Papacharissi, Z.: The self online: the utility of personal home pages. J. Broadcast. Electron. Media. **46**, 346–368 (2002)
69. Tandoc, E., Ferrucci, P., Duffy, M.: Facebook use, envy, and depression among college students: Is Facebooking depressing? Comput. Hum. Behav. **43**, 139–146 (2015)
70. Mehdizadeh, S.: Self-Presentation 2.0: Narcissism and Self-Esteem on Facebook. Cyberpsychol. Behav. Soc. Netw. **13**, 357–364 (2010)

Analyzing and Using Wikipedia

DOI Links on Wikipedia
Analyses of English, Japanese, and Chinese Wikipedias

Jiro Kikkawa[1(✉)], Masao Takaku[2], and Fuyuki Yoshikane[2]

[1] Graduate School of Library, Information and Media Studies,
University of Tsukuba, Tsukuba, Japan
jiro@slis.tsukuba.ac.jp
[2] Faculty of Library, Information and Media Science,
University of Tsukuba, Tsukuba, Japan
{masao,fuyuki}@slis.tsukuba.ac.jp

Abstract. In this paper, we analyzed Digital Object Identifier (DOI) links among English, Japanese, and Chinese Wikipedias (hereafter, enwiki, jawiki, and zhwiki, respectively), which possibly work as a bridge between the Web users and scholarly information. Most of the DOI links in these Wikipedias were revealed to be CrossRef DOIs. The second most-referenced in jawiki were JaLC DOIs, whereas those in zhwiki were ISTIC DOIs. JaLC DOIs were uniquely referenced in jawiki, and ISTIC DOIs tend to be referenced in zhwiki. In terms of DOI prefixes, Elsevier BV was the largest registrant in all languages. Nature Publishing Group and Wiley-Blackwell were also commonly referenced. The content hosted by these registrants was shared among the Wikipedia communities. Moreover, overlapping analysis showed that jawiki and zhwiki share the DOI links with enwiki at a similar high rate. The analysis of revision histories showed that the DOI links had been added to enwiki before they were included in jawiki and zhwiki — indicating that the majority of DOI links in jawiki and zhwiki were added by translating from enwiki. These findings imply that the DOI links in Wikipedia may result in multiple counts of altmetrics.

Keywords: Scholarly communication · Digital Object Identifier (DOI) · Wikipedia · Altmetrics

1 Introduction

Along with the fast-growing digitization of scholarly communication, all people can easily, immediately get scholarly information through the Web nowadays. In such an environment, Digital Object Identifier (DOI) is absolutely necessary to identify each electronic document. DOI is the best-known international standard infrastructure that assigns persistent and unique identifiers for any type of objects [1]. As of November 2015, the total number of DOIs are approximately 130 million [2]. CrossRef is the largest DOI Registration Agency [3]. It reports

A. Morishima et al. (Eds.): ICADL 2016, LNCS 10075, pp. 369–380, 2016.
DOI: 10.1007/978-3-319-49304-6_40

that Top 4 referrers of DOIs assigned by CrossRef (i.e., CrossRef DOIs) are academic literature databases (i.e., Web of Knowledge, Serials Solutions, ScienceDirect, and Scopus) and the 5th largest referrer is Wikipedia [4]. Wikipedia is a free, collaboratively edited, and multilingual online encyclopedia. As of February 2016, there are 246 language Wikipedias that include English (enwiki), Japanese (jawiki), and Chinese (zhwiki) [5]. According to Alexa Internet, Wikipedia was the 7th most viewed website in the world in 2015 [6].

Therefore, as typified by Wikipedia, open websites seem to build and enhance a bridge between Web users and scholarly information through DOI links. Furthermore, it is assumed that these connections redound to make the best use of scholarly information — not only by researchers or specialists, but also by more various people such as students and general public.

However, few studies have attempted to analyze scholarly information, including DOI links, referenced on Wikipedia. In other words, which publishers or academic societies have content that is highly referenced on Wikipedia? What are the differences in referenced contents among other Wikipedia languages? How and when was the scholarly information written on Wikipedia? These viewpoints are important for understanding characteristics and meanings about DOI links that are referenced on Wikipedia.

Thus, we aim to answer the following two research questions:

– RQ1. Which publishers or academic societies have content that is highly referenced on Wikipedia?
– RQ2. Does the highly referenced content vary among Wikipedia languages, or is it very similar to other languages?

To answer these research questions, the present study analyzes DOI links on enwiki, jawiki, and zhwiki. It reveals which kinds of scholarly information are referenced on these Wikipedias. The reasons why this study set targets on enwiki, jawiki, and zhwiki are as follows:

– Because enwiki is the largest language version of Wikipedia, it is meaningful to identify its influence on jawiki.
– If some similarities or common points are observed between jawiki and enwiki, we should check whether the similarities with enwiki are also seen on other language Wikipedias — or are peculiar to jawiki.
– jawiki and zhwiki have some similarities in that both are Asian languages, and they are equal in quantity of articles. Thus, we also use zhwiki.

2   Related Work

2.1   Analyses of Academic/scientific Citations on Wikipedia

Nielsen [7] analyzed referenced journals in English Wikipedia (as of April, 2007) and checked the correlation to their Journal Citation Reports Impact Factor, a measure of journal influence. As a result, the Top referenced journals were

Nature and Science. Journals in the field of astronomy were highly referenced. Not all of the journals had high Impact Factors.

By using DOIs, Lin & Fenner [8] analyzed references of articles published in a series of open access journals by PLOS (Public Library of Science) on the Top 25 language versions of Wikipedia (as of March 2014). As a result, 4.13 % of all the PLOS articles at the time were referenced on Wikipedia, and 47 % of them were referenced on Wikipedia other than English version. They argued that "the number of referenced PLOS articles on Wikipedia highly correlates with the number of active users that are associated with that Wikipedia".

The "Extract academic citations from Wikipedia" tool [9] is used to extract identifiers (such as DOI, PubMed, ISBN, and arXiv) on Wikipedia. The tool was developed by Halfaker from Wikimedia Foundation. Halfaker et al. analyzed and showed the amount of each identifier on English and Dutch Wikipedias (as of June 2015). The most referenced identifier was ISBN, and the second most-referenced identifier was DOI; their amounts change over time [10,11].

The "Wikipedia DOI citation live stream" [12] is a service that collects DOI links on Wikipedia and shows them as real-time streams. This service displays which DOI links are referenced from which Wikipedia pages.

The "Wikipedia Cite-o-Meter" [13] is a service developed by Wikimedia Tool Labs. This service shows the reference status on a prefixes basis — in 100 language versions of Wikipedia. For example, it illustrates how PLOS contents (prefix:10.1371) were referenced on Japanese and English Wikipedias.

In summary, past studies have investigated scholarly information on Wikipedia from the viewpoint of journal titles [7] and that of specific publisher's contents [8]. Although these studies showed interesting results, investigations from viewpoints of publishers and academic societies seem to be lacking. On the other hand, existing services focus on the number of DOI links on Wikipedias, but it is not clear how they overlap among different Wikipedia languages.

2.2 DOI Usage Analyses by CrossRef

CrossRef analyzed its access log about DOIs and reported their referrers. According to the CrossRef Blog [14], as of 2014, the 8th largest referrer was Wikipedia. It revealed that users actually click DOI links. CrossRef also reported that (as of 2015) Wikipedia was the 5th largest referrer, which followed four academic literature databases (Web of Knowledge, Serials Solutions, ScienceDirect, and Scopus) [4]. In addition, the Top 10 Wikipedias that were most frequently accessed were (in decreasing order) English, English (mobile), German, Japanese, Spanish, French, Russian, Chinese, Italian, and Portuguese.

The "DOI Chronograph" [15] is a service about referrers of CrossRef DOIs, which is supplied by CrossRef Labs. This service shows the number of clicks on the basis of DOI link, referrers' domain names, and referrers' sub-domain names. However, this service is not from all access log data — but from small sample data.

2.3   Analyses of Wikipedia External Links

Tzekou et al. [16] analyzed external links on English Wikipedia (as of October, 2009) to investigate their decay and distribution in the English Wikipedia articles. Their results showed that roughly 18.3 % of external links were dead links. However, they noted that the majority of external links on Wikipedia were reachable, because very few articles contained a considerable amount of dead links and approximately 77.3 % of Wikipedia articles did not have dead links.

Sato et al. [17] investigated characteristics of external links and dead links on Japanese Wikipedia (as of April, 2011). As a result, they pointed out that (1) approximately 11 % of external links were dead, (2) contents hosted by the domains edu, co.jp, and go.jp had a high rate of access failures, and (3) many access failures occurred on contents hosted by newspaper-company websites.

3   About DOI

The DOI is an infrastructure that provides resolvable, persistent, and interoperable links. Each DOI consists of a prefix, a slash (/), and a suffix.

A prefix is assigned to a particular DOI registrant, such as publishing companies or academic societies. DOI registrants assign suffixes to their contents and register DOIs through DOI Registration Agencies (RAs). There are 10 RAs.

Some RAs that handle scholarly resources (such as journal articles, books, and datasets) are CrossRef, JaLC, ISTIC, and DataCite. JaLC is the only RA in Japan, ISTIC is a Chinese RA, and DataCite is an RA for research data. As of April 2016, there are 76,944,396 DOIs registered by CrossRef (CrossRef DOIs); 23,422,068 DOIs by ISTIC (ISTIC DOIs); 6,614,478 DOIs by DataCite (DataCite DOIs); and 1,401,144 DOIs by JaLC (JaLC DOIs).

The DOI also provides hyperlinks (DOI links) by adding DOI after "http:// doi.org/" or "http://dx.doi.org/." DOI links redirect to each original content's URI.

4   Materials and Methods

4.1   Datasets

In this study, we analyze DOI links on enwiki, jawiki, and zhwiki. To extract DOI links (as well as the page and the namespace written by these languages) from Wikipedia, we made use of the English dump file on March 4, 2015; the Japanese on March 13, 2015; and the Chinese on March 4, 2015.

In particular, we used extraction conditions that URLs of external links contained "doi.org" in the el_to column of externallinks.sql or the prefix of interwiki links equaled to "doi" in the iwl_prefix column of iwlinks.sql[1]. Thereafter, we removed non-DOI links. Table 1 shows the overview of our dataset.

---

[1] These two are provided in SQL file formats. Externallinks.sql contains page ids (el_from column) and URIs (el_to column). Iwlinks.sql contains page ids (iwl_from column), interwiki prefix codes (iwl_prefix column), and interwiki links (iwl_to column).

Table 1. Dataset overview

Language	No. of total DOI links	No. of unique pages	No. of unique DOI links
enwiki	1,474,230	166,490	519,736
jawiki	28,799	9,750	25,444
zhwiki	36,669	9,676	28,177

4.2 Methods

In this study, we performed a detailed analysis of DOI links on each language Wikipedia through the following three analyses:

Prefix-Level Analysis. We counted each prefix to clarify which registrant's content is most commonly referenced.

Overlap Analysis of Unique DOI Links Between Two Language Wikipedias. To analyze the overlap of unique DOI links between two different language Wikipedias, we used their difference set and product set. The former refers to DOI links referenced only in one language or another; the latter refers to those referenced in both languages (as Fig. 1 illustrates).

Comparison of DOI Links Through Interlanguage Links and Page-Revision Histories. Some DOI links seemed to be added to enwiki, before they were first added to jawiki or zhwiki pages. Thus, we extracted common DOI links through the following four steps:

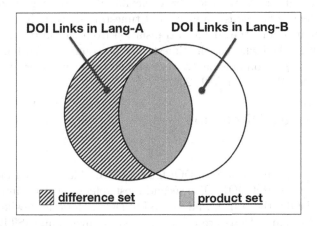

Fig. 1. Overview of the overlapping analysis of unique DOI links between two language Wikipedias

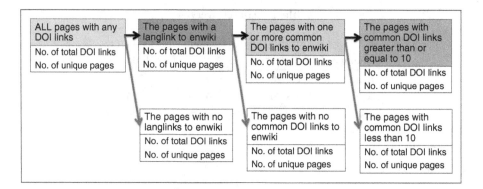

Fig. 2. A workflow of comparison of DOI links between different Wikipedia languages

- **STEP1**: We extracted DOI links, written in main namespace pages on each language Wikipedia (see Fig. 2: *"ALL"*).
- **STEP2**: We extracted the pages that have interlanguage links [18] to enwiki (i.e., correspondent pages) and DOI links written on these pages (see Fig. 2: *"The pages with a langlink to enwiki"*).
- **STEP3**: We extracted the pages that have common DOI links with the correspondent page — and the DOI links written on these pages (see Fig. 2: *"The pages with one or more common DOI links to enwiki"*)
- **STEP4**: We extracted the pages that have 10 or more common DOI links with the correspondent page (see Fig. 2: *"The pages with common DOI links greater than or equal to 10"*). Figure 3 shows an example of a page with common DOI links between jawiki and enwiki. This extraction condition, sharing 10 or more DOI links, was set on the basis of data observation.

We analyzed whether the extracted common DOI links were added to jawiki or zhwiki through the translation from enwiki. We used page-revision histories [19] to identify the edit summary and timestamp. We judged whether the edit summary mentions the edit as a translation from enwiki by manual. Moreover, we distinguished whether the timestamps on common DOI links that were first added to corresponding pages were earlier than jawiki or zhwiki. In the analysis, we used Wikipedia API [20].

5   Results and Discussion

5.1   Overview

Table 2 shows the number of total DOI links for RAs. Most of DOI links in these Wikipedia are CrossRef DOIs. The second most-referenced DOI links in enwiki are mEDRA DOIs; those in jawiki are JaLC DOIs; those in zhwiki are ISTIC DOIs. Note that JaLC DOIs are not referenced in zhwiki, and ISTIC DOIs are not referenced in jawiki. In other words, the scholarly content in Japan tends to be referenced in jawiki, the content in China tends to be referenced in zhwiki.

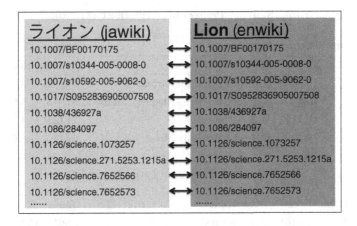

Fig. 3. An example of common DOI links between jawiki and enwiki

Table 2. The number of total DOI links for RAs

RA	enwiki	jawiki	zhwiki
AIRITI	2	0	0
CrossRef	**1,463,052**	**27,900**	**36,202**
DataCite	464	13	6
ISTIC	101	<u>0</u>	44
JaLC	9	549	<u>0</u>
mEDRA	647	5	9
OPOCE	176	2	3
Public	367	6	25
Error	9,412	324	380
Total	**1,474,230**	**28,799**	**36,669**

5.2 Prefix-Level Analysis

Tables 3, 4, and 5 demonstrate Top 5 prefixes in enwiki, jawiki, and zhwiki, respectively. The top-ranked prefix in these Wikipedias is 10.1016 (Elsevier BV) which accounts for about 15 %. Additionally, Nature Publishing Group (prefix:10.1038) and Wiley-Blackwell (prefix: 10.1002, prefix: 10.1111) are also common registrants in Top 5 prefixes.

Springer+Business Media (prefix: 10.1007) and American Chemical Society (prefix: 10.1021) are the common Registrants in two languages. From these findings, it is evident that a few common registrants in these Wikipedias host the majority of referenced contents.

Table 3. Top-5 Prefixes in enwiki (n=1,474,230)

Rank	Prefix	Registrant	Count	%
1	10.1016	Elsevier BV	245,360	16.6
2	10.1038	Nature Publishing Group	97,943	6.6
3	10.1007	Springer Science+Business Media	87,107	5.9
4	10.1111	Wiley-Blackwell	71,629	4.9
5	10.1093	Oxford University Press	67,657	4.6

Table 4. Top-5 Prefixes in jawiki (n=28,799)

Rank	Prefix	Registrant	Count	%
1	10.1016	Elsevier BV	4,565	15.9
2	10.1021	American Chemical Society	1,915	6.6
3	10.1007	Springer Science+Business Media	1,796	6.2
4	10.1002	Wiley-Blackwell	1,497	5.2
5	10.1038	Nature Publishing Group	1,497	6.2

Table 5. Top-5 Prefixes in zhwiki (n=36,669)

Rank	Prefix	Registrant	Count	%
1	10.1016	Elsevier BV	5,165	14.1
2	10.1021	American Chemical Society	2,588	7.1
3	10.1086	University of Chicago Press	2,530	6.9
4	10.1038	Nature Publishing Group	2,327	6.3
5	10.1002	Wiley-Blackwell	2,180	5.9

5.3 Overlap Analysis of Unique DOI Links Between Two Language Wikipedias

Table 6 illustrates overlaps between two Wikipedias per unique DOI links. For instance, "jawiki-enwiki" refers to the set of jawiki and enwiki in this table. Then, their difference set is constituted of the DOI links that are written in jawiki but not written in enwiki, and their product set is constituted of the DOI links that are written in both jawiki and enwiki. Each percentage is the proportion of the set of DOI links to jawiki.

From the product sets, overlaps to enwiki are 79 % in jawiki and 93 % in zhwiki. While zhwiki has more DOI links than jawiki, the overlapping ratio to enwiki is higher than jawiki. The product sets "enwiki-jawiki" and "enwiki-zhwiki" are small, compared to enwiki (about 5 %). The product sets of "jawiki-zhwiki" to jawiki and "zhwiki-jawiki" to zhwiki are also small, so overlapping ratios between jawiki and zhwiki are low. These findings indicate that many

DOI links might be added by translating from one to another — in the case of "jawiki-enwiki" and "zhwiki-enwiki." On the other hand, a consideration has been made that there are few DOI links added by translating from jawiki to zhwiki, and vice versa.

Table 6. Results of overlapping analysis of unique DOI links between two language Wikipedias

Target	jawiki - enwiki	enwiki - jawiki	zhwiki - enwiki	enwiki - zhwiki	jawiki - zhwiki	zhwiki - zhwiki
difference set	5,259	499,551	2,022	493,581	20,774	23,507
%	20.7	96.1	7.2	95.0	81.6	83.4
product set	20,185	20,185	26,155	26,155	4,670	4,670
%	**79.3**	**3.9**	**92.8**	**5.0**	**18.4**	**16.6**
total	25,444	519,736	28,177	519,736	25,444	28,177
%	100.0	100.0	100.0	100.0	100.0	100.0

5.4 Comparison of DOI Links Through Interlanguage Links and Page-Revision Histories

Table 7 shows the number of DOI links and pages concerning common DOI links between enwiki and other Wikipedia languages — through the workflow described in Fig. 2. Table 8 reveals that about 88 % of the common DOI links in the corresponding pages in jawiki were added by translating from enwiki.

Table 7. The number of DOI links and pages concerning common DOI links between enwiki and other Wikipedia languages

Language	ALL No. of total DOI links	No. of unique pages	The pages with a langlink to enwiki No. of total DOI links	No. of unique pages	The pages with one or more common DOI links to enwiki No. of total DOI links	No. of unique pages	The pages with common DOI links greater than or equal to 10 No. of total DOI links	No. of unique pages
enwiki	1,474,230	166,490	–	–	–	–	–	–
jawiki	28,799	9,570	26,987	9,118	20,599	7,122	6,133	327
zhwiki	36,669	9,676	35,099	9,351	31,161	8,579	12,915	634

Thus, there are a lot of DOI links in jawiki by translating from enwiki. While about 85 % DOI links in zhwiki were added with no information about translation in edit summaries, approximately 12 % remaining DOI links were identified by

Table 8. The number of DOI links that is identified as translation from enwiki or other language page by using edit summaries

Language	The pages with common DOI links greater than or equal to 10 No. of total DOI links	%	The pages translated from enwiki No. of total DOI links	%	The pages translated from other language page except English No. of total DOI links	%	Unknown No. of total DOI links	%
jawiki	6,133	100.0	5,413	88.3	49	0.8	671	10.9
zhwiki	12,915	100.0	1,479	11.5	408	3.2	11,028	85.4

translating from enwiki. This discrepancy seems to have occurred due to the difference between translation guidelines.

Figure 4 is an example of edit summary that is recorded in "ライオン (Lion)" (Lion) page of jawiki. It mentions the edit is translation from Lion page of enwiki and specifies its revision of original page.

> - (cur | prev)○   18:27, 10 November 2010 4 K (talk | contribs) ..
> (116,036 bytes) **(+95,384)** .. *(en:Lion (07:18, 18 October 2010 UTC)*
> から抄訳している) (undo | thank)

Fig. 4. An example of edit summary that mentions translation from enwiki

While the translation guideline in jawiki [21] requires mentioning of the source language and article when jawiki translates from other Wikipedias, the translation guideline in zhwiki [22] does not require such mentioning. Therefore, in zhwiki, it is difficult to identify DOI links through translations from enwiki.

Table 9 shows the number of DOI links that were added to enwiki before they were first added to the page. There are about 98 % DOI links in jawiki — and about 99 % DOI links in zhwiki — that were added to the page. Thus, the majority of DOI links in zhwiki are thought to be written through derived enwiki.

Table 9. The number of DOI links that were added in enwiki before they were first added to the page

Language	The pages with common DOI links greater than or equal to 10 No. of total DOI links	%	The DOI links were added in enwiki before they were first added to the page No. of total DOI links	%	Unknown No. of total DOI links	%
jawiki	6,133	100.0	6,024	98.2	109	1.8
zhwiki	12,915	100.0	12,808	99.2	107	0.8

6   Conclusion

In this study, we analyzed DOI links on English, Japanese, and Chinese Wikipedias to answer the following two research questions:

- RQ1. Which publishers or academic societies have content that is highly referenced on Wikipedia?

Most DOI links in these Wikipedias were CrossRef DOIs. The second most-referenced DOI links in jawiki were JaLC DOIs, whereas those in zhwiki were ISTIC DOIs. JaLC DOIs are uniquely referenced in jawiki, and ISTIC DOIs tend to be referenced in zhwiki. In terms of the analysis of prefixes, Elsevier BV is the largest registrant in all languages.

Also, Nature Publishing Group and Wiley-Blackwell are commonly referenced. The content hosted by these registrants is shared among the Wikipedia communities.

- RQ2. Does the highly referenced content vary among Wikipedia languages, or is it very similar to other languages?

Overlapping analysis showed that jawiki and zhwiki share the DOI links at a similar high rate with enwiki. An analysis of revision histories showed that the DOI links were added to pages in enwiki, before they were added to the corresponding pages in jawiki and zhwiki.

This analysis means that the majority of DOI links in jawiki and zhwiki were added by translating from enwiki. These findings imply that the DOI links in Wikipedia may result in multiple counts of altmetrics.

Acknowledgments. This work was partially supported by JSPS KAKENHI Grant Number JP26330362.

References

1. The International 2016, DOI Foundation. Digital Object Identifier System. http://www.doi.org/. Accessed April 12, 2016
2. The International 2016, DOI Foundation. Key Facts on Digital Object Identifier System. https://www.doi.org/factsheets/DOIKeyFacts.html. Accessed June 19, 2016
3. The International: DOI Foundation. (2016). doi:Registration Agencies. http://www.doi.org/registration_agencies.html. Accessed April 12, 2016
4. Geoffrey, B.: Strategic Initiatives Update (2015). http://www.slideshare.net/CrossRef/geoffrey-bilder-crossref15. Accessed April 12, 2016
5. Wikimedia Foundation. Wikipedia Statistics - Site map (2016). https://stats.wikimedia.org/EN/Sitemap.htm. Accessed April 12, 2016
6. Alexa Internet. Alexa - wikipedia.org Site Overview (2015). http://www.alexa.com/siteinfo/wikipedia.org. Accessed April 12, 2016
7. Nielsen, F.A.: Scientific citations in wikipedia. First Monday **12**(8), 795–825 (2007). http://doi.org/10.5210/fm.v12i8.1997

8. Lin, J., Fenner, M.: An analysis of Wikipedia references across PLOS publications. In: altmetrics14 Workshop at WebSci, June 2014. http://doi.org/10.6084/m9.figshare.1048991.v3

9. Halfaker, A.: Extract academic citations from Wikipedia (2016). https://github.com/mediawiki-utilities/python-mwcites. Accessed April 12, 2016

10. Mietchen, A., Klein, M., Taraborelli, D., Halfaker, A.: Usage of Digital Object Identifiers across Wikimedia projects, July 2015. https://wikimania2015.wikimedia.org/wiki/Submissions/Usage_of_Digital_Object_Identifiers_across_Wikimedia_projects. Accessed April 12, 2016

11. Wikipedia. Research: Scholarly article citations in Wikipedia (2016). https://meta.wikimedia.org/wiki/Research:Scholarly_article_citations_in_Wikipedia. Accessed April 12, 2016

12. The International: DOI Foundation. (2016). doi:Registration Agencies. http://www.doi.org/registration_agencies.html. Accessed April 12, 2016

13. Wikimedia Tool Labs. Wikipedia Cite-o-Meter: Find citations by publisher in Wikipedia (2011). https://tools.wmflabs.org/cite-o-meter/. Accessed April 12, 2016

14. Bilder, G.: Many Metrics. Such Data. Wow. - Crossref Blog (2014). http://crosstech.crossref.org/2014/02/many-metrics-such-data-wow.html. Accessed April 12, 2016

15. CrossRef Labs. 2016, DOI Chronograph. http://chronograph.labs.crossref.org/. Accessed April 12, 2016

16. Tzekou, P., Stamou, S., Kirtsis, N., Zotos, N.: Quality assessment of Wikipedia external links. In: Proceedings of the 7th International Conference on Web Information Systems and Technologies, pp. 248–254 (2011). http://www.dblab.upatras.gr/download/nlp/NLP-Group-Pubs/11-WEBIST_Wikipedia_External_Links.pdf

17. Sato, S., Yoshida, M., Ambiru, T., Itsumura, T.: Characteristics of external links and dead links in Japanese Wikipedia. J. Jpn Soc. Inf. Knowl. **21**(2), 157–162 (2011). http://doi.org/10.2964/jsik.21_06, in Japanese

18. Wikipedia. Help: Interlanguage links - Wikipedia (2016). https://en.wikipedia.org/wiki/Help:Interlanguage_links. Accessed April 12, 2016

19. Wikipedia. Help: Page history (2016). https://en.wikipedia.org/wiki/Help:Page_history. Accessed April 12, 2016

20. Wikimedia Foundation. API: Main page - MediaWiki (2016). https://www.mediawiki.org/wiki/API:Main_page/en. Accessed April 12, 2016

21. Wikipedia. Wikipedia:翻訳のガイドライン. (2016). https://ja.wikipedia.org/wiki/Wikipedia:%E7%BF%BB%E8%A8%B3%E3%81%AE%E3%82%AC%E3%82%A4%E3%83%89%E3%83%A9%E3%82%A4%E3%83%B3. Accessed 12 April 2016. (in Japanese)

22. Wikipedia 維基百科:翻譯守則(2016). https://zh.wikipedia.org/wiki/Wikipedia:%E7%BF%BB%E8%AF%91%E5%AE%88%E5%88%99. Accessed April 12, 2016, in Chinese

Cross-Modal Search on Social Networking Systems by Exploring Wikipedia Concepts

Wei Wang[1(✉)], Xiaoyan Yang[2], and Shouxu Jiang[3]

[1] School of Computing, National University of Singapore, Singapore, Singapore
wangwei@comp.nus.edu.sg
[2] Advanced Digital Sciences Center, Singapore, Singapore
xiaoyan.yang@adsc.com.sg
[3] School of Computer Science and Technology,
Harbin Institute of Technology Harbin, Harbin, China
jsx@hit.edu.cn

Abstract. The increasing popularity of social networking systems (SNSs) has created large quantities of data from multiple modalities such as text and image. Retrieval of data, however, is constrained to a specific modality. Moreover, text on SNSs is usually short and noisy, and remains active for a (short) period. Such characteristics, conflicting with settings of traditional text search techniques, render them ineffective in SNSs. To alleviate these problems and bridge the gap between searches over different modalities, we propose a new algorithm that supports cross-modal search about social documents as text and images on SNSs. By exploiting Wikipedia concepts, text and images are transformed into a set of common concepts, based on which searches are conducted. A new ranking algorithm is designed to rank social documents based on their *informativeness* and *semantic relevance* to a query. We evaluate our ranking algorithm on both Twitter and Facebook datasets. The results confirm the effectiveness of our approach.

1 Introduction

Social Networking Systems (SNSs) such as Facebook and Twitter have become the platforms for people to share their interests and activities, to socialize and to interact with others. Consequently, these SNSs contain a huge amount of information from different modalities. For example, a post in Facebook or a tweet in Twitter may contain both text and images. We call such a post or tweet a cross-modal *social document*. Typical users in social networking systems have interest in multiple modalities: a user may want to search relevant images given a piece of text or retrieve relevant text descriptions given an image. Therefore, a cross-modal search service that retrieves relevant social documents (e.g., text or image) from different modalities is needed, especially in the context of Big Data in SNSs. In this paper we study cross-modal search over two modalities, i.e., image and text.

Most of the current SNSs only provide search service within single modality, i.e., intra-modal search. Moreover, the keyword-based intra-modal search over

© Springer International Publishing AG 2016
A. Morishima et al. (Eds.): ICADL 2016, LNCS 10075, pp. 381–393, 2016.
DOI: 10.1007/978-3-319-49304-6_41

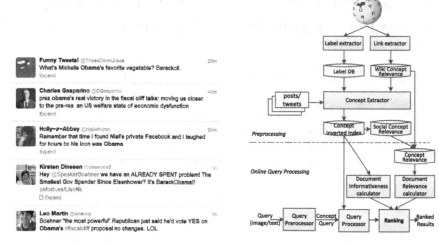

Fig. 1. Screenshot of tweets returned by searching 'Obama' in Twitter taken on 1/1/2013

Fig. 2. System overview

text is insufficient in handling information retrieval on SNSs. For example, Fig. 1 shows the results of search using keyword 'Obama' in Twitter shortly after the U.S. president election of 2012. From the user's perspective, results related to 'Barack Obama' are probably expected for this query. The search results are, however, generally ranked based on popularity and timestamp. Considering the content of returned tweets in the results, the fifth one contains the most relevant information, but is underrated by the search service. The search results also include tweets that contain little useful information like the third one. Such insufficiency in text search is partially caused by the characteristics of text documents on SNSs, which tend to be much shorter and noisy compared with common web documents. Such short text brings new problems to traditional text retrieval methods. For example, it is difficult to differentiate a key term (e.g., 'Obama' in Fig. 1) from other terms based on their tf (term frequency) values, as most words (terms) appear only once in a short document. Besides the insufficiency in text retrieval, current search services in most SNSs do not support image queries.

To solve the issues stated above, we propose to exploit Wikipedia concepts and convert social documents from different modalities into a common concept space. Based on this uniform data representation, a novel concept-based cross-modal search method is proposed. The intuitions of our approach are as follows: *First*, representing data using Wikipedia concepts, which have well-defined semantics, allow us to measure the semantic relevance of social documents more precisely, and therefore improve the quality of search results. For example, if we rank tweets in Fig. 1 according to relevance of concepts extracted from them, the fifth tweet would be ranked much higher than the third one, as it contains word 'Republican' representing concept relevant to *Barack Obama*. *Second*, concept representation can alleviate search ineffectiveness incurred by synonym and polysemy, which are more serious in the context of short text. With the help of Wikipedia corpus, we can extract concepts associated with social documents accurately so that documents described with synonymous/polysemous words can be related/differentiated. *Third*, we can support image queries over text and images more efficiently. By annotating images (and text) with concepts, relevant social documents can be retrieved as long as they share similar semantics (concepts) with the query image. *Last*, concepts can help filter uninformative documents in social networking systems. A novel *informativeness* measure is proposed that leverages concepts in documents, document length and popularity. A major drawback of exiting methods that use Wikipedia concepts to measure document relevance is that they calculate concept relevance merely from knowledge base like Wikipedia, which may not capture the emerging and trending topics in SNSs. To address this, a novel concept relevance measure is proposed that integrates information from both Wikipedia and samples of recent social documents.

2 Preliminary and System Overview

Definition 1 (Concept). A concept is defined as the representative of an Wikipedia article. Each Wikipedia article describes a unique concept. The title of each article is used as the concept name.

Besides titles of articles, Wikipedia provides many surface forms (aliases) for each concept through link anchors, redirect pages and disambiguation pages. The surface forms help define synonyms of a concept, which are useful in search. For example, the surface forms of concept *Apple Inc.* consist of 'Apple Inc.' from article title, 'Apple Inc' from redirect page title and 'Apple' from disambiguation page title and link anchors.

Definition 2 (Concept Relevance). Concept relevance is a similarity measure of the semantic relevance between two concepts, with value in $[0, 1]$. A larger value indicates two concepts are more relevant.

We define concept relevance considering factors from two domains: Wikipedia and SNSs. In particular, two types of concept relevance measures are defined: the Wikiepdia-based relevance r_w and the social-network-based relevance r_s. The overall concept relevance r is the combination of r_s and r_w.

Definition 3 (Wikipedia Label). A Wikipedia label [11] is a key-value pair, in which the key is a concept surface string, and the value is a list of concepts called senses that share the surface form.

Definition 4 (Document Informativeness). Document informativeness is a measure of quality of information contained in social documents. A larger value indicates a social document is more informative.

Problem Definition. The *cross-modal search* problem is defined as two sub-problems:

1. *Concept Relevance Calculation*: given two concepts a, b and documents containing these two concepts, calculate the relevance $r(a, b)$ of a and b.
2. *Cross-modal Social Document Ranking*: given a query (text or image), rank the social documents based on the concept relevance and the informativeness of each document.

System Overview. Figure 2 shows the overview of our cross-modal search system. It consists of two components: *preprocessing* and *online query processing*. The preprocessing part first extracts Wikipedia labels and page links from Wikipedia articles. It then builds the label dictionary (for text conceptualization) and calculate Wikipedia concept relevance. Social documents are fed into the concept extractor, which recognizes the concepts in each document and builds an inverted index for each concept. The inverted index serves for concept retrieval and social concept relevance calculation. In the online query processing part, the query concepts are extracted from an intra-modal search, in which concepts of top-ranked documents relevant to the query are used as query concepts. All documents containing at least one query concept are returned by the inverted concept index. These candidate documents are ranked according to their informativeness and relevance to the query. Data from other modality than text and image can also be supported in our system as long as intra-modal search for that modality is available.

3   Concept Relevance Calculation

Let a denote a concept. Given two concepts a and b, we consider documents containing a and (or) b to decide their semantic relevance. Let A denote the set of documents that a appears. We define concept relevance $r(a, b)$ as,

$$r(a, b) = 1 - f(A, B) \tag{1}$$

where $f(A, B)$ is a distance function defined over sets A and B. We use existing distance functions for $f(A, B)$, since it is not the focus of this paper to define new distance functions. In this paper, we apply Normalized Google Distance [2] (NGD, Eq. 2)[1] on document sets, which is a widely used semantic similarity measure [4,12,16].

$$f(A, B) = \frac{\log(\max(|A|, |B|)) - \log(|A \cap B|)}{\log|W| - \log(\min(|A|, |B|))} \tag{2}$$

Let A_w denote the sets of Wikipedia articles that concept a appears as a link. According to (1), the *Wikipedia-based concept relevance* r_w is defined as $r_w(a, b) = 1 - f(A_w, B_w)$.

---

[1] We have tried different similarity measures such as cosine similarity. NGD performs the best.

However, Wikipedia articles are not sufficient to capture the semantic relationship between two concepts. The relevance of some concept pairs are time-dependent. For example, concept *Barack Obama* and *Mitt Romney* were less related before 2012, but were highly related around October 2012 during president election. Few articles in Wikipedia mentioned both of them together before November 2012. As a result, the relevance of these two concepts is underestimated when only considering Wikipedia articles. The top related concepts of *Barack Obama* are about the 2008 president election while *Mitt Romney* is out of the top 10 related concepts based on Wikipedia articles. We need documents from other domains to reflect relevance of concepts from trending events.

Social networking systems convey rich information about trending topics and are thus widely used to improve tasks like image retrieval [3,13] and personalized recommendation [6] etc. Let A_s denote the set of social documents where concept a appears. We define the *social network-based concept relevance* as $r_s(a,b) = 1 - f(A_s, B_s)$. Although r_s reflect relevance of concepts involved in trending events well, it is not sufficient to use r_s along. This is because the accuracy of r_s depends on the quality of conceptualization tool and the size of sampled social documents.

To overcome the problems of r_w and r_s, we define a novel relevance measure r that combines these two. In particular, we consider r_w as the long-time relevance and r_s as the short-time one, which is used as a complementary relevance measure to r_w for trending concept pairs. Based on this intuition, we define the concept relevance r as

$$r(a,b) = (1 - \xi(a,b))r_w(a,b) + \xi(a,b)r_s(a,b) \tag{3}$$

which is the weighted sum of r_w and r_s, and $\xi(a,b)$ is the weight function representing confidence of r_s defined as,

$$\xi(a,b) = \begin{cases} 0 & \text{if } r_s(a,b) \leq r_w(a,b) \\ \frac{2}{\pi}\arctan(\frac{\pi \cdot \omega}{2} \cdot \min(|A_s|,|B_s|)) & \text{if } r_s(a,b) > r_w(a,b) \end{cases} \tag{4}$$

The intuitions are as follows: (1) When $r_s \leq r_w$, a, b are less mentioned in social documents than in Wikipedia articles. In such a case, we rely on Wikipedia articles, which are more reliable than social documents, to decide concept relevance and set $\xi(a,b) = 0$, i.e., $r = r_w$. (2) When $r_s > r_w$, consider the following two extreme cases: When $\min(|A_s|,|B_s|)$ is very small, we are likely to get a large value for r_s according to NGD. This happens and is validated in real world SNS dataset[2]. Such r_s is not reliable and should be assigned low confidence. When $\min(|A_s|,|B_s|)$ is large, a and b must co-occur frequently so that $r_s > r_w$. In this case, a and b form trending concept pair and r_s should be assigned high confidence. Therefore, we use a normalized arctan function with range $[0,1]$ to define $\xi(a,b)$ (Eq. 4), which increases monotonically with $\min(|A_s|,|B_s|)$, i.e., we assign higher confidence to r_s when $\min(|A_s|,|B_s|)$ is larger. When $\min(|A_s|,|B_s|)$ is large enough, we have $\xi(a,b) \approx 1$, i.e., $r = r_s$. ω is a small coefficient (we used 0.003 and 0.009 in our experiments).

---

[2] Details are discussed in the experiment section.

4   Cross-Modal Social Documents Ranking

In this section, we describe the social documents ranking process in our cross-modal search system. In particular, we present details of query conceptualization, informativeness measure and document relevance calculation. Finally, an online query processing algorithm is presented.

4.1   Preprocessing: Query Conceptualization

In preprocessing, social documents are fed into the concept extractor, which recognizes concepts contained. Each document is then represented by a set of Wikipedia concepts. To support cross-modal search, we also need to convert the original query into a set of Wikipedia concepts. Wikipedia provides a broad range of concepts to describe queries. The main idea of query conceptualization is to utilize intra-modal search to find concepts relevant to a query.

For *image query*, following [8], we retrieve similar images using state-of-art content-based image retrieval(CBIR) method, which compares the query image with images in social documents based on image features such as color and shape. Concepts in top similar images are used as the context of the query. To select representative query concepts from its context, we measure the *stickiness* of each concept c to a query q defined as,

$$stickness(c, q) = \sum_{c' \in C, c' \neq c} r(c, c') \times w(c), \quad w(c) = \sum_{d \in D, c \in d} s_i(d) \tag{5}$$

where C is the context of q. $w(c)$ is the weight for concept c, which is the sum of intra-modal search scores (i.e., s_i)[3] of documents that contain c. D is the set of similar documents to q. The top k(e.g., $k = 3$) concepts with largest stickiness scores are used as the query concepts in our system.

For *text query*, we first try to detect query concepts by looking up the Wikipedia label dictionary using keywords in the query. However, text queries usually contain few words (e.g., $2 - 3$), which is not sufficient to serve as context for concept disambiguation. Therefore, we use intra-modal text search supported by Lucene[4] to retrieve similar social documents, and use concepts in top-ranked documents to form the context for disambiguating query concepts. If no concept is detected from the query text, we then follow image query conceptualization and select top k concepts from the context according to their stickiness scores.

4.2   Document Informativeness

To filter uninformative social documents, we propose a novel document *informativeness* measure that considers factors from three perspectives: document

---

[3] For image query, we use the cosine similarity calculated based on image features as the intra-modal search score. For text query, we use *tf-idf* similarity as the intra-modal search score.

[4] http://lucene.apache.org/.

concept ratio, length and popularity. Given a document d, its informativeness $i(d)$ is defined as

$$i(d) = i_c(d) \times i_l(d) \times i_p(d) \tag{6}$$

where i_c is the normalized concept ratio, i_l, the normalized document length and i_p, the normalized document popularity.

Document Concept Ratio. Given a document d, let $n(d)$ denote the number of distinct concepts d contains and $N(d)$ the total number of concepts mentioned in d. We define concept ratio d_c of document d as, $d_c = \frac{n(d)}{N(d)}$, and apply Gaussian function on d_c as normalization to measure the impact of concept ratio, and define i_c as,

$$i_c(d) = \frac{1}{\sigma_c\sqrt{2\pi}} e^{-\frac{1}{2}(\frac{d_c-\mu_c}{\sigma_c})^2} \tag{7}$$

For $N(d) = 0$, we set $i_c(d) = 0$. $i_c(d)$ aims to capture the percentage of distinct concepts over all mentioned in social documents. This would help to filter two types of social documents: those without any concept, and those with (many) duplicate concepts. Based on study of tweet dataset, we set $\sigma_c = 0.4$ and $\mu_c = 0.3$ in our system, which work well on real dataset.

Document Length. Let d_l denote the length of document d in terms of number of words. Similar to i_c, we apply Gaussian function to model the effect of document length, and define $i_l(d)$ as,

$$i_l(d) = \frac{1}{\sigma_l\sqrt{2\pi}} e^{-\frac{1}{2}(\frac{d_l-\mu_l}{\sigma_l})^2} \tag{8}$$

In our system, we set $\mu_l = 20$ and $\sigma_l = 15$. i_l helps to filter documents with too few (many) words.

Document Popularity. Let d_p denote the popularity score of a social document d. In our system, we use number of retweets of a Tweet in Twitter and number of likes of a post in Facebook as d_p. We define $i_p(d)$ as,

$$i_p(d) = log(d_p) \tag{9}$$

4.3 Document Relevance

Given a query q and a social document d, we propose a novel document relevance measure $r(q,d)$ to capture the semantic relationship of q and d based on concept relevance and document informativeness, defined as,

$$r(q,d) = \sum_{c\in C(q)} w(c) \sum_{c'\in C(d)} f^*(c') \times r(c,c'), \quad f^*(c') = \frac{2}{\pi}\arctan(\pi/2 \cdot f(c'))\tag{10}$$

where $C(d)$ is the set of concepts in d and $C(q)$ is the set of concepts in q. $w(c)$ (Eq. 5) is a boost factor of c. $f^*(c')$ measures the impact of frequency of concept

---

Algorithm 1. onlineSearch(q, I)

Input: q, (text or image) query; I, inverted index mapping concept to documents that
   contain it
Output: R, search results containing top ranked documents
   1. $S \leftarrow \emptyset$ //candidate document set
   2. $C(q) \leftarrow$ extractQueryConcepts(q);
   3. $S \leftarrow$ getCandidateDocuments($C(q), I$)
   4. **for** each $d \in S$ **do**
   5.   calculate $score(q, d)$ according to Eqn. 11
   6. $R \leftarrow$ rank documents in S based on $score(q, d)$

---

c' in d, where $f(c')$ is the number of occurrences of c' in d. $f^*(c)$ assigns larger weight to a concept c with larger $f(c)$, as c is likely to be the main topic of a document when it appears more than once. Notice that $f^*(c)$ nearly converges to 1 when $f(c) > 3$, as we do not want to distinguish concepts that appear many times. *idf* scores of concepts are not used since it is already captured in the distance function (NGD).

4.4 Social Document Ranking Based on Document Relevance and Informativeness

Given a query q and its concept set $C(q)$, we first retrieve social documents that contain at least one concept $c \in C(q)$ as candidates S. Candidate documents $d \in S$ are then ranked based on $score(q, d)$ defined as

$$score(q, d) = \mathrm{r}(q, d) \times i(d) \tag{11}$$

which combines d's relevance to q (Eq. 10) and informativeness (Eq. 6). The top ranked documents are returned as the search results of q. The detailed online cross-modal query processing is presented in Algorithm 1.

5   Experiments

We conduct extensive experimental studies on our cross-modal search system. First, we compare the effectiveness of different relevance measures. Second, we evaluate the effectiveness of cross-modal search using two SNS datasets. Nine researchers from computer science domain are invited to rate the experimental results.

We use the English Wikipedia dump released on 1/11/2012, which contains about 3.7 million articles. Wikipedia-Miner [11] is applied to extract Wikipedia labels. Similar as [5], we filter meaningless labels whose keys contain only chronology words (e.g., '100 BC'), numbers, stop words and phrases starting with 'A list of'. Finally, we construct a Wikipedia label dictionary with 9,091,347 entries.

Datasets. We collect data from *Twitter* and *Facebook*. For Facebook, we only have access to posts of Public Pages. We prepare a list of English public pages

Table 1. Statistics of datasets

	# Document	# Image	Publish time
Twitter	2,159,889	188,906	Dec. 2012
Facebook	1,714,891	551,217	Oct. 2012

Table 2. Mapping of concept relevance

Label	Relevance value range
Very related	$(0.75, 1]$
Related	$(0.5, 0.75]$
Less related	$(0.3, 0.5]$

from Facebook's Public Page Directory[5], and crawl 50 posts published in October 2012 from each of these pages via Facebook's API. For Twitter, we prepare a list of $193,926$ Twitter users, and use Twitter4J[6] to crawl tweets of these users. For each user, we crawl 100 tweets published in December 2012. The statistics of the two datasets are summarized in Table 1.

Social Document Conceptualization. We apply Wikipedia-Miner to extract concepts in social documents. For each document, concept mentions are detected by looking up the Wikipedia label dictionary. Disambiguation are conducted by analyzing the consistency between concepts and the context. For example, if concept *iPad* and *iPhone* have appeared in the context, then word 'Apple' would probably mean *Apple Inc.* instead of *Apple (fruit)*. For social documents that are too short to serve as context for concept disambiguation, we use all social documents of the same publisher as the context.

5.1 Evaluation of Concept Relevance

To validate the design of concept relevance r (Eq. 3[7]), we compare it with r_s and r_w in terms of precision in reflecting semantic relationship of concept pairs. We divide all concept pairs (a, b) into 5 groups based on their minimum occurrences, i.e., $\min(|A|, |B|)$. For each group, 40 concept pairs are randomly selected from each dataset such that $r_s > r_w > 0.3$[8]. Then the invited researchers are asked to rate the relevance of each concept pair. Three types of labels are provided: *very related*, *related*, and *less related*. The ground truth label of each pair is decided by majority voting.

Given relevance values $(r, r_s$ and $r_w)$ of a concept pair, its label is decided according to Table 2. We compare it with the ground truth label and report the accuracy in Fig. 3. Accuracy of a relevance measure r is defined as follows: Let $n_i(r)$ denote the number of corrected labeled concept pairs in group $i (1 \leq i \leq 5)$ based on r. We report $\frac{n_i(r)}{40}$ as accuracy for r in group i. From Fig. 3 we can see that when $\min(|A_s|, |B_s|)$ increases, the accuracy of r_s increases while that

---

[5] http://www.facebook.com/directory/pages/.

[6] http://twitter4j.org/en/index.html.

[7] For $\xi(a, b)$ (Eq. 4), we set $\omega = 0.009$ for Twitter and $\omega = 0.003$ for Facebook.

[8] Concept pairs with $r_w \leq 0.3$ are not considered as they are usually not related. Concept pairs with $r_s < r_w$ are also not considered as we have $r = r_w$ if $r_s < r_w$ (Eq. 3).

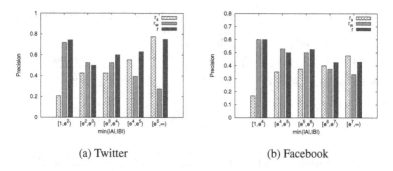

(a) Twitter   (b) Facebook

Fig. 3. Comparison of concept relevance measures.

of r_w decreases. This confirms the intuitions behind the definition of r. When $\min(|A_s|, |B_s|)$ becomes large, which indicates that the concept pair is a trending topic in SNSs, the accuracy of r_w becomes low as r_w cannot reflect the semantic relationship of trending concept pairs well. Therefore, larger weights are assigned to r_s when $\min(|A_s|, |B_s|)$ increases as in Eq. 4, which makes it more important in r (Eq. 3). When $\min(|A_s|, |B_s|)$ is small, r_s is less reliable than r_w and therefore plays a small role in r. Overall, the integrated concept relevance r has the highest accuracy and proves to be most effective relevance measure among the three.

5.2   Evaluation of Cross-Modal Search

We study the effectiveness and efficiency of our proposed cross-modal search method on processing text queries and image queries respectively. Let Q denote the query set. For evaluation of search effectiveness, we use $Precision@k$ as the evaluation metric, defined as:

$$Precision@k = \frac{\sum_{q \in Q} N(q, k)}{|Q| \times k} \tag{12}$$

where $N(q, k)$ is the number of relevant items in the top k results for query q.

We compare our concept-based cross-modal search method (denoted as CCS) with two baselines: (1) CDS [8] is most related to CCS. It is also a concept-based cross-modal search approach that uses the vector space model in Lucene[9] to retrieve social documents after converting them into concept vectors. (2) Indri[10] is an advanced search engine based on a combination of language modeling and inference network. It supports pseudo relevance feedback based query expansion method that outperforms the vector space model provided by Lucene.

Text Query. For evaluation, we prepare 20 text queries by randomly selecting concepts from Twitter and Facebook data. Each query contains 1 to 3 concepts

---

[9] http://lucene.apache.org/.
[10] http://www.lemurproject.org/indri.php.

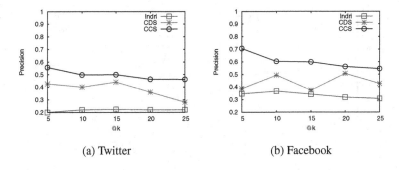

(a) Twitter   (b) Facebook

Fig. 4. Evaluation of search effectiveness on text queries

with topics covering celebrities (e.g., Lady Gaga), news (e.g., US School shooting) and etc. Similar as in TREC Microblog track, we test the precision for all (highly) relevant documents. The invited researchers are asked to label the relevant documents in the top k ($k = 30$) results. A document d is labeled as relevant to a query q if q is mentioned in d and d is informative.

The results are shown in Fig. 4. Two concept-based methods CCS and CDS perform better than Indri. This is because converting text queries into concept queries helps disambiguate the intent of user queries better. Further, concept-based methods can detect synonyms of keywords in queries easily by exploring surface forms of concepts. On the other hand, Indri's query expansion method would suffer from over-expansion such that the topic or intent of a query drifts. It would also suffer from ranking uninformative documents with repeated query keywords high. Among the concept-based methods, CCS performs better than CDS, as CCS considers both concept relevance and informativeness when retrieving documents. The performance of CDS is not as stable as that of CCS. The precision curve of CCS goes up and down over different k, indicating some randomness in the ranking of results. Overall, CCS outperforms the two baselines CDS and Indri by achieving the highest precision on both Twitter and Facebook.

Image Query. We prepare 20 image queries for evaluation by randomly selecting images (with improper ones filtered) from Twitter and Facebook data. Besides CDS, we compare CCS with Lire [9], a content based image retrieval method using Color and Edge Directivity Descriptor (denoted as Lire-CEDD). The invited researchers are asked to label the relevant documents in the top k ($k = 10$) results. Figure 5 shows the results. We observe similar trends as for text queries. CCS outperforms CDS and Lire-CEDD on both Twitter and Facebook with the exception of *precision*@3 on Facebook. This is because Facebook has a larger image dataset which contains more visually similar or nearly duplicate images. Lire+CEDD retrieves those nearly duplicate images in the top few results and achieves high *precision*@3. However, its performance decreases a lot when k increases. Similar to text queries, the performance of CDS is not stable as shown in Fig. 5.

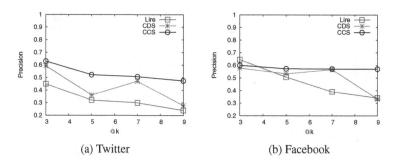

(a) Twitter   (b) Facebook

Fig. 5. Evaluation of search effectiveness on image queries

6   Related Work

Cross-Modal Search. Previous papers [1,7,14,15,17] tried to learn to map functions or project matrices to transform data in different domains represented by a feature vector into a common space, where traditional similarity functions such as cosine can be applied. The major drawback of these methods are that the mapped space usually does not contain semantic information, i.e., it is difficult to explain the features in the common space. [10,15] annotated image and text document with a semantic vector, with each ordinate representing the probability that the document contains a predefined concept. Considering annotation cost, only some high-level concepts, such as music, history, were used in the semantic space.

Wikipedia Concept Relevance. Wikipedia has a broad range of topics. Each page could be used as a concept. [12] applied the Normalized Google Distance [2] to compute concept relatedness. Although Wikipedia is updated frequently, the concept relatedness calculated based on Wikipedia data only still cannot capture the relatedness of concepts from hot events. Thus, we combined relatedness computed from Wikipedia and Social Network data as an improved measurement.

7   Conclusions

In this paper, we propose a new cross-modal search method for SNSs. We exploit Wikipedia to convert all data into a common concept space, in which we rank social documents based on their semantic relevance with respect to a query. We propose a novel concept relevance measure that integrates information from both Wikipedia and social network data. An informativeness measure is also proposed to filter uninformative documents in SNSs. Experimental results show that our proposed measures and cross-modal ranking method largely improve the search quality.

Acknowledgements. This research was funded by the National Research Foundation, Prime Ministers Office, Singapore, under its Competitive Research Programme

(CRP Award No. NRF-CRP8-2011-08). Xiaoyan Yang was supported by the research grant for the Human Centered Cyber-physical Systems Programme at the Advanced Digital Sciences Center from Singapores Agency for Science, Technology and Research (A*STAR).

References

1. Bronstein, M.M., Bronstein, A.M., Michel, F., Paragios, N.: Data fusion through cross-modality metric learning using similarity-sensitive hashing. In: CVPR, pp. 3594–3601 (2010)
2. Cilibrasi, R., Vitányi, P.M.B.: The google similarity distance. IEEE Trans. Knowl. Data Eng. **19**(3), 370–383 (2007)
3. Cui, P., Liu, S., Zhu, W., Luan, H., Chua, T., Yang, S.: Social-sensed image search. ACM Trans. Inf. Syst. **32**(2), 8 (2014)
4. Han, X., Zhao, J.: Structural semantic relatedness: A knowledge-based method to named entity disambiguation. In: ACL, pp. 50–59 (2010)
5. Hu, J., Fang, L., Cao, Y., Zeng, H.-J., Li, H., Yang, Q., Chen, Z.: Enhancing text clustering by leveraging wikipedia semantics. In: SIGIR, pp. 179–186 (2008)
6. Jiang, M., Cui, P., Liu, R., Yang, Q., Wang, F., Zhu, W., Yang, S.: Social contextual recommendation. In: Chen, X., Lebanon, G., Wang, H., Zaki, M.J. (eds.), 21st ACM International Conference on Information and Knowledge Management, CIKM 2012, Maui, HI, USA, October 29 - November 02, pp. 45–54. ACM (2012)
7. Kumar, S., Udupa, R.: Learning hash functions for cross-view similarity search. In: IJCAI, pp. 1360–1365 (2011)
8. Liu, C., Wu, S., Jiang, S., Tung, A.K.H.: Cross domain search by exploiting wikipedia. In: ICDE, pp. 546–557 (2012)
9. Lux, M., Chatzichristofis, S.A.: Lire: lucene image retrieval: an extensible java CBIR library. In: MM, pp. 1085–1088. ACM (2008)
10. Magalhães, J., Ciravegna, F., Rüger, S.M.: Exploring multimedia in a keyword space. In: ACM Multimedia, pp. 101–110 (2008)
11. Milne, D., Witten, I.H.: An open-source toolkit for mining wikipedia. Artif. Intell. **194**, 222–239 (2013)
12. Milne, D.N., Witten, I.H.: Learning to link with wikipedia. In: CIKM, pp. 509–518 (2008)
13. Popescu, A., Grefenstette, G.: Social media driven image retrieval. In: ICMR, Trento, Italy, April 18–20, p. 33 (2011)
14. Qi, G., Aggarwal, C.C., Huang, T.S.: Towards semantic knowledge propagation from text corpus to web images. In: WWW, pp. 297–306 (2011)
15. Rasiwasia, N., Pereira, J.C., Coviello, E., Doyle, G., Lanckriet, G.R.G., Levy, R., Vasconcelos, N.: A new approach to cross-modal multimedia retrieval. In: ACM Multimedia, pp. 251–260 (2010)
16. Shen, W., Wang, J., Luo, P., Wang, M.: Linden: linking named entities with knowledge base via semantic knowledge. In: WWW, pp. 449–458 (2012)
17. Zhen, Y., Yeung, D.-Y.: A probabilistic model for multimodal hash function learning. In: KDD, pp. 940–948 (2012)

Suggesting Specific Segments as Link Targets in Wikipedia

Renzhi Wang[(✉)] and Mizuho Iwaihara

Graduate School of Information, Production, and Systems,
Waseda University, Kitakyushu 808-0135, Japan
ouninnyuki.ips@asagi.waseda.jp, iwaihara@waseda.jp

Abstract. Wikipedia is the largest online encyclopedia, in which articles form knowledgeable and semantic resources. Links within Wikipedia indicate that the two texts of a link origin and destination are related about their semantic topics. Existing link detection methods focus on article titles because most of links in Wikipedia point to article titles. But there are a number of links in Wikipedia pointing to corresponding segments, because the whole article is too general and it is hard for readers to obtain the intention of the link. We propose a method to automatically predict whether a link target is a specific segment and provide which segment is most relevant. We propose a combination method of Latent Dirichlet Allocation (LDA) and Maximum Likelihood Estimation (MLE) to represent every segment as a vector, then we obtain similarity of each segment pair, finally we utilize variance, standard deviation and other statistical features to predict the results. Through evaluations on Wikipedia articles, our method performs better result than existing methods.

Keywords: Wikipedia · Link suggestion · Text mining · LDA

1 Introduction

Wikipedia articles are edited by various volunteers from all over the world, with different thoughts and styles. One of Wikipedia's characters is the featured articles. Wikipedia includes many high quality articles that reach the standard of featured article criteria. These articles are usually edited by experienced authors and checked by Wikipedia's administrators. Featured articles are supposed to be well-written, comprehensive, well-researched, neutral and stable. Wikipedia is structured via a number of links between different articles, which imply that the two linked articles are closely related. Majority of links within Wikipedia are pointing to article titles, and only small fractions point to segment titles. However, when readers browse topic via links, sometimes they are only interested in certain segments while the link itself is pointing to article titles, so the readers will probably get lost in such long articles. To avoid such situations, administrators and editors often modify link target text from an article title to a specific segment title. Figure 1 shows an example that an editor modified the link target from the article title to the a specific segment. In article "Super Mario 64" there is a link, first pointed to article GameCube, then the editor corrected the link to the segment "Controller".

© Springer International Publishing AG 2016
A. Morishima et al. (Eds.): ICADL 2016, LNCS 10075, pp. 394–405, 2016.
DOI: 10.1007/978-3-319-49304-6_42

Like *Wave Race 64*, *Super Mario 64* was re-released in Japan on July 18, 1997, as *Super Mario 64 Shindō Pak Taiō Version* (スーパーマリオ64 振動パック対応バージョン). This version adds support for Nintendo's Rumble Pak peripheral and includes the voice acting from the English version.[78][79] In 1998, *Super Mario 64* was re-released in Europe and North America as part of the Player's Choice line, a selection of games with high sales sold for a reduced price. The game was later released on the Wii's Virtual Console service in the United States on November 19, 2006, and in other territories the following weeks.[80] This release adds compatibility with the GameCube and Classic controllers, and enhances the resolution to 480p.[51]

link:Gamecube#Controller
Link to segment

link:Gamecube
Link to article title

Article | Talk

GameCube

Controller [edit]

Main articles: GameCube controller and WaveBird Wireless Controller

Nintendo learned from its experiences – both positive and negative – with the Nintendo 64's three-handled controller design and went with a two-handled, "handlebar" design for the GameCube. The shape was made popular by Sony's PlayStation controller released in 1994 and its follow-up DualShock series of gamepads introduced in 1997. In addition to vibration feedback, the DualShock series was well known for having two analog sticks to improve the 3D experience in games. Nintendo and Microsoft designed similar features in the controllers for their sixth-generation consoles, but instead of having the analog sticks parallel to

Fig. 1. Wikipedia links

Current link detection methods are focused on article titles [1, 2, 6, 9, 10]. They often first generate a candidate set for an article by utilizing existing connections of articles, then rank all articles in the candidate set, and select the most similar article as the final result. But in our case, it is hard to generate a candidate set by using existing connections, due to shortage of links that point to segment titles. Besides, the length of segment texts are usually short, so it is necessary to improve vector representation of segment texts, so that we can obtain better similarity comparisons between segment pairs which helps in candidate set generating process.

In this paper, we discuss the following link suggestion problem: Given a link source, which is a position in a Wikipedia article, we find the most related link target, which is either a whole article, or a segment in an article.

Our approach employs Latent Dirichlet Allocation (LDA) [4] method for topic detection, where segments are represented as vectors of word probabilities. To improve accuracies of conventional LDA-based methods, we combine LDA with Maximum Likelihood Estimation (MLE) in a nonlinear way. We compute semantic similarities on the segment level. It is hard to predict whether a link should point to a segment, by only using similarities between segment pairs. We compute similarities between one target segment and all the segments in another article, to obtain similarity distributions in one article. We define statistical features based on these similarity distributions. Then we use a classifier to determine whether the link should point to a specific segment rather than the whole article. When we confirm that the link should point to a segment, we compare the similarities between segment pairs to find the most related segment. Our evaluation results show that our method is effective and improve accuracy over popular TF-IDF methods.

The rest of this paper is organized as follows. Section 2 shows related work. Section 3 introduces our assumption and proposed method. In Sect. 4 we describe our dataset in detail, explain our experimental process and we present evaluation results in various situations. In Sect. 5, we address a conclusion and future work.

2 Related Work

Automatically discovering missing links in Wikipedia has been discussed in the literature. Sisay et al. [1] propose a method which can rank pages using co-citation and page title information. They use LTRank to identify similar pages and select top similar articles as the prediction results. This method needs the organizational structures of the articles; LTRank is not suitable for detecting links at the segment level, because there are not enough segment-level links.

Junte proposed a method utilizing TF-IDF and the vector space model to detect document-to-document links and anchor-to-BEP links [16]. Best Entry Point (BEP) is similar to our task. The best entry point here is a specific article belonging to a general article. The difference is that Junte's work is still focusing on the whole article, while our task is to detect the best segment in an article. Junte's research regards the source article as the query and selects top-K similar articles as the result. Then a deep-first iteration is repeated to find the final result. This method uses TF-IDF and the vector-space model to compute similarities. But TF-IDF is heavily affected by corpus construction.

David et al. [7] proposed a machine learning-based link detector to detect links between Wikipedia articles. In their method, they did not simply evaluate textual similarity between two articles, but for each article pair, they evaluate five features: link probability, relatedness, disambiguation confidence, generality, location and spread. Then they train a classifier, for predicting whether there should be a link between an article pair. Its result was much better than other similarity-based methods.

3 Proposed Algorithm

3.1 Data Collection

As the world's largest encyclopedia, Wikipedia is organized as a large, complex network, where articles are connected by interlinks. Given a target, we assume that an interlink from a target article to another article assists complementing the content of the target article, by incorporating the content of another article. In order to utilize this link structure for incorporating the contents of the linked articles, we construct a suitable corpus for the target article. Given a target article A, we regard the union of all the articles that A links to and A itself as the corpus. Certain links may point to a specific segment, but we include its whole article in the corpus. Wikipedia featured articles are less erroneous and stable, so they are suitable for our experiments. Our dataset consists of randomly sampled featured articles. Since our objective is to suggest a segment-level link, we decompose the articles in the corpus into segments based on their logical structures, such as paragraphs. The following steps are operated on segments.

3.2 Representing Segments as Vectors

We argue that linked articles bring additional information to the central article and affect the topics of the central article. The LDA model [3, 4] is a popular model that can extract topics from the corpus. Figure 2 shows the structure of LDA model, where documents are regarded as topic distribution and topic is regarded as a word distribution. A document d is sampled from a topic distribution θ, and a topic z is represented over words by word distribution ϕ.

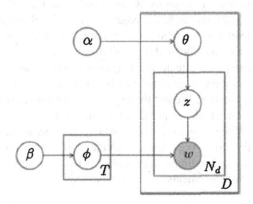

Fig. 2. LDA generation process

So we can obtain the probability of a term in a document by the following formula

$$P_{LDA}\left(w|d,\hat{\theta},\hat{\phi}\right) = \sum_{z=1}^{K} P\left(w|z,\hat{\phi}\right)P\left(z|\hat{\theta},d\right) \tag{1}$$

Here, $\hat{\theta}$ and $\hat{\phi}$ are the posterior estimates of θ and ϕ, respectively. LDA does not perform very well on long tail words, so there are a number of variants over the basic LDA model. One of the variants is to combine LDA and Maximum Likelihood Estimation. The authors of [7, 8, 13–15] utilize linear combination of word-level probability from LDA, document-level probability and collection-level probability to smooth the results. The document-level probability and collection-level probability are obvious parts which can be observed by simple term occurrences. The LDA model can extract the word probability from latent topics which can be regarded as latent part. However, the existing methods adopted a linear combination of obvious part and latent part. But in the assumption of LDA, the word probability of the document is based on the corpus while the document-level probability is based on the current document, so linear combinations may not be the best choices, because it is ad hoc to current corpus. To optimize the combination method, we propose the following nonlinear combination of the obvious part and latent part:

$$p(w|D) = \frac{1}{e^{\alpha N_d} + 1} \left[\frac{1}{e^{-\beta N_d} + 1} P_{ML}(w|D) + \frac{1}{e^{\beta N_d} + 1} P_{ML}(w|Coll) \right]$$
$$+ \frac{1}{e^{-\alpha N_d} + 1} P_{LDA}(w|D) \tag{2}$$

Here, N_d is the number of terms appearing in the segment. The first part of the formula is the probability of the word appearing in the document by term frequencies. The weight proportion of the obvious part and latent part will affect the word probability. This document-level probability is combined with the collection-level probability by the smoothing parameter β. We adjust the value of β to optimize the obvious part. Smoothing parameter α is to adjust the ratio of the obvious part and latent part. By these two formulae, we can obtain the probabilities of all the words in the corpus. People utilize perplexity to evaluate the language model. The perplexity is smaller when the fitness between the model and data is better. In our experiment, we need to determine the best parameters. We put the experiment data into the formula and select the parameters based on which the perplexity is minimal.

We represent each segment as a vector, whose element is the probability of the segment generating the word. We could use all the words in the corpus as elements of the vector. But to reduce the dimensions of the vectors, we only select words which appear in more than three segments.

3.3   Obtaining Similarity Distributions

After representing each segment as a vector, we use cosine similarity to measure the similarity between two segments. We need to evaluate the similarity distribution between segment SA in articles A and each segment in article B. So for SA in article A, and the link from SA that point to article B, we compute the similarity between SA and each segment in B.

3.4   Feature Extraction

A Wikipedia interlink points to an article title or a segment title. As Wikipedia's guideline[1] specifies, a link should point to a segment title when the link source and the link target segment are remarkably similar and describe more details. Simply comparing the similarity between segment SA in articles A and segment SB in article B, and the similarity between SA and article B is not a good idea, because the segment SB of the link target is a part of article B, hence they are related, and it will greatly affect the results. To solve this problem, we adopt the following assumption.

Assumption: If segment SA has a link to segment SB, then SB should be the most related segment with SA in article B, and the other segments in B are just slightly related with SA. In other words, if we rank the similarities between SA and each

---

[1] https://en.wikipedia.org/wiki/Help:Link#Section_linking_.28anchors.29

segment in article *B*, then the similarity between *SA* and *SB* should be a prominent outlier. If segment *SA* is linked to article *B*, then all the segments in *B* should be slightly related with *SA*, but there is no obvious outlier.

Based on this assumption, we construct our feature set to incorporate statistical features on segment similarity distributions. We introduce the following features from three aspects.

Range of similarity distribution. Similarities between pairs of segments are measured by segment vectors based on either TIFIDF or LDA. One article consists of multiple segments, so we obtain a vector of segment similarities for one article. We note that similarity values are so diverse between articles. Therefore, we characterize these similarity vectors by descriptive statistics of similarity distributions of the following: The number of the segments in the article, and maximum, minimum and mean of the similarity values of the segments in the article.

Dispersion of similarity distribution. Based on our assumption, if a link points to a segment, there will be at least one segment in the link target article which is highly similar to the link source. In an ideal situation, if the link points to an article title, not a specific segment, then the similarities of all the segments in the article toward the link source segment are close between each other, so the dispersion of these similarity values is small. Thus dispersion of similarities within one article is an important clue for determining whether the link should be on the article level or segment level. Thus we introduce the following features: variance, standard deviation, and coefficient of variations. These features are derived from statistical properties of the distribution of segment similarities in one article.

Outliers. According to our assumption, if a link points to a segment title, then it is more likely that there exists an outlier segment, having an outstandingly larger similarity than other segments. We adopt the conventional concept of outliers such that, if the difference between one segment and mean is more than the double of the standard deviation, then we believe the segment is an outlier. If the difference is more than triple of the standard deviation, the segment is a large outlier. In this paper, we use the number of large outliers in one article as a feature.

3.5 Prediction

We train a classifier based on the above features to predict whether a target link points to article title or a specific segment. The features we introduced are statistical measures on similarity distributions, which do not have obvious linear relationships. So we utilize the nonlinear classifier model random forest [5] as our classifier.

When the target link is predicted as pointing to a segment, we need to determine which segment should be pointing to. In this step, instead of simply selecting the most similar segment as the result, we also require that the selected segment must be an outlier in the similarity distribution.

4 Experimental Evaluation

4.1 Dataset

Featured articles are considered to be high-quality articles in Wikipedia, and they are well organized and maintained. We adopt links from featured articles as our golden standard, assuming that they are appropriately given, so that these links point to segments when there exist specifically relevant segments in the target articles. We randomly selected 2000 featured articles as our dataset (Table 1).

Table 1. Dataset infomation

Dataset	Count
Articles	2000
Segments	16204
Links pointing to segments	3351
Links pointing to article titles	334048

There are totally 3351 links pointing to segments and 334048 links pointing to article titles. We use these links as our reference data. The ratio between the segment links and article links is nearly 1:100. This ratio is rarely observed in most of articles, because the average number of links in one article is 41, so most of articles just have article-level links. We divide the dataset into small subsets, to control the ratio between positive and negative samples, where positives are segment-level links. We use the random forest classifier for our prediction.

4.2 Experiment Preparement

Imbalanced dataset. From the dataset, we observe that the ratio between positive and negative samples is imbalanced. We need a careful setup for training, because the classifier tries to adjust the parameters to put all samples into the correct classes. If negative samples are overwhelming majority, the positive samples could be regarded as invalid values by the classifier. There are two approaches to tackle this problem. The first one is randomly sampling negatives to balance positives and negatives, then train using this sampled set. But its disadvantages are obvious. This sampling process will lose a large number of effective data. The lost negative samples will cause learning errors, degrading precision.

Another solution is resampling positives until positives and negatives are balanced. But it can cause overfitting easily, and it does not help the classifier to learn positive samples, because resampling does not increase new positive samples, instead just balancing the dataset by repeating addition of small positive samples.

In this paper, we use sampling negatives to balance the dataset. We randomly sample negatives several times, and train the classifier. On the prediction results, we calculate average precision, recall, and F1-score.

4.3   Feature Importance

Before we test in the dataset, first we have to measure whether our features are effective to distinguish the positive class. We use correlation analysis methods to test relationship between each feature and the reference data. Mann-Whitney is a nonparametric test of the null hypothesis that two samples come from the same population against an alternative hypothesis, such that a particular population tends to have larger values than the other. The test results are shown in Table 2.

From this test we can find max similarity, mean similarity, variance, standard deviation, small similarity outlier are related to the reference classification. But in our assumption, the large similarity outlier should be related. For further analysis, we performed Two-Sample Kolmogorov-Smirnov test. This is a nonparametric test for equality of continuous, one-dimensional probability distributions that can be used to compare a sample with a reference probability distribution (one-sample K–S test), or to compare two samples (two-sample K–S test). The results are shown in Table 3.

Table 2. Mann-Whitney test on features

Feature	Significance	Decision
Element count	0.454	Retain
Max similarity	0.018	Reject
Min similarity	0.423	Retain
Variance	0.023	Reject
Mean similarity	0.002	Reject
Coefficient of variation	0.611	Retain
Standard deviation	0.023	Reject
Small similarity outlier	0.010	Retain
Large similarity outlier	0.079	Reject

Table 3. Kolmoogorov-Smirnov test on features

Feature	Significance	Decision
Element count	0.227	Retain
Max similarity	0.000	Reject
Min similarity	0.636	Retain
Variance	0.000	Reject
Mean similarity	0.001	Reject
Coefficient of variation	0.714	Retain
Standard deviation	0.000	Reject
Small similarity outlier	0.821	Retain
Large similarity outlier	0.612	Retain

We can see in Table 3 that the small similarity outlier is not very effective, but from these two tests, we can see variance and standard deviation are strongly effective. So the test results support our assumption. These importance results indicate that our features are effective and the classifier is expected to distinguish segment links via these features.

4.4   Baseline

Previous researches are all focusing on linkability to article titles, not targeted to segments. Since there is no preceding work, we choose our baseline based on a simple idea that if words in a link source occur in an article title, then the link should point to the article title. Otherwise, if words in a link source occur in a segment, then the link should point to the segment. If words occur in multiple segments, then the most frequent segment is considered as the target of the link.

4.5   Classification Results

Our first step is to determine whether a link should point to an article title or segment. To test our method in different ratios of positives and negatives, we controlled the ratio from 1:1 to 1:100. In each dataset, we use one half data to train and the other half data to test. At the ratio of 1:1, we randomly selected links of positives and negatives. For the ratios from 1:10 to 1:100, we changed the number of articles from 15 to 43. The results are shown in Tables 4, 5, 6, 7 and 8.

Table 4. Pos: Neg = 1:1

Ratio of Pos: Nag = 148:150, links are randomly sampled.

Pos: Neg = 1:1	Precision	Recall	F1
Our method	68.4 %	73.9 %	71.1 %
Random result	50 %	50 %	50 %
Baseline	61 %	57 %	59 %

Table 5. Pos: Neg = 1:10

Ratio of Pos: Neg = 128:1258. Links are from 15 articles

Pos: Neg = 1:10	Precision	Recall	F1
Our method	16.5 %	64.4 %	27 %
Random result	10 %	50 %	16.6 %
Baseline	13.3 %	47.2 %	20.7 %

Table 6. Pos: Neg = 1:20

Ratio of Pos: Neg = 144:2963. Links from 32 articles

Pos: Neg = 1:20	Precision	Recall	F1
Our method	5.3 %	70.2 %	9.8 %
Random result	5 %	50 %	9.0 %
Baseline	5.1 %	55.8 %	9.3 %

Table 7. Pos: Neg = 1:50

Ratio of Pos: Neg = 128:5959. Links from 38 articles

Pos: Neg = 1:50	Precision	Recall	F1
Our method	2.5 %	67.2 %	4.8 %
Random result	2 %	50 %	3.8 %
Baseline	2.1 %	45 %	4.0 %

Table 8. Pos:Neg = 1:100

Ratio of Pos: Neg = 47:5796. Links from 43 articles

Pos: Neg = 1:100	Precision	Recall	F1
Our method	1.4 %	57.1 %	2.1 %
Random result	1 %	50 %	1.9 %
Baseline	1.1 %	41 %	2.1 %

The second step is to determine which segment is most relevant to the link source. In our method, for a link in the source segment the most similar segment is selected, based on cosine similarities between two segments. After that, we calculate whether the most similar segment is an outlier in the entire similarity distribution. If the outlier is satisfied, we select the segment as our prediction result. We randomly selected 48 links which point to segments from 15 articles. We compared our method with the random selection of segments and the algorithm such that the similarity function of (2) is replaced by TF-IDF. The result is shown in Table 9.

Table 9. Predicting the most related segment

Average segment count = 8	Accuracy
Our method	41.6 %
Random result	12.5 %
TF-IDF	24.2 %

4.6   Discussion

From Tables 4, 5, 6, 7 and 8, the results show that our method is most accurate to predict links pointing to segments. Our method performs better than the baseline. Correlation analysis shows that our statistics features on similarity distributions are effective, to capture patterns when segment-level links occur.

Our method works well when the positive and negative samples are balanced to 1:1. However, even though we already use the sampling method to balance the dataset, the influence of imbalance data is still strong. We can find that when the ratio of positives and negatives is more than 20:1, precision goes down significantly. We still need to improve to deal with imbalanced datasets, since most of the real world data is imbalanced.

Regarding Table 9, the experiment is to select one segment from eight choices, and our method shows a superior result to the conventional TFIDF method by 16 percent in accuracy. That means our representation of segment texts is effective.

As our dataset is imbalanced, we can observe that the sampling process is very important in our method. Table 10 shows that if we ignore the sampling process, the F1 score decreases a lot.

Table 10. Pos: Neg = 1:10

Ratio of Pos: Neg = 128:1258. Links are from 15 articles			
Pos: Neg = 1:10	Precision	Recall	F1
With sampling process	16.5 %	64.4 %	27 %
Without sampling process	10.5 %	46 %	17.1 %

5   Conclusion and Future Work

In this paper, we proposed an LDA-based algorithm to represent segment texts as vectors, and determine whether links in Wikipedia articles point to a related segment, or article title. We believe that our research is the first work of link detection on segment level. Our approach is combining the LDA model with MLE with a nonlinear combination. Our result shows that our nonlinear combination performs better than TFIDF method. But it can still be improved, we currently use document length to smooth the obvious part. Further improvements over parameter optimizations can be expected.

We introduced statistical features on segment similarity distributions, to train a classifier for predicting whether a link points to segments or article titles. Our method performs well when the dataset is balanced. In future work, we plan to design a strong feature to improve accuracies when the dataset is much imbalanced. New features such as word embedding [11, 12] are also under our consideration. We also try to utilize category hierarchies when selecting the most related segment.

References

1. Adafre, S.F., de Rijke, M.: Discovering missing links in Wikipedia. In: Proceedings of the 3rd International Workshop on Link Discovery, pp. 90–97(2005)
2. Besnik, F., Katja, M., Avishek, A.: Automated news suggestions for populating wikipedia entity pages. In: Proceedings of the CIKM 2015 Proceedings of the 24th ACM International on Conference on Information and Knowledge Management, pp 323–332(2015)
3. Blei, D.M., Moreno, P.J.: Topic segmentation with an aspect hidden markov model. In: Proceedings of SIGIR (2001)
4. Blei, D.M., Ng, A.Y., Jordan, M.J.: Latent dirichlet allocation. J. Mach. Learn. Res. **3**, 993–1022 (2003)
5. Breiman, L.: Random forests. Mach. Learn. **45**(1), 5–32 (2001)
6. Knoth, P., Novotny, J., Zdrahal, Z.: Automatic generation of inter-passage links based on semantic similarity. In: Proceedings of the 23rd International Conference on Computational Linguistics, pp. 590–598, August 2010
7. Lavrenko, V., Croft, W.B.: Relevance-based language models. In: SIGIR 2001, pp. 120–127 (2001)
8. Liu, X., Croft, W.B.: Cluster-based retrieval using language models. In: Proceedings of the 27th International ACM SIGIR Conference on Research and Development Information Retrieval, pp. 186–193 (2004)
9. Milne, D., Ian, H.W.: An effective, low-cost measure of semantic relatedness obtained from wikipedia links. In: Proceedings of the AAAI Workshop on Wikipedia and Artificial Intelligence: an Evolving Synergy, Chicago, pp. 25–30 (2008)
10. Milne, D., Ian, H.W.: Learning to link proceeding. In: CIKM 2008 Proceedings of the 17th ACM Conference on Information and Knowledge Management, pp. 509–518(2008)
11. Mikolov, T., Sutskever, I., Chen, K., Corrado, G., Dean, J.: Distributed representations of words and phrases and their compositionality. In: NIPS 2013, pp. 3111–3119 (2013)
12. Mikolov, T., Chen, K., Corrado, G., Dean, J.: Efficient estimation of word representations in vector space. In: ICLR 2013 Proceedings of Workshop at International Conference on Learning Representations (2013)
13. Xing, W., Croft, W.B.: LDA-based document models for ad-hoc retrieval. In: Proceedings of the 29th ACM SIGIR Conference, pp. 178–185 (2006)
14. Wang, R., Wu, J., Iwaihara, M.: Finding co-occurring topics in wikipedia article segments. In: Tuamsuk, K., Jatowt, A., Rasmussen, E. (eds.) ICADL 2014. LNCS, vol. 8839, pp. 252–259. Springer, Heidelberg (2014). doi:10.1007/978-3-319-12823-8_26
15. Zhai, C., Lafferty, J.: A study of smoothing methods for language models applied to ad hoc information retrieval. In: Proceedings of the 24th ACM SIGIR 2001, pp. 334–34 (2001)
16. Zhang, J., Kamps, J.: A content-based link detection approach using the vector space model. In: International Workshop of the Initiative for the Evaluation of XML Retrieval, pp. 395–400 (2009)

Author Index

Aizawa, Akiko   137, 144
Allen, Robert B.   212, 218
Amagasa, Toshiyuki   251
Anand, Vishwaraj   98
Asato, Noriko   63

Boamah, Eric   21
Bootkrajang, Jakramate   127
Bowen, Judy   37
Brittle, Collin   51
Buranarach, Marut   257

Chai, Don Tze Wai   245
Chaijaruwanich, Jeerayut   127
Chansanam, Wirapong   231
Charin, Nanthiya   57
Charoenkwan, Phasit   127
Chen, Chao-Chen   180
Chen, Yinlin   51
Cheng, Wei-Chung   180
Cochrane, Euan   225
Crestani, Fabio   311
Cunningham, Sally Jo   37, 45

Foo, Schubert   92

Giachanou, Anastasia   311
Goh, Dion Hoe-Lian   98, 188
Guo, Yan Ru   188

Han, Feng   98
Hansen, John H.L.   77
Hatano, Kohei   269
Hinze, Annika   45
Ho, Shinn-Ying   127
Hongwarittorrn, Nattanont   257

Inkeaw, Papangkorn   127
Ishita, Emi   269
Iwaihara, Mizuho   394

Janchian, Chadaphon   57
Jiang, Shouxu   381
Jiang, Tingting   51

Kageura, Kyo   150
Kamiura, Naotake   85
Kaushik, Lakshmish   77
Kawai, Yukiko   167
Kikkawa, Jiro   369
Kitagawa, Hiroyuki   251
Komamizu, Takahiro   251
Kong, Xiaoyu   98
Krataithong, Pattama   257
Kristianto, Giovanni Yoko   144

Lee, Bo Eun   212
Lee, Chei Sian   98, 325, 339, 351
Lee, Chu Keong   245
Lee, Jiyoung   212
Leenaraj, Bhornchanit   57
Liebetraut, Thomas   225
Liew, Chern Li   21
Lin, Jiaping   16
Luca, Edward   275

Marukatat, Sanparith   127
Mather, Paul   51
Merčun, Tanja   104

Na, Jin-Cheon   285
Nakano, Yu   157
Nakatoh, Tetsuya   269
Narayan, Bhuva   3, 275
Nichols, David M.   37, 45
Nii, Manabu   85

Oard, Douglas W.   77
Ohshima, Hiroaki   110

Pang, Natalie   92
Perianin, Thomas   137

Phetwong, Watcharee   57
Pingo, Zablon   3

Rechert, Klaus   225
Rungcharoensuksri, Sittisak   203

Salaba, Athena   104
Sangawan, Abhijeet   77
Sawangsire, Krisorn   57
Seki, Yohei   297
Senuma, Hajime   137
Sesagiri Raamkumar, Aravind   92
Shimizu, Toshiyuki   157
Sin, Sei-Ching Joanna   325, 339
Song, Hanna   212
Speer, Julie   51
Supnithi, Thepchai   257

Takaku, Masao   369
Takayama, Michiaki   269
Takeda, Naoto   297
Tan, Sang-Sang   285
Tanaka, Katsumi   110
Teo, Winston Jin Song   351
Theng, Yin-Leng   325
Topić, Goran   144
Toth, Bryan   77

Tuamsuk, Kulthida   231
Tu-Keefner, Feili   10

Varathan, Kasturi Dewi   311

Wang, Renzhi   394
Wang, Wei   381
Wang, Yuanyuan   167
Wee, Joan Jee Foon   245
Wehrle, Dennis   225
Wertheimer, Andrew   63

Xie, Zhiwu   51

Yada, Shuntaro   150
Yamanaka, Takahiro   85
Yang, Xiaoyan   381
Yang, Yi-Ting   180
Yoshikane, Fuyuki   369
Yoshikawa, Masatoshi   157
Yu, Chengzhu   77
Yumoto, Takayuki   85

Zhang, Jing   16
Zhao, Meng   110
Žumer, Maja   104

Printed in the United States
By Bookmasters